FALKLANDS - THE SECRET PLOT

by

CARDOSO, KIRSCHBAUM AND VAN DER KOOY
Translated by Bernard Ethell

To Peter & Diana
Christmas 1989

Virginia

PRESTON EDITIONS

Falklands - the secret plot
by
Cardoso, Kirschbaum and
van der Kooy

First published in 1983 by
Sudamericana/Planeta SA
Buenos Aires, Argentina.
17 editions in Spanish.
English edition first published
in 1987 by
PRESTON EDITIONS
5, Creek Road, East Molesey,
Surrey, UK.

ISBN: 1 870615 05 0   Hardback
          1 870615 00 X   Paperback
© 1983 Sudamericana/Planeta SA
          (Editores)

CONTENTS

PREFACE

The original idea behind writing this book was certainly simpler than the end product. The book was the result of a long "newspaperman's vigil," which began in the small hours of April 2nd 1982, while awaiting confirmation of the landing of Argentine troops in the Falkland Islands. That night was fraught with fatigue and anxiety. For the 74 days which followed, we enjoyed privileged access to scenes in the drama which it was our job as representatives of the press to report. It was during this time that we worked on the plans for our project, though without finalizing them.

Throughout that time, wherever we found ourselves - the fleetingly-recovered Falklands, Buenos Aires, New York or Washington - as well as before each episode we covered, we reminded each other of the vague promise that "some day, we must sit down quietly and write about all this." To be frank, with the pressure of work, the motivation could easily have evaporated. There would then have been nothing to show for it.

But the single fact of having to face that final defeat and humiliation taught the whole Argentine nation a few home truths. It made us, as writers, realize that the project, which at first had been just a diversion and a pleasant dream, was now a necessity.

Though we gained little from it materially, it presented us with a real challenge: *to prevent the propaganda of the victor from becoming the official history of the vanquished.*

Many aspects of the military operation of April 2nd were to receive far harsher censure from many on the Argentine side than could ever have been conceived by the cleverest British propagandists. As is the case with other ordeals suffered by much-castigated Argentina over the past decade, all that can be done now is to look at what happened in the hope that it may never recur.

The project only reached its final form after several revisions. Shortly after 14th June 1982, we thought of several alternative approaches, and proceeded by trial and error. One of these methods was extensive interviewing of the leading figures in the story, followed by a narration of the events and incorporating a rough attempt at their analysis.

We rejected this approach because of its obvious limitations. Impelled to relate much of what we had experienced from a global perspective, our first decision was to reconstruct the political and diplomatic aspects of the conflict, and to exclude the military side. We agreed we were no experts on the latter. Furthermore we assumed that the war had been such a trauma for the Military that any objective assessment of it from that quarter was out of the question.

Here we were mistaken. we found we could keep to the limits we had set ourselves only partially. The political and military aspects of the events preceding and following the recovery of the islands proved inseparable. The separation we had envisaged could not be sustained. On the contrary, we often had to immerse ourselves in events on the battlefront. This was good in that it made us realize our misjudgement of the armed forces. We could complete our reconstruction largely because many officers of various ranks shared our view that it would be useful to write a history of this national humiliation.

Nevertheless, it is essential to put it on record that we make no reference in the following pages to the capabilities of different types of aircraft, missiles or ships, or to the merits of having deployed or not deployed combat forces in any given area. This book recounts the story of the men involved: their frailties and dignity, their generosity and ambition, their rights and their wrongs - and it describes the final outcome, to which the sum of all these qualities inexorably leads us.

A certain dash of immodesty - the consequence of having occupied ring-side seats for the spectacle - made us presume, falsely, that we had perfect knowledge of at least the most significant events.

At the end of those days of euphoria, depression and death, we believed we had a story outline which would make for swift and sure completion. This was a delusion: as we progressed with the investigation, we discovered a certain unpublished history of the war. It was then that we decided to write on the theme of that "secret plot" which answers many, though not all, of the questions which persist over this conflict with Great Britain.

We soon realized that to achieve a satisfactory result, it would not be enough merely to rely on our memories and the notes we made at the time, nor even the testimonies we were gathering. Our progress would still be impeded by a lack of documentation to support the story. Still, once we had overcome the initial mistrust and apprehension of those who acted as our sources, we managed to penetrate that world of reserve, secrets and ciphers which hid the truth of what had happened.

In the course of a hard year's work, many people provided us with this information. We strictly preserved the anonymity of most of them, though we have named certain of our sources. Our account is based on testimonies, dialogues and unpublished documents which help to reconstruct the history of the war from the overthrow of Roberto Viola to the fall of Leopoldo Galtieri a few days after the surrender of Port Stanley.

Our method was to interview ex-officials at length in order to obtain the broad thrust of the argument. Then we would cross-check and compare versions of events and decisions. We used the same method in Washington and New York when speaking to many of the principal members of the Reagan administration involved in the negotiations between Argentina and Great Britain - as well as other personalities who took part unofficially in the drama. From some of our contacts we accepted unpublished, often confidential, documents on the events of the war.

There were enthusiastic guides who directed us to people we wanted to meet and helped us to clarify this or that episode. It was also evident that sometimes we found ourselves on false trails which inexorably led us to spurious versions of these events.

Naturally the burden of our work involved the development of events in Argentina itself. This was our main focus. Though many excellent books have been published on the subject, we sincerely believe that none of them present such a complete view of the *Argentine* perspective of the war as does the one we have written.

Such an assertion should be justified:

1. This book does not claim to be the "definitive version" of what happened. First, because in history no such thing exists, and secondly because our investigation has both the richness and the weaknesses inherent in a work of journalism. It is more extensive and exhaustive than are accounts in newspapers and magazines, but in the end it is still a work of journalism. We ask the reader, when judging this work, to remember that we are not academic historians, but journalists reporting on a period of history.

2. It will also be noted that in some areas the analysis lacks depth. We shall not try to justify our evident failings here, but we must mention some of the limitations which bound us. As our investigation progressed, we found that some purported facts and versions of events supplied by some of the witnesses interviewed did not tally with those from other sources. Rather overwhelmed by the sheer mass of data collected, we decided on the spur of the moment to deal only with selected aspects of this issue, in order that the book might actually get completed.

3. We have not here discussed the foundations of the Argentine claim to sovereignty over the archipelago. This seemed unnecessary because our starting premise was that the Argentine people have long believed this aspiration to be justified.

Many men and women encouraged us and collaborated with us - giving us long hours of their time and invaluable advice. We wish to offer them our deepest gratitude, though we regret that we cannot mention most of their names.

Some, however, we shall identify. This list is headed by our wives - Alicia de Bianco, Silvia Fajre and Dora Young - who helped actively in the work. They were our keenest critics - inflexible *and* well-intentioned. Furthermore, they lived with our obsession for over a year, making light of their own infinite tolerance.

We are also indebted to our colleagues, Ernesto Jackson, Roman Garcia Azcarate, Juan Carlos Bairo, Carlos Sarraf, Jorge Viejo, Alicia Muzio and Horacio Perez. Their assistance was invaluable. They, together with all those contributors left unnamed, are completely blameless over the final contents of this book.

The mere existence of this work is ample reward for our efforts. But if it also contributes to the debate on the Falklands War and helps to clarify its significance, we shall have fulfilled our greatest aspirations.

Oscar Raul Cardoso
Ricardo Kirschbaum
Eduardo van der Kooy

Buenos Aires, July 1983.

PUBLISHERS' ACKNOWLEDGEMENTS

Cover design: Linda Sullivan.

This book is set in Times Roman 10pt on equipment supplied by:
The Desk Top Publishing Centre,
57a Hatton Garden,
London EC1N 8JD.

Hardware: Apricot XEN-xi and postscript laser printer.
Software: Microsoft WORD and Aldus PAGEMAKER.
PRESTON EDITIONS would like to thank the DTP Centre for
invaluable help in the speedy production of this work.
Printed in Great Britain by J. W. Arrowsmith Ltd., Bristol BS3 2NT

PRINCIPAL CHARACTERS IN ORDER OF APPEARANCE

Anaya, Admiral Jorge Isaac.....*Member of Argentine Junta and Navy Commandant*

Lombardo, Vice-Admiral Juan Jose.....*Argentine Commander of Naval Operations*

Viola, Lt Gen. Roberto Eduardo.....*ex-President of Argentina*

Galtieri, Lt Gen. Leopoldo Fortunato.....*President of Argentina and Army Commandant*

Perez De Cuellar, Javier.....*UN Secretary-General*

Kirkpatrick, Jeane.....*US Ambassador to the UN*

Schlaudermann, Harry.....*US Ambassador to Buenos Aires*

Figueroa, Gustavo.....*First Secretary, Argentine Foreign Ministry*

Mallea Gil, Brig. Gen. Miguel Angel.....*Argentine Military Attache in Washington*

Walters, Lt. Gen. Vernon.....*White House Foreign Affairs Adviser, now US Ambassador to UN*

Haig, Gen. Alexander.....*US Secretary of State*

Takacs, Esteban.....*Argentine Ambassador in Washington*

Lami Dozo, Brig. Gen. Arturo Bisilio.....*Member of Argentine Junta and Air Force Commandant*

Costa Mendez, Nicanor.....*Argentine Foreign Minister*

Roca, Eduardo.....*Argentine Ambassador to the UN*

Menendez, Col. Bernardo.....*Official, Argentine Ministry of the Interior*

Menendez, Maj. Gen. Mario Benjamin.....*Chief of Operations of the Army General Staff and Argentine Military Governor of the Falklands*

Williams, Anthony.....*British Ambassador to Buenos Aires*

Molteni, Atilio.....*Deputy to Argentine Ambassador in London*

Quijano, Raul.....*Argentine Ambassador to the OAS*

Luce, Richard.....*Minister of State at the British Foreign Office*

Henderson, Sir Nicholas.....*British Ambassador in Washington*

Davidoff, Constantino.....*Argentine entrepreneur*

Pym, Francis.....*British Foreign Secretary after invasion*

Parsons, Sir Anthony.....*British Ambassador to the UN*

Ure, John.....*Under-Secretary for the Americas, British Foreign Office*

Woodward, Rear-Admiral John.....*Commander of British Task Force*

Belaunde Terry, Fernando.....*President of Peru*

Daher, Brig. Gen. Americo.....*Argentine Chief of Staff, Falkland Islands*

Moore, Maj. Gen. John Jeremy.....*British Commander of Land Forces, Falkland Islands*

Chapter 1

THE FATEFUL PACT

"Lombardo, it's Anaya speaking. Could you come to the Officers' Club?"

"Yes, of course, Sir," was the reply.

In fact, a few minutes before the call from his superior, Vice-Admiral Juan Jose Lombardo had assumed the position of Commander of Naval Operations: a bureaucratic post in time of peace, but a key one in a war. Since the period of tension in 1978, when Argentina risked a military confrontation with Chile over the Beagle Channel, war had reverted to being what it always had been for the Argentine armed forces in the Twentieth Century: not much more than an abstraction within the private fantasies of the Military. But none of this worried Lombardo that 15th December, 1981: within the peculiar power structure of the navy, the command of naval operations was a sure step on the road that led to the top of the pyramid - the titular head of the navy itself.

Although the Vice-Admiral did not know it that day, when he received the invitation from Admiral Jorge Isaac Anaya his personal destiny was changed together with that of the whole country. For Lombardo it was a special day that he would never forget. For the great majority of Argentines, on the other hand, that day was lived like any other. With absolute indifference they had observed the outcome of a palace intrigue that toppled yet another President of the Nation - a president who, after all, had not been elected. Lt. Gen. Roberto Viola was a serving officer who had laboured patiently for years to reach the *Casa Rosada*, the presidential palace, yet he was not even able to enjoy his power. His fleeting administration lasted barely nine months. His successor was Leopoldo Fortunato Galtieri, Commander-in-Chief of the Army. Galtieri had accepted this post from the hands of the puppet Viola in order to control the Army's internal affairs. Argentine history is plagued with such paradoxes: thus Viola discovered himself a victim of the man he himself had chosen as heir, whom he had placed above other candidates, considering him the least dangerous of them all for his

1

purposes.

The newspapers of that day speculated on the composition of the new cabinet to accompany the expansive Galtieri. The spectre of hard orthodox monetarism - softened during Viola's time - floated before the mind's eye of the suffering Argentine people. Adalbert Krieger Vasena, ex-official of the Ongania Government and ex-head of the *Banco Interamericano de Desarrollo*, as well as Alvaro Alsogaray were mentioned by rumour-mongers as possible successors to the Economy Minister, Lorenzo Sigaut. Alsogaray was an irredeemable admirer of the market economy and of the "iron fist" of Margaret Thatcher, who was perceived as managing the economy of her own country without regard to the social cost. Sigaut had attempted a clumsy and incomplete break with the economic programme of Jose Alfredo Martinez de Hoz. The latter had been a virtual president of Argentina - with an office in the Treasury, the Palacio de Hacienda - ever since the assumption of power by the Military following the coup of March 1976.

The heat weighed down on the people of Buenos Aires that day even more than the news. The *Multipartidaria*, a group of the five most important political parties in the country (*Justicialismo, Union Civica Radical, Intransigente, Desarrollismo and Democracia Cristiana*) had thrown on the deaf ears of the authorities a new claim for "immediate elections - and without conditions".

More appealing for the mass of Argentines, however, and with a better chance of fulfilling their expectations was the approaching lottery at the end of the year - because a lucky break could end the penury of many a citizen - or else the football match between the *River Plate* club (with Alfredo Di Stefano as technical director and Mario Kempes as star), and the modest team: *Western Railway*. Western Railway is typical of the many football clubs that grew up next to the railway tracks which were themselves laid out during long years of management by the British in Argentina.

Lombardo hurried to attend the meeting with his superior, thinking that he would receive orders to make ready the Sea Fleet for further operations during the recently-announced "Naval Year". Perhaps, too, he would hear some reference from Anaya to the political situation - but this was rather improbable because this man occupying the top post in the hierarchy was hardly communicative.

Lombardo gestured a greeting and tried to speak, Anaya stopped him, his face stern and inexpressive.

"Look, Lombardo," said the Commandant, Anaya, by way of introduction, "what I am going to say is absolutely confidential, strictly confidential - do you understand?"

Lombardo's thoughts became concentrated as the flamboyant

Commander of Naval Operations made the assurances of understanding his chief, Anaya, required. His thoughts centered on an idea he had treasured for some time and had secretly desired more than anything else in the world: an operation to recover the islands of Picton, Lennox and Nueva presently in the possession of Chile. The timely mediation of Pope John Paul II in the 1978 crisis had thrown overboard the dreams of many among the Argentine Military for such an *"act of liberation"*.

"I order you," said Anaya, resorting to a formula that left no margin for error, "to prepare a plan for an Argentine landing in the Falkland Islands. You are to be the first to know about this. It would be wise, therefore, for the people you choose to work on the plan to keep their mouths shut. Secrecy is vital. Do you understand me?" he demanded, with his customary taste for repetition.

The newspapers of that day also commented on the election of the Peruvian, Perez de Cuellar, as Secretary-General of the United Nations. This took place after a never-ending series of vetoes which had put the two Argentine contenders out of the race: Carlos Ortiz de Rozas, a diplomat of solid reputation who led the Argentine legation in London, and Alejandro Orfila. The latter's secret hope was an ambitious scheme to change his post of titular head of the Organisation of American States (OAS) - which he had held since the days of the government of Isabelita, ex-President Peron's widow - for that of the *"Crystal Palace"* of the United Nations Building in New York.

The episode passed unnoticed by the Argentine public. All this seemed merely another episode in international bureaucracy, too distant from the life of anyone in these southern latitudes. Scarcely four months later it would be understood that this was far from the truth.

Lombardo, hardly able to simulate any enthusiasm for Anaya's order, called together his closest colleagues. At the meeting were the chiefs of naval aviation, Carlos Garcia Boll; of the fleet, Gualter Allara, and of the marines, Carlos Busser.

The men did their utmost not to arouse the least suspicion over their work. Moreover, they took special care not to alert the Naval Intelligence service itself. This they did by dusting off a plan from the archives that had been worked out by Anaya himself in 1977 during his command of the Sea Fleet, while under the command of the then head of the navy, Admiral Emilio Eduardo Massera. On that occasion, Anaya had proceeded in open violation of the chain of command - according to the military rule-book - since he delivered the plan to the Commandant without even notifying its existence to his Chief of Naval Staff, Vice-Admiral Antonio Vanek. Vanek was, of course, furious to discover this move by his subordinate.

That first year of the Military Government's *Process of*

National Reorganisation was the scene of a sordid and at times brutal confrontation between the ambitious Massera and the President of the Nation, Lt. Gen. Rafael Videla. At one time during this battle, Massera actually delivered a formal request to the Junta for a military force in order to proceed to recover the Falkland Islands. In the same way, he demanded of his peers that they should take the responsibility for "excesses" committed during the repression of the leftist guerrillas. His real intention, however, was to make life impossible for Videla - a man who loved the trappings of power, and who, underneath a cloak of humility and false bonhomie ruthlessly maintained a political and economic system whose consequences the Argentines would suffer for decades.

Videla saw himself heading for a difficult rupture. On recovering somewhat, he arranged to meet two of the generals who had worked on the arduous task of elevating him, an obscure officer, into the principal and uninvited inhabitant of the Casa Rosada. They were: Roberto Viola - at that time Chief of Army General Staff - and Jose Rogelio Villareal, Secretary General of the Presidency. Together, they devised a scheme to enable Videla to check the political ambitions of "Black Massera".

In a reply, drawn up in carefully chosen language, they recorded the "community of aspirations" among the army, navy and air force over the Falkland Islands and recognition of the "importance of the matter". But - and here was the snag - the documentary reply required overall details of the plan for the naval capture of the territory before "taking a definite decision." Massera saw through the ploy and accepted the inevitable with all the nobility to be found in a game between swindlers - for Massera's naval force had no real plan at all. He dedicated himself instead to thinking up new pitfalls to put in Videla's path. Still, conscious of the need not to leave his flank exposed, he nevertheless ordered Anaya to work on the plan. It was a way of being prepared in case the army at some time wanted to turn his manoeuvre into some kind of boomerang. There is no evidence that Massera mentioned the Falklands question again to the Military Junta until his retirement in 1979.

Anaya, on the other hand, transformed the undertaking into a personal quest. "With that project of his under his arm he became Commander-in-Chief," recalled a comrade and friend. The result of the work to which Anaya obsessively dedicated himself was converted - in 1982 - into the basis of the operation of April 2nd.[1]

On December 20th of that year (1981), two days before Galtieri showed off his Presidential sash for the first time, Lombardo flew from Bahia Blanca to Buenos Aires. In his briefcase he carried papers recording the preliminary measures needed for putting Argentine troops on the Falklands. They were in handwritten form, so as to avoid having to use typists or perhaps leaving marks of letters on some typewriter roller.

Lombardo also bore with him some reasonable doubts to lay before the Commandant. The requirements of the operation obliged him to have recourse to the influential Naval Intelligence, (SIN), in search of a quantity of data needed in his calculations for the undertaking. Details were required on the depth of the coves around Port Stanley, on the state of the beaches and their suitability for amphibious landings, and on the access roads to the capital and its airport. SIN had had all this information for a long time, but it was essential for them to have the reassurance of the Commandant's authorisation. Any Intelligence officer who read the list of Lombardo's requirements would be most suspicious.

Anaya waited for him, as was his habit, seated at his desk with his hands spread out and his face muscles set in a mask which betrayed not the least emotion. With hardly any of the opening formalities - their shared interest being enough - Lombardo began his briefing. He ended with the conclusion: the recovery operation could indeed be undertaken with relative ease, considering the existing naval strength. But he emphasized that two factors were absolutely essential: tactical surprise and strategic secrecy.

With "tactical surprise," it would be possible to reach the coasts of the Falklands without the inhabitants becoming aware of it and the operation would thus be "clean" - a euphemism for an absence of bloodshed. If as well, they managed to preserve "strategic secrecy" the British would not then reinforce their military posture on the islands, which scarcely amounted to 40 Royal Marines and an old ship - the *Endurance*. To cap it all, this ice patrol vessel was on the point of being decommissioned by the Royal Navy as part of the economy measures planned by the government in London.

While he threshed out his data and his proposal, Lombardo prepared himself mentally for the difficult questions he was thinking of putting to his superior. The truth is that the experience the Argentine Navy had had in working out such plans left a lot of room for scepticism. This was justified even if for no other reason than that the navy's initiative could be blunted or annulled upon being received by the Junta. In which case the prospect of having worked in vain did not amuse Lombardo very much, any more than that of having his own particular enthusiasm squashed.

Anaya's reaction, who this time decided not to hide the discomfort that his subordinate's questions produced in him, confirmed to Lombardo that he had been right to put those questions.

"Sir," said Lombardo formally, "are forces of all three services taking part in the operation or only those of your own?"

"It will be an action by the whole armed forces," replied Anaya.

"In that case it seems to me that I should at least talk to General Osvaldo Garcia," noted Lombardo, seeking tacit authorisation to discuss the problem with the commander of the 5th Army Corps stationed in Bahia Blanca. It was not just his anxiety at being the possessor of a unique secret that motivated Lombardo's request. He actually did believe that the moment had come to involve senior staff of the other armed forces in the development of the project.

"No, no - certainly not!" said Anaya. "Don't do it until expressly authorised, and that will not be before I have spoken to General Galtieri," explained the Commandant, raising his voice to squash all doubts that he meant what he said. Lombardo nodded agreement, but decided not to let his superior off the hook, and fired off another difficult question:

"Admiral - what is going to happen after we've taken the islands?" he inquired.

"Don't you worry about that, because that's not your responsibility," was the cutting reply. "Limit yourself to working on the plan to take the islands; the rest can come later".

At the time, Anaya did not explain to Lombardo but he was sure that Galtieri would be no obstacle to bringing the project forward - for Galtieri had been his close friend, a comrade in the ups and downs of power and a partner in the last coup. Furthermore, the subject had arisen several times in conversation when they were planning the overthrow of Viola. The Commandant of the Navy had pointed out what an important thing the recovery of the islands would be for his branch of the services. This he had done during the same sessions in which he had used his notable influence over Galtieri to convince the General that he was, indeed, "the man the country needed". Galtieri, seduced by the idea of power, limited himself to agreeing on each occasion. After all, wasn't it essential to have the support of the navy within the Junta in order to succeed in dislodging Viola?

Galtieri rose to the Presidency by means of an increasing influence that he exerted over his subordinates - it was not like the style of leadership of Presidents Alejandro Lanusse or Juan Carlos Ongania. He grew by virtue of the contrast with the shadowy military presence shown by Viola, whom all saw more as a politician.

"Galtieri," recalled a general who served under his orders, "imposed his authority by his presence alone. He was a real soldier. Viola, on the other hand, preferred to stay in his office."

Supported by such facts as these and by his impressive physique, some of the obliging civilian "advisers" who always hang about Commanders-in-Chief thought up and promoted a sort of campaign to create a parallel between this descendant of Italian immigrants and the legendary General Patton, American hero of World War II. In fact, little except a few facial features and the straightforward language they both used could be deemed common to them both. Galtieri had been a mediocre officer his whole career and, according to many who dealt with him, his promotion to general could only be explained in terms of the turbulent epoch he happened to live in.

One fact concerning his career frequently cited by his critics is that he was given a scholarship by the US Army in 1960 in order to do a course in advanced engineering - his military specialism. In fact, he was the only one in the group of Latin Americans on the course who *failed*. It is well known how difficult it is to fail on these exchange programmes, which are designed more to "strengthen links between the institutions" than to improve the professional skills of the military from "peripheral" countries.

In any case, at the time he seized power, Galtieri had only a one-dimensional view of Argentina and the world - certainly a simple one but for that reason an easy one to grasp firmly. He believed, as much as Anaya, that it was necessary to restore political power in the country and to revitalise the military machine which was showing unmistakable signs of exhaustion. In Galtieri's world, grey areas hardly existed and therefore on the question of his country's international alignment he supported a solid alliance with the United States. This was a country for which he felt an almost limitless admiration - as well as a great nostalgia for the year he had spent there, even though it was not notable for its success.

Argentina had to re-enter the Western World without any vacillation. Confident of the approval of North America, the Military Government could consolidate itself and inaugurate a political and military force which would ensure the historic survival of the regime even under a new democratic facade. All this he attempted to outline after attending a gigantic barbecue organized in Victorica, La Pampa.

Being already Commander-in-Chief of the Army, Galtieri travelled to the United States in August 1981. Having been invited by his American colleague, General Edward Meyer, he stayed for ten days. Between meetings and receptions, in decisions that still showed signs of his having been an army volunteer, he sought to involve the effective presence of Argentina in United States foreign policy.

The country was engaging in a polemical debate at that time on the advisability of participating in the setting up of a Multinational Peace Force in Sinai. This was to be part of the Camp David agreement signed by Egypt and Israel, with the US acting as guarantor. The Egyptian Foreign Minister, Boutros Ghali, first raised this possibility with the Argentine Government during a visit to Buenos Aires at the beginning of July. Days before, in Washington, Jim Buckley, US Assistant Secretary of State for Strategic Affairs and Defense, had met representatives of various countries in order to discuss with them the assistance their respective governments would be expected to give. Present at the meeting, besides those of Australia and Uruguay, was the Argentine ambassador.

Also just before August, there arrived in Buenos Aires, as an envoy of President Reagan, the US ambassador at the UN, Jeane Kirkpatrick. She sounded out the Argentine Military about their attitude to the American request. The positions they took up were crystal clear: the army looked forward to co-operating with the request as a sign of friendship towards the United States, while the navy and air force certainly showed reluctance.

For his part, President Viola took a stand against the proposal, making his own suggestion, which was outlined by his Foreign Minister, Dr Oscar Camilion. For the latter, supporting the rather unsubtle customs of American diplomacy would not be a simple matter. One was not only dealing with special envoys like Jeane Kirkpatrick, whose arguments might be well received by her uniformed Argentine questioners. One also had to counter the efforts of the permanent members of the US Embassy in Buenos Aires.

The lobby for securing the dispatch of troops to Sinai was unmasked. In this political game, Claus Ruser, deputy to America's ambassador, Harry Schlaudermann, became notorious. Almost daily he would peddle the plan to some general, admiral or brigadier. Ruser, a man with the tact of a bull in a china shop, zeroed in on the then Chief of the Army General Staff, Major General Vaquero, with whom he had formed a close friendship. Vaquero, an officer whose ubiquitous role brought him equally near to Viola and Galtieri - even at the most critical moments - promptly conveyed his American friend's arguments to his Commandant. Camilion felt himself so besieged by this sort of indirect strategy by Ruser that he began to consider asking the Government to declare him *persona non grata*.

The idea was finally discarded - what Viola needed least was another area of conflict with a Junta openly seduced by the siren calls from the north. Instead, a discreet approach was made to Schlaudermann, who had no alternative but to curtail the activities of his over-zealous subordinate. In any case, Galtieri heard about the incident and the episode contributed to a deep antagonism for Viola's Foreign Minister which he was beginning to develop.

8

Furthermore, on this matter Galtieri always listened to the advice of his personal secretary, Colonel Norberto Ferrero, who had served in the Argentine Embassy in Brazil when the head of the mission was the same Camilion.

Already, during his earlier visit to the United States in August 1981, Galtieri had heard a very suggestive remark concerning the then chief of the Argentine diplomatic corps. At a reception for the Commandant, an Argentine diplomat had made a humorous reference to Camilion. "The thing is," he pointed out with a smile, "the Foreign Minister has one grave defect: he's got a big mouth."

Instead of some more appropriate reply, he received Galtieri's observation: "The Foreign Minister has much graver defects than that!"

The *Justicialist Party* (Peronist) and the *Union Civica Radical*, declared themselves against the sending of Argentine troops to the Middle East, while in the main, the parties of the centre and right, favoured Galtieri's policy of supporting the American scheme. The latter parties considered that an Argentine presence in Sinai would restore the complex bilateral relationship with the United States. This had deteriorated largely due to the international campaign for human rights during the Presidency of the Democrat, Jimmy Carter. Meanwhile, critics on the other side asserted that the national interest did not permit the country to form part of a multinational force which excluded the Europeans, Africans and Asians - which amounted to half the West and all the Non-Aligned countries as well as the Group of 77.

The historical precedents were rather ambiguous as the record of Argentine foreign policy appeared to support the argument of those in favour just as much as those against.

In the middle of June 1950, the Security Council of the UN raised with the Argentine Government the possibility of providing combat forces for the South Korean front. The Peronist Foreign Minister at the time, Hipolito Paz, rejected the idea completely. In 1965 it was the *Radical*, Miguel Angel Zavala Ortiz, who adopted an identical posture upon being requested by the Organisation of American States (OAS) to send troops to the Dominican Republic.

On the other hand, in 1962 the naval ships, *Espora* and *Rosales* formed part of the fleet which blockaded Cuba, whilst in Buenos Aires the 10th Army Brigade was made ready. In the so-called "Football War" of 1969, which concerned Honduras and El Salvador, personnel of the army and air force intervened in a cease-fire mission. Over the ending of the Six-Day War between the Egyptians and Israelis, Argentine officers of the three services acted in the role of observers.

In reality, to have added her troops to the multinational force in Sinai, Argentina would have compromised herself by moving further to one side in the East-West superpower confrontation. This, of course, was precisely what Galtieri was seeking in those days, so he did not spare any efforts to bring about an Argentine presence in the Middle East.

On Friday November 14th, the army chief dined in the exclusive New York restaurant, *Le Cigne*, located on Park Avenue. At his table was a group of Argentine diplomats and military personnel with duties in that city. Galtieri sat at the head, flanked by ambassadors Gustavo Figueroa, Juan Carlos Beltramino and by the military attache, Brig. Gen. Angel Mallea Gil, among others. With extreme caution, the civilian officials explained to Galtieri the reasons why it would not pay Argentina to accede to Washington's request. The diplomats, nevertheless, were careful to produce an explicit assessment when they noticed that Galtieri had sunk into silence, giving the impression that he was waiting for the right moment to make his views known. And this is, in fact, what occurred.

At a certain moment, Galtieri put his glass on the table and declared: "Gentlemen, Argentina *must* be present in Sinai. Today I have notified Meyer of this." (Meyer was his American counterpart). An almost total silence descended over the group at the table as the diplomats exchanged furtive glances. Nobody ever touched on the subject again.

The following morning, before returning to Argentina, Galtieri confirmed to a group of American reporters who questioned him about collaboration with Reagan that: "For the Argentine Army, there is no problem in giving that support because we can give it and much more." He had expressed the same thoughts at his last official meeting - with Assistant Secretary for Economic Policy, Paul Roberts - a few hours before leaving.

Galtieri was already back in Buenos Aires when, on a Sunday evening, a certain corpulent gentleman with a large face and sharp features arrived in the country. The press detected his presence only forty-eight hours later. But this was not unusual, for the man's professional life was always cloaked in the utmost secrecy.

The Lieutenant General and itinerant ambassador, Vernon Walters, arrived in Argentina as a personal emissary of President Reagan. The choice of envoy was the right one. This ex-deputy director of the CIA and indefatigable reader of history has a profound knowledge of the traditions and realities of Latin America. Spanish is one of the nine languages he manages with total fluency. Besides, he is a drinker of enviable capacity and has forged solid friendships with numerous Latin American military officials on countless gastronomic occasions.

Walters had the matter of Sinai on his agenda and his journey was arranged - not by accident - when Foreign Minister Camilion found himself present at the annual Assembly of the UN. Nevertheless, for Washington the priorities had changed. The US Government had properly calculated the adverse consequences for their cause thrown up by the public debate and did not want them to lie in the way of further opportunities for co-operation in other no less important issues.

The Washington representative attended a dinner at the Presidential residence in Olivos on Monday evening, accompanied by Ambassador Schlaudermann. There were, apart from Viola, the Chiefs of Staff of the three services, the Secretary-General of the Presidency and the Argentine ambassador in Paris, Gerardo Schamis (a close friend of Walters) as well as certain more junior officials.

Walters, with his usual note book and ball-point pen, explained that the United States was hoping for the formation of a Latin American group for Sinai, but suggested that it could wait until a rotation of personnel was required there.

He was speaking of bilateral relations and without subterfuge threw on the table the issue of the "anarchy" which was subverting Central America and the chances of co-operation in this area. No-one was surprised at Walters' openness. Scarcely a few weeks beforehand, Galtieri had been very explicit in Washington: "Perhaps it may not be possible to send troops to the Middle East, but with Central America we shall do a better job."

The true significance of Walters' presence in Argentina remains, like his personal history, shrouded in mystery. For example, the Labour MP, Tam Dalyell - one of Margaret Thatcher's most fiery critics - maintained in his book on the conflict in the South Atlantic[2] that:

"Walters was in Buenos Aires, intermittently, for many days, between October 1981 and February 1982. He discussed, *inter alia*, the establishment of a *South Atlantic Treaty Organization*. He also discussed the advantages for such an organisation of an island-base in the Falklands, somewhat along the lines of Diego Garcia. However, the understanding was that the agreement on Hemispheric and other grounds should be between the United States and Argentina, the bulwark of American policy in the South Atlantic, and not between the US and Britain. Asked by the Argentine Military what Britain would do, the American replied to the effect that the British would *huff, puff and protest, and do nothing*, with the implication that the Americans could soothe ruffled British feathers."

What is certain is that in the period mentioned by Dalyell, only one visit by Walters was recorded. Nevertheless, this military ambassador specialises in making secret journeys - witness the title of his first book of memoirs, *Discreet Missions*[3]. Other testimonies, too, point in the same direction as that of the Labour MP:

In a work by Commander Marshall Van Sant Hall of the US Navy on the political results of the Falklands War[4] which was prepared for the College of Naval Warfare, it is stated that when Lt. Gen. Galtieri assumed the Presidency in December 1981, he offered much assistance to President Reagan. This strengthening of inter-American relations put Galtieri in close contact with the itinerant American ambassador, Vernon Walters. According to a persistent rumour, President Galtieri used the ex-deputy head of the CIA, Vernon Walters, to sound out US policy in the case of an Argentine recovery of the Falklands. General Walters repeatedly spoke of a hypothetical request for US neutrality with the precondition that the Argentines would not kill British people on capturing the islands. It might have been by intention or coincidence, but the Argentines scrupulously avoided any casualties of British or islanders during the invasion.

Walters, on being interviewed for this book in Washington, denied that during his contacts with the Argentines they, at any time, hinted at his intentions regarding the Falklands. Nevertheless, he acknowledged that he did believe firmly that the defence of the South Atlantic could only be undertaken with the co-operation of the coastal states, specifically Argentina, and thus he promised to put this fact on record.

On the other hand, the idea of a security pact for the South Atlantic after the model of NATO, was one of his dearest dreams and had been encouraged by the strategists of the Military Government's *Process of National Reorganisation* since its beginnings in 1976. However, the reluctance of Brazil in this matter for fear that the zone might formally become involved in the confrontation between the superpowers impeded its creation. There were, too, the difficulties of forming an alliance of this nature requiring South African involvement as well as the chronic problems of Argentine-American relations in recent years, and several other factors besides.

Of the matters on Walters' agenda that he had brought to Buenos Aires which we have been able to verify, that of Central America went deeper than that of the multinational force for Sinai. When Reagan took over the American government and transformed his country's policy in that region into a sort of "anti-Soviet crusade," he already knew that the Argentine armed forces were embarked on a covert campaign of the same type. Argentina had tried unsuccessfully to avoid the overthrow of the Nicaraguan dictator, Anastasio Somoza, providing him with arms and money until the end. Then advisers were sent to Honduras and Guatemala. These were experts in counter-insurgency, a speciality which experienced an enormous growth in Argentina after 1976. Galtieri also arranged help for the remnants of the Somoza regime in exile in their efforts to bring down the new government of the Sandinista Liberation Front.

This peculiar foreign undertaking of the Military Government was conceived in 1979 by the Chief of Staff of the Army. It stemmed from the hypothesis that Argentina could: "...occupy the vacant spaces in the continental struggle against Communism," that, according to military analysis, was leaving the Carter administration with its policy on human rights short of allies. It is certain that this course of action also caused the Military to throw a protective veil over the Bolivian dictatorship of General Luis Garcia Meza - which did not please Reagan. But equally, the Americans saw an extremely useful tool in this voluntary ideological commitment by the Argentines. Buenos Aires was in a position to assume, given funds and material support from Washington, a degree of participation in the crisis, that Reagan could not demand from his own people without running the risk of triggering a storm of public criticism.

This was a central theme in Walters' negotiations, and even more crucially in the meeting in New York which Camilion had with Alexander Haig. The latter mentioned to him that one could not even discount the possibility of a new blockade against Cuba.

As the negotiations between Buenos Aires and Washington progressed, Galtieri returned to the United States in early November in order to attend the Assembly of American Army Chiefs. Nevertheless, the atmosphere in the American capital was not yet as sympathetic to his case as Galtieri might have wished. Reagan's government viewed with concern the deterioration in the relations between President Viola and the Junta. The Argentine ruler retained a high credibility among the United States leadership, which was mindful of his undertakings, some public, others confidential, to democratize his country. Nobody in Washington thought that co-operation in Central America and democracy were incompatible.

A few days before Galtieri's arrival, Ambassador Schlaudermann sent the State Department a long cable in which he minutely detailed the power struggle taking place at that time in Buenos Aires. The army commandant was received on November 1st by the Argentine ambassador, Esteban Takacs, a businessman turned diplomat, who invited him to stay at his residence. However, Galtieri preferred to take a suite at the luxury Watergate Hotel, arguing that his colleagues would be there and that he would be able to maintain contacts as protocol required.

Takacs was evidently concerned at Galtieri's activities but, above all, he wanted the visitor to be aware that the Reagan administration was not ignorant of the leadership crisis that was approaching in Argentina. For that reason he persuaded Mallea Gil, a military attache possessed of a certain political intuition, to put the matter to Galtieri and invite him to a strictly private discussion at the embassy. The following morning, Galtieri went over to the embassy building and met the ambassador behind closed doors. The latter, speaking as elliptically as he was able, tried to give the visitor a picture of the situation, taking into account his visitor's susceptibilities and his own desire not to appear a meddler. Galtieri listened attentively but at the end said only: "I'll attend to it," thus leaving Takacs in a fog.

Mallea Gil was stubbornly insistent on making more of his commandant's visit than was required for the inter-American meeting. This immediately seduced Galtieri, who showed himself amenable to each of the military attache's suggestions over the various lunches and dinners with military and political figures from the American establishment.

Mallea Gil knew his way around the Washington jungle. He himself was a scholarship-holder and graduate of the Military Academy at West Point and had the US General Meyer among his passing-out companions. He was also able to count on the advice of another "expert," the exiled Nicaraguan, Francisco Aguirre, editor of the *Diario de las Americas*, which is published in Miami. This is a conservative Hispanic publication, furiously anti-Castro in its editorial policy. More than once Aguirre was denounced as an agent of American Intelligence. One Argentine diplomat who in those days was assigned to Washington later remarked: "No-one ever knew what were Aguirre's objectives or what part he was playing, but one could find him any day of the week visiting the office of the Argentine military attache talking about Central America."

A luncheon was given in Galtieri's honour at the Argentine embassy. Mallea thought of every detail with praiseworthy care even to the point of deciding *not* to invite his naval attache, Vice-Admiral Oscar Franco, and air attache, Brigadier Oscar Pena, on the excuse that the deference was to a man of the *army* already cast as a future Head of State.

Mallea's gesture did not go down well with his colleagues, but the exalted rank of those at the table masked his rudeness. The list was long and included: Caspar Weinberger, US Secretary of Defense; Richard Allen, National Security Adviser to President Reagan; Thomas Enders, Assistant Secretary of State for Inter-American Affairs; Jeffrey Briggs, his deputy - as well as William Middendorf, a wealthy businessman rewarded by Reagan for his financial contributions to his campaign by the ambassadorship to the OAS. There were also Paul Roberts,

Assistant Secretary for Economic Policy; Edward Meyer, Commander-in-Chief of the Army; John Marsh, Secretary for the Army and Alejandro Orfila, Secretary-General of the OAS. Finally there were were Vernon Walters and Raul Quijano, the Argentine ambassador to the OAS.

Galtieri, with his broad gestures and pompous pronouncements, was making himself the centre of attention. With singular determination, he forced himself to speak in English, a language of which he scarcely knew the rudiments. Takacs had suggested to him that it would be better to use Spanish, but Galtieri took no notice. This, anyway, gained him the sympathy of the Americans for trying. Weinberger was thrilled with the General and let Ambassador Quijano know it. To crown his performance, Galtieri rose to his feet for the toast and described what he imagined to be the indissoluble alliance between Argentina and the United States:

"Argentina and the United States will march together in the ideological war that is beginning in the world," he confidently affirmed. He added that: "in foreign affairs, Argentina has a major part to play in the world, and it must not limit itself to a secondary role." These words had the desired effect, for in American ears they were equivalent to a ratification of the Argentine intervention in Central America.

For Galtieri it was the consummation of a project meticulously carried out. Part of this consisted in the inclusion in his retinue of Generals Albert Valin - who had already lent his advice to Somoza's National Guard during the civil war - and Mario Menendez, an officer who had the reputation of having participated in the *Operativo Independencia* in the Argentine province of Tucuman, during the repression of the leftist guerillas there.

At the end of the luncheon, a swarm of reporters cleverly alerted by Mallea Gil was waiting for the guests to leave. Richard Allen was overcome by his own rhetoric and described Galtieri as having a "majestic personality." This generous description lost all credibility a few weeks later when Allen was obliged to resign his post for not adequately explaining certain gifts received from a Japanese publication. These consisted of a thousand dollars and two Seiko watches - worth hardly 175 dollars each - a poor compensation for losing one of the most influential political posts in the world: that of National Security Adviser to the American Government.

But Allen was not alone in revealing his enthusiasm. Another who did as much, though more cautiously, was Weinberger: "He is very impressive," he admitted. A few days later, the *Christian Science Monitor* announced in its editorial that: "Galtieri....is a tough and shrewd strategist and potentially a warm ally of the United States".

The "spoilt child of the Americans"[5] as Galtieri described himself after the war, had acquired a definite image. Galtieri believed all the praise bestowed on him quite literally and so, glimpsing idyllic and unlimited horizons opening up between the two countries, lost no time in getting into action. Straight away the Government in Buenos Aires announced a credit of fifteen million dollars to El Salvador. Almost simultaneously, Reagan obtained from Congress the authorisation to renew his country's military assistance to Argentina - although this was conditional on the presentation of his certification which, in fact, never materialized. This assistance had been suspended since 1978 by the "Humphrey-Kennedy" amendment by which "the grave and systematic violations of human rights" committed by the Military in Buenos Aires were penalized.

Reagan and his colleagues had conceived a vast scheme for countering presumed Soviet-Cuban influence in Central America and also countering the support they insisted was being given to the Sandinistas and the insurgents in El Salvador and Guatemala. A key element in that programme was an agreement with the Argentine Junta, whose evident head was Galtieri.

The pact made funds and intelligence available to Argentina in order to impede the aid for guerrillas in El Salvador and Guatemala coming from Cuba via Nicaragua. For its part, Washington would hamper Sandinista actions against Honduras, finance counter-revolutionary groups in Nicaragua and co-ordinate action with its exiles in neighbouring countries. Galtieri delighted the Americans with the idea of winning over to the cause the legendary Eden Pastora. This ex-Sandinista commander, a defector from the Nicaraguan Government, was at that time exiled in Costa Rica and was active in destabilizing the regime set up by his one-time comrades.

Later, certain newspapers such as the prestigious *New York Times* would denounce this scheme, explaining that it was Galtieri's advice that caused the CIA to undertake the patient courting of Pastora.

Until the last few months of 1982, Argentina was the principal source of finance and training of the anti-Sandinistas, but after the Falklands episode, the Reagan administration had to increase its own covert operations in the face of Argentina's desertion.

Before returning from his second journey to the United States, Galtieri had the pleasure of being received by Vice-President George Bush. On Saturday November 7th, on a cold, rainy and foggy evening, Galtieri set off from Manhattan for the military airport from which he had to fly back to Buenos Aires. Nobody in his entourage, nor he himself, expected the news that awaited them at the air base. An official from the Argentine consulate had been sent there to deliver an "urgent and secret" telegram, sent from the Casa Rosada, which informed them of the sudden illness of President Viola.

Galtieri, his wife Lucy on his arm, arrived smiling at the spacious airport lobby where he received the message. His expression, and that of his wife, suffered a sudden transformation. In an almost hysterical reaction, according to some witnesses, he detached himself from Lucy, lit a cigarette, walked a few yards and sank into an armchair. He remained there some forty minutes, his head in his hands, his eyes fixed on some distant point in the room, alone and silent.

Hardly a day after Galtieri's arrival in Buenos Aires, Viola entered the Military Hospital with an acute case of arterial hypertension. From that moment the outline of a new political crisis in Argentina began to take shape. November ended amid uncertainty brought about by the President's illness.

On Saturday 14th, Galtieri stated that: "It did not pass through the minds of the Junta to replace Viola," but on that occasion he was not entirely sincere. The country sensed the inevitable change at the apex of power. At that stage, Galtieri began to design a new power structure for the army which, later, would support him on his Presidential adventure.

Exactly one week later, Viola relinquished power, ceding it to his Minister of the Interior, Major General Horacio Tomas Liendo. He would never recover it. Viola still believed in his own possible return, however. Nevertheless, he was not unaware that the navy, which had disapproved of his appointment, was pressing for a change. Still, he was not persuaded that Galtieri would be involved in any plan to displace him.

Viola always saw Galtieri as a simple man without great aspirations. He was accustomed to describing him privately as: "A good soldier, a good troop commander. He knows nothing about politics. He is uncivilised, rudimentary..."

In support of this impression, the ex-President recollected a conversation he once had with the general which took place on the occasion when Galtieri was notified that he would succeed him as army chief.

"General," Viola advised him, "you must maintain contact with politicians, with trade union leaders. Get out of the barracks a bit, get informed about the problems, and what's going on."

"No, those things are not for me." was Galtieri's reply, given in his habitual genial tone: "I don't get mixed up in those tiresome things that I don't understand anyway."

On December 3rd, a medical bulletin reported an improvement in the President's physical health. His political health, however, had got decidedly worse. Twenty-four hours later, Galtieri set out a new structure for the army, designed in accordance with his interests, which had nothing to do with developments since 1976 under the successive shadows of Videla and Viola. It was not, certainly, an ideological change, but rather one of management styles, ambitions and personal loyalties.

Galtieri got rid of five generals. Two of the dismissals seemed crucial to his plan. With Antonio Bussi out of the way, Galtieri could lay to rest the ghost of an alternative choice inside the regime. Such rivalry would always be promoted by that general who had in the past unleashed a wave of authoritarianism and caprice on Tucuman. Without Jose Rogelio Villareal, moreover, *"Violism"* was deprived of contacts with the political leadership. Also displaced were Reynaldo Bignone, Eduardo Crespi and Carlos Martinez, three obscure officers.

Galtieri chose to surround himself with men like Cristino Nicolaides and Juan Carlos Trimarco, none of whom were known for their political skill, and for whom the "natural commands" of the barracks seemed the only points of reference they could understand. With that army, Viola saw his hope of returning to the Casa Rosada finally vanishing. The coup was in the making and the army had put all its command structure at the service of the operation.

In reality, for many, the fall of Viola had begun even before his appointment, which was delayed by more than ten days by the disapproval of the then Commandant of the Navy, Admiral Armando Lambruschini, a man whose most prominent characteristic was his obedience. With this as a precedent, and the six months wait between his designation as Head of State and his assumption of office, Viola began his Presidency already a spent force. Moreover, Viola sought to impose a pale and tepid adaptation to the monetarism of Martinez de Hoz, and surrounded even that attempt with a flaccid political management and a vague tendency towards liberalization.

While this was taking place and paralysis, a product of Viola's style, was spreading to large parts of the Government, power moved rapidly out of the President's hands. On December 2nd, Galtieri met ex-President Videla in his office of the Commander-in-Chief and asked his opinion on the possible outcome of the power crisis. Not even then did Videla abandon his evasive manner, preferring not to risk unconditional support for his sick friend.

Next day, Galtieri spoke several times to Anaya, who had at least three telephone calls, and then finally resolved to break it to Viola that his luck had run out. The new strong man of Argentina preferred not to face up to the deed himself. After all, it was difficult for him to topple someone who in a way had opened the road to power for him.

Instead of going himself, he sent a series of emissaries. The first was General Llamil Reston on Saturday the 4th, then Hugo Martella on

Sunday the 5th and finally Vaquero on Monday the 6th. The three officers tried to persuade Viola that it was advisable that he should present his resignation because his frail health would prevent him from dealing with the urgent needs of Argentina in that difficult period.

No one actually asked for the dismissal of the President directly. This was simply because the uncomplicated laws governing the *Process of National Re-organization* did not take into account the possibility of the Junta demanding the resignation of a President. There was only provision for voluntary removal or for resignation. Viola, who was one of the architects of the *Process* - and sheltered behind it while he could - knew the argument inside out: "Let the Junta ask for my resignation in writing and for political reasons, not for illness" - was the last thing Viola said to Vaquero.

Finally, on Monday the 7th, Galtieri sent a message to the President, who was shut away in Olivos, announcing that he would visit him the following day to solve the leadership crisis. That same day, at the Comandante Espora air base, Admiral Anaya presided over a ceremony for the arrival of five Super Etendard aeroplanes, the first of a total of fourteen acquired from France.

On Tuesday at 10 pm, Galtieri went to the Presidential residence. Newspaper reports of the day indicated that the meeting lasted until past midnight. In fact, everything was much briefer. Viola and Galtieri sat face to face, with a small coffee table between them. The dialogue began in a roundabout way - Galtieri made an allusion to how well the President looked - but then Viola took the initiative: "Well, General, what do you want us to talk about - illness or politics?" he said.

"Well, er ... we might talk of illness," was the reply.

"Why are we going to talk about illness?" insisted the questioner.

"Well....because a decision has to be taken," stammered Galtieri.

"Then I repeat to you that I am not ill. But you and I know that this is useless, because *I* say this and *you* maintain the opposite. Suppose, General, that you convince yourself that I am not ill? Could we start again from there?" said Viola, determined to give no respite to his political murderer.

"No," admitted Galtieri in a faint voice, unusual for him.

"Then don't let us fuck about. Why the shit do you want to talk about illness? Let's talk about politics," snapped Viola in exasperation.

On Wednesday the 9th, Galtieri and Viola renewed the conversation. The President left a resignation of no more than a page in length in the hands of the Commander-in-Chief of the Army. It was a text following a pattern set by two predecessors in the office, Juarez Celman and Ortiz - in which he indicated clearly that he was retiring for political reasons and not for health.

That evening Galtieri dined at the private residence of Anaya, situated in the northern part of greater Buenos Aires. Also present were the men who shared responsibility for the air force: Brigadier General Omar Graffigna and the man designated to succeed him on the 17th of the month - Brigade Major Arturo Basilio Lami Dozo. Here the decision was made: the Military Junta would name the next President.

Viola's obstinacy in not wanting to make his exit in a quiet manner backstage irritated Galtieri as much as Anaya. They had both hoped to be able to avoid, at least to all appearances, a public display of their palace intrigue and so limit the damage to the Military. But if that was how Viola wanted to be overthrown, then that is how it would have to be.

The announcement of the decision of the commandants was almost symbolic. It fell to Admiral Anaya, during an end-of-year reception customarily organised by the navy to entertain the press. In a severe and monotonous voice, and with an almost perverse expression, Anaya told the country that: "Time and available procedures for dealing with the crisis are exhausted," which sealed the fate of the sick President.

At the party, Galtieri strolled around exultantly, without abandoning his glass of mineral water, an unusual drink for him. He made a point of visiting every part of this reception of the Commander-in-Chief of the Navy, which was taking place on the 13th floor of the *Libertad* building. A journalist, betrayed by what was present in the collective unconscious, called Galtieri "Mr President," whereupon the General carelessly fell into the error of a brief "usurping of duties and honours" and did not correct his obsequious questioner.

Before retiring, Galtieri let out an ecstatic: *"Let's go, Argentina!"* And at least one of those present questioned whether such a voluminous figure would even be able to pass through the double doors of the room.

That same Thursday evening, the then Secretary-General of the Army, Major General Alfredo Saint Jean, was sent to Olivos to tell Viola that twenty-four hours later he would have to present himself at the *Libertador* building, the headquarters of the Army Commander-in-Chief, where the Military Junta would receive him. The dialogue between the President and the commandants was brief - hardly a last vain attempt to find an honourable settlement to the crisis. Not even thirty minutes passed before he was invited to retire to another office and to await a further summons. Ten minutes later he returned to the interview room to be notified of his removal. Galtieri was already the new *de facto* President of the Argentines.

The outcome in reality seemed to provoke more excitement abroad than in Argentina itself. The country continued functioning without obvious disturbance: people lived through the New Year festivities, and the radio and television - especially the latter - discussed other countries and other personalities.

The foreign press reacted with sarcasm and concern. *Le Monde* spoke of the "tragi-comic ballet that the generals of Buenos Aires perform around the Casa Rosada," and affirmed that Galtieri was "pro-American," which would herald the return to Argentina "...of those who possess the big stick." The American newspapers presented the information without embellishment, with the exception of the *Washington Post*, which described the new President as "hard line."

Galtieri was the son of a modest Italian family which had lived in the suburbs of Buenos Aires. At 55, Galtieri was above all an ingenuously ambitious man. He had a quick and explosive tongue: "I am going to the front!" he said on December 22nd, upon assuming the Presidency. He was simple and emotional, as was demonstrated on one of his journeys to the United States where he insisted on visiting Hollywood and Disneyland.

In tune with his rudimentary ideological principles - such as those of all military endeavour - Galtieri imposed an expansive style. This was in accordance with the role which he believed Argentina had been assigned in the international community. "He believes that the world revolves around the Argentine Republic and that the Argentine Republic revolves around him," Viola said about him.

Many visitors were impressed by his habit of receiving them wearing short sleeves settled in an armchair behind his desk, a glass of whisky in his hand - often with his feet on the table. His wife Lucy had great social aspirations, frequently expressed in an apparent interest in art and painting, which she had tried for years to cover with a varnish of refinement. All this was in vain however, for the provincial life of the barracks had branded him - he was a man defeated in the struggle against his own intellectual sloth.

Galtieri knew that he was arriving at the Casa Rosada with a country coming apart at the seams, with deep social divisions and a yearning for political change. He was convinced that before anything else he would have to reform the broken power structure. In particular, he felt that it would be essential to have some resounding triumph in order to give impetus to the military regime which was struggling to survive. For that reason he went round a number of the larger ministries, without much of a plan in mind. He placed much emphasis upon the Foreign Ministry, since he supposed that in foreign policy he might find a key to the success of his strategy.

The new President, through Saint Jean, who was pulled out of the ranks of the army to be Minister of the Interior, made contact with Nicanor Costa Mendez. This was a man with credentials compatible with Galtieri's plan and with a nostalgia for the Falklands which recalled the early days of the fledgling republic. They also shuffled names of certain other candidates, among them a friend of Costa Mendez' childhood, the lawyer and consultant of multinational companies, Eduardo Roca. Both were linked with the relatively new but influential Argentine Council for International Relations, one of the keys of the Argentine establishment.

The newspapers began to speculate about the appointment of one or the other. On one occasion Roca and Costa Mendez decided to lunch in the restaurant of the Plaza Hotel, a daily meeting place of many powerful figures in Argentina. "Let them see us together," said Roca to his friend, "and draw any conclusions they want; it will not be one of *them* that puts us out of the competition."

During the meeting, between greetings to others at the table and jokes on the same theme, the old companions of student days made a close pact:

"You are going to be Foreign Minister," began Costa Mendez mistakenly to Roca, "and I Ambassador to the UN; I very much want to have a spell in New York," he slyly proposed.

"I agree, Canoro," Roca smilingly accepted, "but if you go to the Palacio San Martin I shall be the one who has charge of the mission to the UN," he responded. This, in fact, would be the final outcome - Roca could see the future more clearly. A few days later, Galtieri informed Costa Mendez of his selection as Foreign Minister and imposed two priorities on the ex-ambassador to Chile and ex-Foreign Minister of President Organia. These two priorities were the Beagle Channel and the Falklands. For his part, Costa Mendez made his acceptance conditional upon an assurance that the Military Government would not embark on a war with Chile. This prompted an ironic remark, but also a veiled warning from the President: "I called for a hard man, and it turns out that a soft one has come."

Anaya and the navy felt seduced by the presence of Costa Mendez in the Palacio San Martin. The naval chief - an obsessive man - perceived one more green light to add to those he sought in order to push forward his cherished idea to possess the Falklands. The air force was also satisfied: Costa Mendez was one of the men to whom commandants turn, from time to time, to obtain advice. In 1978, Costa Mendez had edited the part of the document, *The Political Bases of the Air Force*, dedicated to international policy. This was one of the key documents employed in working out the political programme of the Military Junta and in which he defended the inclusion of Argentina in the "Christian West."

For the rest, Anaya knew that Galtieri - his friend - would not fail him. He was certain of this because the President never flinched before adventure. The *"Fateful Pact,"* as it was described by one ex-President, was already under way.

NOTES

1. In an interview in the course of researching this book, General Horacio Tomas Liendo, ex-Joint Chief of Staff, affirmed that that organization, "never prepared a contingency plan for occupying the Falklands." Liendo assumed the title of Joint Chief of Staff in 1980, after the Military Junta decided to reactivate it, since it did not function in military terms during the so-called "struggle against subversion."

2. *One Man's Falklands* Tam Dalyell, MP, appendix A, pp. 133-4. Cecil Woolf, London, 1982.

3. *Misiones Discretas* Lt. Gen. Vernon Walters, Editorial Planeta, Barcelona, 1981.

4. *Argentine Policy in the Falklands War: The Political Results*, Commander Marshall Van Sant Hall, USN Naval War College, USA Chapter II, pp. 23-4, 1983.

5. Newspaper, *Clarin*, April 2nd, 1983. In a report of an interview with Leopoldo Galtieri by Juan Bautista Yofre, entitled "Galtieri speaks of the war."

Chapter 2

THE TEST IN NEW YORK

A new spirit was circulating in the armed forces, softening the impact of President Viola's removal. Galtieri's assumption of power was a reassuring signal to the fractured military edifice and meant that in spite of growing difficulties, the Government's continuity would be preserved. But until when? 1990 was an appropriate year to hand over the reins of power to civilians, always provided, of course, that they scrupulously respected the rules of the game.

From the point of view of the new occupant of the Casa Rosada, the unwritten pact with Anaya would open broad options for his leadership policy. In exchange for support for the Falklands project, Galtieri received the naval chief's backing in throwing out Viola from the Presidency. Now, Galtieri calculated that he was ready to set in motion the first stage of his plan: to get the army firmly in power, neutralizing the influence that the navy had acquired in recent times, and to a lesser extent, that of the air force.

Colonel Bernardo Menendez, an official at the Ministry of the Interior who acted as a liaison officer between the Casa Rosada and political and trade union leaders, proposed in a handwritten memorandum, three central points of strategy for the Commander-in-Chief and President. First, an end to so-called "feudalism," thus breaking the mechanism by which military cabinet ministers - and consequently some civilians also - were loyal first to the commandant of their arm of the services and only then to the President. Secondly, to reverse the "system of loyalties" in the provinces, so that the respective governors might report to the Casa Rosada, and not to the army, navy or air force, as was happening up till then. Thirdly, to create a political force which, with a strong national network, would support the Presidential candidature of Galtieri *in the future*.

Although at this point in the story, Menendez did not know of plans to land in the Falklands, that adventure might very well have been later included to give a final impulse to that strategy. "Triumph in the

25

Falklands might have historically justified the Government of the armed forces," said the Colonel in all sincerity during the research for this book.

Galtieri had given his naval chief the green light and the latter would not want to lose a minute. It was time to formalise the project in the Junta in order to be able to begin co-ordinating plans, something Lombardo was demanding insistently.

That opportunity arrived on 29th December. The three commandants found themselves in the small cinema of the Condor building, the headquarters of the air force. They were presiding over the award of insignias to newly-appointed brigadiers. Afterwards, with the excuse of an end-of-year celebration, Galtieri, Anaya and Lami Dozo went up to the fifth floor to take a glass of champagne in the air chief's office.

They made small talk until Anaya and Galtieri threw the Falklands idea on the table. Inside twelve months, they said, one hundred and fifty years of British occupation of the archipelago would be completed. The Government of the armed forces had to try to ensure that by that time the blue and white flag would fly over Port Stanley.

Basilio Lami Dozo did not raise objections, but instead cursed his luck. He had only been head of his service for a few days but he had already been a protagonist in the overthrow of a President. Now he was faced with a proposal to land in the Falklands. The air chief had projected a rather different image to the other military leaders in the conduct of political affairs, and in fact seemed an adaptable man and less wedded to rigid military ideology in the eyes of the political parties.

In this informal way, the Junta advanced towards its crucial move. Although the essential decision was not taken that hot afternoon, the final step was not long in coming.

Anaya was not happy and he said as much to Galtieri at a celebration on the night of January 1st. For the army commandant, who had still not informed even his Chief of Staff about the plan of action, had authorised contact with General Osvaldo Garcia, Commander of the 5th Corps, although the actual substance of the matter was not to be revealed. He also told Anaya that General Mario Benjamin Menendez, Chief of Operations in the General Staff, would be Governor of the Falklands if the operation was successful - something that both commandants took for granted.

Naturally, Garcia and Menendez did not know the fate to which their chief had assigned them. They were appointed *"in pectore* - like the Pope does with his Cardinals" - as one of the participants in the story described it.

Garcia's ignorance of the matter that Lombardo had in hand posed an additional difficulty. The admiral resorted to subterfuge in order not to postpone joint planning further. He visited him, using as an excuse his recent promotion as Commander of Naval Operations in Puerto Belgrano. In the conversation with the general, he let fall the necessity of discussing "plans of support" between his land and sea forces.

The chief of the 5th Corps was certainly intrigued by this spontaneous offering from the admiral. The geographic closeness of Argentina's largest naval base and his own army command obliged them to live at close quarters, and he presumed that Lombardo wanted to make a social gesture. He also thought that something might be up in Buenos Aires, thought he could not put his finger on it exactly.

A quick review of matters pending brought him inevitably to the "Chile Question" - primary responsibility of his large battle unit, whose influence extended over all South Argentina and to the region of the southern Andes. And he was right. The naval chief presented to him a series of considerations regarding the frontier dispute with the Chileans. He told him that they had to work with their eyes open to an apparent sudden increase in tension with the government of Augusto Pinochet. "The political and international situation is so difficult that at any moment we can be assigned to some new task like this," argued Lombardo, looking the general straight in the eye.

Both chiefs agreed to put joint planning in hand and examined the problems realistically. Lombardo thought that joint training in helicopter transport and communications was necessary. There were very serious difficulties: the army would be taking a new batch of conscripts at the end of February and, as if that were not enough, that year the work was the responsibility of the 5th Corps. These recruits would only be ready to do technical work by April and only by that month could they be considered moderately trained, or perhaps even later. Lombardo warned that at this rate there would be no appreciable progress and so he returned to the fray with Anaya. The latter asked him to be patient, as a decision would be taken soon.

On January 6th, the commandants sorted the matter out. They insisted on bringing the action forward in the event of the failure of the next round of negotiations with Great Britain due to take place in New York on February 27th and 28th.

Anaya also made a formal request: the embassy in London ought to be occupied by an *admiral* when the landing was undertaken, and he proposed Rudolfo Luchetta, Governor of Santa Fe, and an ex-naval attache in London.

Why did he raise this question, which at first sight appeared so unexpected - as if dragged in by the scruff of the neck? The naval commandant's idea was that an admiral would be in a better position than a civilian to explain to the British armed forces the meaning of the

27

Argentine military operation. It would count more with his British counterparts if he could talk the same language in technical and political terms. The naivete of that proposal demonstrated very well the Argentine Military's view of the world: they were reducing a problem of British foreign policy to an "understanding between the armed forces" - as if the British Military were installed at 10 Downing Street, in the same way as Argentina's were in the Casa Rosada.

A day later, the newspaper, *Clarin*, in its political commentary, revealed the proposal to swap Ortiz de Rozas for Luchetta[1]. At first the leak was attributed to the Foreign Affairs Ministry, seeking to expose the manoeuvre. But in fact, the information was not from there but from sources close to the Junta. The replacement of Ortiz de Rozas, it was considered, could alert the British. Until that moment, the efforts of this diplomat had perceptibly improved the dialogue with London and surely his removal would disturb the British Foreign Office, which would rush to find the hidden reasons for the replacement?

Six days later the commandants made the final turn of the screw in their plans for the landing. Galtieri notified Garcia, and Lami Dozo appointed Brigadier Sigfrido Plessl as his delegate on the small staff for the operation.

The President informed the Foreign Minister, Costa Mendez, about the navy's request and asked him to remove Ortiz de Rozas from London. It was evident at that time that Galtieri did not want to have any sort of clash with his principal ally, Admiral Anaya, and was disposed to give way to the majority of the requests he might make. Costa Mendez did not agree to the removal of his ambassador from Great Britain in order to replace him by a military officer. He must avoid making any change, he told Galtieri, at least until an important post could be found for Ortiz de Rozas, given that he occupied one of the highest ranking posts among the Argentine ambassadors. But Galtieri cut him short, saying: "Offer him Italy."

Ortiz de Rozas could not imagine what was happening in Buenos Aires. On the 12th, when he returned after a dinner at the Belgian Embassy in London, he was given a message that Costa Mendez had called during his absence. On the next day, he contacted the Foreign Minister. The following dialogue then took place:

"I wanted to say to you that due to an irreversible decision of the Junta, you have ceased to be ambassador in London. An admiral will be coming in your place. This, Carlos, has nothing to do with yourself or your diplomatic conduct, which has never been called into question by the commandants".

Costa Mendez had fired off a terrific broadside in the sensitive ears of the diplomat. In spite of the dressing up that the Foreign Minister had used to soften the blow, the impact was clear.

Disturbed, Ortiz de Rozas replied drily: "What is the reason, Canoro?"

"A decision of the Junta. I can offer you the Embassy in Italy," the Foreign Secretary tempted.

"You have nothing to offer me. At this stage in my career I don't want tourism....." replied the ambassador, who, convinced that his fate was no longer in his own hands, counter-attacked: "I could be Ambassador to the United Nations, which is also vacant."

Costa Mendez left the matter to be answered another day.

The reply, when it arrived, was negative. In exchange for London, it was suggested that he could take charge of the Argentine negotiating mission at the Holy See in the Papal mediation over the Beagle Channel. Ortiz de Rozas was not displeased at this new prospect. But he arranged to travel to Buenos Aires to talk about the matter personally. He quickly set off for Paris, where he changed planes and flew on in a Jumbo of Air France to Argentina. When he met Costa Mendez on Monday 18th, the situation was still tense. The Foreign Minister made an effort to humour him.

Finally, the matter of the replacement was set on one side. It was necessary to talk about the future, which was really the purpose of the meeting. The Foreign Minister explained that the Junta's idea was that Luchetta, who had resigned the Governorship of Santa Fe, should go to London. For his part, he could go to Rome and at the same time take charge of the negotiating mission with the Pope.

There was one serious difficulty: they both knew that the Holy See would view unfavourably the combining of both diplomatic functions in one envoy. But they had to convince the commandants, who thought that the objection Costa Mendez was bringing up was a device to impede the change of ambassador in London. The Papal Nuncio in Buenos Aires, Monseigneur Ubaldo Calabressi, was therefore consulted, and the Argentine Ambassador to the Holy See, Jose Maria Alvarez de Toledo, was brought in to sound out the Vatican Secretary of State, Monseigneur Agostino Casaroli, officially. In both cases the reply was negative.

At the same time, Ortiz de Rozas was given notice that he would be received by Galtieri on January 20th at 12.30 pm at the Casa Rosada. He would be offered charge of the mission in the Papal mediation on the Beagle Channel, replacing Guillermo Moncayo, whose work did not satisfy Galtieri and Costa Mendez.

On the day of the interview with the President, whilst Ortiz de Rozas was getting ready in his flat in the Avenida Alvear, he received an unexpected telephone call. It was the British Ambassador in Buenos

Aires, Anthony Williams, who was calling. This diplomat had heard rumours about an admiral being sent to London and he clearly explained to Ortiz de Rozas that his government, "viewed with displeasure" the appointment of a military officer as ambassador. The Argentine replied that he took note of the message, but that he was not the right person to receive it. Williams replied that he would immediately contact the Foreign Ministry.

There then began a race between Ortiz de Rozas and Williams. The Argentine wanted to arrive first at the Palacio San Martin in order to alert the Deputy Foreign Minister of the unexpected conversation with the Englishman. When he sat down in front of Ros and began to explain to him what Williams had been saying a few minutes earlier, a secretary came into the office to say that, without having asked for an appointment, the British Ambassador had arrived asking for an urgent interview. Learning that Ros was in a meeting - the secretary did not tell him that Ortiz de Rozas was there - Williams said he would take a walk around the Plaza San Martin and return in ten minutes.

Ortiz de Rozas then told Ros that the British ambassador's argument was weak, as there already was a mission in London headed by an admiral - that of Venezuela - and that *he* had managed things quite satisfactorily.

On the other hand, the appointment of a military officer to London was only a rumour, until then only reported in the newspapers. Williams then entered and informed Ros of his concern about the replacement of a civilian for a military officer in London. He indicated that though the Foreign Office would not reject a request to send another ambassador, his government was not pleased with the appointment.

Meanwhile, Ortiz de Rozas went to the Casa Rosada to meet Galtieri. Whilst he waited for the President to emerge from a Cabinet meeting, he asked one of the officers to put him in telephone contact with Costa Mendez: he wanted to talk to him before the interview with Galtieri. This was done: the Foreign Minister, informed of the British pressure - in fact, he had already spoken with Ros - decided to accompany the ambassador during the first part of the conversation with the President.

"Let the English stop bothering us," Galtieri exploded on hearing about Willams' action, "because we have the right to name anyone we like as ambassador in London. Now we shall have the chance to work something like this on *them....*" He ordered Costa Mendez to comply literally with the Junta's instructions on the matter. The Foreign Minister departed a few minutes later and left Galtieri and Ortiz de Rozas alone.

The conversation concerned the formal offer from Galtieri to head the negotiating delegation in the Vatican. Ortiz de Rozas accepted, on condition that he had freedom of action and that his chain of command should be to the Foreign Minister and the President - exclusively and in that order.

"I want to have your authorization to use that red telephone," he added, indicating the one the President had in his office. The "red line" was fundamental for some decisions that did not admit of intermediaries during the complex negotiations with Chile. Encouraged by the mood of cordiality Galtieri was showing, Ortiz de Rozas asked expressly that the channel with the Holy See, manned by a single officer, be suspended. In that way duplication in the conversations with the Pope's representative could be avoided.

Galtieri again agreed. As the idea that Ortiz de Rozas might go to the Rome embassy was now discarded, he thought of sending him to Paris, but that would mean removing Geraldo Schamis, an ambassador who used to boast of his friendship with the commandant of the air force and with the American, General Vernon Walters, ex-Deputy Director of the CIA and friend of the Argentine Military. Later, with the war on, the Walters-Schamis connection would be used assiduously.

Enchanted with the President's understanding attitude, Ortiz de Rozas wanted to put the finishing touches to his contribution and offered to brief Galtieri on the negotiations with Great Britain over the Falklands - without knowing that he was putting his head under a guillotine. He explained that bilateral relations with London had improved after the prolonged absence of an Argentine ambassador, and one could sense the goodwill of Margaret Thatcher's Conservative Government in the negotiations with Buenos Aires, but that these good intentions had a limit. He considered that in resorting to the ploy of taking into account the "wishes" of the inhabitants of the Falklands, the British were using a delaying tactic. He remembered a conversation he had had in London with the Foreign Secretary, Lord Carrington, in which the latter had appeared surprised that the negotiations with Argentina were not progressing, because the problem "had no political importance" for the United Kingdom.

The ex-Foreign Minister Camilion had arrived at the same conclusion when he met Carrington in New York in September 1981. "For the British, the Falklands are item 242 in the order of priorities in foreign policy," the then Minister had said.

Continuing with his briefing, Ortiz de Rozas predicted that the negotiating procedure would last a long time....

"In a word, would you say that the British will not answer us until the year 2000?" asked Galtieri.

"In effect, yes," replied the ambassador.

Galtieri, in his only published report after the war[2] asserted that Ortiz de Rozas gave his opinion concerning an eventual Argentine landing in the archipelago, indicating that there would be no British counter-attack if the military action was carried out "cleanly." He said that the British "would not even have to twist an ankle." The ambassador, on the other hand, completely denied being informed about the landing: "I should have opposed it firmly," he said to the authors. He also denied having used the words Galtieri attributed to him.

Ortiz de Rozas stayed a few more days in Buenos Aires, before returning to London, and examined the memorandum prepared by the Argentine Foreign Secretary for delivery to the British Ambassador. This document contained the Argentine proposal for the negotiations in New York.

The manoeuvre by the British Ambassador, Williams could easily have turned on warning lights for the Argentines. Costa Mendez took the British ambassador's message very seriously and tried to press for the change to be dropped, but Galtieri subordinated it to Anaya's requirement. The Foreign Minister then sent an emissary to Lami Dozo to ask him to convince Anaya of the futility of the step he was proposing. This way turned out to be best, for the air force chief, knowing that his friend Schamis could be unseated in this affair, being forced to give up his embassy in Paris, accepted the Foreign Minister's arguments and managed to prevent Ortiz de Rozas' transfer. The latter would remain in London, but would also take charge of the Beagle Channel problem. Luchetta, meanwhile, would have to agree to be Argentine ambassador to the Italian Government.

Whilst all this negotiation was taking place, those entrusted with the military planning met for the first time. General Garcia had to cancel his vacation on the Atlantic coast to take charge of the project. In the first meeting, the general made a veiled criticism of Lombardo. This occurred when the admiral informed him that he had been working on the plans since December and that that had been the reason for his proposal for a programme of joint action with the army. As he was the most senior of the three officers, the head of the 5th Corps assumed the leadership of the operation. The first task was to draw up a *Strategic Military Directive* for delivery to the three commandants. One of the members of the working party at the time commented on the paradoxical situation in which they found themselves: "We are working out the orders that we ourselves should have received from our superiors!" he said. They decided to specify the closing date for the operation. "*D-Day*" would be July 9th. The landing and the recovery of the islands would last until "*D Plus 5*", which meant that the whole thing would take five days. Later those dates were changed and *D-Day* was fixed for May 15.

The three members of the planning team supposed that these plans had been worked out with one of the world powers. They quickly discarded the Soviet Union as a possibility, because the navy was always raising the spectre of Russian submarines in the South Atlantic. This had caused the navy to recommend, in conjunction with the South African Government, an agreement to form a strategic alliance in the region with the participation of the United States. According to the prevalent opinion among the Military, one of the solutions to the Falklands question would consist in offering Washington a naval base in the islands. But that was a matter for the Foreign Affairs Ministry. At that time, the latter only had instructions to "turn the screws" on London to obtain some results in the next round of talks.

"In January," declared Costa Mendez during discussions with the authors, "we knew absolutely nothing about the military plans that were being prepared. I only knew that the tension would gradually increase." With that purpose in mind, he drafted the memorandum to be delivered to the British on January 27th which also accorded with a request from London that it should receive details of the matters the Argentines wished to raise with sufficient notice - as if the Argentines knew them properly themselves! Three days before handing over this document, the reporter, Jesus Iglesias Rouco, revealed in his column in *La Prensa* that the Government would press Great Britain to agree to a firm negotiating timetable which would finally settle the issue of the islands in favour of Argentina. He said that the conditions that Buenos Aires would demand would be "firm and clear" and that if London did not accept them, or did not respond within a certain period, Argentina would break off the discussions.

He also stated that the United States would support Argentina in any action, not excluding military action, to recapture the archipelago. Only the first part of this information turned out correct.

The long document entitled: *The Argentine Position* that Costa Mendez delivered to the British ambassador - a copy of which was obtained for this book - stated in its most salient paragraphs that: "The recognition of Argentine sovereignty over the archipelagoes (i.e. the Falklands, South Georgia and the South Sandwich Islands) is a fundamental principle." And he reaffirmed that that recognition "continues to be a requirement *sine qua non* for the solution of the dispute."

He also made reference to resolutions 2065 (XX), 3160 (XXVIII) and 31/49 of the United Nations, underlining that the latter "concede due attention to the interests of the inhabitants of the islands, in the context of the negotiations to which they invite both Governments. The decisions of the world organization at no time refer to the *wishes* of the islanders, because the dispute concerns only the Argentine and

33

British Governments."

Finally he made the following concrete proposal:

"On the assumption that the question of sovereignty over the Falkland Islands, South Georgia and the South Sandwich Islands must be solved peacefully, finally and rapidly in the interests of the parties to the dispute and of all others concerned in its solution, the Argentine Government proposes, in order to expedite matters, the establishment of a permanent negotiating commission, which will meet during the first week of every month, alternately, in each capital, and will be charged with maintaining continuity and impetus in the negotiations, not allowing them to be relegated to desultory meetings without clear objectives and concrete results.

"Its technical and political standing would permit the rapid and thorough treatment of the matters under discussion, and enable it to make proposals to the governments. This commission would have one year's duration. It could be discontinued at any time by either party, with prior notice."

"The Argentine Government will consider the future of the negotiations in the light of the reply which the British Government makes to this proposal, hoping that that will be given before or during the next round of negotiations that are to take place in February 1982."

This, then, would be the proposal to which Great Britain would have to respond. In fact, the document was based on an official Argentine declaration of July 27th 1981, during Camilion's term of office. Simultaneously, the small military committee was actively continuing to develop itsr plans, which were completed in outline on February 15th.

That month found the Argentine Government wholly absorbed in three issues: (a) the strengthening of ties with the Reagan administration; (b) consolidation of the personal political strategy of President Galtieri and (c) the negotiations with the British, which would be the final test for the military option that was being prepared in secret.

The honeymoon with Washington already had substance but also a cost: open participation in Central America. The same day on which the British patrol vessel, *Endurance*, was mooring in the Argentine port of Mar del Plata and Ambassador Williams was declaring that he noted: "a certain impatience on both sides to resolve the Falklands question," the ABC television network of America threw a grave accusation at the Argentine Military. The American Broadcasting Corporation, which had one of the best teams in the Central American region, announced that Argentine troops were forming a company of "freedom fighters" in the struggle against the Nicaraguan Government. The Foreign Minister of the Sandinistas, Miguel D'Escoto, turned the screw once more by asserting that the military regime in Buenos Aires was involved in a "conspiracy to overthrow" his government.

This offensive remark was not gratuitous. Washington was preparing the largest and most ambitious operation yet against the Sandinistas and the Salvadorean guerillas. Moreover, it would have legal cover under the auspices of the OAS, if it could succeed in getting that forum to apply the *Inter-American Treaty of Reciprocal Aid,* with the argument that an "extra-continental threat" was manifest in the region.

According to the magazine, *Newsweek,* the operation was called *Plan Charlie* and consisted in "a right-wing, pan-Latin American *Army of Peace* headed by Argentina that would be able to push the left-wing guerillas of El Salvador inland towards Honduras, where the army of that country would crush them in a pincer movement."

The Foreign Affairs Ministry in Buenos Aires replied, denying everything, and describing these reports as: "imaginary and untrue." While Costa Mendez was summoning the Argentine Ambassador, Marcelino Chuburu Lastra, back to the country in order to express the Military's displeasure at D'Escoto's accusations, the Argentine representative in Washington revealed that his government gave "strong support to many United States initiatives in the Hemisphere." Takacs was not a man to speak for the sake of it. He knew perfectly well that he was complying literally with the memorandum drawn up in December to improve relations with the U.S.

That document[3], made public later by the Argentine press, had been drafted by General Mallea Gil, and proposed a series of successive steps from the engagement of a lobby in Washington to visits to the American Secretary of Defense, aimed at bettering relations with the White House. Of that memorandum, they only carried out two proposals: the withdrawal of ambassadors from Havana and from Managua.

By then Galtieri had rapidly begun to savour the pleasure of power and imagined popularity, a product perhaps of keeping his eyes half closed.

A gigantic barbecue at La Pampa for all centre-to-right politicians in Argentina marked the beginning of his campaign. But it would be with the Falklands that that still nebulous project would take definite shape.

Galtieri obtained authorization from the Junta in early February to inform Costa Mendez of the military plans for the recovery of the islands. The Foreign Minister proposed that a working party should be formed to study the scheme and develop possible alternative strategies, but the President required total confidentiality. The round of talks in New York was now approaching and its results would determine the direction of events.

The Deputy Minister for Foreign Affairs, Enrique Ros, would head the delegation. He would be accompanied by Ambassador Carlos Lucas Blanco, Director of the Falklands Department at the Foreign Affairs Ministry, and a military consultant, an expert in the field. From London, Ambassador Ortiz de Rozas flew to New York, with his military adviser Atilio Molteni. The British sent Richard Luce, Secretary of State at the Foreign Office, who was replacing Nicholas Ridley. For the meeting in New York, Luce was accompanied by Ambassador Williams and by members of the legislative council of the Falklands.

A few days before the departure, the Argentine ambassador to the OAS, Raul Quijano, ex-Foreign Minister of the Peronista Government and a cautious man, arrived in Buenos Aires. Costa Mendez called him to discuss the Central American crisis and to prepare the agenda for the next visit to Argentina of Thomas Enders. Enders was Assistant-Secretary for Inter-American Affairs at the Department of State.

At a luncheon for two, the Foreign Minister took the opportunity to sound out Quijano's opinion on the Falklands. He put the question to him like an exercise:

"What would happen if we landed in the Falklands?" Costa Mendez asked him.

"To negotiate or to stay there?" queried the ambassador.

"If we go there, it will be to stay," replied the Minister.

"It would be madness!" exclaimed Quijano, abandoning his habitual reticence.

The day of his departure, Ros asked for patience and trust "in that the decisions the Government takes are the best, given the circumstances, taking into account not only the past but also a vision of the future." The Deputy Foreign Minister was a man with great ability to talk without saying anything. Judged as an able professional by his colleagues, Ros had the virtue of constantly keeping his mouth shut and was a specialist in avoiding leaks. Nevertheless, he lacked initiative. He stuck almost obsessively to his instructions and did not move a millimetre from them - an attitude for which he would be criticized, as much by the Secretary-General of the United Nations as by the American negotiators during the war.

The conversations in New York did not depart from the tradition of these sterile contacts. Luce indicated that the duration of the negotiating commission, as proposed by Argentina, "was not realistic." He was also keeping to the instructions given him by his chief, Lord Carrington, which consisted in firmly resisting any pressure to impose a limit to the dialogue. London was not totally opposed to the setting up of a Permanent Commission, but rejected discussion of sovereignty because the "kelpers" were totally opposed to introducing that question.

He delivered a working paper, giving the British point of view on the role of the Permanent Commission, in which no mention was made of the frequency of meetings, but the Argentines strongly pressed for a reply to the idea of monthly meetings and a period of one year to resolve the dispute. In any case, the document did not contain a concrete proposal from the British Foreign Office. It was hardly a *working paper* in fact[4].

The British strategy consisted in delaying any definite action and preventing the negotiations from having a date of expiry. The British delegate agreed with his Argentine colleague in maintaining strict confidentiality over the British document, as this was a draft unseen even by the Conservative Cabinet, Parliament as a whole and the lobby of the Falkland Islands Company, though he obviously did not mention the latter.

Ros and Luce shook hands on February 28th. The following day they issued a joint communique which said that the meetings "had taken place in a cordial and positive atmosphere. Both parties re-affirmed their decision to find a solution to the sovereignty dispute and to consider in detail the Argentine proposal to make better progress in that direction. They agreed to consult their governments."

Neither of the two knew that the countdown would begin hardly twelve hours later.

NOTES

1. *Clarin* Newspaper, January 7th, 1982 pp.14-15.
2. *Clarin*, April 2nd, 1983, report of Galtieri interview (cited above).
3. *Movimiento* Magazine, Year 1, No.5, p.30.
4. *Falkland Islands Review*, p.40, Paras 135-6.

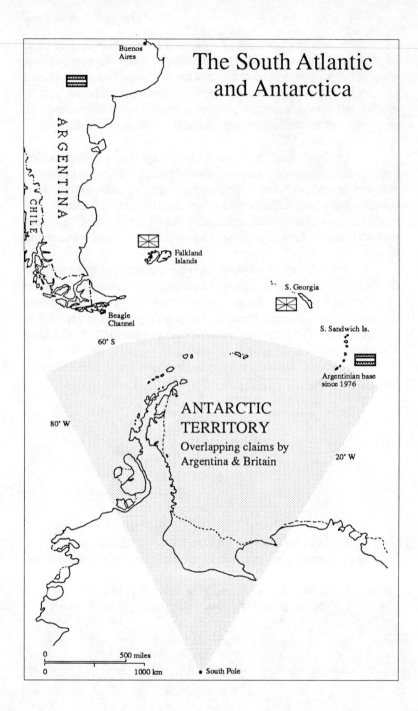

The South Atlantic
and Antarctica

Buenos
Aires

ARGENTINA

CHILE

Falkland
Islands

S. Georgia

S. Sandwich Is.

Beagle
Channel

60° S

Argentinian base
since 1976

80° W

ANTARCTIC
TERRITORY

Overlapping claims by
Argentina & Britain

20° W

0   500 miles
0   1000 km   • South Pole

Chapter 3

"MENENDEZ, HOW IS YOUR ENGLISH?"

Costa Mendez warned that the communique from New York would come like a bombshell among the Military. Its insipid and colourless text would not only further reinforce the distorted and defeatist image the High Command had of the Argentine international negotiating team, but more seriously, the failure of the new round of talks with the British would undoubtedly promote the military option for resolving the dispute with London[1]

His concern also arose from the forseeable reaction by the Military faced with the lack of results and he feared that this would weaken his own position with the commandants. Any challenge, public or private, made to the conduct of diplomacy, would damage his negotiating position in two important forthcoming dialogues. First, he had to journey to Brasilia to convince his colleague, Ramiro Saraiva Guerreiro, of the advisability of working out a common position on the Central American crisis; and on his return he was to receive Thomas Enders, Assistant Secretary of State for Inter-American Affairs, one of the architects of the Hemispheric policy of Ronald Reagan's government.

For the Argentine diplomats - at that stage all experts in the sterile acrobatics of talking to the British - the result in New York was expected and did not count as a failure. Inwardly they thought that the unsatisfied expectations for the meeting had been out of proportion, although they nourished the small hope of obtaining an early reply to the scheme proposed on January 27th to Ambassador Williams by Argentina.

Ros, a punctilious bureaucrat, had agreed the text of the statement with Luce, his counterpart at the Foreign Office, who time and again avoided any commitment, forever deferring his responses until after consultation with London. Ros, as much as the London-based diplomats: Ortiz de Rozas, Molteni and Blanco acted from a different standpoint to Costa Mendez. They were simply unaware of the plans developing at the heart of the Military for recovering the Falklands and South Georgia. Although they had heard and read rumours about these operations, they attributed everything to a "psychological manoeuvre" of the intelligence services of the armed forces.[2]

By midday on March 1st, Costa Mendez already had confirmation of the adverse military reaction to the negotiations. He had received two telephone calls, one from the Casa Rosada and the other from his Navy Commander-in-Chief. The President was very disappointed with the results from New York.

The Foreign Minister underlined in pencil the paragraphs of the text that he considered most irritating for the Junta. He pointed out that the climate of the meeting had been "cordial and positive" and he also pointed out an omission: South Georgia and the South Sandwich Islands had been excluded from the dispute. This last point was difficult to explain. Up to that time, the British interpretation of the dispute was unintentionally favourable to Argentina. London characterised South Georgia and the South Sandwich Islands as "Falklands Islands Dependencies," which helped Buenos Aires to justify its claim that they should be included in the overall negotiation on sovereignty. That position changed after April 2nd 1982, and the British Government began to maintain that it would only negotiate on the Falklands themselves.

Costa Mendez decided that he ought to produce a quick and forceful reply, which would act to soothe some hot heads, but at the same time not give the game away to London. He summoned Gustavo Figueroa, his influential Cabinet Secretary, to his office and discussed with him the drafting of a unilateral declaration which he would take to Galtieri.

As well as Costa Mendez and Figueroa, the Director-General of Policy at the Palacio San Martin, Federico Erhardt del Campo, took part in the drafting, and would later take the lead in a hard line at the Buenos Aires Foreign Ministry during the war. Erhardt del Campo, *Pirincho*, as he was nicknamed by friends, had been strongly marked in his development by *Catholic Nationalism*, in whose liturgy the Falklands cause occupied a privileged place. These features did not fade away during his later progress through the ranks of *Desarrolismo*.

Confronted by the need to calm the nerves of the Military who, in their turn, were concerned to cover themselves with glory,[3] the diplomats drafted their statement. In this they warned Great Britain that the absence of replies to the Argentine proposals and the constant delays would leave the way clear for a unilateral decision by Buenos Aires.

The first draft prepared concluded in this way: "Moreover, if this does not happen, that is if no British reply is forthcoming, Argentina reserves the right to put an end to the proceedings and choose the procedure, as prescribed by the Charter of the United Nations, that best suits its interests." The reference to the mechanisms of the international organisation - an implicit renunciation of the use of force as set out in the Charter - was the subject of a long discussion. On the one hand, it was thought to "soften" the warning, and on the other, if one looked for it, London could perceive a clear message of what could happen in the future.

If the British read this declaration in the correct way, relating it to other signs that were in the air, they might decide to reinforce the island defences. Thus the prospect of recovery by force could be seriously affected because of an indirect indication of Argentine intentions. Taking everything into account, it was decided to drop any mention of the United Nations from the paragraph.

Drawn up in this way, the communique had the same effect on sensitive military ears as their favourite martial music; for international public opinion, heedless of the grumbles from the South Atlantic, it was to signal the beginning of the countdown.

Costa Mendez had a meeting with Galtieri and this strengthened his impression that the failure of the talks in New York had disturbed the domestic military front. The President was worried because Anaya was taking advantage of the opportunity to speak of the "weakness of the Foreign Ministry" before his admirals and that involved the executive authority. He therefore recommended that the text be toughened, to which Costa Mendez agreed.

The final paragraph of the communique of the afternoon of March 1st ended thus: "Moreover, if this does not happen, Argentina reserves the right to put an end to the proceedings and to choose freely the procedure which best suits its interests." When Figueroa faced the television cameras to read his declaration, Ros was preparing to board a Jumbo Jet of Aerolineas Argentinas to return from New York to Buenos Aires. The Deputy Foreign Minister did not even dream that the "cordial and positive atmosphere" he had agreed upon that morning on the 25th floor of the UN Plaza building had transformed itself so abruptly. Reclining in a soft seat in the first class, he saw the lights of Manhatten fade away - that island he had loved passionately since heading the Argentine diplomatic mission to the United Nations.

His surprise was great when on arriving at the international airport of Ezeiza, and before disembarkation, a *protocol* official from the Foreign Ministry entered the cabin and delivered to him, without comment, the text of the declaration that was broadcast the previous night. He read it rapidly and could hardly hide an expression of annoyance. Nevertheless, he was grateful for the foresight of his colleagues that enabled him to avoid a confrontation with the reporters then waiting for him in the air terminal, alerted to the unexpected turn of events.

He found it hard to believe what had happened. At this stage in his life he was used to the great causes that the various military regimes obliged so many diplomats to plead - in particular this last one. Nevertheless, he could not tolerate coming off badly in an international negotiation. Next day, he had lunch with Lucio Garcia del Solar, ex-ambassador to the UN, and one of the promoters of Resolution 2065, which obliged Great Britain to sit down at the negotiating table. At the lunch, Ros complained bitterly:

"They screwed me!" He said. "I agreed with Luce to maintain maximum confidentiality and this communique destroyed that agreement. We are in the wrong; we broke it."

The Deputy Foreign Minister arrived at the lunch after receiving a telephone call from Luce. The latter, who had also irritated Parliament, was furious. He reminded Ros that the Argentine declaration went against the New York understanding that the proposals discussed would be kept under strict secrecy until the respective governments were consulted. He added that Argentine threats would make any progress difficult. It had to be made clear that the question could only be solved "through peaceful negotiations."[4]

It is difficult to know up to what point this episode influenced the later behaviour of Ros, who then became a notorious hard liner in Argentine diplomacy during the conflict. When, on two occasions he was responsible for conducting negotiations in the United Nations to find an end to the hostilities, he was many times criticised by foreign colleagues and also some compatriots, for his inflexible attitude. On one occasion, even the Secretary-General of the UN, Javier Perez de Cuellar, mentioned the difficulty of his relationship with Ros. In the middle of May 1982, a colleague in the Argentine Foreign Service in New York risked the following irony on Ros's style: "He who burns himself with the soup blows on everything until the dessert, and Enrique is no exception to the rule."

For his part, Luce had already taken his political soundings before speaking to Ros. He and his chief, Lord Carrington, did not believe in the likelihood of an Argentine military action such as certain signs in the air were suggesting. He thought that Buenos Aires would have no appetite for openly defying British power. To help clear his doubts he had spoken to Enders in Washington about it. The Assistant Secretary of State, who a few days later would fly to Argentina, undertook to transmit a "verbal message" to the Buenos Aires Military urging them to keep things calm. Enders had thus agreed to be charged with this task by the representative of Britain, the ally of his own country.[5].

Did he know the Argentine diplomatic position in these negotiations with Luce? The British Minister of State was careful to discuss matters when he met the Argentines in the United Nations on his journey to Washington from New York. The meeting with Enders was arranged to discuss the situation in Central America, a region that was Luce's responsibility at the Foreign Office.

The aggressive unilateral Argentine declaration shook the British Government. Parliament was heavily lobbied by the Falkland Islands Company, a firm which controls the homes and livelihoods of the kelpers of the Falklands. The Foreign Office sent urgent messages to its ambassadors in Washington, Sir Nicholas Henderson, and in Buenos Aires, Anthony Williams. They were ordered to make contacts with Enders and Harry Schlaudermann, the American representative in Argentina. The move was intended to indicate that Her Majesty's Government was willing to seek a solution to the dispute, but that it was impossible to negotiate against a background of threats.

On March 3rd, Luce was grilled in the House of Commons, withstanding a barrage from the Members and with the memory in mind of his predecessor, Nicholas Ridley, who had been severely attacked in the same Chamber, on December 2, 1980, after a journey to the Falklands. One of the Members asked Luce:

"Did you notice the rather aggressive declaration in the Argentine press yesterday? Can you assure us that all necessary precautions will be taken to ensure the protection of the islands against an unexpected attack?"

Luce took a pause before replying. His eyes rose to the Strangers' Gallery of the House of Commons and searched the diplomatic area until he spotted a familiar face. His gaze rested on the man in charge of the Argentine negotiations in London, who had just arrived from a meeting in New York and was now watching the debate.

"We have no doubt about our sovereignty over the Falkland Islands, and no doubt about our duties to the islanders," replied Luce, addressing himself as much to Argentina as to the Members. "The statement to which my right honourable Friend referred causes me and my right honourable and noble Friend deep concern, especially as the discussions last week were held in a friendly and cordial atmosphere. Yet they have been followed by a statement that is most unhelpful. It causes me deep anxiety and it is not helpful to the process of finding a solution to the problem." he added.

Earlier he had stated: "Without any shadow of a doubt there will be no contemplation of any kind of sovereignty without consulting the wishes of the islanders or without the consent of the House."

"Action threatened in the Falklands," headlined the *Guardian* on reporting the Argentine communique. Jimmy Burns, from Buenos Aires, said in the influential, *Financial Times*: "Great Britain is warned on the Falklands," and the circumspect, *Times* indicated: "Argentina increases the pressure," underlining that "the decision to insist on the matter in aggressive terms carries the stamp of General Leopoldo Galtieri..... but it is still not clear if he seeks to obtain a satisfactory reply from Great Britain or if in fact he is using the affair to gain support inside Argentina."

Enders arrived in Buenos Aires on Sunday March 7th. Costa Mendez was waiting for him with open arms. The American Under-Secretary had his own reasons for being pleased with Argentina. The outrageously sycophantic posture of the Argentine Military towards Reagan, whose triumph they celebrated as their own, derived from agreements made with Galtieri, who promised them heaven and earth.

The Chief of the Argentine diplomatic corps had flown to Brasilia to try to convince the Brazilian Government to join Argentina in its offensive on the leftist Salvadorean guerillas and the Sandinistas in Nicaragua. Although Costa Mendez returned with empty hands - Saraiva Guerreiro listened courteously to the enthusiastic arguments of his Argentine colleague, but then pointed out the standing difference of opinion - Washington saw in this Argentine gesture confirmation of its will to co-operate.

Acting as a pawn of the United States, the Argentinian Army was involved in the crusade against changing the status quo in El Salvador, Guatemala and Honduras, although they wished to help overturn the situation in Nicaragua. "A hundred Somozas are better than one Sandinista," army officers used to say to reporters, in a tone which tried to be humorous. But it was no joke.

Enders arrived, therefore, at a propitious moment to weave his most ambitious scheme, which would enable troops of an inter-American force to be placed in the interior of Nicaragua. At the same time, Galtieri bragged to his generals in his own exaggerated tones about the magnificent relations with Washington. Before a select audience, the exuberant commandant announced:

"Secretary of State Haig and Secretary of Defense Weinberger want to come to Argentina. Vice-President Bush wants to come." He made a deliberate pause, preparing for the final flourish of his oration, and in order to make it more forceful he brought in an Italian word for emphasis: "*Anche* (even) Reagan himself!" he declaimed.

What doubts could Enders himself have about the attitude that the Argentine Government would adopt when it was proposed to them to urge the summoning of a consultative meeting of the Inter-American

Treaty of Reciprocal Aid (IATRA) against Nicaragua?

The military regime had prepared a complementary counter-proposal for Reagan: for the first time they would bluntly put the Falklands question to an American envoy of Enders' level. This dialogue would have to be much more thorough than in the previous contacts that the Foreign Minister had had with American officials and politicians.

Nevertheless, Costa Mendez clearly knew that he could not put all his cards on the table. The Argentine plan at this stage consisted in gradually involving Washington in its conflict with London, while yielding on some sensitive questions of special interest to Reagan and his government. The Argentine Foreign Minister had initiated a series of contacts at different levels in the American establishment. He first received a group of members of the House of Representatives, to whom he mentioned the importance to Argentina of regaining sovereignty in the southern archipelago. The address was delivered in the Palacio San Martin, and presented in deliberately vague terms in order not to contain clues to the real intentions. Nevertheless, that precaution turned out to be unnecessary: the American Congressmen, who had included Argentina as part of a tour in the winter vacation, did not have the least idea where those remote and frozen islands were. Costa Mendez did not consider this a limiting factor in his plans however, and a little later he bent the ears of Senators Howard Baker, Ernest Hollings and Paul Laxalt in the same way.

All this occurred in the first days of January 1982, when Galtieri's administration was hardly settled in, although the plans for the Argentine landing in the Falklands were going full steam ahead. The American Senators were impressed by Galtieri's personality. He was always inclined to curtail protocol and use more direct and less conventional methods. Moreover, the fact that the President forced himself to speak in his clumsy English awoke sympathy in his questioners. During the luncheon at the Casa Rosada which Galtieri shared with the Republican Senators, Baker and Laxalt, and the Democrat, Hollings, he did not broach sensitive matters.

Costa Mendez took on the task of softening up the Americans. He gave a careful presentation of Argentine claims over the archipelago, subtly emphasizing that the US had always maintained a neutral stance on the dispute over sovereignty. So long was his statement that Baker jokingly interrupted Costa Mendez saying,"That's enough; don't the Argentines talk of anything but the Falklands!"

The arrival of Enders would give the Argentine Government the chance to continue this diplomatic initiative. At that time it did not cross the minds of any of the responsible officials in the military administration that the United States might oppose an Argentine action.

45

At most, their neutrality would be more sharply defined but Washington would never leave Argentina in the lurch.

With the tall American's appearance, things began to move. A warm relationship sprang up between Costa Mendez and Enders, kindled by many affinities, including religion, as they were both Catholics. Moreover, the wives of the two officials rapidly became friends and the two couples enjoyed a very pleasant evening together - at the home of Costa Mendez. This was a comfortable flat in the heart of Palermo Chico and a short distance from the American ambassador's residence, where Enders stayed during that visit.

The United States proposed, through Enders, that Argentina be one of a group of countries to promote an application under IATRA for the Central American situation to be used to justify the formation of an Inter-American force. There is strong contemporary evidence for the existence of this proposition, later corroborated by the circulation of a confidential document of the National Security Council[6] and by testimonies gathered by the authors in the United States. Argentina, above all the Army High Command, totally agreed with the American point of view on Central America and had no difficulty in satisfying Reagan's request.

Notwithstanding the importance that the Americans and Argentines gave it at that moment, the Central American crisis was not the only important matter that Enders had on the agenda which he brought to Buenos Aires. The Argentine-Chilean dispute over the Beagle Channel also worried the Reagan administration. It is true that, since the intervention of John Paul II, the chances of a frontier war breaking out had receded, but the absence of a definite solution, in particular the failure of Argentina to accept the Papal proposal of December 12, 1980 caused tension between the two countries to underly all relations concerning the American Hemisphere.

This picture of the situation generated another political problem for Washington. In spite of his enthusiasm for rewarding his new and willing friends in South America, Reagan had still not been able to re-establish military assistance to Argentina. This had been prohibited since 1978 by the Humphrey-Kennedy amendment to the law governing American foreign aid. Congress had authorized it, but it required prior written certification from the President that the original reason behind the ban, that is, "systematic violation of human rights" had disappeared, or was on the way to disappearing. Much as Reagan wished to comply with this requirement, he could not pay such an excessive political price.

On Chile there was a similar prohibition and in this case the chances of convincing Congress to end the sanction were plainly remote. Reagan knew it, and Augusto Pinochet did not trouble himself to make things easier. On the contrary, for he refused to extradite the military officers implicated in the assassination of ex-Foreign Secretary Orlando Letelier, after a request from an American court. Thus, while the threat of a war between the two neighbouring states continued, Washington could not afford the luxury of appearing to reinforce militarily one or other of the opposing sides.

On the other hand, there is no doubt that the Foreign Affairs Ministry of the Argentine military regime put a major effort into an attempt to secure the annulling of the Humphrey-Kennedy amendment from the moment it came into force. There was no contact, official or unofficial, between the United States and Argentina in which the latter's representatives did not seize the chance to bring up the matter in a manner intended to make clear that "national pride" was wounded and immediate amends were required.

It is not that the ban had even been effective. The French, Israelis and the British, among others, filled the gap left by the American suppliers. This permitted the Argentine Military to spend in the year 1980 more than $3000 m. on armaments[7]. From any point of view except the military, the lifting of the amendment could not be considered a priority for the nation. But for a government like Argentina's, the ban was an affront and a major obstacle in the way of the international legitimacy it never stopped seeking. Besides, the experts admitted, American-made armaments had always been preferred by the Argentine officers, since they offered more sophisticated technology and, in addition, better financial terms were possible.

Reagan had the power to deliver to the Military what it longed for, but the Junta had to make an effort, and this perspective caused Enders, in his first meeting with Costa Mendez to put to him his country's concern at the lack of a solution to the dispute with Chile. Costa Mendez tried to reassure him about his government's behaviour, being especially careful to emphasize its fidelity to the undertaking to negotiate with the Pope's assistance. Enders wanted to be convinced and chose a moment in the conversation to put a direct question:

"Can you assure me there will be no war?" he asked.

"Of course I can!" replied Costa Mendez, knowing that, at least for the moment, the meridian of military interest did not pass through the Beagle Channel. This was one of the confirmations for which Enders had journeyed to Buenos Aires.

The Assistant Secretary also had in mind the charge of his British colleague, Richard Luce. It has always been accepted by those who have investigated the war in the South Atlantic from whatever angle, that Enders' journey marked a milestone on the road to the Argentine-British confrontation. There has also been speculation on

47

how far the behaviour of Reagan's envoy had contributed to the *green light* that Galtieri and his colleagues believed they saw coming from Washington, thus finally convincing themselves of the viability of the scheme for a military repossession.

The report of the post-war committee of inquiry headed by Lord Franks says that:

"Mr Enders visited Buenos Aires from Sunday March 7th to Tuesday March 9th 1982 and met, among others, President Galtieri and Dr Costa Mendez. The newspaper *La Prensa* reported that he had been given a very full report on the progress of the Falklands negotiations. The British ambassador in Buenos Aires reported that his information from the American Embassy was that Mr Enders had not taken the opportunity specifically to advise the Argentines to keep the temperature down, but Mr Enders himself subsequently asked that Mr Luce be informed that he had raised the matter both privately with Dr Costa Mendez and publicly, stressing the strategic and human aspects of the problem, both of which had to be resolved for a successful outcome. Although the Argentines had been somewhat non-committal, they had not given him the impression that they were about to do anything drastic."[8]

Argentine sources recorded that Costa Mendez took advantage of a meal offered by the US Ambassador at his residence - at which he had to be present as a matter of protocol - in order to speak face to face with Enders on the Falklands question. At the dessert stage, the host and Enrique Ros, also present, gracefully manoeuvred themselves in order to leave the way clear for Costa Mendez and Enders to have a private conversation. This turned out to be frank: Costa Mendez informed him that the Argentine Government could not continue to tolerate British delaying tactics, and that the Military were extremely restless because of London's attitude. In that context, he stressed, the communique of March 1st had not been simply another warning.

It is then reported that Argentina planned a vast diplomatic offensive that would culminate in the UN General Assembly in November of that year. Although the Argentine Foreign Minister did not enter into too many details, he left no doubt that tension would increase. (He was thinking of moving by stages if Britain persisted in its delaying policy. The plan included such measures as a reduction in the level of diplomatic representation, cutting the supply of Argentine fuel to the islands and also discontinuing the regular flights which link them with the mainland.)

The Argentine Foreign Minister had tried to ascertain what the American attitude would be, faced with this problem. "Hands off!"

would have been, according to Buenos Aires sources, the certain reply from Enders. This would have been nothing new. Those two words defined the traditional policy of the United States on such matters - a country which never entered into any affair of competing claims of sovereignty. In any case, Costa Mendez believed he saw in the message (from Enders) a confirmation of American disinterest - a decisive point in the Argentine military plans.

Consultations in Washington during the authors' investigation threw up a significantly different version to that which the Argentines remember. American diplomatic sources affirmed that it was Enders - during his first formal contact with Costa Mendez at the Palacio San Martin - who raised the matter and indicated the United States' concern for the continuation of a search for a negotiated solution, especially in the light of the latest Argentine communique. These sources also emphasised that what Costa Mendez and other Argentine officials said at no time suggested that the Argentine Government was considering settling the dispute by means of force.

In a conversation with Enders, which took place in his office at the Department of State in early May 1983, the authors specifically asked him about his expression - "Hands off!"

On that occasion Enders confirmed that he did not recall using it, Nevertheless, he asked one of his assistants to search the archives for the report of his visit. A little more than a week after this interview, the authors received a telephone call in Buenos Aires in which they were assured that, from the notes, it appeared that the Assistant Secretary had not used those words. On the contrary, he had employed various prescriptions to urge the Argentine Government, through Costa Mendez, to pursue negotiations with the British.

Nevertheless, there is another episode in the visit of Enders to Buenos Aires, also of significance, in which the versions offered by the two sides coincide a little less in the details. On the second day of the stay, the same one on which he went to the Casa Rosada to meet Galtieri, the American envoy received a detailed report on the Argentine-British dialogue (which was referred to in the Franks report). Deputy Foreign Minister Ros was his host at the Palacio San Martin, and on concluding his lengthy presentation, he emphasized the feeling of national frustration after seventeen years of fruitless negotiation, pointing out that one could not expect that: "The patience of the Argentine people will last forever."

Why a statement like that from an official of Ros's seniority did not sound a warning note in the ears of the Americans is something which does not seem to have a satisfactory explanation. Washington sources explained the situation by saying that the language used by Ros was not infrequent in diplomacy when someone wanted, as the Argentines then did, to stress the impatience of his government on some question. Nevertheless, the flippancy in interpretation of the signals given by the Argentine Foreign Ministry appears unflattering.

Whatever may have been the case, this posture of the US envoy, or the perception of it by Argentine officials, became, in private, one of the most pressing arguments of the Argentine Government for proceeding with the plans for military action. Certainly this was not the only recourse of those who pointed to American neutrality (then in force), as a sort of protective umbrella over the operation. Other reports, arriving by military routes, were resting on the desk of the army commandant. General Mallea Gil, even if there is no evidence that he knew of the plans for the Falklands landing, nevertheless believed that the Argentine presence in Central America was of vital importance for the *putsch* that the Americans were organizing in Nicaragua.

At that stage the Argentine involvement with American strategic planning was little less than total. Enders himself, before leaving for Chile, pointed out in Buenos Aires that: "Argentina is very concerned at the situation Nicaragua and El Salvador are experiencing," and affirmed that: "Argentina would want to be present in an active way in any action that is taken." Immediately afterwards he qualified: "Nevertheless, I would not suggest by that, the participation of Argentina in the formation of a military force in the region."

From the practical point of view, Enders was a blind for the Argentine Military, who were already operating in Central America. The visit also hid the desire of Buenos Aires to unite with other countries - Chile and Colombia were among the remaining candidates - in sponsoring the application of the Rio de Janeiro Treaty for collective Hemispheric security.

A few days later, on March 14th, Costa Mendez ordered his staff to examine the possibility of organizing a meeting of the consultative body - the Conference of Foreign Ministers of IATRA. The task fell upon Marcelo Huergo, an intelligent official of middle rank considered an expert on the ramifications of the Rio Treaty, who had served twelve consecutive years in Washington. He had served in the Argentine mission to the OAS, in the embassy, and also - with special permission from the Foreign Service - as Chief of Staff to the Secretary-General of that organization: Alejandro Orfila.

His ex-chief was in fact in Buenos Aires. Orfila arrived in early March in Argentina to make political contacts. This extremely able ex-ambassador to the White House, appointed by Juan Domingo Peron, was bringing with him an ambitious scheme: to act as a bridge between the military regime and the civil institutions. Orfila belonged to the Washington establishment and he only had to lift the telephone to communicate with many of the offices where power resided.

"Alex," as the diplomatic and political elite of Washington called him, was a man with political aspirations. He was not tainted by the military regime when he secured the post of Secretary-General of the OAS during the trauma of Senora Peron's Government. The original plan of Orfila's advisers was to take advantage of his stay in Buenos Aires in order to renew political contacts, above all with the Peronistas, and to mix a little in military circles. Then he would take a trip to the Falklands, where he thought of arriving on April 14th, the Day of the Americas, in order to broadcast a statement. Those plans changed rapidly when his political antennae detected something in the air.

On March 6th, from his home town, Mendoza, Orfila declared that the Falklands were Argentine, and prophesied: "It will not be long before that corner of national territory flies the flag of the Fatherland." Some time later he would regret, if not the content of his declaration, at least the occasion on which he made it, because many interpreted it in the light of what had happened, as a sign that the Secretary-General of the OAS had been informed previously of the operation - something which he denies.

Orfila maintained many contacts with political and trade union leaders, in particular with Lorenzo Miguel, Secretary-General of the sixty-two Peronist organizations, and with Antonio Cafiero, ex-Minister of the Economy under Isabel Peron. Later he was received by the top rank of Argentine politics - "I met the full *Multipartidaria*," he recalled, when he conversed at a dinner given in the large apartment of Ricardo Yofre, a lawyer and a man possessed of an enviable list of civil and military contacts.

The result of these conversations convinced Orfila that something was about to happen. He was right. By then the ship *Buen Suceso* of the Argentine Navy was approaching Stromness Bay in South Georgia. The fuse had no safety device; it only had to be lit for the explosion to follow.

Brigadier General Mario Benjamin Menendez received an order to present himself before the Commander-in-Chief. He was not surprised. That March 2nd was no different from any other Tuesday. Galtieri used that day of the week to attend to Army affairs and to listen to reports from those in charge of the various departments of the General Staff.

As Chief of Operations, Menendez had some reports to make concerning the induction of new conscripts just settling down to military life, and certain other minor matters. Either because of his seniority or by some other curious military logic, Galtieri was accustomed to receive him at the end of the afternoon.

That day, Menendez had hardly read the newspaper headlines. He had only lingered a few moments over the reports of the strongly-worded communique issued by the Argentine Foreign Ministry. This had threatened London with a break in negotiations if they persisted in their delaying tactics over the Falklands dispute.

He entered Galtieri's office, where the President received him in his shirt-sleeves. Well-drilled, Menendez began to report on the matters he had in hand while the Commandant regarded him fixedly. When he had finished, Galtieri rose and paced the office. He then said:

"Very well, sit down, Menendez; now I'm going to talk."

The subordinate did as ordered, believing he would receive instructions on the matters in hand.

"Tell me, Menendez; how is your English?" Asked Galtieri.

"Not too bad, sir. The same as when I accompanied you on your trip to the United States," replied the Chief of Operations, trying to contain his surprise.

"Good. Brush it up. You're going to need it."

"Why?" asked Menendez, knowing that this was exactly what Galtieri was waiting to hear following such enigmatic advice.

"We have taken the decision to recover the Falklands by military means and the Junta have approved my proposal that you should head the military government of the islands," announced the commandant. He then paused.

Menendez was surprised and excited in equal measure. "Look sir," he confessed, "at the moment I can't think about this; I really am astonished. It's such a wide-ranging matter!" He managed to stammer.

Pleased with the effect achieved - there is a natural tendency to dramatize *great moments*, and Galtieri was the last man to be an exception to this rule - the commandant went on to explain the plan in overall terms:

There would be a garrison of 500 men that he would command, which would act almost like military police. "There will be someone from the air force and the navy," added Galtieri vaguely, "a couple of Pucara planes, two or three ships - that's for the security of the air and sea space, you know....."

Without waiting for comments, Galtieri added: "Your post here will remain unfilled, because when the situation is consolidated in the islands, you will return to the General Staff. I want you to continue being my Chief of Operations," he promised.

"When do you think I shall return to the mainland?" Asked

Menendez.

"You will stay on the islands until November or December at most," speculated Galtieri.

"What do you think will be the British reaction after we recover the islands?" asked Menendez almost unintentionally, still stunned by the vista which the commandant had opened up.

"That is not your problem," was Galtieri's sharp reply, which he followed up with a hidden warning: "you just concern yourself with preparing to govern. The rest is up to the Military Junta and the ECI, who are already working on it."

This was the classic reply of a superior dicomforted by a question from a subordinate. For every problem that seemed difficult of solution there was an ECI (Combined Forces Liaison Team) dedicated to seeking that solution - though usually without even a hint of success.

"Yes, General," Menendez acquiesced. "Who can I speak to about this?"

"To nobody. The secret is absolute," was his order. Nevertheless, he explained that the ECI which was working out all aspects of the operation, was composed of General Garcia, Admiral Lombardo and Brigadier Plessl.

"Can I speak to them?" Menendez timidly asked.

"No, not even to them! The secret is absolute," Galtieri energetically reiterated, while he lit up another *Galaxy*.

The two men continued turning the matter over for another half an hour and the commandant began to realize that his subordinate had sunk into insecurity and isolation.

Finally he agreed to him making a sole contact with the Chief of the Army General Staff, Major-General Jose Antonio Vaquero: one of the few senior officers *au fait* with the plans.

The brand new - but still secret - military governor left the office. He did not know whether to jump for joy or ask the earth to open up and swallow him. He had many doubts, the scale of which he did not even want to know about, but Galtieri's assurance about the success of this operation calmed him. The commandant's affirmation that the situation would be consolidated quickly also calmed him from time to time.

But neither did he deny himself growing feelings of pride. Now another Menendez would enter military history and surely he would do better than his uncle Benjamin, who rose against Peron in 1951, or his cousin Luciano Benjamin, who revolted against Viola in 1979 - an affair which ended neither in sorrow nor in glory?

Menendez had experience of war, or at least he believed sincerely that he had. He had helped to root out the guerillas in Tucuman.

Of course, that was another type of war - for which the army and its officer corps had been prepared. He had assembled the forces which had been victorious over the left-wing People's Revolutionary Army. In passing, he had also taken advantage of the campaign to crush any expression of dissent among the Military - but that was another story.

To military nostrils that campaign had had the smell of heroism - but the martial melody of trumpets at some imagined victory parade broke Menendez's daydream....

Two days later, he asked to speak to Vaquero. He was impatient to discuss with someone the secret that was suffocating him. His superior received him in the afternoon.

"What do you want, Menendez?" asked Vaquero drily - he had the habit of getting straight to the point.

"I was with General Galtieri last Tuesday. He spoke to me about the Falklands operation," said Menendez, introducing the subject.

"Ah... he told you."

"Yes. Tell me, General, how do you see this business?" he continued, seeking the advice of his immediate superior.

"Look, Menendez; I don't think you should worry too much," replied Vaquero, guessing the pre-occupations of his Chief of Operations. "The British have been with this problem for a long time and they don't know how to come out on top. The fact is that they are going to shout a lot, get annoyed and appear tough, to satisfy internal public opinion. It will certainly be a difficult negotiation and we shall have to give them the moon. But remember, Menendez, England doesn't know what to do with the Falklands. They find them expensive and far away. Those 1800 inhabitants give them endless trouble."

Vaquero's naive analysis did not convince Menendez, but after all, it was the word of his superior. Perhaps the Chief of the General Staff was unaware of Galtieri's actual plans. Without doubt Vaquero was the odd man out in the military establishment. He had always survived the various recurrent crises in the army and floated like a cork when the waters got rough during the overthrow of Viola. But Menendez wanted assurance and insisted further:

"Look, sir, the truth is that what General Galtieri told me a few days ago has left me worried. Perhaps you can tell me this....it's just an assessment because I don't know....but up till now there is no indication that the negotiations have collapsed. Certainly there are difficulties - but the world believes we are negotiating. For the United Nations, we are certainly negotiating."

"No, no, Menendez...if you have these doubts, let General Galtieri know about them," Vaquero advised, ending the conversation.

He would have to wait until the following Tuesday to raise

those questions. Given the order of strict secrecy, he had to continue his daily duties in order to dissemble among his colleagues.

Nevertheless, some signs were discernible for sufficiently suspicious observers in army circles. Possessed of this secret information, only someone like Menendez would be in a position to understand the long harangue that Galtieri had poured out to the Generals in one of the first meetings of the year for the High Command.

In the forceful, almost violent tone which characterized him, the commandant had said two things of importance on that occasion:

1. That the commanders must: "maintain the logistic and operational capabilities of the forces, since military force could be used during the coming year either in the Beagle Channel or in the Falklands, or in both places simultaneously." The preamble to this surprising message was an allusion to the hardly perceptible progress in the negotiations both with Great Britain and in the Papal mediation over the problem with Chile.

2. That he would dedicate himself to politics. Galtieri, at the Gargantuan barbecue that he had given in Victorica, was moved by the co-operation of right-wing politicians who aspired to inheriting the regime. Those 13,000 people who swallowed the meat, offal and *empanadas*, on that hot afternoon on the pampa encouraged Galtieri in his secret wish to transform himself into a popular leader. But he had to earn his spurs. Accordingly, the army chief demonstrated to his commanders some of the points of the game. He told them: "As President, I am going to make politics. Don't ask me to keep to the rules in this. Don't be surprised, fellow generals, if I raise one arm, or two at the same time....."

It was as if every Argentine military uniform contained a breast bursting with the private wish to emulate Juan Domingo Peron. Events in Argentina during the last few years have provided more than enough examples of this. Almost always there are the same ambitions, but never the same talent. Galtieri was no exception, and Messianic aspirations had become part of his outlook.

But only now did Menendez begin to link his new knowledge with what he already knew. Therefore when Galtieri again received him he began to put to him the need to speak as "great and thinking people," in a tone and with such words as are unusual in the master-servant relationship that the two men held.

"Be brief, Menendez. What do you want to say?" said Galtieri, cutting him short.

"Look, General, I spoke to General Vaquero and put to him certain points, but he directed me to you. The question is: "What are going to be the direct or indirect consequences that Argentina will suffer after the military action?"

"Menendez.....you mustn't concern yourself with that. In the Junta, we have already thought about it in co-operation with the Foreign Minister. That has all been studied. Concentrate on being the Military Governor."

At these words of Galtieri, Menendez stopped worrying. Inhibited by his subordinate role, he replied:

"That's clear enough, Sir. I shall think no more about it. I will think simply in the terms of a Military Governor."

Galtieri ended that conversation with some recommendations: he asked him not to form a very large team because "Governing the Falklands is a nonsense." He repeated that he was required to safeguard secrecy. He authorized him to make contact with the working group preparing for the landing only when he received an explicit order to that effect. Once on the islands, added Galtieri, problems had to be reported through General Garcia, head of the 5th Army Corps whose headquarters were in Bahia Blanca. When he concluded his conversation with Galtieri, Menendez relaxed. If everything worked out as the commandant described it, it wouldn't be a war. It would be an outing.

The key documents ratified what Galtieri and Vaquero told Menendez. Basically, the *Strategic Military Directive*[9] worked out by the Junta, set out, in the first place, an operation limited in time by the withdrawal of Argentine troops from the islands. The initial forecasts envisaged *D-Day* as fixed for the second half of May, the landing to be completed five days later.

For that reason, the day *D plus 5*, which represented the maximum time that the operation of occupying the islands could last, had to be on May 25th. This was a day of special national significance and therefore a propitious one for the armed forces to broadcast from the Falklands their message announcing the restoration of the nation's territorial integrity.

In the period that followed, various alternative diplomatic courses of action were suggested:

(a) A very intense bilateral negotiation with Great Britain in order to convince Her Majesty's Government of the *fait accompli*.

(b) The *fait accompli* to be accompanied by concessions to British subjects. These would range from indemnities to the Falkland Islands Company and to islanders who wished to emigrate; to offers of close economic co-operation with British companies. These companies might wish to exploit the petroleum deposits of the southern basin with Argentina, as well as the stocks of fish and krill.

(c) The United States to be involved in the negotiation, either directly or as a guarantor of the agreements that might be achieved.

(d) To work on the countries of the Western World, especially those of the EEC, in order that, together with the United States, they might assist in convincing Great Britain that there was no going back and that the situation had to be accepted.

(e) To intensify contacts with the Soviet Union, China and countries of Eastern Europe in anticipation of possible problems in the United Nations.

This plan was obviously based on the assumption of an almost total absence of British military reaction, or at least, the absence of any *overwhelming* reaction - such as that which actually did take place.

From the original documents of the Junta two points clearly emerge:

1. If Great Britain did react to the landing, it was assumed it would be in a fashion intended to force negotiation. It would therefore only send a small symbolic force. In that eventuality, it was envisaged that an army, air force and naval contingent of not more than 600 to 700 men should be left on the islands, under the command of a colonel. That Argentine garrison would serve as a deterrent to the Royal Navy to prevent recovery.

This deduction was straightforward and simple, so simple, it was later proved, as to be truly naive. Its starting point was the well-known supposed weakness of Margaret Thatcher's government which was being shaken by an important economic crisis. The British surface fleet was being progressively sold off in order to make way for Trident nuclear submarines. What would Britain be able to send to the Falklands, at 8,500 miles from London? Only a small force, surely.

2. Great Britain, it was assumed, would prefer or would accept negotiation until it was convinced that the question of sovereignty was no longer open for discussion. It would then seriously evaluate the situation in order to decide whether to attempt a re-occupation by force.

"No other assessment will be made for the moment." the document said.

But this central argument worked out by the Argentine Foreign Ministry was based on the "super-power hypothesis." This assumed that the United States would actively intervene in the search for a peaceful solution, thus accepting its responsibility as the Western super-power.

Costa Mendez had pressed this thesis upon the members of the Junta using examples like Suez in 1956, when Great Britain and France

57

launched a joint task force against Nasser, in reprisal for the nationalization of the canal. In that episode, President Eisenhower and his Secretary of State, John Foster Dulles, obliged the aggressors to suspend the attack. He also recalled the American pressure on Israel *not* to destroy the 3rd Egyptian Army, when it was surrounded in the Sinai desert during the Yom Kippur war. Finally he raised that super-power role played by the United States in its action during the skirmishes between El Salvador and Honduras; and between Peru and Ecuador.

The case of the Arab-Israeli war was a seductive argument for the Military. It was a good example of a war begun by one country (Egypt), knowing that a military victory would be impossible. The central assumption was the expectation that military aggression would be followed by a super-power intervention to bring the parties to the negotiating table. However, in this case, the reality is that the South Atlantic is remote and the Middle East was not.

The key, therefore, to the success of the Argentine action in achieving Britain's acceptance of the futility of an armed counter-attack, was the United States - whose intervention the Argentines would receive with pleasure.

In the middle of March, Buenos Aires was a boiling cauldron of rumours. The newspapers were saying that in the circles of power a landing in the Falklands was being prepared. But reactions were sceptical, and editors prudently did not confirm the story.

On March 11th, a Hercules C-130 of the Argentine Air Force made an emergency landing at Port Stanley airport, in East Falkland. The excuse of the plane's captain was that he had detected faults in the huge aircraft when he was flying towards the Antarctic base of Vice-Comodoro Marambio, where there is a landing strip. He told the suspicious British authorities that it was a logistics flight for a detachment carrying out an Antarctic programme that year. In Buenos Aires the news did not receive much attention, and was not linked for a moment to any eventual landing.

Was it an intelligence operation intended to check the conditions on the ground for landing the Hercules transports? These aircraft would later have the hard task of sustaining the air bridge set up between the continent and the islands. If this was so, were there not already enough reports in the hands of the Air Force Commandant upon the matter? Such reports were regularly supplied by the military pilots of the State Air Lines (LADE) carrying out scheduled journeys. Was it worth risking the security of the operation in this way?

It is difficult to get to the truth about this forced landing, although one cannot discard the possibility that the emergency may have been authentic. What is certain is that at that time, the Falklands operation had not finally been decided upon.

The British embassy, which was carefully monitoring Argentine attitudes, immediately informed London about this strange episode. Mark Heathcote, the First Secretary at the British mission in Buenos Aires, sent a coded cable to his headquarters, evaluating the appearance of the Hercules C-130 in the islands. Heathcote, a diplomat of genial manner, and a great beer-drinker, had replaced the efficient David Gozney on the Falklands desk. That British official was "believed to have had independent lines to the Joint Information Committee for his news. What happened to this intelligence, when it reached Cabinet Office is not known."[10] However, it is clear that the British authorities did not consider it as a danger signal[11] even though the question certainly worried the Argentine charge d'affaires in London, who was acting without the benefit of instructions from Buenos Aires on the matter of the Falklands.

When he heard about the emergency landing, he called the air attache in London, Commodore Viola, to his office. They discussed the affair, but the latter convinced Molteni that the landing was nevertheless on one of the designated alternative airports that the Hercules planes could use when they travelled to Marambio from Rio Gallegos. The pilot, Viola assured him, only used Port Stanley in accordance with the flight plans for such occasions.

On the other hand, the *Latin American Weekly Report*, a private service to the press published in London, said after describing the landing in its edition of 19th March, that: "Observers in Buenos Aires hint that the incident was planned. With rumours of a possible Argentine invasion of the islands, the reasoning is that the air force is testing the possibility of disembarking troops on the islands with Hercules aircraft. The landing occurred just after Alejandro Orfila, the Argentine Secretary-General of the OAS, had predicted that *the Argentine flag will soon fly over the Falklands.*"

The diplomats at the Palacio San Martin did not give great importance to the incident either. Up till then the only ones who knew of the military plans were: the three Commandants; the Foreign Minister, Costa Mendez; the Chief of the Army General Staff; the three senior officers who worked on the plans and the future Governor of the archipelago.

The coming crisis of the scrap metal dealers would cause a good number of diplomats to be included in that select circle.

NOTES

1. For General Juan Enrique Gugliamelli, a critic of the Argentine politico-military conduct of the war, "the success or failure [of the negotiations in New York] depended on setting in motion the plan to occupy the islands. "From *La Guerra de Malvinas. Falsos supuestos politicos conducen a la derrota* in *Estrategia*, No. 71/72, p.33, Buenos Aires.

2. In fact there are testimonies regarding the warning of Ambassador Ortiz de Rozas to Luce (during an aside at the negotiations) on what could occur if London delayed its reply. In a conversation with the authors, the ambassador admitted that that warning was certainly made, but was not based on a previous knowledge of the military action. In the same way, an interview Ros had with Perez de Cuellar in the United Nations building in the same period of the negotiations with Great Britain was not an anticipation of what would occur scarcely a month later.

3. The Commandant of the Navy, Admiral Anaya, protested to Galtieri at what had happened in New York.

4. *Falkland Islands Review*, Report of a Committee of Privy Counsellors (Franks Report), p.39. London, 1983.

5. The expression used by Luce in his interview with Enders was: *keep things cool*, on referring to the Argentine attitude in the negotiations with Great Britain. Quoted in Franks Report, ibid.

6. The *New York Times*, 6 April 1983.

7. Instituto de Estudios para la Paz, Stockholm, 1981.

8. Franks Report, ibid. p.42.

9. The *Strategic Military Directive* was repeatedly cited as much as the *Strategic National Directives* in various interviews during the investigation by the authors.

10. *The Battle for the Falklands*. Max Hastings and Simon Jenkins, p.59, London 1982.

11. The Franks Report, which makes an exhaustive compilation of the evidence prior to April 2nd 1982, does not mention the secret telegram sent by Heathcote.

Chapter 4

"OPERATION ALPHA"

The spacious office in the Palacio San Martin which faces the calle Arenales was the venue that March 19th of a meeting of Foreign Minister Costa Mendez and his closest colleagues: there were Deputy Foreign Minister Ros; First Secretary Figueroa; and Ambassador Arnoldo Listre, the Director of International Organizations at the Palacio San Martin. Marcelo Huergo spoke on the subject of IATRA and Nicaragua - a theme which kept the diplomatic leadership awake and would provide legitimacy for a combined military operation in Central America.

Tom Enders' recent visit, when he had strengthened ties of friendship with Costa Mendez, would be followed by that of Caspar Weinberger, the influential Pentagon chief to whom the Argentine Military, with an ingenuous and mistaken conception of American policy, assigned a power little less than total. That visit of Weinberger was the long-cherished dream of Miguel Mallea Gil, who had made himself the man in the Government with most influence in Washington, more even than that formally exercised by Ambassador Takacs. The latter pressed for Weinberger's visit to Buenos Aires, working in tune with Mallea Gil, whom he consulted at every step.

Huergo's thorough presentation was abruptly cut short by the entry of the spokesman of the Palacio San Martin in order to put to Costa Mendez a proposal concerning a declaration upon a landing of a group of Argentine workers on the island of South Georgia. Costa Mendez, with his spectacles on his nose, looked fixedly at the unfortunate official. Slowly, as if explaining a difficult problem to a child, he said: "If those who have landed did indeed raise the Argentine flag then they did so on national territory. The Foreign Ministry has no comment to make." The Minister usually kept his best poker face for moments like this. But on this occasion he really would have to comment. The fuse had been lit and now nothing could halt the final explosion.

South Georgia was the first act of the escalating drama that culminated in the Argentine-British conflict. Two powerful influences were at work in this incident. First, the violent British reaction, encouraged by the Admiralty and the hawks of Margaret Thatcher's Conservative Party. Secondly, the sermonizing of the Argentine hawks over the presence of the workers on the island - which was sustained *ad nauseam* - and their later sermonizing during the action by the Argentine marines. The Buenos Aires Government also perceived the episode as an opportunity to justify a landing on the Falklands themselves.

The results of the authors' investigation suggest that two operations were superimposed on each other. One was the perfectly legal operation of Constantino Davidoff in dismantling the whaling station of the Christian Salvensen Company according to the terms of a contract signed in 1979. The other was *"Operation Alpha"* - the code name for the stationing of a military detachment in South Georgia. This was to have the appearance of a scientific base - similar to that successfully set up at Thule in the South Sandwich Islands during the first months of the Military Government.

The Argentine Foreign Ministry was perfectly *au fait* with the plans of the entrepreneur, Davidoff, as part of the transaction had been arranged at the Ministry, and the plans had also been supported by a note sent to the Commander-in-Chief of the Navy in August 1981. This had been under the signature of Ros, at that time deputy to the Minister, Camilion. The Deputy Foreign Minister was responsible for analysing the diplomatic implications and, above all, the consequences of the Argentine presence in South Georgia for negotiations with Great Britain.

The temptation for a repetition of *Operation Thule* was ever-present in the Argentine Navy's contingency planning. In 1974, when Adolfo Savino took charge of the Defence Ministry - Peron was at that time President - he appointed military officers to work on the project for the first time. He summoned three officers, one from each of the armed forces. It was in this way that the then Captain Lombardo became a government official, and was designated Director General of Policy. He began to work out a plan for increasing the Argentine presence in the southern islands. The idea was to install a base in the South Sandwich archipelago to mark the eastern extreme of the zone on continental Antarctica claimed by Argentina. Such a base had been attempted several years earlier, but the project was aborted because a strong tidal wave had struck the area when the ship approached the islands.

Lombardo pursued the matter, but without much response. He first explained the plan to President Peron, then to Isabelita, the widow of the popular deceased leader, until in 1976 when, with the Military in power, the reaction he was looking for seemed to be coming about. The Foreign Ministry was then in the hands of Vice-Admiral Cesar Guzzetti, who was doubtful about the repercussion that the Argentine action could have on the dialogue with London.

In spite of this attitude of the Foreign Minister, Lombardo still managed to promote his idea. The scientific detachment was installed in December 1976. The Palacio San Martin considered it a good idea to test the reaction of the British Labour Government. Argentina maintained only cold relations with this Government in spite of suggesting the re-opening of negotiations with Great Britain over the Falklands. On the 20th of the same month, a helicopter of *HMS Endurance,* the patrol vessel, detected the Argentine landing. This ship supplied the British in the region and would fulfil a significant role in the crisis of April 1982.

The episode, which included an exchange of protest notes, was kept secret. A meeting of the respective heads of the negotiating teams in Buenos Aires (Hugh Carless), and London (Rafael Gowland), was called. The Argentines had no interest in allowing the affair to go public. They wanted to avoid upsetting future discussions with the then Junior Minister at the Foreign Office, Edward Rowlands, due to arrive in Buenos Aires the following February. The British, for their part, wanted to restore links with Buenos Aires where a government friendly to the City had expelled Peronist populism and would defeat the left-wing guerillas.

Naturally, there were intelligence reports indicating that the Thule landing would be the prologue to an action in the Falklands[1]. The views of the Joint Intelligence Committee were based on the belief that a British action to eject the Argentines from Thule would cause a reaction by the Military Junta. It may have been for such military considerations, or in the interests of safeguarding the precarious dialogue between the two countries, that both governments decided to maintain confidentiality in the affair.

It was only in May 1978, as a result of pressure from the Parliamentary lobby on behalf of the Falklands Islands Company, that the matter finally exploded in London. No verbal sparks passed between the two foreign ministries. It was a game between two players who knew their cards. Some months before, the Navy Commander-in-Chief, Admiral Massera, had delivered a plan for a landing in the Falklands to the Military Junta, this the army had managed to get shelved. The fleet had also intercepted Bulgarian fishing boats, one of which they had fired on. The then naval attache in London, Rear-Admiral Anaya, drew the attention of the Foreign Office to the incident.

But in the end, *Operation Thule* turned out perfectly well. Argentina could henceforth count on the physical presence of a scientific base on the island and the reaction in London had been a calm one: they had not even cancelled Rowlands' visit to the Falklands. Nor were the discussions with his counterpart at the Palacio San Martin cancelled. This was a certain Captain Gualter Allara, who later, by some diabolic twist of fate, commanded the task force that landed on the archipelago.

With such precedents it was not out of the question for the Military to think of South Georgia. Nevertheless, a small incident in December 1981, caused them to realise that the mood at the British Foreign Office had changed substantially.

That month, Davidoff, aboard the ice-breaker, *Almirante Irizar*, travelled to inspect the installations that his workers were to dismantle on South Georgia. This was in line with the terms of the contract signed with the Salvensen company. He sent a letter to the British Embassy in Buenos Aires advising them that he would make the voyage and set off on December 16th - one day after Lombardo received the order from Anaya to prepare the plan for a landing in the Falklands. Nevertheless, Davidoff and Lombardo were unaware of each other's plans. On his arrival at Leith in a ship of the Argentine Navy, the British Antarctic Survey, based at Grytviken, sounded the alarm. The British Governor of the Falklands, Rex Hunt, immediately demanded the expulsion of Davidoff - a suggestion the Foreign Office ignored; although they did ask the entrepreneur to legalize his entry into South Georgia by going to Grytviken to have his papers stamped. Great Britain protested at the incident and in an interview with Costa Mendez, the latter said he had no knowledge of Davidoff's journey, nor of what had occurred.

Months later, when the Argentine Foreign Secretary was informed by President Galtieri of the plans for the Falklands, Costa Mendez made an evaluation of the episode. His immediate reaction was to think how Anglo-Argentine friction in South Georgia would affect military planning, and perhaps its security. The backwash of Davidoff's southern voyage faded away, but the Palacio San Martin asked for information from the navy about the objectives in dismantling the whaling stations. Ros was charged with verifying all the details. It was then that *Operation Alpha* appeared riding on the apparently purely commercial intentions of Davidoff.

The plan did not differ substantially from that carried out on Thule. It involved the establishment of a scientific station on South Georgia. This test would undoubtedly be more telling than the one in the South Sandwich Islands however. South Georgia was not as inhospitable as Thule, and in any case it already had a scientific base supported by the British Antarctic Survey. But now that the decision had been taken to make a military move on the Falklands in May or June, any international incident with Great Britain, should it occur, would undoubtedly be prejudicial to Argentine interests.

Although by then, Ros had no information on what was being planned for the Falklands, he showed Costa Mendez that *Operation Alpha* would militate against success for the programme of negotiations proposed to London and about to take place in New York. The Foreign Minister agreed with his subordinate's analysis. But as always, the reasoning of these two men was entirely different. While Ros thought in terms of negotiations, Costa Mendez had in mind the plans of the Military Junta. He naively believed that the reins of diplomacy would remain in his hands; consequently the opening of a flank on South Georgia would be equivalent to providing an opportunity for the British.

Taking advantage of a gathering in the Foreign Ministry, Costa Mendez asked for a meeting with Vice-Admiral Leopoldo Suarez del Cerro, Head of the Joint Chiefs of Staff. At this gathering, Argentine strategy in relation to the Papal mediation in the dispute with Chile was being analysed with the military high command. It was in early March and the waves raised by the Argentine communique of the 1st of the month were still very high. Suarez del Cerro was informed in minute detail about *Operation Alpha*, and he was appraised by Costa Mendez of the problems that such friction could produce for Argentina. The officer promised to raise the Foreign Minister's concern with his commandant.

Operation Alpha was, as already seen, also of personal concern to Lombardo. It was his greatest pre-occupation until he received assurances that it would actually take place at the end of the southern summer of 1981/82 - or at the latest by the beginning of the following autumn. Lombardo was satisfied. He could now tell his superior that something would be done, that the "professional" frustration that they all felt in not going to war with Chile in December 1978 would now be mitigated by the action in South Georgia.

Certainly it was not the same. At the time of greatest confrontation with the Chileans, war was on the point of breaking out. Only an almost providential storm delayed an Argentine commando operation that was going to be executed on the islands in the Beagle Channel. After this meteorological interruption, Pope John-Paul II intervened and separated the parties. South Georgia was, therefore, only a minor objective for many of these officers who believed they had been educated for war and yet had finished up forming irregular commando groups to carry out hardly more than policing tasks.

But when Lombardo received the order to make preparations for the Falklands, he immediately called to mind *Operation Alpha* and now began to delay its execution with the same energy that he once had employed in its promotion: "One can't talk about South Georgia in April and the Falklands in July," he reflected with reason. Lombardo set out his arguments in a note to his chief, Anaya, warning as a corollary that if one carried out *Alpha* - "we will lose the surprise factor" - an essential for any plan to recover the archipelago.

The reply of the Navy Commander-in-Chief to Lombardo's request was positive. The action on South Georgia would be cancelled - this in spite of the fact that the personnel who were going to execute it had already been chosen and appointed by Lombardo. Now, in March, Costa Mendez received similar assurances of *Alpha's* cancellation.

But was it really cancelled? In the course of this investigation, the first of certain testimonies which emerged indicated a suspension, not a cancellation of the operation - and a transference of responsibility to the Chief of Operations of the Naval General Staff. As with everything to do with SIN (naval intelligence) the way forward was surrounded from this point onwards with thick fog.

For the moment it can be said that, in spite of an apparent decision in relation to *Alpha,* formally acknowledging the anxieties of Lombardo and Costa Mendez, the Davidoff operation nevertheless continued receiving enthusiastic support from the navy. Consequently the Argentine naval transport, *Bahia Buen Suceso* was chosen to convey the men charged with the dismantling work.

Another significant fact which appeared, time and again, in the testimonies gathered by the authors, is the link between Constantino Davidoff and the navy. This was presumably a result of transportations arranged to various parts of the coast by naval vessels. In December 1981, he proposed the voyage to South Georgia on the *Almirante Irizar* through the Chief of Naval Transport, Captain Palau. According to the testimonies, Captain Palau forwarded the request, with a recommendation, to Edgardo Otero. The latter then had the responsibility - shared with Rear Admiral Eduardo Morris Girling, chief of SIN - for *Operation Alpha*. Davidoff's first trip included a visit to Antarctica and then three days' stay in Port Leith to tour the abandoned whaling stations, when between November and March, South Georgia is virtually uninhabited. Some of the officers consulted suggested that the naval detatchment of his ship could well have carried out military relief work at the same time.

On March 9th, Davidoff informed the British Embassy that 41 workers would go to South Georgia in a ship which set sail two days later. There were no objections at that time.

When the *Bahia Buen Suceso* entered the bay of Stromness, an article of an unusual nature was published in the British press. The correspondent of *The Guardian* in Buenos Aires, Jeremy Morgan, stated in an article entitled: "British concessions in the Falklands," that the British representatives in the negotiations, "...have apparently acceded to a new procedure...that still has to be approved by the Cabinet."

Morgan's analysis, undoubtedly extracted from sources at the British Embassy in Buenos Aires, added a new element of confusion to the landscape. The political team that accompanied Williams in his *"bunker"* in calle Agote - one of the most aristocratic districts of Buenos Aires - could have deliberately leaked this information to soothe the feelings of the Argentines. When the article was published, the British diplomats based in Argentina had the latest high-level data on hand. They knew perfectly well that there was no possibility in the near future of London accepting the system proposed by Argentina. They were also in possession of Davidoff's communication on his voyage to South Georgia.

The workers at Leith raised an Argentine flag, in a ceremony without much pomp. According to military sources, this act had previously been agreed by Davidoff with the Navy[2]. The incident unfolded in this way:

According to the British, there were military *and* civilian personnel on the rocky beaches of South Georgia. The blue and white flag fluttered on the end of a broken oar like an improvised mast, attached to the turret of an electricity generator. Shots were heard, and naturally, not one of the immigration requirements were complied with. The Chief of the British Antarctic Survey team asked the Argentines to lower the flag, which they did. Williams met Costa Mendez and warned him that the incident was a serious matter for the British Government. A similar message was received in London by the Argentine charge d'affaires to whom it was suggested that it would be advisable for the Argentine authorities to distance themselves from this "provocation" by the scrap metal workers. But even before this interchange was made public, the British Foreign Office and the Ministry of Defence agreed to send *HMS Endurance* with a platoon of Royal Marines to dislodge the Argentine party. The *Endurance* was an armed patrol vessel that in a few more months would be withdrawn from the area as part of an economy drive by the Conservative Government.

The situation thus began to escalate dangerously. Costa Mendez informed the British ambassador that the Argentine ship would leave the place. The formula was ambiguous: in announcing that the *Bahia Buen Suceso* would leave Leith, he did not definitely state that the ship would remove all the scrap metal workers landed there. In Buenos Aires, on the other hand, it was affirmed that there were no representatives of the Military among the workers with Davidoff. However, the chief of the British Antarctic Survey base informed London that some of the Argentines that were on South Georgia wore the uniform of the marines and that there were fifty to sixty civilians. Those wearing uniform, he said, did not carry arms.

Far away from what was happening on that frozen island,

Lombardo had taken a few days' vacation in order to refresh himself before undertaking the final stage in the preparations for the landing on the Falklands. As a senior officer, he knew that the major responsibility for the success of the action would fall on the fleet and the marines. Stretched out on the sand of the exclusive Uruguayan beach, *La Mansa*, at Punta del Este, a place used by those with money and by the Argentine Military for its summer breaks, he enjoyed the March sun which was still very warm. He had decided to buy the Buenos Aires newspapers only every other day in an attempt to distance himself from the complexites that awaited him in his home country, and confined himself to listening to the sensational Uruguayan radio broadcasts.

It was in one of these that he learned of the irregular expedition to South Georgia. He felt disconcerted but he realised that the *kick-off* had taken place. A plane took him to Buenos Aires scarcely a few hours later, and from the airport he made straight for the *Libertad* building, where he asked for an urgent meeting with Anaya.

The latter told him that the navy would give protection to the scrap metal workers on the island, that the British reaction had been "very tough" and that the reply of the Argentine Government to the "threat" would be in a similar vein. Not a muscle moved on the inexpressive face of the commandant when he ordered his subordinate to bring forward the plans for the landing in the Falklands. Lombardo did not raise objections, even though this order would mean a massive amount of extra work. Anaya did not reveal to him at that moment when *D-Day* would be, but it was clearly not far away.

It was March 20th. The initial plans had included the use of naval transport ships, but these were not to be found in port: *Bahia Buen Suceso* was involved in the South Georgia operation, *Bahia Paraiso* was sailing towards the same area with a contingent of marines to protect the scrap metal workers; and a similar course had been adopted by the ice-breaker, *Almirante Irizar*.

Lombardo got on with things straight away and his first efforts produced a surprise. Among the reports he asked for and received was one which confirmed that some navy personnel had accompanied Davidoff's workers. On examining the names of these men, he discovered ten who had served under his command up to October 1981. They were men - mostly tactical divers - whom he had himself chosen for their professional skill to take part in *Operation Alpha*.

But that month, Lombardo had received a request from Vice Admiral Vigo, asking him to transfer these ten marines to his command. No explanations were given for the request, to which Lombardo agreed, but he supposed that Vigo needed them for intelligence work in the possible conflict zones with Chile. The Chief of Naval Operations had not thought about it again until he saw the roll and recognized the names. The doubt was obvious: had *Operation Alpha* really been cancelled?

Quite a few of those taking part in this episode spoke of it as having the most obscure origins in the whole story of the Falklands conflict. There was also one who spoke of independent action by Anaya in relation to the Military Junta.

Argentine diplomacy tried, meanwhile, to extricate itself from the situation. In London, Molteni went to the Foreign Office to explain that Davidoff had acted on his own responsibility, that the ship had now set off from South Georgia leaving behind a good part of the equipment unloaded in the old whaling station; and that although the *Bahia Buen Suceso* was in the Argentine Navy, it had nevertheless been on charter under an entirely commercial contract. This meant, added Molteni, that there was no deliberate political intention to increase tension on the part of the Argentine Government.

The affair had echoes in Port Stanley where a group of islanders painted phrases like "A tooth for a tooth" and "UK OK" in toothpaste on the windows of the offices of the Argentine State Airlines (LADE). They also replaced the Argentine flag, which hung on the front of the small building, with the Union Jack. The officials of the Falkland Islands Company (FIC) were nervous. It is even difficult to breathe in the Falklands without the FIC knowing.

The hostile attitude to Argentina in the capital of the archipelago did not amount to anything serious or even novel in itself. There had previously been reports of animosity towards employees of the State Airlines, State Gas, and State Petroleum (YPF) who were working there, without it becoming well known. But the political situation they described was totally different. The Argentine intelligence sources rapidly transmitted the news and the Foreign Minister formally protested about the incidents.

He met Ambassador Williams and conveyed a verbal protest to him. Later, as is *de rigueur*, he would deliver a document containing the terms of his protest, but in the meeting with Costa Mendez he admitted that there were still some Argentines in Port Leith, and warned that any action that might be taken against them would inflame public opinion.

Contacts between the Foreign Minister and the representatives of the Crown in Buenos Aires were turning more sour and more difficult. Mutual recriminations monopolized the discussions and the tension increased. So much so that Costa Mendez had ceased using his impeccable English with Williams, thereby obliging him to speak in Spanish. On the day of the protest about the incidents in Port Stanley, Deputy Foreign Minister Ros and First Secretary Figueroa were also present. At one moment, Costa Mendez was so exasperated that he said to the

Englishman:

"And you're staying *mozzarella* ("mum")," he said, accompanying the phrase with a gesture of sealing his lips.

Disconcerted, Williams naively inquired.

"What is *mozzarella*?"

Ros, until that moment silent, felt himself obliged to come to the aid of the ambassador in his own language.

Formal though his reply was, it nevertheless equalled Williams' ingenuousness:

"Mozzarella is a kind of cheese used in pizzas."

He appeared set on continuing his didactic culinary explanation, but an impatient gesture from the Foreign Minister interrupted him. Williams left the Palacio San Martin without having any idea why the conversation had acquired that momentary cryptical slant.

Pressured by the FIC lobby in London and with Parliament in a state of great irritation, Richard Luce made an effort to soothe feelings. He reported that the *Bahia Buen Suceso* had left South Georgia with the major part of its personnel on board, but that a reduced contingent of scrap metal workers still remained on the island. "We are making arrangements," he emphasized, "to ensure their early departure."[3] The Minister's optimism was not shared by the Members who discharged their rhetorical artillery without pity. This of course, included that of the Labour Opposition. A memorandum drafted at the time by the Argentine charge d'affaires and addressed to Costa Mendez, recorded the diplomatic point of view on the attitude of the British Foreign Office. The document, classified as secret, stated that the Foreign Office, through Luce's speech to Parliament, tried to reduce the apprehensions generated by the South Georgia incident and to put the situation in perspective. It also stressed that Luce's intervention "did not produce the desired effect..." since "...not only the Opposition, but also the Conservative benches severely questioned the official attitude, and enlarged the scope of the question, linking it with the Falklands negotiations, with revelations after the meeting in New York, and with the British Government's defence policy."

A curious coincidence occurred while the debate was taking place in the Commons. The *Bahia Paraiso* turned towards South Georgia, navigating this time under complete radio silence. An elite group of troops of the Argentine Navy, known in the struggle against the guerillas as *Los Lagartos* (The Lizards), would disembark a few hours later to take up positions among the whaling installations in order to protect the Davidoff workers from any eventual action by British forces.

At the same time, Margaret Thatcher's Cabinet approved the deployment of *HMS Endurance* against the same group of scrap metal workers. Her instructions were to put in at Grytviken before approaching the spot where the Argentine intruders were.

Both governments were approaching a point of no return without either of the parties managing to take the necessary steps to reduce the tension. The impasse had unforeseen implications. On March 22nd, Costa Mendez received a *speaking note* from the British Ambassador whose unusually threatening language was to be interpreted virtually as an ultimatum. Among other things it said:

"Ministers have agreed that *HMS Endurance* should continue to South Georgia in order to remove the remaining Argentines.

"The continued Argentine presence at Leith, contrary to Dr Blanco's previous assurance that the ship and party would depart, leaves us no option but to take this action. The Argentine workforce are at Leith illegally and we cannot allow them to remain. On present plans *HMS Endurance* will arrive ar Leith on 24th March in order to take men on board and return them to Argentina via Port Stanley. Our intention is to conduct this operation correctly, peacefully and in as low a key as possible. We hope that the Argentine Government will, if they are able to do so, advise the Argentine workmen at Leith to co-operate. We have in mind the need to ensure that equipment landed at Leith is properly safeguarded.

"We deeply regret that this action is being forced on us. We had hoped that the previous Argentine undertaking that the ship and party would leave, would have allowed the incident to be surmounted with the least political damage. Our hope is that the political consequences, with careful handling on both sides, can continue to be minimised. But it should be quite clear that this situation has not been of our seeking. It has been Davidoff's irresponsible action and the apparent inability of the Argentine Government to take the necessary remedial action which has brought it about.

"We will speak similarly to Argentine Charge d'Affaires in London.

"In view of the considerable public interest in London Ministers will be making a statement in Parliament today on the situation and on the action we are taking. We do not however at this stage intend referring to *HMS Endurance's* role."

The only way out proposed at that time was a suggestion which came from Williams: that the *Bahia Buen Suceso* should return to South Georgia, pick up the workers and take them to Grytviken, where they could enter legally. The British supposed that Costa Mendez had lost control of the situation. The Argentine Foreign Minister had often told

Williams on other occasions that he had had difficulties, particularly with Anaya. Now the overwhelming British reaction had left the Palacio San Martin with no room for manoeuvre in its dealings with the *hawks* of the navy. What followed was the leak reporting the return of the *Bahia Paraiso* with marines who, as would emerge later, were under the command of Lt. Commander [later, Captain] Alfredo Astiz. This officer had fulfilled an important though shadowy role in the repression, taking part in such acts, according to reliable reports, as the kidnapping of two French nuns and an adolescent Swedish girl. In both cases the victims were never found.

At this time, at the Casa Rosada, another psychological manoeuvre was under way. The Secretary of Public Information, Rodolfo Baltierrez, a wide-ranging journalist and diplomat, summoned various reporters to his home in the calle Carlos Pelligrini, trying all the while to arrange that they did not see each other. For this purpose, he used even his own bedroom to keep them separated - such were the numbers of press men that answered his call. At that meeting, Baltierrez let slip the news that the British vessel, *John Biscoe*, had set off from Montevideo, carrying another contingent of Royal marines to reinforce the garrison at Port Stanley.

American intelligence also furnished data to the British naval attache in Buenos Aires, who lacked his own information network. There is a serious possibility that most of the data sent by this office to London was obtained from reading the newspapers and that the only important information came from contacts with American colleagues.[4]

In the select club made up of those preparing the Falklands operation, plans were advancing at full speed. The possibility that Great Britain might send reinforcements became more likely each day. Should London take this step, the Argentines would be confronted with two alternatives:

1. To suspend the plans for the landing once more. This would provoke open unrest between the armed forces, whose co-existence was already decidedly uncomfortable. But Anaya, however, had agreed to support Galtieri's access to the Casa Rosada, only in return for the *green light* on the Falklands. Any further postponement would finish this pact, bringing with it, sooner or later, deep dissension in the heart of the military regime.

2. To continue with the landing, in spite of the possibility that it would meet strong resistance, and might end bloodily for meagre geopolitical returns. The *Fortress Falklands* syndrome was in the forefront of these men's minds who, paradoxically though it may seem, did not in fact believe in any British military reaction after the Argentine

occupation was achieved.

The first decision that Anaya took was to send two missile-carrying corvettes, the *Granville* and the *Drummond*, to the conflict zone. They positioned themselves between South Georgia and the Falklands, preventing the possibility *of HMS Endurance* returning to its natural base.

Another decision fell to Galtieri. When the incident in South Georgia was made public, he authorised Menendez to get into contact with the military group working on the plan. The meetings of this group took place in the office of the Joint Chiefs of Staff. In his first contacts, the future governor gained access to the details of the proposed landing.

The planners' objective was a *clean* operation, that is, without bloodshed if possible. In the discussions that took place, it was said that if Great Britain suffered casualties, the international community would not stomach the Argentine recovery of the islands. On the other hand, if one managed to avoid spilling British or *kelper* blood, even if there were Argentine casualties, the *fait accompli* would be just tolerable for London.

But Menendez had things on his mind other than speculation about possible casualties on one side or the other. He had received the order to prepare to administer the islands, and Menendez was a well-disciplined officer. He chose two colonels, a naval captain and a commodore. The latter was serving in West Germany as an air attache. Carlos Bloomer Reever was a veteran of the Falklands. He had not only lived on the islands as representative of the State Airlines and virtual Argentine ambassador in Port Stanley, but he had been right-hand man to Foreign Minister Carlos Washington Pastor during one stage in the negotiations. It was Bloomer Reever who had managed to obtain secret material in the Foreign Ministry without awakening the suspicions of the diplomats concerned. Moreover, by his efforts the future Falklands cabinet heard a presentation by Colonel Gonzalez Balcarce who had taken part in the New York round of talks when in his role as an official in the Palacio San Martin.

Menendez spoke plainly with all the members of the island government team: "Nobody is to ask anything about what will happen in the future," he prepared them, "because I don't know myself. I have the same doubts as you do but when I expressed them, the reply of *my* superiors was that I should just take charge of the government of the islands. We are working with a view to government. Period."

D-Day had still not been fixed. There had not been a consensus in the Junta for any acceleration of the pace of the crisis. But that Friday,

March 26th, the Military Committee (which included the Junta and President of the Nation, in circumstances when this duty was carried out by a non-serving officer) sat in order to consider the whole dispute in both its military and its diplomatic aspects.

The British feared, with reason as was seen afterwards, that the impasse in the sterile diplomatic attempt to solve the crisis of South Georgia might allow the Argentines to arm a task force to take Port Stanley. But at the same time they found themselves in a blind alley. Margaret Thatcher's supporters were pressing strongly that there should be no withdrawal. On this point the British Admiralty had a significant role to play. Great Britain was in the process of running down its surface fleet. *HMS Invincible*, its principal aircraft carrier, had virtually been sold to Australia; and the helicopter carrier, *Hermes*, was already scheduled to be scrapped.

The bitter struggle inside the Conservative Government culminated in the defeat of those who wanted to sustain the fleet. It was proposed that the surface ships would virtually be replaced by Trident nuclear submarines. In this way the glorious Royal Navy that had fought in all seven seas would be transformed into a mere appendage of NATO. This Argentine crisis suited the Admiralty to a tee. If the incident escalated and the old British lion reacted as it had throughout history, perhaps then the fleet might be saved.

Lord Carrington tried a new manoeuvre to break the Argentine position. He sent precise instructions to Williams to urge Costa Mendez to persuade the Junta to find a way out of the situation. This effort included, it is now clear, pressure on Washington to get the State Department to bring the Argentines into line. Williams, who at this stage of events was going two or three times a day to the Palacio San Martin, delivered a message from his chief. This indicated that London wanted to avoid escalation but that the Argentine Government should be in no doubt that: "British sovereignty would be defended in South Georgia as in any other territory."

Sir Nicholas Henderson, British Ambassador in Washington, received a similar cable that ended: "..... in the final analysis we cannot acquiesce in this infringement of British sovereignty and we are bound to take action to restore the status quo."[5]

That Friday 26th, Williams' contacts with Costa Mendez were unfruitful. The possibility of receiving a special British envoy had finally been dropped and the only thing standing was the suggestion that the Argentine scrap metal workers return to Grytviken, where their white cards (which served as travel documents for Argentines travelling to the Falklands) could be stamped. They would then be able to return to work in Leith. Costa Mendez, advised by Ambassadors Ros and Blanco, asked for time to consult Galtieri and reply. This would be the decisive meeting.

In London that same day, Molteni, who had formed his own idea of the situation, returned to the fray at the Foreign Office. In another interview with Robin Fearn, head of the South America department, he insisted on another possibility for defusing the situation. This would involve Britain accepting the Argentine proposal made in New York concerning the time taken and extent of negotiations. His own view of the friction in South Georgia, was that it was all an audacious and risky Argentine ploy to bring pressure on Great Britain. After all, hadn't similar projects been mooted at the Foreign Ministry ever since the days of Camilion? He supposed that the warlike noises heard in conversations with his English colleagues also formed part of the game. But he believed that finally, as had happened on previous occasions, everything would end well. Before leaving Fearn's office, he thought it opportune to alert him to the risk of: ".....giving excuses to the hawks in Buenos Aires by failing to reply to Argentina's proposal."[6]

The reality was otherwise. The President asked Costa Mendez to summon a meeting which was held by the Military Committee that 26th at night. Galtieri, Anaya and Lami Dozo met with the shared feeling that the South Georgia incident was rapidly reducing the Argentine Military Government's room for manoeuvre. Under pressure from the critical domestic situation (the trade unions were planning to surround the *Plaza de Mayo* in protest against the economic and social policy) and by British intransigence on the other hand, events had arrived at a point from which it would be difficult for the Government to withdraw without jeopardising the bases of their support. Anaya warned his colleagues of this situation and urged them to come to a conclusion. In this game, Galtieri constantly had to take up tougher and tougher positions in order not to be overtaken by the naval chief.

At the time of this meeting the fleet was ready to sail. Two days before, the commander of the expeditionary force, Rear Admiral Gualter Allara, received the order to bring the preparations forward. There were hours of hectic activity in which the armed forces reached a degree of co-ordination rarely seen before and certainly never achieved during the actual conflict.

The speed of events made it necessary to suspend the landing trials that were taking place in the region of the Rio Grande at the southern tip of Argentina.

The sole consideration for the Junta that night was to decide upon immediate action to avoid Great Britain fortifying the Falklands. When Costa Mendez arrived, he found that the commandants had already been meeting for more than an hour and that the following were also present: Brigadier Plessl; Admiral Lombardo; General Garcia and Vice-Admiral Juarez del Cerro, Head of the Joint Chiefs of Staff.

The Foreign Minister was received with smiling faces. Lami Dozo then said to him: "Sit down, Doctor, and prepare yourself. We've already decided on the Falklands." Galtieri explained to him that there was no going back and Anaya then speculated on the "historic" opportunity that was presenting itself.

Costa Mendez limited himself to saying: "If you have already decided to bring forward the operation, it only remains for me to recommend that it be done quickly. There is no time to delay. Intelligence reports could filter out, ending any chance of a bloodless landing."

The political columnist of the newspaper, *Clarin*, Joaquin Morales Sola, said that the Foreign Minister actually encouraged the military decision, egging the Commandants on by saying: "Let's do it now!"

Williams waited all night for a call from Costa Mendez. He stared out obsessively through the window of his residence in the Grand Bourg as the lights of Palermo and the avenida Libertador went out one by one. His second-in-command, David Joy, accompanied him on that anxious evening. On the following day, the ambassador came to a risky conclusion: "The Argentines are playing with us," he said in a coded message to the Foreign Office.

A public declaration by Costa Mendez served as a reply. That Saturday he affirmed that the Government would protect Davidoff's workers. That protection, he added, would not only be diplomatic, it would include sending the *Bahia Buen Suceso* with a party of marines as well as the frigates *Granville* and *Drummond*. The statement did not leave room for many interpretations, and consequently Williams asked for a further interview with the Foreign Minister. This was not granted and in its place one was given to him by Ros. The Deputy Foreign Minister's moderation was evident to the Englishman, who was demanding to know the exact location of the *Bahia Paraiso*. Ros restricted himself to notifying him that the Military Junta had merely modified its instructions to the Palacio San Martin.

The negotiation was thus virtually at an end. The decision to bring forward the landing obliged Costa Mendez to prepare his staff for the diplomatic battles which were to come. As he was convinced that the disagreements would occur mainly in his own area, he decided to summon a meeting in his office of six top-ranking officials of the Palacio San Martin. But he also thought it necessary to preserve the secret and nothing would better ensure the compliance of those who were going to share it than a solemn *mise en scene*.

They arrived at almost the same time at the Foreign Minister's office. They were: Ros, Blanco, Listre, Erhardt del Campo, Felix Pena and Figueroa. Costa Mendez gravely looked straight into the eyes of each one of his subordinates and invited them to sit down on the ancient art nouveau chairs.

"Please, everyone look at the crucifix," he said in a firm voice, while he indicated an image of Christ that hung on one of the walls.

The diplomats exchanged glances of surprise and one of them who had served in the United States believed himself to be reliving a ridiculous session in the Oval Office at the White House, so well related by Carl Bernstein and Bob Woodward. On that occasion, Nixon had asked Kissinger to kneel down and join him in prayer at the conclusion of the Watergate crisis.[7]

Others, on the other hand, supposed that it was all in fun. But they were mistaken. Costa Mendez was not joking with them. He announced that after 112 years, Argentina could be entering a war in that year - 1982. He then demanded from them an oath of silence which each then took. In spite of this however, these six diplomats were not the first within that Ministry to learn of the military plans.

Some days earlier, at 2 pm on the 20th, Galtieri received Eduardo Roca in his office at the Casa Rosada. Roca was the flamboyant Argentine ambassador to the United Nations. It was a disquieting period for this intimate friend of Costa Mendez, though not because of the Falklands - a matter which the Minister preferred to put to one side. He had come, postponing his take-over of the Argentine mission to the United Nations for various reasons, among them a recent gall bladder operation. Now he found himself pressed to go to New York, where Daniel Ortega was on the point of denouncing before the Security Council, Argentina's participation in the preparations to invade Nicaragua. In one of life's paradoxes, Roca would replace Juan Carlos Beltramino, whose head had rolled as a result of his contacts with the group of Non-Aligned countries - this according to assessments made by Argentinian military attaches in Washington.

Roca entered the Presidential office without an inkling of what would be revealed there and thinking only in terms of the formalities that would be exchanged with the Head of State. But he had not taken into account Galtieri's weakness for theatrical roles. After some small talk, the President warmed to his subject, enjoying the impact he was having on his companion:

"Doctor," he said pompously, "I can't let you take up your new post without telling you that Argentina has decided to recover what belongs to it - the Falkland Islands."

Roca could not believe what he was hearing, but he listened attentively to Galtieri's words.

"We are going to recover the islands, though I cannot yet tell you when precisely. We shall try to do it without bloodshed, if that is possible. So there's a great task waiting for you in New York."

Roca returned excitedly to talk to Costa Mendez, who tried to put the solemn Presidential announcement in perspective: "It is not something that is completely decided, Eduardo," the Foreign Minister tried to explain. But he did not manage to convince his friend who on March 23rd flew to the United States, convinced of the imminence of an Argentine military operation.

There, and until April 1st, when his colleague in West Germany, Roberto Guyer, made a stop in New York to confirm the imminent invasion, Roca lived virtually obsessed by the Falklands affair (as the Sandinista denunciation never materialized). This prospect conditioned all his actions and as a result he learnt a few lessons. The first, UN Ambassador Kirkpatrick taught him when he saw her the day of his arrival.[8] The second came from the Argentine military attache, Brigadier General Miguel Mallea Gil, who had travelled from Washington on the afternoon of the 28th to dine with Roca.

The Ambassador to the UN believed, with logic, that Mallea Gil had been informed of his commandant's plans. General Mallea Gil had been one of the driving forces in the Videla presidency and Roca thought: "If Miguel is here and has the contacts that he has with the American establishment, surely he will have used them to sound out the Government."

At 7 pm, according to the best American custom, both men were already sharing a table in an elegant New York restaurant well protected from the intense cold of late winter.

Roca admitted the urgent need to speak to him about the Falklands question which he had felt since his arrival. But as the conversation progressed he got the impression that Mallea Gil was at sea, as if completely ignorant of anything being planned in Buenos Aires. Roca realised he had gone too fast and he was obliged to change the subject abruptly as he arrived at Galtieri's disclosure. In fact, one comment from Mallea Gil even rejected the possibility of an invasion.

The ambassador breathed a sigh of relief that Mallea Gil had not believed a word. He quickly realised the slippery ground he was treading. "Either Mallea is really in on this secret, or he actually knows nothing, in which case he will leave here for Washington and send a cable to the Command describing this conversation." His mistrust was not misplaced. In spite of the close relations that the Ministry and the diplomats maintained when abroad, they always felt themselves to be sitting an examination when meeting the army, navy and air force attaches.

For the moment, British Intelligence did not uncover any concrete evidence that an invasion was being arranged. Afterwards, though, everything had the appearance of having taken place literally under their noses. Lord Carrington harboured suspicions though, and believed the moment had arrived to wheel in his American friend to put the brakes on the Argentines. He sent a message to Washington asking that the State Department attempt to mediate, and at the same time, he urged the Cabinet to order the fleet to be made ready. First a nuclear submarine, *H.M.S. Conqueror,* received orders to set sail for the South Atlantic. It would arrive there on April 13th. Admiral John "Sandy" Woodward began to organize a task force - in case the Argentines dared to defy the old empire.

On March 28th, from Puerto Belgrano, the Argentine fleet set sail. Its destination: the Falkland Islands.

NOTES

1. *Franks Report*, pp. 14-15, London, 1983.

2. During the investigation, the authors repeatedly received confirmation of this relationship between Davidoff and the navy presumably due to the need the entrepreneur had of the logistic support provided by naval vessels.

3. *Franks report.* para 179. Statement of Luce to the House of Commons.

4. There is repeated mention of the relationship between the British Ministry of Defence and its naval attaches on the one hand and the American embassy in Buenos Aires. In the Franks Report, it says that on March 23rd 1982, the British embassy in Buenos Aires reported, on the basis of information from another embassy, that all the submarines at the naval base of Mar del Plata had recently put to sea... p.59.

5. *Franks Report*, p.57.

6. Results of investigation by the authors.

7. *The Fall of Nixon.* Carl Bernstein and Bob Woodward.

8. Results of investigation by the authors concerning this meeting. This is explained in detail in the chapter *"Neither votes nor vetoes!"*

The Junta at prayer. Left to right: Lami Dozo, Galtieri, Anaya (AP)

Costa Mendez at the OAS (AP)

Chapter 5

"GOOD MORNING, FELLOW ARGENTINES!"

The telephone rang insistently in Government House for the whole day that April 2nd. From 2 pm onwards, the line between Buenos Aires and Washington had been open because Reagan had wanted to contact his Argentine colleague, Galtieri. By 10 pm the efforts of US diplomacy had still not been successful.

The Argentine President was certainly very busy that day. The imminent military operation worried him constantly. He spoke intermittently with Anaya and with Lami Dozo, and almost continuously with Costa Mendez. The prospect of a discussion with Reagan discouraged Galtieri, as he was afraid that it might result in him having to cancel the plans to recover the archipelago. In the morning he had received the US Ambassador, and that brief and tense conversation had revealed the full pressure Washington was bringing to bear on the Military Government. One of the objectives of the visitor, a US embassy source later reported, was to make sure that the Argentine President waited for a telephone call.

Schlaudermann, without resorting to too many diplomatic devices, inquired directly of the President about the possibility of military action in the Falklands. The Ambassador's question was not based on purely personal speculation. Behind his inquiry lay the formidable US and British Intelligence machines, which had arrived at the conclusion that an Argentine military incursion was imminent. The British Ambassador in Washington, Sir Nicholas Henderson, had, for the previous 48 hours, been in permanent contact with the US State Department in order to keep them informed of the latest news. Later, Secretary of State Alexander Haig, already in possession of data of his own which corroborated the English alarm, sent a personal message to his colleague, Lord Carrington.

The Franks Report indicates that:

"Mr Streator, the US Charge d'Affaires, delivered a message from Mr Haig to Lord Carrington undertaking that the US Government would do all it could to help. Mr Haig said that the US Ambassador in Buenos Aires had been instructed to urge Dr Costa Mendez to take no steps which would aggravate the crisis. Mr Haig added that he thought that the US would have a greater chance of influencing Argentine behaviour if they appeared not to favour one side or the other. Later in the day, Mr Streator delivered a message to the Prime Minister from President Reagan saying that his Government shared British concern about apparent moves against the Falkland Islands and would contact the Argentine Government at the highest levels to urge them not to take military action."[1]

Galtieri felt very uncomfortable before his American questioner and in a temperamental reaction, snapped: "We are not going to tell you, Ambassador!" Schlaudermann, for obvious reasons, preferred not to prolong the interview and hurried to his car and to his headquarters in the calle Colombia. Nervous and pale, the ambassador spoke with Haig and conveyed to him his own certainty that the Argentine Military would definitely embark on the operation.

The truth is that the US envoy in Buenos Aires could not overcome his astonishment. His embassy had followed the course of the Argentine-British encounter in South Georgia in detail - to the point that, on March 30 at a meeting with Costa Mendez, Schlaudermann had offered the good offices of his country in order to assist in finding a solution to the dispute.

"We accept mediation if the US takes up the question of the Falklands, South Georgia and the South Sandwich Islands. We want a global agreement," was the reply of the Argentine Minister. Schlaudermann explained that he had no authority to decide on such a grave matter and that he would have to consult with his government - which effectively killed off that embryonic initiative.

At 10.10 pm, the telephone in Galtieri's office rang again. The President did not hide his annoyance when he was informed that Reagan again wished to speak to him. At first he insisted on avoiding the conversation, but Costa Mendez was present at the time and pressed him to accept the call: "General," he said, "it is the President of the United States. If Brezhnev speaks to him, *you* cannot deny him."

Within a few minutes, the Presidential Office was transformed into a communications centre. Costa Mendez demanded to have Secretary Roberto Garcia Moritan, of the Foreign Ministry there so that he might act as interpreter, even though Galtieri would be trying to speak directly in his halting English. Lt. Col. Bauza, a military specialist in communications serving in the Presidential palace, installed three telephones and an extension, so that those involved could listen simultaneously to the conversation between the two Heads of State. One was for Galtieri, one for his Foreign Minister, the third was used by the interpreter and the extension was connected to a large tape recorder.

The President glanced at his watch before accepting the call from Reagan. It was after 10 pm, and the military operation in the Falklands was now beyond the point of no return. Little more than an hour later, the first tactical divers would be landing on the Falklands beaches. Feeling able to deal with any contingency, he picked up the receiver and signalled the operator that he would accept the call.

During the research for this book, the authors had access to the minutes of the Spanish version of this dialogue. It included not only the substance of the discussion between the two Heads of State, but also indicated the manner in which the discussion took place. These minutes left out only certain formalities and repetitions such as the question: "Do you understand me, Mr President?" a device both employed at the end of each part of their dialogue. This was done in order that there could be no misunderstanding on the recordings made at each end of the line. On the basis of this document provided by an unimpeachable source, it is possible to reconstruct the conversation:

"Mr. President," Reagan began, "I have reliable news that Argentina is about to adopt force in the Falkland Islands. As you will understand, I am very worried about the repercussions such an action would have. I want to express to you, Mr. President, the concern of the United States in this matter and the need to find an alternative to the use of force."

"First of all, Mr President, I want to thank you for your concern." Galtieri countered. "I want to remind you," he began to explain, "that my country has always maintained a favourable attitude towards negotiations in this dispute with Great Britain. This is demonstrated by seventeen years of fruitless discussion under the auspices of the United Nations. We have conducted these negotiations with a nation which, more than a century and a half ago, used force to usurp a territory which by right belongs to Argentina. Our negotiating position remains the same - but the patience of the Argentine people has a limit. Great Britain has threatened Argentine citizens legitimately going about their business in South Georgia, and my government has an obligation to protect them. Besides, the United Kingdom persists in ignoring Argentine claims in order to put an end to the negotiation and has not responded - in spite of our insistence - to the last proposal that we formulated in order to speed up the process. I want to repeat to you, Mr. President, that our negotiating stance has not changed."

"I understand, Mr President, but I consider it essential to continue the discussions and to seek an alternative to force," Reagan insisted in order to put on the pressure immediately afterwards.

"Believe me, Mr President, I have good reason to assure you that Great Britain would respond with force to any Argentine military action."

"Argentina has always been in favour of a peaceful solution to this dispute," replied Galtieri, and he began to lay down his own conditions: "It will only be possible to find the alternative you seek, Mr President, if there is recognition on the part of the United Kingdom of Argentine sovereignty over the Falkland Islands. And that recognition would have to be explicit and public," he added, so as not to leave any doubt.

"I understand your position, Mr President, but it is very difficult for the United Kingdom to effect such a recognition immediately and in present circumstances - that is to say under the threat of military force," Reagan tried to argue. "My government is ready, Mr President, to offer its good offices to get the discussions going again so as to reach a solution to the problem. If your government finds it convenient, I can send Vice-President Bush to Buenos Aires in order to hold discussions and begin to find a negotiated solution to the situation." added Reagan, playing his strongest card. "Besides," he added, "We could find an adequate formula under the aegis of the United Nations. Ambassador Kirkpatrick is ready to assist both parties in this process. You know Ambassador Kirkpatrick well, Mr President, and you know it would be possible to work in this way." Reagan tried with Galtieri.

But the Argentine President was at that moment beyond all temptation, for he persisted with his previous arguments:

"I appreciate your offer, Mr President, but I want you to understand that we have been negotiating fruitlessly for seventeen years in the United Nations. There are all those resolutions of the General Assembly, such as 1514, 2065 and others which repeatedly call on the parties to seek a negotiated settlement to this sovereignty dispute. Throughout, Mr President, the United Kingdom has turned a deaf ear to those calls. Only last February, my government delivered a new proposal, in New York, to the British representatives. This was an example of the Argentine willingness to negotiate and it took into account the relevant United Nations resolutions. Up till this moment, we have received no reply from London. Nevertheless, we await it with patience in the desire to find a peaceful solution."

"That may be so, but it will not escape you, Mr President," Reagan said, renewing the pressure, "that a conflict of this nature will have repercussions in the whole Hemisphere and will create a situation of grave tension. Besides, it will occur at a time when our joint efforts to improve bilateral relations are bearing fruit - after the difficulties we experienced during President Carter's administration. The special relationship that exists today could suffer gravely. It is necessary, Mr President, to find a peaceful solution and to avoid the use of force."

"The Argentine Government, Mr President, values its relationship with the United States wholeheartedly. For that reason, remember that it was not my country that sought this situation. Indeed it was merely seeking a solution, and one can still be found this very night if Great Britain recognizes Argentine sovereignty over the Falklands," Galtieri replied, closing all leeway to Reagan's efforts.

"Such recognition would be impossible at this moment," Reagan said, in an effort to drag out the conversation. "If the alternative is an Argentine landing, the United Kingdom will make a military response, I assure you, Mr President.

" What will happen to those two thousand islanders, Mr President?" Reagan asked.

"Rest assured," said Galtieri, trying his best, "that the Argentine Government will expressly offer all guarantees to the inhabitants in the Falkland Islands. They will keep their liberty, their free will and their property. They will be able to remain on the islands or emigrate to Great Britain, as they wish. They will be able to opt for Argentine or British citizenship and will be able to emigrate to the United States if they desire." In this last offer, Galtieri rashly over-reached himself in generosity, since Reagan had not mentioned the possibility of receiving the *"kelpers"* in his own country, nor was there any reason for him to do so.

"Mr. President," said Reagan putting on the pressure again, "I believe that it is my obligation to bring to your notice that Great Britain is ready to respond militarily to an Argentine landing. This has been made known to me by the United Kingdom. Furthermore Mrs Thatcher, a friend of mine, is a very determined woman and she would have no other alternative than to make a military response. The conflict will be tragic and have grave consequences for the Hemisphere."

"I repeat, Mr President, that Argentina did not seek this situation, and the desire of Argentina to negotiate has been unmistakeably demonstrated over seventeen years of discussions," replied Galtieri briefly.

The possibilities having been virtually exhausted, Reagan began to admit defeat before the crushing weight of reality:

"I understand from your words, Mr President, that Argentina reserves the right to use force. I want to make clear, therefore, that the relationship between your country and mine will suffer gravely. American and world-wide public opinion will take a negative attitude to an Argentine use of force. Besides, the effort I have made to restore our relationship will be severely affected. Great Britain, Mr President, is a very close friend of the United States and one will see the new relationship that Washington has with Argentina - achieved in full view of American public opinion and after a long effort - irremediably prejudiced."

"Argentina really regrets this situation, Mr President, but the reality is that the capacity to negotiate and the peaceful disposition of my country have limits. The Falkland Islands are one of the last cases of colonialism in the world, and, in particular, on the American continent. We have not arrived at this point without having already exhausted all attempts at negotiation. We have not been responsible for this situation. The English are not, nor have they ever been, our enemies. I would like to ask, Mr President, if the United States could lend all its support so that the situation may be overcome in the best way possible. It is essential that the United States understand the extremity to which Argentina has now arrived. My country and government hope that the United States may act as a friend of Britain and Argentina equally in order to be able to resolve the present situation," declared Galtieri, wishing to mitigate the effect of his rejection upon the American President.

"I can only say that I regret not having been successful in conveying to you my concern over the effect of this situation on the future of the Hemisphere. I tried to make a good case in order to persuade you not to resort to the use of force. I could hardly fail to contact you precisely because of the consequences of this Argentine action," Reagan replied, admitting his failure, but also managing to leave an implied threat.

"Argentina and the Argentine people, Mr President, thank you for this gesture; and Argentina and its people hope that the United States will understand their position. I am deeply grateful to you, Mr. President, and I sincerely hope that this dialogue may continue," Galtieri said in a tone that showed that this was more than a formality.

There followed a couple of paragraphs of farewells which, according to a Presidential source, were cold.

Reagan put down the telephone as if he had said something which had not been understood by his colleague. The message had not reached its destination. Galtieri, for his part, concluded the conversation convinced that this had been a well-meaning gesture by Reagan, but without grasping the real significance of the call.

All the lights of Government House were on at that hour and the substance of Reagan's message spread quickly among the officials of the Presidency and the Ministry of the Interior. The Assistant Secretary of the Ministry, Colonel Menendez, spoke every 15 minutes with General

Saint-Jean by internal line in order to keep up with the news. This army lawyer was still greatly excited by news of the military operation which he had received that very lunchtime, when leaving with the Minister of the Interior to attend a reception given by the Argentine Chamber of Advertisers. He was not the only one in the Government bereft of information. The Minister of the Economy, Roberto Alemann, was only informed of the news at six in the evening, hardly five hours before the beginning of the operation.

Menendez was a little displeased, because he recalled the meeting of March 27th, held in secret in a downtown apartment with a group of trade union leaders who were preparing a protest march for the 30th. He had met Lorenzo Miguel, Roberto Garcia and Miguel Unamuno, and having concluded his briefing as planned, the senior official of the sixty-two organizations asked him: "Colonel, what is happening over the Falklands?"

"Nothing will happen, rest assured!" the officer had replied with a complacent air.

That April 2nd, the Under-Secretary of the Ministry of the Interior began to understand some of the things that had been happening on the previous few days. The end of March had not been very auspicious for Galtieri's government. The economic deterioration had produced a momentum in the behaviour of the trade unions who had been largely passive until then and it was difficult to control. The union leaders aligned in the *CGT Brasil*, and within the Peronist orthodoxy, started a massive mobilization, in effect a show of strength.

The prospect of such protest generated a debate in the heart of government. There appeared two clearly opposing factions: that of Nicolaides and Vaquero, who saw the march as a form of subversion; and that of the Minister of the Interior, who advised that the problem should be faced with political tact, without recourse to repressive measures. Galtieri found himself between these two opposing positions, which in spite of many meetings could not reach agreement. The President, of course, was inclined towards a hard line with the demonstrators. Galtieri feared that the march might become uncontrollable and degenerate into a popular revolt that would threaten the stability of the Military Government. Nor did he forget that, barely 72 hours hence, the *Proceso Militar* would at last revive when the recovery of the Falkland Islands commenced.

The President ordered the Federal Police to place themselves under the authority of the Army Commander-in-Chief and so relieved the Ministry of the Interior, who would normally have commanded that security force. The subsequent repression was ferocious. In Mendoza, for example, police action under the jurisdiction of the 4th Army Corps at that time commanded by General Llamil Reston, resulted in a worker dying of bullet wounds. In spite of having previously maintained the opposite, the Minister, Saint Jean, expressed the opinion at a luncheon of the Chamber of Advertisers that the trade union march amounted to "subversive gymnastics."

During these hours the Argentine embassies in London and Washington were following events carefully. In the British capital, Alfredo Molteni, the charge d'affaires, read the newspapers eagerly because they were his best source of information. (Ortiz de Rozas had been sent on the Argentine mission concerned with the Beagle Channel dispute. His attempts to return at the time of the crisis in South Georgia had been blocked.)

Molteni had filed an article by Michael Fidman in *The Times*, published during the last days of March, in which he asserted that: "The Argentine Military are unpredictable," and foresaw a "possible invasion of the archipelago."

Contact between the embassy in London and the Palacio San Martin hardly existed. In the first place, the Junta had made the military operation a matter of total secrecy, organized and planned by an elite group. Secondly, communications between the two capitals were not simple. At that time, Molteni had spoken only a couple of times by telephone to Gustavo Figueroa, the First Secretary in the Foreign Ministry, who gave him no clue as to what might happen. Besides, the Argentine representative in London was rather apprehensive about that sort of call, and he was not wrong either. The communications used by the Argentines could be perfectly well understood by the British, as was soon realized.

At any rate, anxiety was becoming apparent in all the members of the Argentine mission. Molteni was uneasy and worried, and he viewed with some distrust the changing activities of the naval attaches, Admiral Raul Gonzalez and Captain Alfredo Febre. On March 30th, Gonzalez advised him about South Georgia; "If it continues like this, we shall have some news soon." On Wednesday the 31st, he received a call from the manager of Aerolineas Argentinas in London, which finally opened his eyes. The official informed him that flights between Argentina and London had been suspended, Molteni immediately contacted the manager of the London branch of the Banco de la Nacion Argentina and warned him about the availability of funds in the event of an incident in the Falklands.

The same almost feverish activity was to be seen among the officials of the Latin American desk at the Foreign Office. About mid-day on April 1st, Ray Whitney, Conservative Member of Parliament, called at the Argentine Embassy. There he spoke with Molteni and formally proposed to him that a representative of the United Kingdom should be sent to Buenos Aires, or anywhere else for that matter, to meet with a corresponding senior diplomat from Argentina. Molteni was surprised at the offer and only managed to ask: "And who would you send?" Whitney proffered the name of John Ure, Under-Secretary at the Foreign Office, and then those of Francis Pym and Richard Luce, the Minister of State who had negotiated in New York with the Argentines and who had replaced Nicholas Ridley. In 1979, Ridley had nearly been expelled from Argentina on the initiative of the then Deputy Foreign Minister, Carlos Cavandoli: after a visit to the Falklands, he had had some scathing remarks to say on the situation of human rights in Argentina.

Molteni did not commit himself, and suggested that perhaps Ambassador Ros was the person to speak to, but deferred any further discussion because he felt intuitively that the situation in the South Atlantic would no longer permit that type of negotiation.

Whilst this contact was taking place between Whitney and Molteni, the British Cabinet was in deep discussion. Humphrey Atkins, who was covering the absence of Lord Carrington, visiting Israel, reported on the most recent events occurring in South Georgia. An intelligence group had produced a report on the war preparations of the Argentine armed forces and predicted the possible launching of a military operation on midday of the 2nd. The report indicated: "There is no evidence that the Junta has decided on an invasion," but there was "the certainty that an unusual co-operation between the three branches of the armed forces had taken place and of their active participation in an amphibious working group." The report estimated that the joint Argentine forces had acquired sufficient operational capacity and logistic support to mount an invasion.

By mid-morning of that April 1st, the British precautionary measures were taking on a new dimension. The Defence Committee announced to the Prime Minister that an Argentine military action was beyond question being planned for the following day, but that: "One still cannot determine the intentions of the Military Government." The Committee urged fresh diplomatic efforts: "The Government of the United States can play an important part." But at the same time it pressed for preparations for the military alternative: a large naval force would be needed to confront the Argentine contingent.

In Washington that same morning the Argentine Ambassador at the White House, Esteban Takacs, received a call from his US colleague, Jeane Kirkpatrick. The latter was forthright and told him that no doubts remained about the imminence of an Argentine operation on the archipelago. "I was absolutely astonished. I had not the least information on the matter," he confessed later. Without doubt there had been a marked lack of communication between Buenos Aires and the outside world - a dangerously secret handling of the affair.

Takacs knew nothing that April 1st, but on the other hand, twenty-four hours earlier, perhaps somewhat less, the Argentine representative at the United Nations had been informed of the military decision. Eduardo Roca spoke on March 30th with Costa Mendez, by *carola*, the nickname that the diplomats give to the telephone used for private conversations. The device scrambles the words into unintelligible sounds, which are then recomposed at the other end of the line. In spite of this, such precautions cannot be absolutely secure and the Foreign Minister resorted to cryptic language:

"Eduardo," he said, "the date of the event will be brought to you by Robert. He is going to Bonn, but I asked him to pass through New York to talk to you. He arrives there tomorrow," announced Costa Mendez. The messenger was Roberto Guyer, Argentine representative in West Germany. Roca could not resist the temptation to ask: "What date, Canoro, the one we have been waiting for since the time of Vernet?"[2] The UN representative, however, was not any less worried than Takacs, and the event seemed so serious and overwhelming that he decided to take very little sleep and, at half past four in the morning, well wrapped up to protect him from the intense cold, he was already pacing the arrivals lobby of John F. Kennedy airport. Hardly had Guyer disembarked from the plane than he told him that the landing would be made in the early hours of the 1st. They had breakfast together and neither of them thought of taking a minute's rest.

In Washington, Takacs received a call from Assistant Secretary Enders inviting him to go as soon as possible to the office of his chief, Alexander Haig. The Argentine diplomat agreed, put on his raincoat and less than 20 minutes after putting down the telephone he entered the office of the Secretary of State. Haig repeated to him the information that Jeane Kirkpatrick had anticipated hours before, but also offered him the personal intervention of Vice-President Bush to act as mediator. "You will understand, Ambassador, the importance relations with Great Britain have for my country. We do not want a war because perhaps we would not be able to be neutral."

The Argentine diplomat returned to the embassy rapidly and before meeting his military attaches, ran over to himself what had happened. He was almost in a state of shock and could not grasp the events rushing past at breakneck speed. Above all, he was worried about the way the Government seemed to have excluded him from the whole procedure. Later he met Brigadier Ricardo Bonino, Admiral Ruben Franco and General Mallea Gil, and gave them a meticulous account of his meetings, all of which seemed to surprise the officers - at least that was the reaction that they showed as the ambassador outlined the scheme to recover the Falklands by force. In spite of Takacs' recollection, sources close to the centre of those events suggest that at least one of the three attaches, General Mallea Gil, was perfectly *au fait* with events in Buenos Aires, though this could not be confirmed.

Takacs resolved to communicate with the Foreign Minister and in virtue of the delicate nature of the message, he opted to use *carola*. The conversation turned out to be tantalizingly brief:

"Haig offered me the mediation of Vice-President Bush," he said, hoping for a reply.

"Take note," replied Costa Mendez laconically.

The Foreign Minister was pre-occupied with negotiations taking place with the Soviet Union and with China, in case there should be a meeting of the Security Council following the recovery of the Falklands. A first report by Roca - based on an appreciation made by Jeane Kirkpatrick - that had foreseen a British decision not to refer the matter to the UN, was proving mistaken. The British representative at the United Nations had begun to stir things up. Argentina had to prepare itself for an eventual world condemnation. The leeway was certainly narrow: the problem of human rights and the blindness of the Military to international relations had left the country virtually isolated.

On March 30th, Deputy Foreign Minister, Ros had received the Soviet Ambassador to Argentina, Sergei Striganov, at his office. This was a key meeting for the Argentine diplomat because, without expressly saying so, he planted the idea of the need for a veto. This request to Moscow contrasted inevitably with the feeble relationship which the Argentine regime had opted for *vis-a-vis* the Third World, renouncing - more or less - their inclusion among the under-developed countries. That morning of the 30th, Argentine diplomacy performed a carefully prepared manoeuvre. Whilst Ros and Striganov were talking, Costa Mendez left his office and in order to evade the reporters, descended by the corridor of the Palacio San Martin which leads on to the calle Esmeralda, walked a few metres and entered the office of his deputy by a rear door.

The following day, Striganov was again received by the Foreign Minister, who formally requested a veto from Moscow. Shortly afterwards on the same day, Costa Mendez met the representative of the Chinese People's Republic in order to indicate a similar requirement. Soon after these interviews, he sent two coded cables to the Argentine ambassadors in Moscow and Peking so that they might complete the diplomatic initiative that had just begun. The messages, of identical form, read: "The Argentine objective is that the USSR (China) apply its veto in the Security Council to any proposal that goes against the interests of our country."

That same March 31st - and he would repeat it on April 1st - Costa Mendez met the British Ambassador to Argentina, Anthony Williams. The British diplomat, who always seemed to behave as if events were too much for him, was hoping for an Argentine reply to the offer made in London to Molteni to send an emissary from Her Majesty's Government. What he obtained was the following declaration, signed by the Chancellor:

"Since the problem raised is disregard of Argentine sovereignty, I judge pointless the despatch of a person to examine the events in the Georgias since Argentina considers this incident resolved. In fact, the workers there are carrying out their tasks under normal lawful conditions without any breach of the agreement previously reached between our two countries.

"Bearing in mind the antecedents and the course of the negotiations undertaken from 1964 to today we would have accepted the despatch of the representative proposed by Great Britain if his task had been to negotiate the modalities of transferring sovereignty over the Malvinas Islands and their Dependencies to the Argentine Republic which is essentially the central cause of the present difficulties.

"I cannot omit to draw attention to the unusual British naval deployment towards our waters reported in the international press which can only be interpreted as an unacceptable threat of the use of military force. This obliges us to refer to the UN organisation where Argentina will circulate a note on the antecedents of this case."[3]

In fact, Ambassador Eduardo Roca had hardly finished presenting this note when he received a call from Jeane Kirkpatrick, who invited him to take tea at her residence with the British representative, Nicholas Parsons. Roca and Parsons did not know each other, since the Argentine ambassador had been in New York less than a week. A few hours before this call, the Secretary-General of the UN, Javier Perez de Cuellar, had summoned them in order to express his "growing concern regarding the tension in the South Atlantic," but they had arrived at different times and so avoided crossing paths. Later, Perez de Cuellar made a public appeal to both governments.

Roca did not reply to Kirkpatrick's invitation because he really did not know what attitude to adopt. The ambassador had been informed that the military operation had been postponed to the early hours of the 1st because of a storm which blew up around the archipelago, but he imagined that perhaps by that time - the mid-afternoon - the fleet would have begun its final advance towards the Falklands. Negotiations at this stage were suspended, and Roca thought that his meeting with Parsons might be viewed unfavourably in Buenos Aires. He then spoke with Jeane Kirkpatrick and explained to her that it would be better to leave the visit pending for the present, though he accepted the suggestion to go to the UN *Crystal Palace* to make contact, even if only formally, with Nicholas Parsons.

The meeting took place in a small room at the side of the hall used by the Security Council. The conversation was extremely brief and Parsons ended it by excusing himself, saying: "My office has just advised me that a long message is being received from London. If you wish we can meet again tomorrow." He was never able to fulfil this invitation because the message came from the Foreign and Commonwealth Office, advising that reliable information had been received that an Argentine naval force would gather the following morning and confront Port Stanley.

Parsons received the message and read it carefully, but almost immediately he was informed that another telex would be sent in under five minutes. This second message indicated that the British Governor of the Falklands, Rex Hunt, had made arrangements for the deployment of the Royal Marines because there now existed a firm assumption of an Argentine landing. With this last telex in his hand, Parsons set off once more for the *Crystal Palace*, where he successfully negotiated the summoning of a meeting of the Security Council.

That session, No. 2345, provided the British with an occasion to vent their feelings over the Argentine threat. The result was an order from the Council to its President, Kamanda wa Kamanda of Zaire, to urge the parties to the conflict to avoid the use of force, which he immediately proceeded to do. This move also marked the formal entry of the Security Council into the affair, and proved a useful precedent for Parsons to exploit when he came to propose the resolution that would be approved on April 3rd.

Meanwhile in London, Lord Carrington and John Nott, convinced that events had reached the point of no return were debating in the early hours, the advisability of making ready a fleet to be sent to the South Atlantic. Without delay, the Minister of Defence put on alert the naval task force gathered in British ports. He knew that in 48 hours these ships would be able to set sail and also that others, presently on exercise in international waters would be able to join them.

A few hours later contact was made by telex between London and Port Stanley:

London: What do you make of these rumours about Argentines?

93

Port Stanley: We have a lot of new friends.

London: And what about these rumours of invasion?

Port Stanley: Those are the friends I referred to.

London: They have landed?

Port Stanley: Of course.

London: Are you doing business?

Port Stanley: There are no orders yet. We have to obey orders.

London: Whose orders?

Port Stanley: The new Governor's.

London: Argentine?

Port Stanley: Yes.

London: Are the Argentines in control?

Port Stanley: Yes. You can't fight against thousands of soldiers, with enormous naval support. We are only 1800. Keep the line open, please.

At this point in the dialogue, according to one newspaper report,[4] communications were abruptly cut off.

By that time, the Argentine military were already holding the key points of East Falkland. The operation had been accomplished with little difficulty because the stormy weather of the previous day had given way to a pleasant morning with calm seas in the bay where Port Stanley is situated. In spite of all Argentine precautions, the islanders had been alerted to the invasion and had prepared some obstacles. For example, the airport landing strip was covered with vehicles placed across it, and with large, heavy pieces of iron. The troops making the landing had their first casualty that day: Lt Commander Pedro Giachino, who died during the approach to the Governor's residence.

The naval operation went according to plan, with the sole exception of the final part of the journey. The original scheme envisaged entry into Port Stanley after completing a great arc round the south of the archipelago. But this was not to be. The Argentine Military advised that the element of surprise had already been lost, as they had picked up a broadcast message from *Radio Falklands*, made by the only journalist on the islands, Patrick Watts, in which he warned of the imminent landing.

That day was also notable for an incident among the Argentine military leaders themselves. It was a first indication of problems that would arise during the war. The armed forces had doctrinal and operational differences, resulting from the absence of any centralized command structure - and these rapidly became obvious. This had never happened before, for the simple reason that Argentina had fought its last war in the previous century.

The army and the navy arrived at an agreement that the infantry battalions would remain under the orders of General Garcia. Such an agreement was not easy to achieve with the air force, however. The planes of the air force and those of the fleet began to dispute control over the air space of the islands and Port Stanley airport.

At seven in the morning, the runway had been cleared, and one hour later planes were beginning to land. Three and a half hours after that, the Commander of Naval Aviation, Rear Admiral Carlos Garcia Boll, boarded an Electra in Comodoro Rivadavia, to fly to Port Stanley. When he began to fly over East Falkland, his pilot requested permission to descend, which was denied by the traffic controller on land. From the control tower they warned that as the airport had no fuel it would be futile to land the plane there.

Garcia Boll, little inclined to accept what he took for a bluff, made radio contact with the Commander of the Theatre of Operations in the South Atlantic (TOAS), Vice-Admiral Juan Jose Lombardo, in order to give him the news. The latter immediately instructed the Commander of the Fleet, Rear Admiral Gualter Allara, to send a platoon of marines to dislodge the air force contingent from the airport.

While this incident was unfolding, Commodore Luis Guillermo Castellanos was taking part in the ceremony of raising the Argentine flag on the mast before the Governor's residence, whereupon one of his staff made him *au fait* with the embarrassing news. Before even the arrival of the order from Lami Dozo on the mainland, Castellanos set out for the airport and settled the problem by personally authorising the landing of the Electra bearing Garcia Boll. This episode reflects, anecdotally perhaps, the lack of preparation and organization of the armed forces in the face of a military confrontation with one of the Western powers.

Hardly minutes before the landing, Costa Mendez received in his office at the Palacio San Martin a communication from the ambassador in Moscow, Ernesto de la Guardia, who informed him of the moves he had been making there. At 4.40 a note arrived in which the ambassador indicated that he had spoken with Vice-Minister Zemkov and Ambassador Volski. The Soviet Government had affirmed that: "they would give full consideration to the Argentine case," while de la Guardia had left with them the final message that: "Argentina hopes to continue counting on the support of the USSR on this question."

The Soviet language was sufficiently ambiguous to leave serious doubts concerning the veto. Costa Mendez folded the message and put it in one of the pockets of his by now rumpled suit and began a series of communications. First to London: "In a couple of hours there will be news," he said to Molteni. Then to Washington: "The landing has been carried out," he informed Takacs briefly, and finally to New York: "All turned out well. I am travelling today," he told Roca.

At that hour, in London, Margaret Thatcher's ministers were meeting. Nott, a man of few words but firm decisions, gave an account of military movements in the South Atlantic and Lord Carrington, dispirited by what he guessed could be a full stop to his career as Foreign Secretary, described the failure of the latest diplomatic moves, among them Reagan's telephone conversation with Galtieri.

About midday GMT, *HMS Bransfield*, a British Antarctic survey vessel, announced a break in radio communication with the Falklands. It was the first reliable evidence that the Argentines had landed. The news spread like wildfire and Haig himself transmitted it to the "Iron Lady." Almost immediately a message arrived from the British station at Grytviken, South Georgia, and then London was able to establish contact with the cable and radio operator on the Falklands, who only had time to confirm the presence of Argentine forces in the telex quoted above.

At the Argentine embassy in London, Molteni contacted the manager of the Banco Nacion, in order that he might transfer all available Argentine funds before the inevitable blocking of accounts. Some $500m immediately fled to Switzerland. Three times this amount could not be freed, for legal reasons and because of restrictions over withdrawal periods.

Molteni immediately convened a meeting of all the staff of the legation. There remained four diplomats - Fleming, Jaurequiberry, Iglesias, Salvador; some ten officers of the armed forces; and fifty clerks. Having called them all to his office, Molteni launched a fiery harangue: "It is a historic day, the most important in our lives," he managed to make clear, overcome as he was by emotion. After intoning the national anthem, a pragmatic spirit returned to the team, and without losing time Molteni arranged the destruction of all the embassy files.

He did not have to improvise too much because since he had learned of the suspension of flights by the manager of Aerolineas Argentinas, he had been working out a contingency plan for just such an occasion. He had even formed a working group to select all the key newspapers, collect articles published by the British press and record programmes broadcast on radio and television.

Molteni did not use a sophisticated method. He simply took an old boiler which was lying in the attic of the embassy and shifted it to the back yard. He gathered all the documents into this receptacle and after spraying them with alcohol, set them alight. He repeated the operation three or four times and then reflected that the moment should be recorded. He took a small camera and snapped the scene.

A little later, all the military attaches began to arrive at the embassy, many of them not a little surprised at the haste with which Molteni was making decisions. The diplomat feared that the British might take some organized action against the Argentine legation though the attaches did not share this view. They thought that everything would work out eventually, and did not believe that anything untoward would happen in the immediate future. Just like the Military Junta in Buenos Aires, the attaches did not reckon on a violent reaction from Britain.

The naval representative managed to get the point across to Molteni that it was wrong to over-react and think of a war. "We can't stand more than 15 days of combat, let alone think of war," he commented.

Curiously, Councillor Echague, agreed with this opinion. He was better informed than anyone in the embassy, but was always tight-lipped. Without giving any reasons to anyone, he had chosen to spend the night of 1st April in the embassy. This made everyone conclude afterwards that he had had detailed information about the operation.

Molteni continued burning papers and hiding keys until he received a summons from the Foreign Office. It was 2 pm and he was told to present himself three hours later.

He immediately sent a telex to the Palacio San Martin asking for instructions. Molteni believed that at first Great Britain would formalize the break in relations, but feared something more serious. Some days before, a friend and official of the British Home Office confessed to him that due to the incident in South Georgia, the Prime Minister was considering interning Argentine residents.

The news had leaked out through a couple of London newspapers, which were making much of the prevailing discomfort in the Conservative administration, particularly concerning the Argentine Navy. This was because the missile-carrying frigate, *Santisima Trinidad* - which formed part of a group of six vessels which had threateningly approached the scene of the South Georgia incident - had actually spent six months in British ports. The British, therefore, assumed that its commander was aware of the events in South Georgia at the time when his frigate was moored at a British quay.

Full of doubts and fears, Molteni reached the Foreign Office where he was received by Sir Michael Palliser, Permanent Head (with special powers during the conflict). Molteni had not had to wait more than two minutes when an assistant called him in to Palliser's office. There was hardly a greeting.

"I am handing you a formal note of the break in relations. You have invaded British territory." said Palliser.

"Excuse me, but we have recovered what has always belonged

to us." Molteni managed to reply.

"That we shall be discussing in the United Nations and in other places," replied the Englishman, with obvious threatening intent.

"That may be," said Molteni, realizing that the tense exchange of bravura was over.

Before concluding the meeting, Palliser informed him that Switzerland would represent British interests in Argentina. Molteni said that before agreeing to this he would have to consult his Government, after which he returned to his office and sent another cable to Costa Mendez.

Molteni also settled the details for a dinner that was taking place that evening at the embassy - planned several days beforehand - which would be attended by a group of Argentine friends. There was no lack of toasts over the big news, but the meeting was marred by anxiety. The telephone rang insistently and anonymous English voices threatened the imminent explosion of bombs in the vicinity.

Dawn had not yet come over Washington when Takacs was already sitting down to breakfast with the military attache, General Mallea Gil. They discussed the preparations to be made, because they believed that all the negotiating effort over the crisis would fall on the United States. The ambassador spoke several times to New York so that Roca could keep him informed of the options prior to the meeting of the Security Council. Nevertheless, Washington that April 2nd was marked by much uncertainty. This was generated by a dinner Takacs had to offer the same night to the United States Ambassador to the UN, Jeane Kirkpatrick, who had completed her spell as President of the Security Council in March.

And so it was that that day Argentina took possession of the Falklands, so ignoring the advice of President Reagan himself: in this way Argentina defied its principal American ally. With a good measure of logic, Takacs supposed that the social gathering would be cancelled, and that the guest of honour and the others invited would send their regrets. The Argentine diplomat thought that the US Government would be too compromised by Argentina if its officials were to attend. All afternoon counsels were sought in Washington. Wives of diplomats and White House officials who were due to attend exchanged telephone calls in order to get the news as to whether the social evening was on or off. Washington is in fact a kind of court. Social life revolves around power.

Even Roca considered the possibility of not attending, though for different reasons. He let Takacs know as follows: "I don't feel like leaving the office, even for a few hours. Here things are really in the balance and I don't know what may happen." - this in one of the many telephone conversations they had that day. Finally he was convinced by his colleague that he should go and took the shuttle to the capital.

Nevertheless, Takacs' optimism grew as the hours passed. Kirkpatrick called him at mid-day and confirmed she would come, though she said she would be a little late because she had an interview with Ronald Reagan. She did not tell Takacs at the time, but her determination to be present had been "accepted at the highest level." This emerged later from testimonies gathered by the authors during their investigations in Washington.

The decision was, as Kirkpatrick recognized in one of her interviews: "A difficult and delicate question." United States interest in Central America was great and Argentina was behaving like a first-class ally. The ambassador emphasized the necessity for the United States of projecting an image of neutrality, thus ensuring some scope for making an intervention. "Although you may not have believed it, Argentina was very important to us," she explained.

Inaugurating what was to be a succession of confrontations with the US Ambassador to the United Nations, Secretary of State Haig advised a boycott of the gathering. In this way, he argued, the British and Argentines would know on which side United States solidarity lay. In the event of future negotiations, London would count this in Washington's favour and inasmuch as Buenos Aires would accept US intervention of whatever kind they would neither have anything to worry about. Reagan ended by inclining himself in favour of Kirkpatrick's suggestion. The various sources consulted in Washington all agreed on this point.

The first to arrive at the residence of the Argentine ambassador was the Secretary-General of the OAS, Alejandro Orfila. "Are they going to come?" he asked, concerned at the prospect of a mass desertion, and he sat down rather relieved when the host replied with a gesture of assent. Moments later the guests began to arrive and were seated in a room on the first floor of the residence - at round tables decorated with small floral displays. Apart from the guest of honour, there were: Tom Enders, Assistant Secretary of State for Inter-American Affairs; Walter Stoessel, second in line-of-command after Haig; Frank Carlucci, Assistant Secretary of Defense; Edward Meyer, US Army Chief; and William Middendorf, US Ambassador to the OAS.

Events in the South Atlantic dominated the conversation during that tense social evening. Takacs wanted to know what the United States would do in the Security Council, and although he knew it to be inappropriate to put a direct question, he tried to prompt his American guests into making some reference to it. These exchanges were laboured, and an embarrassing silence gradually began to descend over the tables. "It was a horrendous dinner," commented Sonia Adler, one of the guests and editor of the *Washington Dossier*.

The meal, in which the main course was salmon, turned out to be meagre. The tension finally crystallized in Jeane Kirkpatrick's words of thanks: "You Argentines are good at almost everything except governing yourselves," she allowed to slip out, thus doing credit to her reputation for verbal incontinence.[5] In a later interview with the authors she reiterated the opinion.

Kirkpatrick waited until the dessert before informing Takacs that her country would vote in favour of Great Britain in the Security Council. Dissembling somewhat, Takacs nevertheless betrayed on his face the impact of this news. Before he could say anything, the US ambassador offered her personal assistance, repeating what Reagan had said in his telephone conversation with Galtieri. She also invited Takacs and Roca, together with Costa Mendez, who at that moment was flying towards New York, to join her for dinner the following evening. "I hope to see you tomorrow in the Waldorf Towers," would be Jeane Kirkpatrick's farewell.

By attending this dinner party, even though she was not the only US Government official present, Jeane Kirkpatrick acquired a distinctly suspicious reputation in British eyes, and thus she became a target for critics. Sir Nicholas Henderson, British Ambassador in Washington, said to the press that the gesture was: "As if I had attended a dinner at the Iranian embassy the day they took the American hostages in Tehran."

In the early morning of that April 2nd there was to be a prolonged and nerve-racking vigil in Buenos Aires. The newspapers kept their lights burning, and as on great occasions - perhaps the last had been the death of the "smiling Pope," John Paul I - issued several editions. Confirmation of the operation had been picked up only a few hours earlier. On the previous evening one of the present authors made the obligatory trips to the Foreign Ministry and the office of the Commander-in-Chief of the Navy. At that hour, in the Palacio San Martin, they were still insisting on the possibility of reaching a diplomatic settlement. In reality, nobody believed in that possibility and only the professional zeal of Gustavo Figueroa was sustaining this dying hope.

The impression to be gained in the *Libertad* building was very different. Without daring to admit that the operation was already past the point of no return, some officials left open the possibility that some military action was possible. But persistence in a journalistic interview is often an effective way of getting nearer to the truth. The reporter left the office of the Navy Chief with the distinct feeling that the landing would take place that night. But there was no confirmation, no exact corroboration of a "good source" to clinch the story. He had hardly begun writing when he took up the telephone and rang a naval captain with whom he had a good personal relationship: "If the weather is good, the landing will be made tonight. I'm sorry, but you are not going to be able to sleep," the sailor said in jocular tone.

At the Foreign Ministry, Costa Mendez did not even leave his office to dine, in spite of being disgusted at the thought of eating there - for there was no kitchen and one had to go out to buy food in the vicinity. The result was that the food arrived at the table tepid or almost cold. But the special circumstances of those hours set such problems at nought. In this way, Figueroa and two or three assistants remained all night on the first floor of the Ministry, collecting the news, above all that coming from the military commands.

By 10.30 pm, this reporter was once more at the Ministry where other accredited journalists were also mounting vigil. After waiting five minutes or so, Figueroa appeared from behind a curtained door, without jacket, his shirt almost out of his trousers and his face lined with fatigue. He took the visitor by the arm and together they sat on an old and faded sofa near the Salon Dorado.

"Has the landing begun?" was the first question.

Figueroa did not try to reply, still less to say anything untrue. After looking at his watch he confided resignedly: "It's almost happened." The reporter could perceive in him a strange mixture of enthusiasm and apprehension when he added: "Well, boy, now we are going to see what happens."

The first editions of the newspapers, which that day were on the street at 2 am, announced the military action in their headlines, but by nature rather conservative in such circumstances, none of them risked over-forceful statements. "The reconquest of the Falklands begins," headlined *Clarin*, later to amplify it to "Argentine troops land in Falklands," in a subsequent edition. "Operations begin in the South to ensure National Sovereignty," informed *La Nacion* rather more ambiguously. In a later edition it indicated: "Argentine troops begin military action in the Falklands." *La Razon* sought God's blessing with its front page: "The Falklands in Argentine hands. Today is a day of glory."

Surprisingly, Galtieri's ministers were only due to meet at seven in the morning. Some of them arrived at Government House looking rather embarrassed, with newspapers under their arms. Not all officials knew what had happened that morning. Slowly they began filling the *Sala de Situacion*, ironically an area intended by the former President Ongania for the purpose of working out and debating military strategy. In this spot another President would announce the most important action by Argentine arms this century - and without having submitted it to any debate at all.

Half an hour later than arranged, Galtieri's entrance silenced the gossiping and a sonorous "Good morning, fellow Argentines," served to demonstrate the President's exuberant spirits. Galtieri spoke of the conquest but did not go into details. Actually, the eyes of ministers kept resting again and again on Costa Mendez, on whom fell the responsibility of justifying to the world the audacity of the Argentine Military Government. They awaited the Foreign Minister's words as one would a sedative.

Something was already clear. Not all the ministers shared Galtieri's optimism over the operation, although they were careful not to make public any signs of doubt that they might be feeling. Galtieri would not have tolerated it. Perhaps that state of tension was why it was difficult to obtain parallel accounts of what happened from the participants. Some sources stated that Costa Mendez assured the Cabinet that there would be no problems in the UN and that one could count on the Soviet and Chinese veto. Others, among them the Foreign Minister himself, merely spoke of that problem being discussed.

Already by mid-morning, crowds began to gather in the Plaza de Mayo. Not a few officials recalled the ecstatic success of the 1978 World Cup and felt the same magical atmosphere. As if by some beneficent spell, the conflict between the police and demonstrators of March 30th now seemed a distant memory. They were all there, the police smiling and the public well-behaved as in a chapter from science fiction. Some of the crowd enthusiastically chanted the name of Galtieri, and the temptation to join in was stronger than anyone's modesty.

The President appeared on a balcony that seemed larger than ever and said to the multitude that Argentina "...will accept a dialogue after this forceful stand." Nobody knew it then, as confirmation was delayed, but London had ordered the Task Force to make ready to be sent to the South Atlantic while in the United States incredulity prevailed. "I can't believe they have done it," admitted an angry Reagan to reporters in the White House. "Argentina invaded who?" was the question Americans asked when they heard the news on radio or television.

In hardly 24 hours, Argentina had introduced a new chess piece, isolated and unexpected, onto the board of world politics. But after a brief period of astonishment, matters were settling into place.

Optimism was the currency of that day. There was confidence that the imminent diplomatic battle in the UN would end in an Argentine triumph.

In the evening, Galtieri spoke to the nation and confirmed plainly that Argentina had recovered the Falklands "without taking any political calculation into account." The euphoria of those hours drowned the news. No-one paid attention and no-one believed it. And, to judge by the international reaction at least, it was true.

NOTES

1. Falkland Islands Review. Para. 243, p.69.
2. Reference to Luis Vernet, first Argentine Governor of the Falkland Islands appointed in 1829.
3. Ibid 1 Para. 244, p.69.
4. *Clarin*, April 4, 1982, p.5.
5. War for the Falklands. The Full Story. *Sunday Times* "Insight" team.

Menendez sworn in as Governor of the Falklands (AP)

Lombardo and Menendez on the Falklands (AP)

Chapter 6

NEITHER VOTES NOR VETOES

Spring had still not begun on the American East Coast when Costa Mendez and his team of assistants arrived at John F. Kennedy Airport in New York on the morning of April 3rd. The sky was covered by the leaden shades of winter, anticipating what 48 hours later would be the last great snowfall of the season. None of the Argentine retinue associated the weather with any omen, but later one of them was to comment: "The difficulties were in the air," on recalling those hours.

In the south, Argentine troops continued going through their baptism of fire. For the first time this century, they had come up against foreign forces. A few hours after Costa Mendez stepped onto American soil, the Military Junta in Buenos Aires made public Communique no. 12, announcing that South Georgia and the South Sandwich Islands, were, like the Falklands, now under Argentine sovereignty. This time there were three Argentine casualties.

At the airport, awaiting the Foreign Minister, was a large group of Argentine diplomats, including three ambassadors: Roca (UN), Quijano, (OAS) and Takacs (US). Also - a clear sign of how the operation of April 2nd had altered the rules of the game - a swarm of American and British reporters received the Argentine delegation. In other circumstances the television networks would be unlikely to have sent their teams to the airport to cover the arrival of an Argentine official. The visit of the then President Jorge Rafael Videla to attend the signing of the Panama Canal treaties in 1977, for example, passed virtually unnoticed by the American press - but this time things turned out to be entirely different. Argentina had reached the front pages of the newspapers of the world and the prime spots in the television news programmes. A doubtful privilege this, that was only to be conceded during the negotiations, to the incursion of Israel into Lebanon. The news coming from the Falklands, until then one of the least known parts of the planet, obscured even the most notorious international crises, among them that of Central America.

105

It was just this journalistic enthusiasm, so exceptional for the Argentines, that Quijano remarked upon for the benefit of Takacs, whilst Costa Mendez was replying to reporters in his impeccable and colloquial English. This marked the beginning of a siege that lasted without diminishing in intensity for several months. From this the Foreign Minister only managed to escape on many occasions thanks to suitable blocks and interruptions on the part of his First Secretary - invariably attentive to detail. More than this, during the frequent hours of tension, Figueroa took upon himself the responsibility of soothing the inevitable friction between Costa Mendez' assistants and for helping the "chief" as he used to refer to him, over moments of anguish, uncertainty and depression.

The tension scarcely kept the Foreign Minister alert however, weighed down as he was by fatigue. This had been accumulating without let-up and was compounded by jet-lag following almost twelve hours of flight in the Boeing 747 of Argentine Airlines from Buenos Aires to New York. Whilst defending the Argentine cause before American cameras, Costa Mendez had to make mental notes for the conversation he was thinking of having with his childhood friend and now permanent representative at the UN, Eduardo Roca. The most important questions would have to be worked out on the way to the exclusive United Nations Plaza Hotel, where the delegation was housed. Not only did it turn out necessary to bring the work forward (there was an imminent meeting with the ambassadors of the Non-Aligned group of countries and immediately afterwards he had to sit at the circular table of the Security Council) but, worse still, there were few opportunities to have confidential conversations proof against leaks.

He had to accustom himself to the idea that bugs might be permanently tuned to the Argentines' voices. Neither their rooms in the UN Plaza Hotel nor the offices of the Argentine mission to the UN on its 25th floor were safe and everyone knew it. The accommodation could have microphones installed by American intelligence and, though less likely in the case of the embassy, the Argentines always worked on the assumption that a portable receiver, controlled from some neighbouring building, was monitoring conversations inside their diplomatic headquarters. Often, including their contacts with reporters from Argentina, the Buenos Aires envoys would have to speak out loud on some inconsequential subject, while writing and passing messages among themselves on some more delicate topic. At other times they would walk together for one or two blocks along First Avenue seeking the privacy which ironically only the public street could offer them. At such times, the fantasy of spy thrillers became a daily reality.

Costa Mendez exchanged customary greetings and, with Roca

and Figueroa, climbed into the luxurious black limousine that the mission had hired for his stay. The Argentine representative at the UN was more than worried. The Security Council had been in continuous session for more than 24 hours. It had been called at the request of the British Ambassador, Sir Anthony Parsons, as soon as he had confirmation of the Argentine landing at Port Stanley. Moreover, he had already introduced into the agenda the proposal that soon, without any modification, became Resolution 502. In fact, to extract from the Council the minimal concession of a postponement of the vote until the Argentine Minister arrived had required much effort by Roca and his assistants as well as members of the Panama mission. This was the only Latin American state with a seat on the Council and it began to exercise an inflexible and militant solidarity with the Argentine cause.

As if this accumulation of unhappy omens was not enough, the latest soundings of the Argentine representatives among the diplomats in the remaining delegations threw up a distressing picture: the British were getting nearer and nearer to obtaining the necessary nine votes to get their resolution approved. This was thanks to the alacrity with which Parsons had pressed his negotiations with the representatives of the other countries on the Council, in particular with those who were members of the Non-Aligned group. The crisis "struck the Council like lightning from heaven," the British representative recalled later, and he lost no time in reacting.[1]

Roca, a recent arrival to the complexities of the *Crystal Palace* of the UN could not match, still less surpass, the confident footwork that characterized the veteran Parsons' conduct of the British case. Worse still, on the night of April 2nd, the Argentine experienced what he remembers as a "false euphoria" into which he was drawn by the Jordanian ambassador, Hazem Nuseibeh, who assured him that: "Great Britain will not get the necessary votes." In the morning, the first news his assistants provided brought Roca down to earth. Imprinted forever on his memory would be the contempt he would feel for his Jordanian colleague. "He's a double-crosser," he said categorically from then on, each time he referred to Nuseibeh.

The fact is that Roca had still not recovered from a previous illusion, this time provided by the American representative, Jeane Kirkpatrick, who on being sounded out by the delegate the same day as he arrived in New York, gave her forecast that it was: "impossible that Great Britain would bring a crisis in the Falklands to the United Nations."

Roca had arrived that March 24th full of anticipation and found that his closest colleagues, Ministers Nestor Martines and Jorge Herrera Vegas, had gone to great lengths in their zeal to comply with his latest instructions. These had been transmitted to them by telephone before he left Buenos Aires. They had not only obtained the audiences he asked for - the first to accredit himself at the UN and the other with Kirkpatrick - but both were to take place within the first three hours.

Annoyed by the implications of the tight agenda - a most stylishly dressed man, he could not even change the shirt he had worn on the journey - he began to arrange with his assistants the matters that he would develop with Kirkpatrick. Martinez and Herrera Vegas were surprised by the emphasis that their newly-arrived chief put on the Falklands question - it is clear that neither of them knew of Galtieri's intimation to Roca. For these Argentine delegates to the UN, it seemed the most urgent matter was the possibility that Daniel Ortega Saavedra would unleash a public denunciation of the clandestine military participation of Buenos Aires in Central America that same day before the Security Council.

Roca doubted the wisdom of putting the problem of the South Atlantic at the top of the agenda. Would that impatience betray his real anxiety - which he ought to conceal before his American colleague? Finally he recalled the excellent links forged with her and other prominent members of the American Right, since meeting in 1979 at the seminar organized by the businessman Raul Pinero Pacheco. He decided to stretch the margin of sincerity as far as security permitted.

Thus, exactly at midday in New York, Roca entered the office of his friend and opposite number. Wasting hardly any time on formalities and small talk, the Argentine ambassador brought the conversation to the subject that was causing him both excitement and unease at the same time. "The British," Roca told Kirkpatrick, "are making this incident in South Georgia, which is a simple extension of domestic territory, into something of international dimensions, and that is a piece of nonsense."

Roca found the American diplomat a reluctant partner in his argument. On a couple of occasions he had to make an effort to stop her changing the subject to the problem of Central America or the group of Non-Aligned countries. Finally, faced with the Argentine's insistence, Kirkpatrick agreed to ask her secretary to provide a map of the South Atlantic for him in order to demonstrate what he was saying. "We see this as a problem between the Argentines and the British, and do not believe that the United States should intervene," she commented afterwards. This was the American "hands off" policy again.

Nevertheless, Roca was not satisfied by so non-committal a reply; he had come in search of justice and consequently insisted on looking at the possibility of an escalation in the scope of the affair. "In any case," Kirkpatrick then ventured in reply: "it is impossible that Great

Britain would bring the question of a crisis in the Falklands to the United Nations. Here everyone knows how to get in, but no-one knows how to get out in these matters: the British mistrust the United Nations, and with good reason."

Roca thought that this prediction was precisely what he had been looking for. Although nagged by suspicions, never cleared up, that his friend had some aces up her sleeve he allowed the conversation to flow naturally in the way his hostess wanted it to. Anyhow, hadn't he also concealed the decision taken by the Military Junta? Diplomacy, he thought, is in some ways a card game for cheats and is disagreeable when, as on this occasion, one had to play it with friends. But those were the rules.

Before ending the day's work, Roca had dispatched a coded cable with the heading: "For the exclusive attention of His Excellency, the Foreign Minister," reporting and commenting on Kirkpatrick's assertions. After all, weren't the Falklands a colonial problem? Why therefore bring it to an international forum where the term imperialism and all its derivatives had the force of an insult?

Whilst his car covered the distance between the airport and his hotel, Roca found more than one reason to regret that cable of April 3rd, in which he had informed Costa Mendez of the latest events. At precisely that moment, Parsons was proving that it *was* possible for London to defend its case before the UN. At that time too, the Foreign Minister and his assistants were agreeing about the meeting prior to the vote. This had to be held with the ambassadors of the Non-Aligned Countries - the so-called "Non-Aligned Caucus" - and would be of vital importance for the course of events.

Obviously, one would have to continue working for a Soviet or Chinese veto to the British initiative but, after the efforts made in Buenos Aires by Costa Mendez, and in Moscow and Peking by the Argentine ambassadors, this possibility was really remote. There was also the plan for a Panamanian resolution, but its chances were minimal, slanted as it was to coincide with Argentine interests.

Now, in the United Nations Plaza Hotel, Costa Mendez also heard news and opinions from Takacs and Quijano. The first was a man who was well-liked at many levels in the Reagan administration and particularly at the State Department. He brought his Foreign Minister up to date on the latest signs of concern on the part of Washington and everyone agreed that these, perhaps in a few more hours, would give way to some definite move.

This last possibility was the one which privately seduced Costa Mendez. His previous analysis of the military operation indicated that the United States would behave according to its super-power status, intervening in order to prevent a confrontation. It was an argument taken from the lessons of contemporary history - like that of the Suez Crisis in the fifties.

Quijano, the professional Argentine ambassador to the OAS, remembered the opposition and criticism of the Military Government's action expressed by Costa Mendez in Buenos Aires, and limited his role to a technical assessment which he offered only when it was required. Afterwards he would confirm that he found it hard to disguise his pessimism.

Rest was denied Costa Mendez that day as on so many that followed. He descended the thirty floors that separated his suite from the street, and, crossing the hall which connected the mission offices with the hotel, he went first to those offices and then on to the Crystal Palace. Physically to enter into the multinational world of the United Nations from the UN Plaza, it was enough to cross First Avenue, but diplomatic conventions are sometimes irresistible: Costa Mendez, resigned to them, had to get back into the limousine and be driven the 150 yards that separated him from the entrance. This, apparently, is how dignitaries have to arrive.

It was ironic that it had to be Costa Mendez, a sophisticated intellectual who had never made a secret of his strong cultural preferences for the West, nor of his gut rejection to every "Third World" attitude that his own mission might adopt when trying to win agreement for the Argentine anti-colonialist cause in the Non-Aligned forum. It was not only ironic, it was also problematical.

Many of the ambassadors that listened to Costa Mendez that afternoon hardly even knew of the Falklands - beyond what could be read in the latest editions of the New York Times, heard on the television news programmes or seen referred to in cables from their ministries. But they were all perfectly well informed on the violations of human rights in Argentina; on the special links that united the country with South Africa; on how the Argentine Military assisted in the repression in Guatemala, Honduras and El Salvador - and on the positions that Buenos Aires adopted on the Middle East, always siding, as it did, with Israel. Even more, they were perfectly clear on the reluctance of the military regime to support anti-colonialist causes in the international assemblies. Now in this forum their Minister of Foreign Affairs came to defend just such a cause.

Still more, some remembered, as Costa Mendez entered the place, that this was the same man who had said: "Argentina does not belong to the Third World," so that many supposed that Roca, the new UN ambassador came charged with the task of preparing for Argentina's withdrawal from the Movement of the Non-Aligned Countries, of which it had been a full member since 1973.

Roca today denies that those had been his instructions, but concedes that he had been charged by his friend the Foreign Minister to "observe the evolution of the Movement attentively." Both agreed that the latter was "an altar to which one periodically had to go with offerings, without them producing concrete results very often."

In any case, they decided that there would be a period of one year for observation and in it Roca had to examine the possibility of co-operating with the more moderate countries, among them India and Yugoslavia.

In such cases, nevertheless, the view taken of the facts by the parties concerned can be out of proportion to those facts. And the perception the ambassadors of the Non-Aligned countries had of Costa Mendez and of the government he represented was decidedly bad. An intelligent Ugandan diplomat would give, weeks later, the following description to the authors: "Costa Mendez was a man who came to a place in which he did not believe, to say things in which he did not believe - and we didn't believe him either." That relationship got better after a few days, in the same way in which the position of the Argentine Government changed - abandoned by the West which it so admired - and also that of Costa Mendez himself who, he now says, changed many of his convictions and views.

"There were some things that I didn't see then and I didn't want to see," he reflected to the authors on one occasion, "but that changed." If the Foreign Minister of a country is not transformed by a war, who will be transformed?"

The formal exhortation made by Costa Mendez was unfortunate. Pressed by circumstances, he put more emphasis on what he considered should be the behaviour of the Non-Aligned - which was equivalent to giving them a lesson on how to vote - than in detailing the merits of the Argentine cause. Finally, he was not even disposed to answer questions. "The meeting was bad," Roca recalls. "Costa Mendez found at the end of his speech that the only head that nodded was that of the Panamanian delegate." Anyway, the questions that could have been asked would have meant some difficult moments for him to negotiate successfully, since not a few of those present had referred to the unilateral use of force on the part of Argentina.

Although the international system as presently conceived, reserves the right to use force to its powerful members, the smaller countries are apt to oppose strongly what they feel are precedents against the expressed renunciation of violence that all states make which adhere to the United Nations Charter. "For some, to invalidate initiatives like Argentina's in the Falklands is equivalent to mortgaging one's own destiny. What about Guyana and its dispute with Venezuela regarding the Esequibo?" a French diplomat commented later.

Roca remembers that everyone, including Costa Mendez, emerged from the meeting with the Non-Aligned Countries troubled by a new sense of urgency. The attitude of members of the caucus had varied between indifference and hostility, and one could not hope to benefit from a new postponement of the vote. This had been fruitlessly attempted by the Panamanian Foreign Minister, Javier Illueca, who placed himself at the head of his delegation. The only result of his feverish efforts had been the inclusion in the text of the British motion the words: "Islas Malvinas," following each reference to the Falkland Islands.

Better luck accompanied the efforts of the British Ambassador, Parsons. Even in conversation with the Jordanian delegate, while the latter was practising a sort of permanent ambiguity, the delegate from London knew what to do. He put one of his assistants in front of a telephone with orders to find the Foreign Secretary, Lord Carrington. As the latter could not be found, Parsons took the telephone and demanded to speak to the Prime Minister, Margaret Thatcher. The *Iron Lady* has in general a poor opinion of her diplomats - she thinks that almost all of them are capable of negotiating away even the most sacred principles - but Parsons was one of the exceptions to this rigid outlook. Thatcher knew him when he headed the British Embassy in Tehran and he had impressed her as much by his intelligence as by his style. Parsons asked her to make a special effort with King Hussein. Thatcher did not hesitate in acceding to his request, and a little more than an hour after Parsons' manoeuvre on the telephone, Nuseibeh received a telex from Amman carefully instructing him to vote with the British. Parsons knew Nuseibeh's personality very well: not in vain had he had long talks with him in Arabic - the language of Jordan.

With this background, Costa Mendez took his seat at the Security Council table assigned to him according to protocol by the Zairean, Kamanda wa Kamanda, who was President of the Council during the month of April. He showed a degree of uncertainty equalled only by the degree of confidence exhibited by Parsons.

The situation required some daring move, and Costa Mendez conceived of one. He leant towards Roca and impressed on him the necessity of trying once more to obtain the Russian veto. Roca swallowed, rose from his seat and made his way towards the place where the delegates from the USSR were to be found.

He approached ambassador Oleg Troianovski and told him that Costa Mendez would like to speak to him. The Soviet diplomat agreed, rose from his seat and accompanied Roca as far as a lobby on one side of the Council Chamber, where the Minister awaited him. Time was pressing and the Argentine went straight to the point, asking Troianovski if he had received instructions from Moscow to oppose the British motion. "The wheels of time do not favour us, sir," was the elliptical reply. "You will understand that a veto in the Security Council is a matter of extreme importance; I do not decide it, nor even an Assistant Secretary in Moscow, and it is now 2 o'clock in the morning over there," he added after consulting his watch and looking blank. The Russian's reply mixed refusal, courtesy and a certain irony - who can believe that the Foreign Ministry of the USSR sleeps at any hour of the day or night? At the same time it also made it clear what was going to be his attitude minutes later. The formal reply of the USSR to the Argentine request would arrive at the Palacio San Martin on April 11th.

At the same time, an assistant of Parsons, Hamilton Whyte, wagered a bottle of whisky with an American colleague. The latter maintained that the Russians would veto the British motion, but Whyte preferred to stick to the evaluation made by his chief, Parsons. This was that the history of the United Nations showed that the USSR only exerted its power of veto when the subject affected its interests in a direct way. The case of the invasion of Afghanistan in December 1980 was a clear example.

In Buenos Aires, that April 3rd, no-one seemed to share the concern of the Argentine negotiators. On the contrary, there was confidence that the imminent diplomatic battle in the United Nations would result in an Argentine triumph. The Minister of the Interior, Alfredo Saint Jean, summoned the leaders of the political parties to his office to speak to them about the "reconquest" and of the plans of the Military Government for the territory recovered.

The audience for the Minister was not hostile. Already by then all the leaders, without exception, had declared themselves to be in support of the military initiative. It is not that the politicians liked expressing rhetorical sympathy for the de facto Government, but there was no alternative at that moment. One of them even tried a joke. The leader of the Popular Left Front, Jorge Abelardo Ramos said to the Minister in a conspiratorial tone on greeting him: "Very well, General, but now that we are throwing out the Englishman, couldn't we make another effort to throw out the German?" The allusion to his colleague Roberto Alemann, the Minister of the Economy, was clear to Saint Jean, who made a compromising smile, deciding to ignore the suggestion.

The Christian Democrat, Carlos Auyero could not disguise the displeasure that the mandatory nature of the occasion was causing him and he arrived late at the Ministerial meeting. He was taken by a secretary into Saint Jean's office, where the latter was explaining the situation. The general interrupted his discourse, approached Auyero, greeted him and accepted his apologies for the delay. After inviting him to sit down, he took up the thread of his presentation: "As I was saying, gentlemen: the matter is now in the hands of the Security Council of the United Nations. But we have even considered that. There is little chance that Britain will obtain the necessary votes. But even if they do, the Foreign Ministry is making efforts to ensure that the USSR, or China, or both, veto the British motion." Such was the assurance with which Saint Jean pronounced this forecast that no-one in the audience dared to question it.

The scene for the drama in the United Nations was complete. Of the principal protagonists only Ambassador Kirkpatrick was absent, replaced on that occasion by her deputy, Charles Lichenstein, whom everyone nicknamed the "Woody Allen of the United Nations," because of his physical similarity to the actor. This absence at the time of voting only served to increase the criticism of American diplomacy - suspected by the British of being pro-Argentine - and the antipathy which Parsons would maintain for it.

The Security Council has fifteen members, of which five are permanent (United States, USSR, China, France and the United Kingdom), any of which can, by its veto, cause a motion to be cast out. The remaining ten members are chosen for periods of two years and in April 1982 the council comprised: Poland, Spain, Panama, Japan, Togo, Jordan, Uganda, Zaire, Ireland and Guyana.

In order for a resolution like the one the British were seeking to be passed, it was necessary to obtain two thirds of the votes. After a relatively brief debate - according to the tradition of the Council - the voting confirmed Parsons' forecast: the text prepared by the lawyer David Anderson was approved by 10 votes in favour (Great Britain, United States, Japan, France, Ireland, Togo, Jordan, Uganda, Guyana and Zaire). There were four abstentions (USSR, China, Poland and Spain) and only one against (Panama).

Two last, almost desperate manoeuvres of the Panamanians had already ended in failure. Illueca first asked for a fresh adjournment of some two hours in order that the Council could consider the text of a new alternative motion. This proposal was defeated on a procedural vote: it could not obtain the two thirds needed. Then the Panamanians tried to deprive Parsons of his vote declaring that, in accordance with Article 27 (3) of the Charter:

"...in decisions under Chapter VI, [Pacific Settlement of Disputes] and under paragraph 3 of article 52, a party to a dispute [in this case, Great Britain] shall abstain from voting."

Parsons counter-attacked, arguing that the resolution had been proposed under Chapter VII [Action with respect to threats to the peace], a position in which he was supported by the Spanish delegate, Jaime de Pines, whom all respected as an expert on the small print of the Charter and the provisional rules of the Council. Illueca desisted on this occasion from demanding a new procedural vote. Resolution 502 established:

"The Security Council:

Recalling the statement made by the President of the Security Council at the 2345th meeting of the Council on 1 April 1982 calling on the Governments of Argentina and the United Kingdom of Great Britain and Northern Ireland to refrain from the use or threat of force in the region of the Falkland Islands (Islas Malvinas),

Deeply disturbed at reports of an invasion on 2 April 1982 by armed forces of Argentina,

Determining that there exists a breach of the peace in the region of the Falkland Islands (Islas Malvinas),

1.*Demands* an immediate cessation of hostilities;

2.*Demands* an immediate withdrawal of all Argentine forces from the Falkland Islands (Islas Malvinas);

3.*Calls* on the Governments of Argentina and the United Kingdom of Great Britain and Northern Ireland to seek a diplomatic solution to their differences and to respect fully the purposes and principles of the Charter of the United Nations."

Predictably, Costa Mendez hastened to reject the terms of this resolution. The position would alter later when Argentina declared itself as accepting the mandate "in its entirety," stating that it only objected to the British interpretation of it. Nevertheless, the diplomatic defeat and the sequence of events leading up to it were obvious. These were:

1. The idea of the military operation as a *fait accompli*, was invalidated when on April 1st, the President of the Security Council, Kamanda, summoned Parsons and Roca separately in order that they might ask their respective governments to exercise moderation.

2. With the approval of the Resolution, the British, who today consider it "a minor classic of their diplomacy in the post-war period"[2] obtained something more than a mandate which was ignored by the Argentines. By demanding of the parties that they wholly respect "the principles and propositions of the Charter," they gave London the necessary leeway to introduce the principle of self-determination for the islanders into any future negotiations and moreover permitted them to appeal to Article 51 of the Charter:

"Nothing in the present Charter shall impair the inherent right of individual and collective self-defence if an armed attack occurs against a Member of the United Nations, until the Security Council has taken measures necessary to maintain peace and security...."

To this *right* Thatcher would return time and time again, to justify sending the Task Force to the Falklands. This triumph inspired the following conclusion of a leader-writer of the Washington Post: "Great Britain is a power of the tenth rate, but with a diplomacy of the first."

In Port Stanley during this time, the commandant of the Falklands Theatre of Operations (TOM), General Garcia, received Argentine reporters, transported from Comodoro Rivadavia in an aircraft of LADE and spoke to them with evident pride about the territory captured. Among other matters for consideration, he gave the journalists a copy of the third of the edicts issued by the new authorities. In this, the kelpers were assured that from the moment the Argentine troops arrived, they were protected by the rights and guarantees of the National Constitution, especially those contained in Article 14. When one of the reporters observed the curious fact that the armed forces could guarantee rights in the islands which the inhabitants of continental Argentina had been denied for the past six years, his comment received no more reply from the officer than a glacial look.

Parsons and his men consequently received congratulations from London and from colleagues of other countries. In the British mission someone found some bottles of champagne in a refrigerator - remains of a recent birthday party - and they uncorked them to celebrate the triumph.

Costa Mendez, after supplying a long report by telephone to Galtieri, had an early dinner with his assistants in the sophisticated restaurant *La Bibliotheque* half a block from the hotel and opposite the *Crystal Palace*, on Ralph J. Bunche Square. The atmosphere was sad and tense. There Roca and Erhardt del Campo began to outline the possibilities for a negotiated solution within the framework of the United Nations, even speculating on the future presence of UN troops in the islands. That would have necessitated the prior acceptance of the terms of Resolution 502. After a conversation with the President, Costa Mendez knew that the scope for making such a proposal to the Military Junta was non-existent. Galtieri had stated that same day in Buenos Aires: "The Argentine nation under arms has to give battle if it is attacked with all means at its disposal." It was, although no-one knew it at the time, the beginning of an escalating military rhetoric that would only know its limit with the coming of defeat.

Costa Mendez was to have dined that evening with Kirkpatrick, who finally decided not to return from Washington where she had spent the day. Her agenda had lengthened more than was foreseen and the weather did not invite travel. The storm clouds and the inclement cold were growing in the same way as Argentine anxiety.

Ten days afterwards, when the focus of attention in the conflict had moved to Haig's mediating mission, Roca received Ambassador Jose Sorzano in his office. He was an academic and diplomat born in Cuba, and a close collaborator of Kikpatrick's. He came with excuses for Kirkpatrick's erroneous forecast on British behaviour. The gesture served to revive the Argentine's sense of frustration. After all, Resolution 502 was already a sad reality and the Englishman Whyte had richly deserved his bottle of scotch.

NOTES

1. The Falklands Crisis in the United Nations. *International Affairs* Anthony Parsons 1982.
2. "War in the Falklands. The full story." *Sunday Times* Insight Team, 1982.

Menendez greets Galtieri at Port Stanley airport (AP)

Astiz surrenders South Georgia (AP)

Chapter 7

THE HAIG MISSION I - "THE IRAN SYNDROME"

After the diplomatic defeat of the adoption of Resolution 502 by the UN Security Council, Costa Mendez and his team had many reasons for discomfort that April 4th 1982. But there were more reasons than they were yet aware of. It was too early for them to know, but the promising, though precarious "special relationship" between Argentina and the United States had visibly begun to collapse as a consequence of the decision by Buenos Aires to recover the Falkland Islands.

A few, though very influential, officials of the Reagan administration tried to prop it up. The principal figure in this was the Ambassador to the UN, Jeane Kirkpatrick, who always had the ear of the President. Others one can include are General Vernon Walters and Assistant Secretary Thomas Enders. These, by advocating neutrality, at least in that first stage of the dispute between their two allies, faced up to the majority opinion in the State Department: the "Atlanticists", who saw no other priority for American foreign policy than London's cause. The visible head of this grouping was none other than the Secretary of State himself, Alexander Haig.

The first meeting held in the "C" Street building in Washington, once the Argentine military operation was an accomplished fact, demonstrated the overwhelming majority of the Atlanticist tendency. From that meeting had come the recommendation which gave rise to Reagan's decision to add the US vote to Resolution 502. There are some signs that Kirkpatrick, at least, argued fruitlessly in favour of an abstention or for seeking a postponement of the vote. This she did first to the National Security Adviser, William Clark, and then to Reagan himself. When the battle was finally lost she chose to remain in the capital, delegating to her second in command, Charles Lichenstein, responsibility for supporting Great Britain in the Security Council.

An American diplomatic source recalled for the present authors that, apart from Haig, the meeting in the State Department included: Walter Stoessel, Tom Enders, Vernon Walters and Laurence

119

Eagleberger among others. (Vernon Walters, in fact, was on the point of leaving on a mission that would take him to Nepal and Ceylon.) At this meeting, there was frequent mention of the phrase "special relationship". To the Argentine Military this had the aura of some distant dream, but in fact, on these occasions it invariably referred to British-American links. This difference in the perception of their relationship by Argentines and Americans emerged as one of the principal political misunderstandings of the whole dispute. It was one of the obvious causes for Buenos Aires' misreading of the international realities - a speciality of the Military Government.

Right from the start in this meeting, Haig began in his habitual, straightforward style to use tough language to describe the Argentine Military. On at least one occasion he referred to them as "power-mad thugs". What infuriated the Secretary of State most, according to one source, had been Galtieri's lack of consideration for President Reagan when the latter telephoned him on the night the landing took place.

The reality was that those advocating neutrality as a way of enabling Washington to mediate between the parties faced strong arguments to the contrary, at least in terms of internal American politics. Some of the many factors according to sources were:

1. From the beginning, the political fate of Margaret Thatcher would be irrevocably tied to the outcome of the conflict. For Reagan, that fate was of the utmost importance since he considered the Conservative Prime Minister as his most valuable ally - as much politically as ideologically. Testimonies agree that on various occasions during the conflict, Haig reminded the President that the United States and the Atlantic Alliance simply could not afford the luxury of risking the fall of Thatcher's government. It was not accidental, they said, that Reagan described the Prime Minister as "my friend" during his telephone conversation with Galtieri on the night of April 1st - in which he had tried to dissuade the Argentine from taking action.

2. British pressure on the White House and also on Congress was immediate and of great intensity. The British ambassador in Washington, Sir Nicholas Henderson, a man little given to subtlety, used every means available to apply this pressure and as many times as possible. He did not hesitate to criticize Kirkpatrick publicly as well as other officials since he suspected her of "sympathizing with the South American dictatorship." He took it for granted that Washington had no option but to support its "historic ally" in the emergency. From the beginning, in his contacts with the State Department and with the Capitol, he repeatedly hinted that London was starting to suspect the American tardiness in openly condemning Argentina. Any attempt to repeat the Suez episode, he implied, would mean a death blow to the

heart of the pact on which NATO was founded.

3. This argument concerning Suez also arose frequently in the American analysis of the problem. London knew very well that it was appealing to the record. The humiliation the then President Eisenhower inflicted on Great Britain had left both a residue of resentment among the British and a curious historic guilt complex in United States Foreign policy: "Because there has already been a Suez, it wouldn't do to have another."[1] was a phrase already being heard in the State Department, on the Capitol and in the White House.

4. For the Americans, the record of the Military Government in Buenos Aires shows that it made any defence of the Argentine cause difficult, when it did not flatly obstruct it. Jeane Kirkpatrick had attempted an intellectual defence of the "authoritarian regimes," such as Argentina, for their opposition to "totalitarian regimes," such as the Soviet Union and Communist governments in general. Nevertheless, she saw her thesis seriously questioned after the action of the Military Junta in the archipelago. Kirkpatrick had maintained, in an essay which won the respect and interest of Reagan[2] that "authoritarian" governments were more susceptible to the liberalizing pressures brought to bear than were the "totalitarian." Furthermore she credited them, among other characteristics, with lacking territorial ambitions. Galtieri had roundly belied these assumptions by his behaviour: he had shown himself insensitive when faced with a personal appeal by Reagan to avoid the operation. But in addition to this, what for Argentina was a recovery of territory usurped by a colonial power, was interpreted by the Americans as a "clear expansionist adventure".

5. Another factor of importance was the behaviour of the American press. Almost without exception it condemned the Argentine decision from the start of the conflict. There are various explanations for this phenomenon, but virtually all of them agree that the "solidarity of the Anglo-Saxon democracies" weighed as heavily as did the deplorable international reputation of the Argentine military regime. Time and again in the earliest press articles and broadcasting commentaries, references to the record of human rights violations by the Military Junta were made. The fascist character of its ideology and the "historic incapacity" of the Argentines to install and sustain a system of democratic co-existence were pointed out.

As if this were not enough, the reasons Reagan's government had for considering the friendship of this military regime in the *Southern Cone* of South America as in the national interest, were not capable of generating a public consensus. To have said openly that the Argentine Military were conducting the "dirty war" in the name of the USA in Central America would hardly have generated sympathy for the cause of Buenos Aires. An Argentine diplomat who was serving in the US expressed the following stark view in an intimate conversation with the authors in those early days: "It doesn't matter how we feel. The fact is that in the eyes of world opinion, "Operation Malvinas" is consistent with Argentina's "black history" and not with its best traditions. To have used force in a problem of international relations whilst negotiations were in progress, is, for world opinion, consistent with our history of repression. It is consistent with dictatorships, and with the violation of the principle of non-intervention as in in the clandestine incursions in Honduras, El Salvador and Bolivia. To deny this analysis is going to be extremely difficult, if not impossible."

The decision to support Resolution 502, adopted by Reagan's government, seemed to constitute the *coup de grace* for the "neutralists"[3]. But even so, they decided to fight a rear-guard political battle. The reverberations of the confrontation were heard in many spheres. On April 3rd, the day of the Security Council vote, Kirkpatrick's second-in-command, Lichenstein, declared that the United States was disposed "to offer its best offices to bring the parties together in seeking a peaceful solution" to the crisis. Such availability was thereby made much more explicit than had been suggested hardly 24 hours before by Larry Speakes, the official spokesman of the State Department. Speakes had said that a move by Washington could be made "only if it can really help in the dispute."

That same day they began to change positions in the headquarters of the so-called: "Working Group for Special Situations," in which Reagan had nominated as head Vice-President Bush - shortly after the attempt on his own life in March 1981. Thus Haig, who had made no secret of his desire to occupy that post, was slighted. It was in this area where the idea of formalizing an offer to the parties began to gain ground.

The antecedents that Haig had brought to the headquarters of the group were rather discouraging, and in some cases, frankly worrying. London had already made known through Henderson and other channels that it expected a rapid, explicit and complete solidarity from its ally and that in some ways it would receive favourably an American effort which was not designed to pressure the Argentines into complying with the terms of Resolution 502.

On the other hand, the first soundings made of the Argentines threw up an entirely different attitude. Ambassador Schlaudermann met Deputy Foreign Minister Ros in Buenos Aires and they both discussed possible American assistance to the parties in confrontation. Ros sent a report to Galtieri via Saint Jean, who had been in charge of the Foreign Ministry, after talking on the telephone to Costa Mendez in New York that night on the matter. But besides this even-handedness,

Schlaudermann's report recorded that rumours had begun to circulate in the Argentine capital of the intention to ask for a consultative meeting of the Inter-American Treaty of Mutual Assistance, (IATRA), or the Rio Pact - something that Reagan's government wanted to avoid at all cost.

For the Argentine Foreign Minister, this hint by Washington was a first positive sign and motivated him that very cold Sunday to start his second day's work on American soil. Some of his helpers, in particular Eduardo Roca and Federico Erhardt del Campo, were already working on the production of a draft assessing the possibility of an Argentine acceptance of Resolution 502. This would be through a withdrawal of troops in exchange for the stationing on the islands of a force of UN "blue helmets" and the establishment of a transitional administration of the United Nations. Although he was careful not to discourage his staff, this exercise was merely "pyrotechnics" for Costa Mendez. Following his behind-the-scenes soundings on Sunday at the Security Council, he now believed that only an intervention by the United States in fulfilment of its superpower role could set the crisis on the road to a solution. This was the factor on which the Argentine negotiators had speculated so much while planning the political side of the operation.

Two matters were on the Foreign Minister's mind that April 4th: the speech he had to give the following day to the Permanent Council of the OAS and the re-scheduled dinner that he would share that evening with Kirkpatrick. On the first, he worked with Ambassadors Quijano, Figueroa and Erhardt del Campo - the last mentioned being normally in charge of drafting Ministry statements. Costa Mendez took care that he himself translated a statement of the Argentine negotiating stance in addition to one simply in support of the cause. The message was destined not only for an American audience, but directed towards international public opinion in general, and in particular, to official ears in Washington.

In the late afternoon, ignoring the inclement weather, Costa Mendez and his principal assistants arrived at the Waldorf Towers building, which was in the same sector of Manhattan as the residence of the American ambassador to the UN. Strictly speaking, Kirkpatrick lived with her family in a Washington suburb, but she lodged in this apartment whenever her engagements prevented her return to the capital. She also fulfilled a large part of her official entertaining there.

Testimonies of those who participated in this gathering do not completely agree. For Costa Mendez it was an important meeting because some proposals were put forward of possible forms of American assistance. It also provided an opportunity to re-state to Reagan's confidential adviser, Argentina's readiness to receive such American assistance to enter into negotiations with Great Britain.

Roca, on the other hand, remembered the meeting as a "sombre evening". The enormous and cold room in which they dined seemed to be as inhospitable as the weather outside. Besides, Kirkpatrick avoided any definite statement and only emphasized the necessity of finding some possible way for Argentina to comply with Resolution 502. In any case, there was agreement that nothing concrete emerged from the conversation, except for her undertaking to continue advising the President that the US should facilitate the path of negotiations.

On the following day Costa Mendez and his delegation moved to Washington, where he had to speak to the Permanent Council of the OAS, whose meeting he had formally requested. His message to the ambassadors from North and South America, as all official Argentine actions that day, was a careful mixture of pressure and conciliation. The most important and unstated objective of this was to make an impression on the heart and mind of the United States Government.

The Foreign Minister spoke of the hopes of his country to find "an honourable solution." This he would seek to reach "by the path of dignified and peaceful arrangements," but he also denounced the "threat to continental security" that the "British colonial presence" represented. He suggested that the time would soon come for putting the IATRA to the test. In Buenos Aires, at the same time, Ros received the Soviet ambassador, Striganov, who repeated the Soviet intention "to follow closely the evolution of the Falklands conflict."

On concluding his discourse, Costa Mendez received congratulations from some of the ambassadors accredited to the assembly. With the same intention in mind, the United States representative, William Middendorf, approached him and courteously suggested putting the same points to the US Secretary of State. The Argentine, feeling that things were going his way, thanked him for the advice but, almost carelessly, mentioned that he had to return that same afternoon to New York: the United States initiative clearly had to be acted upon.

That day the issue was settled after a meeting of the Working Group for Special Situations decided to recommend to Reagan that Argentine co-operation in "Hemispheric security" and the future of US relations with Latin America were well worth a diplomatic effort. Haig decided to go along with events and, with his usual ambition for starring roles, proposed himself as the right man to sound out the parties in question. If the attempt came off, the kudos would be his and with it a triumph that would be as much his own as that of the Reagan Government.

There was not much opposition to Haig's proposal: in the first place he was the Secretary of State and, formally at least, was the most senior person responsible for the conduct of foreign policy, after the President. Moreover, the possibility of a mediation under Vice-President Bush had been rejected by Argentina on a previous occasion and it would therefore not be right to risk further affront to the figure of the Vice-President.

After this meeting, at his regular afternoon briefing, the White House spokesman formally proposed the good offices of the United States to assist the parties in the conflict. Furthermore, in an improvised press meeting in Reagan's office, the latter appealed to both governments, calling them both "allies" to find a peaceful solution and declared himself prepared to assume the role of "honest broker." Costa Mendez noted these signs, but with the *sang-froid* of the poker player, left for New York all the same.

His spirits in the face of such events went through successive highs and lows that Monday. Now, in the Argentine mission to the UN, the Foreign Minister talked with General Saint Jean, his formal replacement at the Palacio San Martin. They both spoke at length, exchanging news, but at one moment in the conversation lines got crossed.

The Minister of the Interior enthusiastically related to Costa Mendez the results of the meeting with the political leaders, which the leaders of the *Multipartidaria* had also attended. Almost in passing he mentioned that the following Wednesday, General Menendez would take up his duties as the new military governor of the Falklands, and that the party leaders had agreed to go *en bloc* to the ceremony, which undoubtedly constituted support for the Government.

Costa Mendez received this news badly, for it certainly did not help his plans. The politicians' visit would be interpreted abroad as another sign that the military regime considered the situation created on April 2nd as irreversible. This would certainly not help to underwrite any conciliatory declarations. The Foreign Minister tried to persuade Saint Jean, who was accompanied by Felix Pena, the Assistant Secretary for International Economic Relations, of the inadvisability of the plan. He argued against the presence of the politicians almost to the point of exasperation. The officer defended his position inflexibly and when the exchange threatened to degenerate into confrontation, he raised an unanswerable point: "The President is enthusiastic about this decision by the politicians."

As Costa Mendez remembers it today, he began to feel a premonition on putting down the telephone that what he judged as the original intention simply to recover the islands had started to change into something different. He would soon have his fears confirmed.

He persisted with Galtieri, who was extremely disturbed by the defeat in the Security Council. The President said starkly: "The original plans have been modified." The Foreign Minister did not understand exactly what Galtieri was saying. But those changes, the first manifestation of the "Plaza syndrome" that took such a hold on the President was not only a question of words: a page of the Strategic Military Directive that had started the very operation was torn up in those days.

Costa Mendez faced a terrible dilemma: whether to resign or continue. He even began to confide these doubts to his friend and assistant, Figueroa. For a moment he almost gave in to the temptation to abandon ship and face the certain jeers of "traitor to the Fatherland," which so easily fall from official lips, but it was only a doubt, a single obstacle on the road.

On the next occasion the telephone would bring better news. At 11 pm the Argentine ambassador in Washington received a call at his residence from Robert Service, Director of the Office for Affairs of the Southern Cone. The first question the American asked was elliptical:

"How long will your Minister remain in the United States?"

"As long as necessary," volunteered the Argentine.

Later, Service made a formal invitation from Haig for Costa Mendez to come to his office at the State Department on the following day. Takacs did not doubt his superior would agree, but confined himself to saying that he would consult the Foreign Minister. A call to the UN Plaza in New York and then another to Service settled the details.

That night, Costa Mendez slept the sleep of the optimist. After all, in spite of the disagreeable argument during his conversation with Saint Jean, things had turned out better for him than for his British opposite number.

The British Foreign Office that day had announced the resignation of its head, Lord Carrington, who decided to assume full responsibility for "the inability to foresee the Argentine military action," and as he would later explain "because someone had to pay for the national humiliation" inflicted on Great Britain. In fact, Carrington had presented his resignation on Sunday, but Prime Minister Thatcher set aside a period of twenty-four hours to try to convince her colleague that he should withdraw it. In spite of the mistakes that may have occurred, she told him, Carrington's experience would be essential in the days to follow.

But the Foreign Secretary stood firm and reminded Thatcher of the sometimes furious debate in Parliament on Saturday April 3rd. It had been a special session of the House, the first held since the Suez crisis of 1956, during which many of its members became enraged with the Conservative Government and in particular with the Foreign Office which various speakers accused of ineptitude. In the end, his own position had been dramatically eroded[4]. On Tuesday, the appointment of Francis Pym was announced, an experienced politician who had served in the Defence Ministry but not credited with much background in international affairs.

Costa Mendez' good humour did not fail that day in spite of some early setbacks. In the morning he discovered that he could not take the Eastern Airlines shuttle to Washington, because a great snow storm, which had reached its peak the previous night, had put the New York airports of La Guardia (internal) and John F. Kennedy (international) out of operation. The Argentine delegation had to take the train, which took four hours where the plane does it in fifty minutes and is uncomfortable to boot.

The meeting with Haig exceeded all the Argentine's expectations. The two men understood each other well from the beginning; one could almost say that a sympathy sprang up between them. No-one could have suspected then that this personal rapport would end before a month had passed in a most brusque fashion, and in the same office in which it had started.

Haig spoke of the mission President Reagan had entrusted to him: a way of demonstrating his credentials to his companion. He spoke of the interest he had in the crisis in the South Atlantic having an early and peaceful solution. He was, however, careful in speaking of the two allies of his country now confronting each other to show a clear anglophilia that he would continue to demonstrate during the course of the negotiations. But neither did he lose the opportunity to remind Costa Mendez of the importance of preserving the active co-operation that the United States and Argentina had begun to develop in the previous few months in the matter of "Hemispheric security." This was a pompous label that in diplomatic jargon meant the clandestine Argentine intervention in the Central American cauldron.

The Secretary of State is a direct man in spite of his affected language. In political circles, his scant respect for the rules of language is mocked and it is claimed that he boasts of using "the worst English since Eisenhower." Haig did not hesitate to speak of his perplexity, and that of President Reagan, over the fact that such a remote and unknown archipelago was lamentably the cause for a confrontation between two Western countries.[5] But he also spoke of the necessity of Argentine aspirations being adapted to take account of the principles defended by London and cited in particular the British concern for the fate of the inhabitants of the islands.

Costa Mendez decided to let the exchange of views proceed along the lines proposed by his companion. Thus he reiterated the importance that the matter had for Argentines, even in its emotional sense, as much as the will to negotiate that motivated his government.

Within this framework, he said, there would be no problem in satisfying any reasonable demands of the 1800 kelpers.

From that moment, the conversation entered into a frank analysis of the possibilities. Haig began to outline various alternatives that his aides had prepared. These involved the withdrawal of Argentine troops and the return of the Task Force despatched from Portsmouth, but not a re-instatement of the previous British colonial administration. He also mentioned the possibility of setting up an interim government, pending a negotiated solution, in which the parties to the dispute would participate, with the assistance of two "friendly states." He then suggested Canada, Brazil and Colombia as possibilities.

This alternative had scarcely been considered in its broader aspects, but in fact, the negotiations began from that very moment. Costa Mendez countered:

"Why involve more countries?" he asked Haig. Why not form a tripartite internal administration in which, besides Argentina and Great Britain, the United States could assume simultaneously the roles of collaborator with the two parties and guarantor of the accord?"

Haig considered for a moment, bringing a silence to the meeting. Then he enthusiastically replied:

"I like that idea. I'll buy it."

He immediately suggested beginning as soon as possible with drawing up a draft containing the points offering possible agreement.

Thus they began to discuss details. Haig gave a brief description of what in his opinion an interim administration would be like, and without intending it, he described a small monster. The Argentine objected:

"Why so much? They're only 1800 islanders."

"1800" repeated Haig mechanically.

"Yes. The islands are like a big ranch," was the metaphor that the Argentine found and the American immediately understood.

Costa Mendez, in spite of having received the go-ahead from Galtieri to start negotiations, did not want to present Buenos Aires with a *fait accompli* and put a brake on the Secretary of State's enthusiasm, explaining to him that he had to consult his government before moving further in the matter. He would not continue without an express mandate. Haig conceded, not without regret, to the restrictions with which the Argentine had to deal. But he urged him to obtain an immediate reply, since time was a decisive factor.

Costa Mendez left the Department of State and went to the office of the military attache, where several of his colleagues awaited him; Takacs and Figueroa had accompanied him at the meeting. Soon after arriving, using the *carola*, he got in contact with Galtieri. In that conversation he began to give the Argentine green light for what would later be known as the "Haig Mission."

After talking to the Foreign Minister, the President convened the Military Junta, which quickly ratified his initial positive reaction. A new communication with Washington - where the Foreign Minister passed the night - closed the round of consultations. As far as Buenos Aires was concerned, the United States was now formally party to the international dispute. To its military rulers this fact brought with it a warm glow of reassurance.

Outside this inner group at some intermediate levels of the military administration, the possibility of calling a meeting of the IATRA was again raised informally. If up to that moment there had been any real intention of doing so, over and above the desire to get Reagan's government moving by threatening a possible move they wouldn't like, it all faded away during the meeting of Haig and Costa Mendez.

The Secretary of State, careful of the proprieties in such a delicate situation, met the ambassador of the Crown, Sir Nicholas Henderson, on the evening of Tuesday 6th. The latter received the news of the progress made by the American with Costa Mendez without showing joy or displeasure. In this meeting it was agreed that once formal Argentine acceptance had been received, the Secretary of State would immediately travel to London to talk with Prime Minister Margaret Thatcher, thus beginning the peace negotiations.

Afterwards Haig again met the Working Group for Special Situations that Bush presided over. He did it coolly: at this stage, no-one could guess at the possibilities for large-scale success or failure, although only the first of those two outcomes crossed his mind at the time. Those who knew Haig well are sure that the figure of his old chief, Henry Kissinger, and his sparkling shuttle diplomacy loomed large in the fantasies of the Secretary of State at the time.

The same reasons which permitted Costa Mendez a night of refreshing rest - all tension released by the day's success - deprived others of sleep in Buenos Aires. This was the case for Generals Jose Rogelio Villareal and Reynaldo Bignone, who were summoned to appear on Wednesday morning at the Libertador building by the Chief of the Army General Staff, General Jose Antonio Vaquero, but without giving them any explanation for the urgency.

At 8 pm on Wednesday they both arrived at the meeting punctually. Although retired from active service, they continued as military officers and these were days of national emergency. Vaquero informed them of the acceptance of the American offer of mediation and conveyed to them a request from the Commandant-in-Chief: that they should produce a working paper of the army objectives in the approaching negotiations. He made clear it could not be a final text since, as invariably happened in such cases during the process of discussion, the position of the land forces had to be modified by those of the other two forces: the navy and air force.

To say that a Commander-in-Chief *requests* is to resort to a euphemism. Bignone and Villareal got to work immediately in the offices of the General Secretariat. Bignone could not resist, however, one moment of rebellion that he shared with his comrade.

"Look, this fellow threw me out of the army, sent me into compulsory retirement three months ago and now he comes to me for help," said Bignone, in an obvious reference to Galtieri.

Villareal, realizing that the target for this indignation was missing decided instead to supply his friend with the motivation for moving forward:

"It's not for Galtieri, Reynaldo. They got us into this jam, but we have to do it for the country."

They began to study the documentation of the dispute and then, on the basis of some notes, they recorded a first draft. At 7 pm this version had been typed and corrected and the required document finally delivered to the then Secretary-General of the Army, General Jose Gutierrez. The latter read it and enthused about it to the point of congratulating the authors. "It is an important work. I have no experience of this type of document and therefore thank you very much," confessed the Secretary-General, relieved. "But don't go away," he warned them, "Vaquero wants to talk to you."

During this meeting, the Chief of the General Staff advised discussing the contents of the text with Galtieri, and arranged an appointment for the retired officers at 8 am of the next day at the Casa Rosada.

In the middle of the night, Villareal was wakened suddenly by the door bell. He recognised a captain of the Regiment of Cavalry Grenadiers who was the bearer of an urgent message from the President. Between apologies the officer informed him that the appointment with Galtieri had been postponed until 9.30 am. In fact, someone had forgotten to make a phone call. But Bignone, who received a telephone call instead of a visit by an emissary, had no better luck: he couldn't get back to sleep either.

On Good Friday, in the private dining room of the President of the Nation, the two generals were received by a Galtieri still visibly sleepy. In his genial style he had words of praise for the work and showed it by embracing the authors.

The proposal by Villareal and Bignone was in essence simple: The American mediation had to secure:

1. A joint administration of the islands in dispute.
2. Machinery for co-operation in the shared exploitation of their resources.
3. A negotiating mechanism able to resolve the problem of sovereignty in the shortest possible time.

"Tell me," enquired Galtieri, "in your judgment, when should these negotiations be completed?"

"In a prudent period," replied Bignone.

"But in the document, it doesn't specify what a "prudent period is," observed the Commandant-President.

"An agreed period, necessarily," Villareal pointed out.

Villareal and Bignone had analyzed the subject on preparing the document and arrived at the conclusion that to include the proviso of a fixed date at the beginning of Haig's mediation could drive the negotiations into a *cul-de-sac* in advance.

Galtieri shook his head and, taking a red marker, drew a circle round the phrase "prudent period."

"Everything must be concluded, at the latest, when the period of 150 years of English usurpation is completed," he announced in an imperative tone.

"On December 31st [1982] the negotiations must have concluded and on January 3rd [1983] the transfer of sovereignty to Argentina must have been effected," he added, completing the scheme.

Villareal, the most senior officer of the two, objected: "General, I don't believe that that requirement will be accepted by Margaret Thatcher, nor even by Haig as mediator."

The commandant did not like to be contradicted. He rose from his chair and, sticking his thumbs in the folds of his uniform shirt as if it was an imaginary waistcoat, he began to pace the room. After a few moments he said to his embarrassed companions:

"If they think they are going to threaten us with military force they are mistaken. The old British lion is going to learn what the Argentine Army is!"

Bignone and Villareal exchanged an understanding glance. The discussion was finished. In silence they listened again to Galtieri's praises for the work they had done and said farewell to the Commandant. They both left with the certainty of having worked in vain.

The situation of the Military Government had altered totally. The almost complete isolation in which it found itself at the end of March had changed into a ready dialogue with the politicians, who since March 1976 had often been insulted.

That rapprochement paved the way for an unmentioned possibility: to co-operate with the party leaders in order that these leaders might speak for the legitimacy of the Argentine action in the Falklands to the international community, who had reacted harshly to the invasion.

The author of the idea was Rafael Martinez Raymonda, leader of the centre-right *Partido Democrata Progresista* and a one-time ambassador of Viola's government in Rome. Assistant Secretary Menendez readily accepted the proposal, but the Government lacked the necessary contacts to persuade the politicians to mount an action of this kind.

Nevertheless, there were civilians who worked to make the project come off. With the exception of Raul Alfonsin, who rejected the idea that the *Union Civica Radical* should lend men for this enterprise, and the later refusal of the leaders of the *Movimiento de Integracion y Desarollo*, the other leaders adopted the idea enthusiastically.

The situation was a really difficult one: an external front opposed to toleration of the Argentine action, was making the work of the politicians futile even though recognizing the rights of Buenos Aires over the islands. Besides, military ideological inertia was continuing to veto the names of some leaders considered left-wing. Thus, for example, they questioned the *Peronistas* Jorge Vazquez, an ex-diplomat, and Vicente Saadi, an ex-senator, and the *Radical*, Luis Leon, considering them irritants to the armed forces.

The first vice-president of the *Partido Justicialista*, the notary, Deolindo Felipe Bittel, contributed the name of Vazquez when the proposal came up to send unofficial "political ambassadors" abroad. This was an idea having about it a certain slyness: Vazquez had been Deputy Foreign Minister during the Presidency of Hector J. Campora and after the coup of March 1976 had spent a hard time in the cells of the new *de facto* regime. The Military did not approve of a speech he made in 1973, before the OAS assembly, in which he characterized the inclusion of Argentina in a way which contradicted the vague "Western and Christian" model that the armed forces then preferred. In proposing him as an envoy, Bittel knew this would oblige the Government to perform a tacit political "whitewash" on Vazquez, and he confessed as much to some friends. He was right only in part, as Vazquez continued to be included in the Institutional Act which deprived him of his civil rights.

In an extremely frank tone, Colonel Menendez explained to one questioner that he had designed a strategy to overcome the objections of the politicians.

"The troops who are in the Falklands will not feel disturbed if we send those men to represent the country," he argued. The soldiers were concerned with more practical matters than those revealed by the

Assistant Secretary of the Interior. A later presidential verdict encouraged this type of mission - whereupon the objection collapsed.

The first symptoms of political resistance to Galtieri's plans appeared when Saint Jean and Col. Bernardo Menendez formed the delegation that would go to Port Stanley for the inauguration of the Military Governor. The main aim was to achieve the participation of the two constitutional ex-Presidents, Doctors Arturo Frondizi and Arturo Illia. They both made formal objections, but at bottom they did not want to share that "charter" trip which naturally was highly suspect. But the principal party leaders, as well as trade union and business chiefs and representatives of the arts and of the Church, went off to the Falklands.

The popular reaction in the Plaza de Mayo was wrongly interpreted by the occupants of the Casa Rosada. They believed that the support that the recovery of the islands undoubtedly had, had somehow been transformed into a general plebiscite in favour of Galtieri's leadership. That mistake, in which some political parties who shared the "principles" of the Military Government participated, strengthened the idea of launching the President as a new *Caudillo*.

After the war, one of the architects of that project, Colonel Menendez, revealed that one of Galtieri's gravest errors was precisely that fantasy induced by a square overflowing with people. In this situation he had to be very clever to speak to the crowd in such a way so as not to torpedo the negotiations. And that is precisely what occurred: Galtieri went too far in his harangue and while working on the crowd's emotions - being both jeered and applauded at the same time - he went on to promise the impossible.

On April 7th the American peace effort acquired the feverish speed that would characterize it up to the moment of its final failure. In the morning of that day, Costa Mendez, who hardly had enough time available to return to Buenos Aires, had a telephone conversation with Haig. In the first part of the conversation, the Argentine went through the formality of confirming to the Secretary of State that the Junta had accepted his intervention. This was a fact which had already been anticipated at the State Department the previous evening.

Haig, for his part, announced that he would leave that same afternoon for London and that after talking to Mrs Thatcher would travel on to Buenos Aires, in order to continue with the mediation. On that occasion they accepted the need to remain more or less permanently in contact, which, as will be seen later, was scrupulously maintained - a requirement which turned out to be essential during the difficult hours that then awaited them. Reagan had left the crisis in the hands of the Secretary of State and almost unconcernedly took a brief vacation in Barbados, at the house of his friend and old Hollywood colleague,

Claudette Colbert.

For Haig, the prospect of a diplomatic triumph in an international problem of this magnitude - it concerned nothing less than the prevention of a domestic war in the Western World - could have gratified his fantasies, but he understood that the difficulties would be considerable. In order to begin, he had to overcome two minor but irritating problems. The first arose on deciding that contrary to normal practice he would not carry reporters on his aircraft. The men of the press reacted angrily to what they considered a snub and counter-attacked where it hurt the Secretary of State most - his ego. One version said that Haig took that decision for "fear" of the reporters. The worst of these malicious comments was that they were largely true. Haig was far from having that assurance with which his predecessor and ex-chief Kissinger handled the journalists on the various stages of his own "shuttle diplomacy"[6].

While he was still dealing with this episode, he learnt that the aircraft that had been assigned to him lacked the necessary communications equipment and that it would be difficult, if not impossible, to replace it. A machine of the kind Haig required was nevertheless on the point of leaving, carrying some congressmen on an official journey. The Secretary of State had to telephone the chief of the delegation, who did not object to changing aircraft. This second anecdote was also included in commentators' accounts, and was related in a scoffing tone. It was said "nothing is good enough for Haig."

The sophisticated communications equipment for which Haig struggled with the delegates from the Capitol would bring complications right from the beginning. Shortly after leaving for London, a cable brought the news that the Thatcher government had declared the establishment of a Maritime Exclusion Zone of 200 miles round the islands, with effect from the following Monday. From zero hour on that day any Argentine ship or auxiliary naval vessel encountered inside that zone would be considered hostile and attacked by British units. Haig understood that the British decision was directed as much to him as to Argentina to serve as an indication of the spirit in which his efforts would be received by the Conservative Government in a few hours' time.

It was not only the opinion of Thatcher and her entourage. The British attitude in general was ill-disposed to the Haig attempts, because it was not able to understand how the United States could remain in a neutral posture in the face of a confrontation between "British democracy" and "Argentine neo-fascism." The British newspapers of Thursday commented on Reagan's envoy with obvious allusions. The *Daily Telegraph*, for example, remarked in an editorial that:

"Some people may be tempted to liken the emergency visit

being paid to London by Mr Haig to the interventions of one of his predecessors, Mr John Foster Dulles, in the Suez affair, 25 years ago. the comparison would be mistaken because the circumstances surrounding the two crises are different. So too are the American interests involved. In the case of Suez, General Eisenhower was outraged and furious at Britain's action, more particularly because the Eden Government had gone to great pains to keep him entirely in the dark about it. Mr Dulles, who had himself played a major part in pushing Nasser into nationalising the Canal, was fiercely determined from the very start to make Britain back down.

"The American stance over the Falklands dispute is very different [....] there are other factors Washington has to take into consideration besides the simple desire to avoid an outbreak of hostilities. One is that the Argentine military dictatorship is deeply unpopular with most ordinary Americans. They are uneasy at the Reagan administration's plans to use them as allies in its anti-Communist crusade. Nevertheless, Mr Haig will undoubtedly press hard for a face-saving formula. Judging from Mr Pym's firm line in the Commons yesterday, prior withdrawal of Argentine forces will be an absolute British condition."[7]

The *Daily Telegraph* was not mistaken, although on Thursday morning Haig could have believed things would be simpler. In the first meeting he found a most propitious climate for accomplishing his task. The men of the Foreign Office were professional diplomats, without doubt good ones. Even in their first contact, when both groups, the American and British, identified numerous problems difficult of solution, the will to negotiate "was underlying each exchange of ideas." Thus commented one source to the authors during their investigations - a source with access to the minutes of the meeting. The Argentine withdrawal from the islands certainly was not the least of these problems.

But the Foreign Office did not embody Thatcher's thinking, even less Parliament's thinking in those moments in which almost without party differences, it seemed decided to make the Foreign Office the scapegoat for the humiliation which the Argentine action had brought. Carrington's head had just rolled in an attempt to pacify the critics in some measure. Moreover, and although she did not show it in public, the episode of April 2nd only aggravated the Prime Minister's traditional mistrust for her country's Foreign Service.

The five virtually uninterrupted hours that Haig spent at 10 Downing Street in often difficult conversation with Thatcher, were those which really marked the course and tone of the negotiations. Even the minor advances that seemed to have been achieved in the first meeting subsequently became embarrassments.

The Prime Minister was not thinking of negotiating from a position of weakness. She had moderate words of praise for the American effort, but made it clear that this should never overlook the still expected "American support for the cause of liberty." The only solution possible, she argued, was that the aggressor respect the mandate the Security Council had made explicit in Resolution 502, which had received the unanimous support of the democracies - including that of the United States, she reminded him.

This was a dispute which involved, above all, principles: "It must be demonstrated to the world," she said, "that the use of force cannot be used in international relations."

"One cannot allow aggression to pay dividends," was the phrase Margaret Thatcher coined and would repeat time and again during the conflict. Great Britain, and of course her government, had the firm intention of converting the crisis in the South Atlantic into a lesson of history, she assured Haig. And she would do it with the solidarity of the West - or by herself if it was necessary.

The symptoms which that "solidarity" that Margaret Thatcher alluded to in full knowledge of the development of events were particularly clear that Thursday. The Minister of Foreign Affairs in the French Socialist Government, Claude Cheysson, demanded the withdrawal of Argentine troops from the Falklands in the course of a message to the National Assembly. Also revealed was the decision of President Francois Mitterand to suspend the delivery of war materials to Argentina, among them various aeroplanes and spare parts for anti-aircraft missiles in reply to a request from London. As a Socialist Government it was presumably opposed to the survival of colonialism. In spite of this and of never having recognized the British title to the archipelago, France, from that moment, nevertheless began to give significant, active and unchanging support to the United Kingdom. This continued while the conflict lasted. In Washington, meanwhile, the ambassadors of the ten Common Market countries held a meeting and issued a communique condemning Argentina.

Margaret Thatcher made clear, moreover, that even after verification of an immediate Argentine withdrawal, Britain would not renew negotiation without imposing prior conditions. The Argentine claim to sovereignty over the archipelago would not be a basis for a new stage in the negotiations and for the British the "interests and desires of the islanders" would be "of supreme importance." (*Paramount* was another of the expressions that the British Government would make popular in those days).

In their book, *The Battle for the Falklands*, Max Hastings and Simon Jenkins explained that initial phase in the mediation as follows:

"The War Cabinet's initial and sheltered self-confidence undoubtedly played a part in Britain's first response to the Haig mission. Haig brought with him on April 8th only the three themes which were to dominatethe whole negotiating phase: military withdrawal by both sides, an interim administration and a long-term settlement. This last included a job lot of solutions borrowed from successive Falklands negotiations in the past. The Americans also brought an apparent lack of understanding of the essence of the British position, which worried those who met them.

"Haig's team was first briefed by Pym at the Foreign Office. Then, at 6 pm, they walked across Downing Street to see Mrs Thatcher. This was followed by a working dinner, with Nott, Lewin and Acland also present. If Mrs Thatcher appeared to the Americans theatrically intransigent - certainly more so than the Foreign Office - the American approach seemed unco-ordinated to the British. In the wider exchanges, one of them after dinner, Haig seemed heavy-handed in his insistence that America could not have two allies at war, and that Britain had to give him room for manoeuvre. More privately - especially in talks with Mrs Thatcher herself - he hinted that he had to talk tough to impress the Argentines and, it seemed, his own team as well.

The War Cabinet's response left no room for doubt. The nation would return to the negotiating table as and when Argentina honoured Resolution 502. Meanwhile, Britain was sustaining her rights under Article 51 of the UN Charter. For good measure, Haig was deluged with details of the horrors of winter in the South Atlantic and of the need for speed. He left that night overwhelmed by the strength of the British stance - as he admitted to his ambassador during a stopover in Brazil."[8]

The testimonies gathered by the authors agree in pointing out that the main problem he faced was in convincing the Argentines of Margaret Thatcher's inflexibility and of its risks. Besides making this clear in his imminent conversations with the Argentines, the Secretary of State began a process of bringing pressure to bear on Buenos Aires. And here is where the itinerant ambassador, Vernon Walters, found a new confidential mission of the type in which he specialized.

Walters was in Ceylon when he received the order to appear at Haig's mission in London. After a few hours in the British capital, he was despatched to Paris to make a brief visit to his friend, the Argentine ambassador in France, Gerardo Schamis.

Schamis, by stages linked with the civilian and military governments in turn, was a man who had managed to establish solid contacts with several of the key figures of the military establishment. It was his luck to be unofficial adviser to President Roberto Viola, who appointed him to his embassy in France, but also he had a close friendship with Brigadier Lami Dozo, which assisted him in remaining in the post after Galtieri's assumption of power.

He had, furthermore, a reputation as an "international analyst" among the Military and in some civilian circles. A good part of this prestige he consolidated by composing and publishing a short treatise of a rather intellectual nature on the "revolutionary war" which, it presumed, international Communism was unleashing on the West.

Another of his *coups* was to prophesy, before his appointment, the triumph of the Socialist, Francois Mitterand in France, sticking firmly to this forecast even though to his friends in uniform, the latter was, at the least, a disagreeable prospect. Only in the limited and intimate circle of the Military could one refuse to admit the possibility of the rising tide of French Socialism which, however, was conceded by the greater part of the international press. Nevertheless, as far as that went, the Junta had another prophet: the predecessor of Schamis in France, Tomas de Anchorena. This envoy persisted until the last moment in informing the Palacio San Martin that Mitterand was a "political corpse" as his opponent, Valery d'Estaing, would demonstrate in the elections. When this description proved nonsense, the reputation of Schamis became hallowed in the military cabinet.

The diplomat was well viewed by the American establishment, and had formed links with many of its members and in particular with Walters. He had an excellent personal relationship with him, although some sources suggested that this overstated the position. For this reason, the Argentine ambassador to France was chosen as the target in the first American "softening up" manoeuvre, which could very well have been proposed by his friend, the itinerant General Walters.

Walters' stay in Paris was brief, scarcely long enough for a conversation with Schamis at his residence since he had to rejoin Haig's retinue before the Secretary of State set off for Buenos Aires. On the following day, the Argentine ambassador informed his Foreign Ministry, in a coded cable, that the American had spoken to him of the Secretary of State's concern at the absolutely unalterable position of Margaret Thatcher. She found herself "very constrained by her domestic front," in gambling with both her personal political fate as well as that of the Conservative administration which she headed.

Walters also told Schamis that the Prime Minister was sure - and counted on that certainty - that Reagan's government would give her its unconditional support in the end. It would do so because it could not risk her fall and the consequent, and almost inevitable accession to power of the Labour Party, which had undergone a shift to the Left.

Schamis' cable preceded Haig's arrival by a few hours. His team was made up of nineteen people, including a senior representative of the National Security Council, James Rentschler. Of the original group only Laurence Eagleburger was missing - the aide in charge of European Affairs in the State Department had returned to Washington.

For the Argentines, another worrying fact had been the declaration by a spokesman of the British Prime Minister who, shortly after the Secretary of State had departed, announced the British Government's satisfaction that: "Washington and London are completely in accord on the problem."

The plane which brought Haig, who had remained a total of twenty hours in London, made the journey to Argentina with two stops - one in Dakar, and the other in Recife. From both airports the chief negotiator took over the transmission of signals. In the first, he declared that "The next few hours will be difficult because the problem is extremely complex." In the second, when - according to Hastings and Jenkins, he confided to his American ambassador his concern at Margaret Thatcher's inflexibility - he said that it was "the most difficult mission of my career." He explained these matters in a more detailed fashion, and certainly confidentially, in radio conversations conducted on board the aircraft with President Reagan in Barbados and with Foreign Minister Costa Mendez in Buenos Aires.

When Haig set foot at Ezeiza, the airport of Buenos Aires, almost all the forces active in the dispute had stopped, with the exception of military preparations of course, and the world held its breath to see what results the mediation might achieve. Scarcely forty-eight hours before, the Permanent Council of the OAS had interrupted its discussion of the affair in order to facilitate Haig's task. A little later the Secretary-General of the UN, Javier Perez de Cuellar, showed his willingness to assist the parties, but made clear that the results would have to be awaited from the American intervention.

At the airport the American envoy was sparing:

"President Reagan asked me," he said, "to represent him personally in trying to find a solution to the dispute. It is my wish to be a help in seeking a solution, on the basis of Resolution 502, on this my first visit to Buenos Aires. I had the opportunity this week to acquaint myself through Foreign Minister Costa Mendez with the Argentine position. As you know, Argentina and the United States are companions in the Hemisphere with many years of close co-operation. This relationship has become still more cordial in recent times and has a firm foundation. I shall be having important discussions with your President and with Dr Costa Mendez. Thank you."

The Argentine officials, among them the Foreign Minister, in spite of official leaks of a more or less optimistic tone, were worried by unmistakeable signs of British rigidity becoming more evident all the time. As if this were not enough, that Friday, a newspaper reported that American spy satellites were providing intelligence for the British according to the terms of the NATO Pact.

In spite of boasts dear to the military pronouncements of those days, some officers of the General Staff began to suggest the advisability of some degree of flexibility. Certain signs suggest that this was particularly marked in air force headquarters. But there is no record that anyone, openly at least, had gone further than making a tepid and respectful suggestion of this kind, suitably balanced by expressions of confidence in the Argentine cause.

In the headquarters of the Junta, euphoria was growing to its highest point. That sentiment is usually a bad political counsellor, as was demonstrated by the actions it inspired in some of those in power. Whilst Haig slept in his suite at the Sheraton, the Military Attache at the Presidency, Rear Admiral Benito Moya and Secretary-General at the Casa Rosada, Brigadier-General Hector Iglesias - both of whom would have exceptional parts to play in the following days - together with the Secretary of Public Information, Rodolfo Baltierrez, were all extremely busy. They were working on a manoeuvre designed to "give an appropriate setting to the audience that Galtieri would grant Haig," as one official of the Casa Rosada recalled.

The President-Commandant had to receive Reagan's envoy against a background of popular support, his collaborators argued. If this could be achieved, they imagined, one could impress the American, lending support to the image of "Argentine determination," that Galtieri had decided to demonstrate to his visitor. The political scheme conceived by the officials consisted in an apparently simple plan: if Mrs Thatcher was the "Iron Lady," the Argentine leader would be the "Steel President." The political imagination is apt to become infested with such superlatives and grandiloquent figures of speech - as it would in the future with the expression: "People's Solidarity." The plan received the go-ahead from other members of the Government, such as the Minister of the Interior, Saint Jean, and of his second-in-command, Colonel Menendez, in whose political views any show of consensus was displayed to perfection. One may add that after a brief consultation, Galtieri was enthusiastic, and gave the necessary green light for the following steps. From that moment on there was no need to consult anyone else.

At first it was considered calling for a popular meeting for mid-day on Saturday. The appeal would be through the State-controlled TV and radio channels. Then there would be a call for help from the privately-controlled media and the political leaders. But this initial idea was overturned. By any reckoning it would be better if the "patriotic call" came from a non-official source.

Thus is was that various contacts were made with those in charge of the different private sector media until, as had been done on other occasions, Radio Rivadavia, the metropolitan station with the biggest audience, took over the project on its own. Jose Maria Munoz, the popular sports commentator and manager of the company with the broadcasting franchise, gave it no rest on the air, exhorting everyone to gather at 11 am on the following day in the Plaza de Mayo to "demonstrate to Mr Alexander Haig and to the whole world the national unity of the Argentines."

Thus the kick-off took place in this match in which many were to play. In successive interviews given to an array of radio programmes and newspapers, the political and trades union leaders dutifully endorsed the mass meeting. Deolindo Bittel *(Justicialista)*, Carlos Contin *(Union Civil Radical)* and the trades unionists Saul Sabatini *(CGT - Brasil)* and Jorge Triacca *(CNT)* called on their followers to make the square in front of Government House "overflow" on Saturday at mid-day.

In the case of the *Partido Justicialista,* an announcement was made by the highest executive organ of their National Council, that exhorted the *Peronist* masses: "In view of the threat which hangs over the Republic, that at this hour there is nothing more vital than the defence of sovereignty, to gather in the historic Plaza de Mayo from zero hour - 10 am Saturday April 10th."

The official machinery also made its contribution with speed and efficiency, announcing special facilities for traffic and for the parking of vehicles in the adjoining districts. The newspapers for their part published a meticulous drawing of the central zone, detailing the routes providing orderly and continuous access.

About one o'clock in the morning, President Galtieri stepped out on one of the balconies of the Casa Rosada and tried out his oratory on a few hundred enthusiastic demonstrators - the first of a multitude of 150,000 - who had decided to pass the night in the square to be sure of the best places.

"Rest assured, in the absolute certainty that the Argentine people will be well represented by the Government," he promised.

He also exhorted them to remain firmly in their places "to demonstrate to the Americans that the Argentine people are united."

"Fill the Plaza de Mayo and the Republic!" he told them in almost identical language to that used by civilian leaders. And thus he began to feel again - as on April 2nd, but now even more intensely - the pleasant glow of popular acclaim.

Saturday was a frenetic succession of meetings. At 9 am Haig began his preparations for the negotiations, discussing them with Schlaudermann, in order to present himself with his advisers one hour later at the Palacio San Martin. There he had forty-five minutes of conversation with his Argentine opposite number, whilst the remaining officials on both sides began to form informal working parties.

It was not a good beginning, although the discussion turned out friendly. Haig opened fire, explaining that the priority was to avoid a warlike confrontation in the South Atlantic, and that this could only be achieved if Argentina proved flexible - in particular on the matter of fulfilling the terms of Resolution 502. Otherwise, he assured them, given the inflexibility of Mrs Thatcher, war would be a very real alternative. Costa Mendez would recall the vehemence that the American put into his words from the very beginning, and how that disgusted him, although for obvious reasons he was careful not to react.

Haig also spoke of Central America, invoking a new source of pressure that he would employ throughout the negotiations. On various occasions, almost capriciously, the Secretary of State attempted to discuss some specific aspect of the negotiations. He would start to speak in a cryptic and admonitory tone about the Central American crisis and to suggest that there could shortly be an important and unexpected development. In this way he emphasised for his Argentine colleagues the necessity that such an outcome should not happen at the same time as an Argentine-British armed confrontation. He also stressed that it was vital to preserve co-operation between the United States and Argentina in the interests of the security of the Hemisphere.

As to the precise terms in which Haig put the Central American question to the Military Government, one can only establish with certainty that he reported the results of the recent secret journey made by Ambassador Vernon Walters to Havana. There Walters met Fidel Castro and other Cuban leaders.[9] Furthermore, it did not escape the Americans that scarcely twenty-four hours beforehand the Cuban ambassador, Emilio Aragones Navarro had returned to Buenos Aires, after a year in which diplomatic relations with Argentina had remained down-graded to the level of charge d'affaires.

At 11 am, Haig and Costa Mendez moved to the Casa Rosada, leaving the experts of the two delegations to begin examining the first drafts of an agreement brought by Haig from London. In this way, Argentines and Americans entered into what the latter would afterwards call the "Iran syndrome".

The Foreign Ministers did not mention the vociferous multitude gathered before Government House, but that omission did not mean that the visitor was not taking it in.

The Secretary of State was received by a smiling Galtieri, who tried to display his most seductive talents. After the greetings he referred to his admiration for the United States and the happy circumstance that Haig, like himself, was a military officer. This was his cue to explain the "iron-clad will" that inspired "the Argentine Government and people" - whilst General Walters acted as interpreter.

Forming a background to these assertions was the murmur arriving in the Presidential office from outside. The cries of the crowd were: "Patria si, colonia no!" (Fatherland - yes, Colony - no!) and other slogans from a popular political repertory. Some, flavoured by political sympathies, did not hesitate to resurrect calls for Juan Domingo Peron and Eva Peron, and even to make uncomplimentary allusions to the scarcely popular figure of the Minister of the Economy, Roberto Alemann.

That sound brought comfort to Galtieri, who began to justify Argentine rights over the archipelago and then to warn Haig that the armed forces were prepared. They would not hesitate to respond militarily to any British aggression, although that possibility was certainly not desired by Argentina.

This was the cue that the American was waiting for, and he replied by recalling the horrors that are inevitable in any war and indicating the absolute necessity of avoiding them in this case. If Galtieri had taken the advantage of referring to the military status the two men shared, Haig replied that nobody was in a better position than a soldier - as they both were - to know of the tragedy of war. With this as a starting point he followed a line very different from the arguments he had employed with Costa Mendez. During this meeting with Galtieri, as with the others that would take place in the evening, whisky was served, and the speed with which the President drank was phenomenal: "The President's whisky consumption awed and then alarmed the Americans."[10]

When, after more than an hour and a half, the audience was coming to an end, Galtieri - who had made frequent allusions to the "people gathered in the square," suggested to Haig the advisability of using one of the Argentine helicopters for the return journey to the Sheraton in order to avoid any inconvenience. Obviously the object of this mass demonstration would not have been completely achieved if the visitor did not get a panoramic view of the multitude.

An initial suggestion by Haig almost frustrated this ploy: he said he was sure he could make this journey by car without any problem. But on the insistence of the Argentines, particularly that of the President himself, things were left at Galtieri's suggestion. The Secretary of State, accompanied by Schlaudermann and Walters, went to the helicopter parked on the flat roof of the Presidency and, boarding the aircraft were seen off there by Costa Mendez.

The aircraft rose awkwardly and began a brief overflight for the benefit of its passengers. The loudspeakers on the perimeter of the Plaza de Mayo announced the departure of the American and the voices of the crowd rose in a single roar. The scene impressed Haig vividly, and he murmured a few words about Iran, remaining deep in thought for some moments. Although those who planned the scene so carefully did not know it at the time, the effect on the mind of the mediator was completely contrary to their original intention.

The enthusiasm of those in charge in the Government was limitless. After Haig withdrew, Galtieri prepared to go out on the balcony to enjoy his moment of triumph and to deliver a harangue. He insisted on improvising this in spite of his scant talent for oratory. Iglesias, Saint Jean and other officials accompanied him. Someone invited Costa Mendez to join the group, but he chose rather to take himself off - which he did not regret afterwards.

"Let the world know, America, that there is a people with a firm will - the Argentine people! If they want to come, let them come; we shall give battle!" Galtieri shouted to the crowd who received these bellicose phrases with unmistakeable satisfaction. The President described the demonstration as an "open city council" and demanded of Great Britain and its Government "moderation in its words and in its deeds."

In terms of its effect, Galtieri's speech did contain one gaffe. This was when he referred to his position as: "President of the Nation." At that point, unequivocal jeers came from various quarters of the demonstration. That his new popularity did not even reach as far as a total legitimacy did not worry him; much remained to be done, and it would all contribute to consolidating this triumph. Nothing, he told himself, could tarnish the glory of that moment.

While the Argentine savoured that moment, Haig and Schlaudermann, while sharing lunch, were talking about the self same popular demonstration. The Secretary of State was frankly alarmed: the combination of Argentine-style demonstrations and men like Galtieri evoked fearful memories of Hitler and Mussolini in the minds of the Americans. It had been like this during the socio-political phenomenon of *Peronism* and would apparently continue to be so. The many explanations attempted since have not lessened this reaction.

But Haig also remembered another more recent occasion. He spoke to Schlaudermann of Iran, of the Ayatollah Khomeini who appealed to the religious fanaticism of his people. He spoke of the more than 400 days of captivity suffered by the members of the American embassy in Tehran, taken hostage by another multitude in November 1979. At that moment a decision was made by the US representative in Buenos Aires.

Schlaudermann immediately began to get things up to date and put into effect contingency plans for evacuating non-essential American personnel from his embassy. At the same time he made preparations to protect American citizens residing in or passing through Argentina. His plans included evacuation of personnel and their effects as far as possible. If there was any possibility of avoiding it, the American humiliation would not be repeated.

And thus the abyss between Washington and Buenos Aires began to open.

NOTES

1. In a conversation with the authors in Washington in May, 1983, the prestigious American journalist, Ted Szule, veteran expert in American foreign policy, described the "Suez Syndrome" that has troubled the relationship between his country and Great Britain since the episode of the 1950s. On recalling the importance that Costa Mendez placed on this precedent in making his political forecasts, Szule indicated that the American officials read the affair in a completely different sense to that of the Argentine Foreign Minister.

2. The essay entitled: *Dictatorships and Double Standards*, was published for the conservative journal, *Commentary* in its November 1979 issue, during the administration of Jimmy Carter. The text attracted the immediate attention of the then aspiring candidate, Ronald Reagan. In 1983 this same essay served as the title for a book by Kirkpatrick. This contained various works and speeches by the American ambassador to the UN. This last publication was produced by the American Enterprise Institute.

3. The definition: *neutralist sector* belongs to Ambassador Kirkpatrick. In the course of an interview with the authors in Washington in May 1983, she gave her opinion that upon the South Atlantic conflict breaking out, two clearly differentiated sectors had formed in the heart of the Republican administration. One pro-British and another "neutral" in which she included herself. "Argentina did not really have support-

ers," she said then. "If she had, then perhaps peace would have been feasible," she speculated.

4. "Off on a wrong foot", *The Economist*, London, April 10, 1982.

5. Reagan himself would later allude publicly to the Falklands, on April 30, the date on which the United States abandoned its efforts at mediation for "a handful of lost rocks" in the Atlantic. This argument could be useful in public, but did not take account of the view of the islands held by many American military strategists. Rear Admiral Horacio Zaratiegui, for example, quoted an American colleague as describing the islands as "two fantastic aircraft carriers" in an article of his distributed through the Argentine News Agency and reproduced by *La Prensa* on June 16, 1983.

6. "War for the Falklands" *The Sunday Times* Insight Team, London 1982.

7. "Haig is not Dulles" *The Daily Telegraph*. London, April 8, 1982.

8. *The Battle for the Falklands*, Max Hastings and Simon Jenkins, p.107 Michael Joseph, London, 1983.

Article 51 of United Nations Charter establishes that:"Nothing in the present Charter shall impair the inherent right of individual or collective self-defence if an armed attack occurs against a Member of the United Nations, until the Security Council has taken measures necessary to maintain international peace and security. Measures taken by Members in the exercise of this right of self-defence shall be immediately reported to the Security Council and shall not in any way affect the authority and responsibility of the Security Council under the present Charter to take at any time such action as it deems necessary in order to maintain or restore international peace and security."

9. The news regarding Walters' journey to Cuba was first mentioned in testimonies of Argentines interviewed. Later it was corroborated for the authors by responsible American sources during the part of their investigation in the United States.

10. Hastings and Jenkins, op.cit.

Chapter 8

THE HAIG MISSION II - "THE MAD CLAUSE"

Sunday, 11th April 1982 was a long and fruitless day. The choices open to Haig on that day presented a range of problems. He would have to resolve them all if he was to defuse the time bomb of armed confrontation in the South Atlantic. For the Argentines, particularly Galtieri and Costa Mendez, it meant confronting the first doubts over American intervention - an intervention so long sought as a solution to the greatest international crisis Argentina had confronted in the Twentieth Century.

When they resumed negotiations, about 4 pm in the Palacio San Martin, the principal performers were already harbouring their first misgivings. The Argentine Foreign Minister felt little pleased with Haig's line of argument and in particular, the latter's vehement tone. Haig made repeated references - some more or less veiled, others direct - to the importance of Great Britain in the scheme of the Atlantic Alliance and of this alliance for American security and other national interests. The implicit condemnation of the Argentine operation in the Falkland Islands and his insistence on Thatcher's inflexibility were judged by Costa Mendez as less than adequate for someone whose mission depended in large measure on its convincing neutrality.

As for Haig, apart from his discomfort at the mass demonstration in the Plaza de Mayo, he felt frankly irritated by the Argentine arguments, particularly those expressed by Galtieri. He did not understand, as happened with so many other things during these negotiations, Galtieri's reluctance to define the problem in common language. Nor did he understand the rigid posture that he assumed when he spoke of the possibility of war. For Reagan's envoy, this attitude, together with the frequent references to "inalienable rights" which seemed to fill Galtieri's presentation whenever he spoke on the matter, were just further signs of the political unreality pervading the mind of the Argentine Military.

And this was only the beginning. There were difficulties which the Americans did not even dream of encountering, some of them were linked with the strong emotional impact that the Falklands question had for the Argentines historically. There was also the no less emotional reaction that their successful operation of 2nd April produced in Great Britain. When the negotiations began to produce the first drafts of an agreement, Haig and his assistants checked, as did the Argentines, the designation of the archipelago - which itself became a matter of dispute.

At first the State Department mission suggested a double name as employed in the United Nations. As each text was drafted in both English and Spanish, they proposed that in the first case, the description would be *Falklands/Malvinas*, and vice versa for the second. It was not to be, however, and after some discussion, it was decided to opt for description by map co-ordinates[1].

The long working session that began in the mid-afternoon of that Saturday was dominated by certain fundamental questions in dispute. On each, the positions of the two parties seemed irreconcilable. One of the authors' sources who took part in the actual meeting recalled that: "It was a sort of dialogue of the deaf. To listen to Haig and Costa Mendez was astonishing. Officially they were communicating in the same language (English), and the matter under discussion was was common, but in some way the signals were crossed."

To reconstruct that first day of negotiations was - as with all of them - extremely complicated. This is because the exchanges were not orderly and related to different discussion groups. Haig and Costa Mendez sometimes spoke alone and sometimes in the company of their respective advisers. The advisers, in their turn, also began to hold independent meetings on specific points. Moreover, the Argentine and the American each left the table at various points to consult with their respective aides and, in the case of Costa Mendez, to speak to Galtieri by telephone.

This "dialogue of the deaf" as remembered by that diplomatic source centered - according to several testimonies - on the following themes:

(a) To Haig's insistence on the necessity of compliance with UN Resolution 502, the Argentine Foreign Minister countered with a demand for the immediate halting and return of the British Task Force. The latter would not in any case be able to travel beyond Ascension Island. (This is an Atlantic Crown possession leased to the United States, which uses it as a military base. It was from Ascension that the fleet dispatched by Margaret Thatcher's government took on supplies.) This was because beyond Ascension, there would remain a few thousand nautical miles before entering the *security zone* (defined in the Inter-American Treaty of Reciprocal Assistance) and that would oblige

Buenos Aires to summon a meeting of the Organ of Consultation of that pact. Further, he demanded that the United States should verify compliance with the demilitarization clauses of any accord reached.

(b) Costa Mendez offered to link the halting and return of the British Task Force to a withdrawal of Argentine troops, this to be effected in two stages. These men, already numbering 6,000 according to official reports, would be replaced by a reduced contingent of security forces: specifically the Federal Police and the Gendarmerie were mentioned.[2]

(c) Argentina was disposed to accept an interim administration. In principle, Costa Mendez spoke of keeping the recently created military government as a superstructure but afterwards it was felt it would be advisable to reduce its establishment - with some appropriate participation of the islanders. In this way, progress would be made towards a revival of the island councils.

(d) The administrative scheme would be completed by the presence of a Crown Commissioner and an American observer. This would be with the proviso that such an arrangement would be provisional and that it would remain in force only until the end of 1982, at the latest. There would be no possibility of any extension, since that would also be the maximum period for reaching a final solution. The Foreign Minister suggested that once the latter was achieved, the transfer of sovereignty of the islands to Argentina would have to be automatic.

In this way the negotiations reached the sticking points which led to total impasse.

(e) Costa Mendez explained that the negotiation should have as its explicit objective the recognition of Argentine sovereignty over the archipelago and its dependencies,[3] demanding that Washington guarantee that a time limit be recognised. In the Argentine imagination, these negotiations - this time having a definite date for completion - would not be allowed to depart from the legal framework that the United Nations had given them over the space of seventeen years. That meant that the starting point would be Resolutions of the General Assembly such as 1514(XV), 2065(XX) and others.

(f) Argentina desired that the documents be signed in the presence of the United States in order to set up the new bilateral negotiations, and that they should place on record that the negotiations could not affect the principle of "national integrity."

(g) Concerning the islanders, the Argentine Government tried to seduce Haig, and through him, London. They spoke of liberties, unrestricted respect for the identity of the island community and fundamentally, a generous range of economic compensations, particularly for those wishing to emigrate. For Argentina, the possibility of the wishes of the inhabitants being considered did not come into it. This was for the simple reason that there was no going back along the road travelled at the UN where, against the opposition of Great Britain, successive resolutions of the General Assembly had chosen the formula: "interests of the inhabitants," validating the Argentine interpretation. To accept the term "wishes" would have involved entering unfavourable terrain, the greatest threat of which might be the application of the "principle of self-determination."

Any possibility of a speedy accord vanished with the light of dawn that Saturday. Haig communicated with his British colleague, Francis Pym, on more than one occasion, and knew that the road that the Argentines were obliging him to follow would not lead to success. The attempts made up till then with Costa Mendez to get the Argentine position to show some flexibility had not produced any positive results.

The Secretary of State, seeing that the outlook was becoming far from clear, re-introduced a formula into the conversation that permitted the United States to avoid total responsibility in the matter - should the alternative of an armed confrontation prove unavoidable. Great Britain did not accept the continuation of any Argentine administration on the islands, still less one with the characteristics of the military government of General Menendez - a vivid reminder of the humiliation suffered by the British. It advocated the institution of a special interim authority and resurrected the idea of bringing in third countries besides the United States, chosen by the parties concerned. Thus the names of Peru, Colombia and Brazil returned to the pack to be shuffled, along with that of Canada. This last name provoked a strong reaction from Argentina, since that old British Dominion had shown an early and complete solidarity with London, going so far as to withdraw its ambassador from Buenos Aires.

At one time, the possibility of the United Nations providing the transitional authority was raised, but that idea was rapidly discarded. An agreement of that type indicated a return to the Trustee Administration anticipated in the UN Charter whose earlier applications had envisaged that the principle of self-determination for the inhabitants should acquire particular importance.[4] From the OAS the governments of Ecuador, Colombia and Costa Rica had tried something similar - first a mediation by the OAS and then the proposal that that organisation should provide a temporary administration and an Inter-American security force. But every initiative of this type was suspended in order to permit full freedom of action for Washington.

The *Special Interim Authority* did not, in the American view, have to have a time limit, and much less an expiry clause involving an automatic transfer of sovereignty. For the British, that would be equivalent to having to negotiate under pressure. Concerning the question of Argentine sovereignty, the formulas proposed by Haig tried to avoid it entirely. The British had made it clear that they would not consider entering into a dialogue between two parties where one of them claimed to prejudge the outcome.

Ambassador Walters took part in much of the negotiations, but not in all of them. "While he was in the Foreign Ministry, he remained seated in a corner of the room most of the time making notes at an amazing speed, though he actually seemed to be working out his opinions on paper rather than reporting on the discussions taking place," recalled one Argentine negotiator. According to accounts from several sources, Walters left the Palacio San Martin some time that evening in order to meet some local contacts.

If there is agreement on this matter, it is difficult to identify who were his companions in the separate meetings during this first part of the Haig Mission. Walters himself admitted, in the interview held during the investigations for this book, having had various conversations with "his Argentine friends." One of the most likely scenarios is that Reagan's itinerant ambassador was received alone that April afternoon by members of the Junta - including Galtieri. It may have been on that occasion or on another during which he accompanied Haig to the Casa Rosada, that Walters had a particular conversation with the Argentine President. This discussion was of a nature that revealed the spirit then directing the conduct of political and military affairs in Argentina. They were speaking of a matter which would return time and again, namely, the dramatic choices which an armed clash between the protagonists of this crisis would doubtless bring.

Beyond such findings uncovered by the authors, it is certain that, in the days following, the Americans insisted on raising, among forecasts of the outcome of a war between Argentina and Great Britain, the phantom of an overwhelming military defeat - this as a way of bringing pressure on Buenos Aires. In exchanges with Walters, however, the Argentine President always countered with unlimited confidence in his subordinates:

"We are prepared to defend ourselves, General. Don't doubt that for a moment. Argentina does not want war, but it will fight if it is necessary," Galtieri warned the American.

"I know, Mr President," countered Walters, without raising objections. "Bear in mind that the British have a professional army, permanently trained for combat, whilst your men are conscripts with hardly three months instruction."

"Argentine soldiers will give a show of courage, you will see for yourself," insisted Galtieri, who was not disposed to accept the arguments of this military diplomat.

But Walters did not give up and a little later he took advantage of a personal anecdote to return to this delicate question:

"I don't doubt the courage of your soldiers, but I remember my own baptism of fire and I think that bravery itself is often not enough, because war is so terrible. I began my military career as a volunteer, a second class soldier, Mr President, (Walters belonged to the Marines). Like every boy, during my training I had an almost romantic idea of fighting: I longed to be in action. But I remember my first day in battle in North Africa during the Second World War. I heard the machine gun nearby and the explosions of the artillery shells and I said: "My God, no one told me it would be like this!"

Galtieri ignored these comments by his American colleague. Walters could not contain his astonishment, he later confessed. If the Argentine Military were flying in the face of reality at that time - as they were throughout the whole conflict - Haig and his team for their part, were over-exaggerating their warnings. These produced a reaction in the minds of Galtieri and the Junta exactly opposite to that desired. The advice, whatever may have been its intention, was in this way simply transformed into promises of humiliation.

There were other reactions too that Walters obtained from his contacts that day that left his companions in the mission equally amazed. Haig was particularly struck on being informed by the itinerant ambassador that he had gathered concrete evidence that only two of the five Argentine army corps commandants had been notified in sufficient time of the plans for the operation on 2nd April. Taking into account this information gathered by Walters, it is not difficult to work out who his contacts were in the first place.

In a very much less confidential way, the person in charge of the Southern Cone area at the State Department, Robert Service, also sounded out a few opinions while Haig was negotiating with Costa Mendez. For this he met the leaders of the principal political parties, including obviously, those forming the *Convocatoria Multipartidaria*. The meeting took place in the US Embassy. There he again heard arguments in favour of the "recovery," of the Falklands although almost all agreed on the overwhelming need to find a negotiated solution to the crisis so as to avoid bloodshed.

Although they were careful to show their support in public, and to Costa Mendez in private, this backing was little less than united in its formal and lifeless opposition to the Military Junta. This support did not please the Secretary of State either. It deprived him, he reasoned, of another means of applying pressure.

When evening fell over an excited and expectant Buenos Aires,

Haig suggested the possibility of a break in the mediation effort, hinting that as he could not return to London empty-handed, his destination would have to be Washington. This would not be for more negotiations; to speak of a "possible break" was a euphemism for threatening a complete rupture. It was then that, after a telephone call by Costa Mendez to the Casa Rosada, the Argentines conveyed an invitation to the visitor to a further meeting with Galtieri.

The invitation referred to the "bond" that precariously linked the parties, which had not broken, even under the greatest strain.

Galtieri faced the new meeting with Reagan's envoy in even better form than in the morning. The crowd which he had addressed from the balcony of the Casa Rosada acted on his spirits like a powerful stimulant. As if this was not enough, the dream of becoming a popular civilian leader like Peron was made more vivid by the words of his advisers, which affected his nervous system like a combination of alcohol and drugs.

In particular, the Minister of the Interior, Saint Jean, the Secretary-General of the Presidency of the Nation, Brigadier-General Iglesias, and the Military Attache at the Presidency, Rear-Admiral Benito Moya - all assured him of a certain future of unlimited triumphs. There is, after all, no more convincing argument than that which one wishes to hear.

Why not allow oneself to feel like this? It was a long way from the dull professional life of an army officer to the role of the "strong man of Argentina." And the President-Commandant believed himself to have travelled it that day once and for all. Nevertheless, he soon found that the causes of so much euphoria did not impress Haig, or if they did, the effect only served to make dialogue more difficult.

The Secretary of State was expecting that this high-level effort in Argentina would rapidly produce the minimum concessions to permit the mediation to continue. But this was an unfounded hope. There was no way of raising the points in dispute directly because Galtieri intended to formulate his own warnings to the representative from Washington.

The multitude at midday was Galtieri's principal argument. If the Americans pressurized him, he could show them that he could play the same game. He demanded that Argentina should receive the same treatment that the United States gave to Great Britain, pointing out that his country would not accept the role of servant to the West. When talking of the mass demonstration of which he had offered Haig a privileged panoramic view, he expressed a concern about a possible budding anti-Americanism in Argentine public opinion. He recalled the inevitable precedent in the forties - graphically described by the phrase: "Braden or Peron"[5].

From that moment, the dialogue was transformed for some time into boasts and accusations, which were more or less veiled and more or less formally polite.

One example was mention of Galtieri's charge concerning American satellite information on which the British Task Force could presumably count, something which the envoy categorically rejected. And the threat of reaching an impasse clearly appeared once more.

In increasingly more direct language, Haig spoke of the "absurdity" of a war and of how the negotiating proposals of Argentina, if accepted by Margaret Thatcher, would be equivalent to her "political suicide" - something the West could not "tolerate." This was the reply to Galtieri's request for equity. As a government spokesman would indicate days later to a group of reporters: "The United States has allies, but considers some to be more allies than others."

Haig returned to demanding concessions from Argentina, stating that only in this way could the time be gained that would be necessary to avoid the failure of his mission. It was essential to procure concessions in order that he might return to London, otherwise that journey would lack any meaning.

This was another significant moment because, at about 10 pm, Galtieri, the man who had hitherto spoken as if he was the sole representative of the national will implicitly admitted, without perhaps noticing it, that it was necessary to consult his colleagues in the Military Junta on the matter of the flexibility Haig was demanding. An hour later, Jorge Isaac Anaya and Basilio Arturo Lami Dozo arrived at the Casa Rosada and Galtieri took his leave in order to meet his colleagues. The scheme for the division of power adopted by the Military in March 1976 was never of great help to the country in its international relations.

The debate at the heart of the Military Junta was hard fought. As he would do until the end, Anaya firmly maintained that the operation of 2nd April had not been carried out to deliver the fruits of conquest onto a negotiating table and that in any case the American threats did not deserve to be taken into account.

The British fleet would not reach the South Atlantic; Reagan simply could not afford the luxury of abandoning a country like Argentina, while the Soviet Union was once more knocking at the door of Central America; the national will of all Argentina was at stake - as had been demonstrated that very midday, Galtieri boasted.

Lami Dozo presented the air force view of matters which, though thinly disguised, was in opposition to that of Anaya, his navy colleague. It was necessary, he said - in order to sustain the alternative of peaceful negotiations - to be flexible as the Secretary of State required. After all, hadn't they realized before accepting Haig's intervention that he would inevitably expect to gain some concessions? Hadn't they also foreseen the necessity of calming the effects on British pride of the armed attack on the islands? In order not to give rise to questions, the commandant of the air force stated that his position was the result of soundings he had made a few hours earlier among his senior officers.

Galtieri was trapped in the crossfire, not because he had a third alternative to those already presented, but because in his mind he partly shared the arguments of both. Like Anaya, it horrified him to think of a withdrawal, but the idea of depriving himself of American assistance did not appeal to him either, nor of increasing criticism of Argentina in Washington.

They continued discussing these variants for a few minutes, but there was not enough time. Finally, they agreed to deliver a document to Haig setting out the Argentine position in order that he might have something to show to the British, thus permitting him to gain the time that he said he needed. Out of politeness, they would try to accommodate the requirements in their draft.

Anaya, however, would not give way and in fact applied another turn of the screw. He made his condition for joining any consensus that active participation by the Military be invoked in the preparation of any document. In other words, he demanded the presence of a delegate of his own to demonstrate once more the mistrust that the Argentine Military felt for diplomats. Allusions to the "paederasts of the Foreign Ministry," were frequent in the camp jargon of those days. There was no way of denying this request although it obviously also obliged the other commandants to nominate their own personal delegates. It was another expression of the principle of "33 per cent of the power for each arm of the forces," inaugurated in 1976 by those in charge of the Military Government.

This opened the door for the entry onto centre stage of three men trusted by the commandants: General Iglesias, Admiral Moya and Brigadier Miret. If Galtieri referred many times to the Military Junta as his "Senate," the delegates of that body were the private "parliament" of Costa Mendez, functioning in the negotiations until the end. Inclining towards irony, Argentine reporters nicknamed them "The Three Marias," and to foreigners who knew them during the travels of Costa Mendez, they became known as "The Three Stooges"[6].

Each one of the three played an important part at various moments in the dispute - very often with different responsibilities from each other - but none of more significance than that of Moya. In a short time this naval officer, at that time Military Attache to the Presidency, displaced Iglesias in Galtieri's preferences.

155

While the crisis developed and defeat loomed more clearly, Moya transformed himself into an indispensible figure for the troubled President, whom he rescued from the depression which afflicted the leader ever more frequently.

Moya, an officer whose fifty-second birthday was only six days before the fall of Port Stanley, belonged to naval aviation, whose command he assumed a few months after the war - before going into retirement[7]. Like many of his colleagues, he had passed through American training institutions - in his case to study the tactics of anti-submarine warfare. But his forte had been intelligence activity - lending his services as much to Naval Intelligence (SIN) as to State Intelligence (SIDE) during the repression of subversion. This last assignment was one of the most fraught of his career, since, according to various witnesses he led internal confrontations with his then chief, General Carlos Martinez. It was Anaya who, after the fall of Viola, got him the post of military attache.

For his part, Miret was the commandant's man of trust *par excellence*, and was considered the most political of those surrounding Lami Dozo. For the two years of 1966 and 1967, he served as air attache in Great Britain with the rank of Vice-Commodore. But he began to figure in the circle of power after he was named Assistant Legal and Technical Secretary to the Presidency of the Nation, in March 1976. From there he went to the Commission for Legislative Assessment, and afterwards to the Planning Secretariat.

Iglesias enjoyed Galtieri's confidence - at least until May, 1982. This he gained mainly for his work as Assistant Secretary General of the Army. From that position he collaborated in working out the commandant's political plans. His career was spent within military units, until reaching the rank of general and consequently he did not become much known to the public at large.

At 1 am on Sunday it was clear that the failure of the mission had not been avoided. The only result was a brief document of hardly five points, containing what the Argentines called "minimum requirements." Haig warned Costa Mendez that it repeated various demands that Great Britain considered unacceptable, such as the immediate cancellation of the Exclusion Zone, which would be in force from the following day - this before any withdrawal of Argentine troops. Similarly, there was the demand to suspend economic sanctions such as London had already applied and which the EEC had announced on Saturday. Galtieri thus made clear the Junta's unwillingness to negotiate under pressure.

In the eyes of the State Department officials, the only thing to emerge as a half-hearted sign of flexibility was the fact that the draft memorandum suggested that Argentina would accept a British refusal to recognize its claims of sovereignty prior to negotiations. For compensation, the document contained provisions to ensure that the Argentine flag would continue to fly over the Falklands during the interim and that the form of administration during this transition period should guarantee effective control by Buenos Aires.

At this point in the discussion, the Argentines warned the Secretary of State that Argentina would feel at liberty to petition for a meeting of the Rio Pact from the moment any naval blockade round the Falklands was mounted - which she would consider an aggression.

This started a new discussion. The Americans argued forcefully against such a decision, which really worried them. They did not want insoluble problems to aggravate still more the crisis affecting the Inter-American system.

Haig made it clear that his government considered that the provisions of IATRA did not apply in the present situation. The main provision was the reciprocal obligation of signatory American states to lend assistance in the case of attack upon one member by an extra-continental state. The explanation for this lay simply in the historical American interpretation of that security treaty. In the American view, one could not speak of extra-continental aggression when the original use of force had, on April 2nd, been Argentina's responsibility. This deprived Argentina of being able to claim the rights of a country under attack.

Contrary to what the dialogue so far might suggest, Haig, at the end of that long day, told Costa Mendez that he would take a flight to London the following morning. Even so, he made it clear that he was going to start a new round of talks with Margaret Thatcher under the worst possible conditions. Breakdown had been avoided on that occasion, but it was impossible to disguise the true outcome. The Secretary for Public Information, Rodolfo Baltierrez, appeared at a quarter past one to the sleepless government reporters to confess laconically: "There was no agreement."

Haig's aircraft set off for London at 9 am. Shortly before, the Secretary of State had heard Mass at the Church of the Holy Sacrament *(Santisimo Sacramento)*, where he recognized Jose Alfredo Martinez de Hoz among the Faithful, and shook hands with him.

On the plane, one of the passengers recalled, the atmosphere was frankly depressing. In the exchange of ideas during that eighteen hour flight, Haig nearly exploded with anger several times when he recalled his conversations with Galtieri. The chance of avoiding conflict was slight in the opinion of the Secretary of State, and he made this known to President Reagan in a radio communication.

The main points of that conversation were later leaked to the press by the polemical columnist, Jack Anderson, and so a speculation shared by the President and his special envoy became public - a clear indication how they saw the question. In one part of that discussion they both asked themselves if Margaret Thatcher would feel that vengeance could be satisfied, and her political needs met, when the cannons of her Task Force sank an Argentine ship.

But the political position of the Prime Minister had been strengthened since the Secretary of State saw her a few days earlier. An opinion poll conducted at the time showed that 83% of the British public considered that sending the fleet was a proper response to the Argentine military action[8]. There was no risk now that the Conservative Government would fall, at least in the short term.

Moreover, if the peace-making effort by Washington had never been completely welcome in London, now, at this stage of events it was frankly resisted. Many newspaper articles spoke openly of the possibility of "American betrayal," and the editorials demanded Reagan's express and final solidarity.

The scene which awaited Haig at Heathrow airport was a symbol, not very difficult to interpret as such, of what was to follow. There was simply no one in authority to receive the American envoy at 5.40 am on that Monday, April 12th. Under pressure, the officials of the American Embassy themselves had to organize a fleet of cars to transport the Secretary of State and his team to the luxury Churchill Hotel where he stayed. The long hours of the flight and the work began to have a critical effect on Haig's constitution - the sudden changes in time zones were hindering his sleep - and there were suggestions of the re-emergence of an old heart condition.

But Haig's ambition was, at least until that moment, stronger than any other consideration. As one of those taking part sharply commented: "There was always the Nobel Prize for Peace, around which they circled, like a merry-go-round, all trying to get the prize."

A new and prolonged day of negotiations was begun during which Pym received his colleague with references to the Prime Minister's inflexibility. There were also unfortunate rumours circulating in Parliament and in the Conservative Government about Washington's hesitation in supporting its Atlantic ally.

As to the practical aspects of the conflict, the discussion centred on a few variants:

1. The idea of an Argentine-British condominium in the islands was not turned down flat. Pym even reached the point of publicly accepting the possibility, but its implementation would involve over-

coming many obstacles. It was difficult to imagine the form in which two nations on the point of going to war - and with open mutual resentment - could work together so directly in such a project. On the other hand, it would not satisfy the basic question which for the Argentines continued to be that of sovereignty. In any case, as some newspaper commentators of those days pointed out, the idea of the condominium seemed useful only from the viewpoint of the islanders, and even then there was no certainty of gaining their general acceptance.

2. The idea of a United Nations *interim authority* had been rejected by Buenos Aires, but there was also a proposal having broadly similar characteristics, this time under the aegis of the OAS. But this body gave rise to strong suspicions for the British, besides which the presidents of Mexico - Jose Lopez Portillo, and of Ecuador - Osvaldo Hurtado, had in any case declared themselves in support of the Argentine demands. As if this was not enough, that same Monday had seen the failure of an attempt by the group of English-speaking Caribbean countries to obtain a condemnation by the Permanent Council of the OAS of Argentina's military action, an episode which culminated in the withdrawal of all the Latin American ambassadors from the discussions.

3. The proposal for getting help from third-party countries: an equal number being chosen by each party in the dispute - plus the United States - turned out more promising. Alternatively, a tripartite authority with the involvement of Washington alone, was also suggested. The American Government could thus act not only as a buffer between the two parties but also offer safeguards for their national interests. This last alternative began to emerge as the most likely formula.

In order for the question of sovereignty to be settled at some future date, the British Foreign Office always made it clear that no fixed period for discussion would be acceptable. In the first place, this was because fixing a closing date implied a prejudgement of the results of the negotiations. A method had to be found of avoiding the danger that an Argentine decision might take the situation back to the origins of the crisis, as could happen if the agreed procedure did not follow the path desired by Buenos Aires and she rejected it.

Furthermore, the agreements to be reached had to protect explicitly and in the most satisfactory manner that could be found, "the wishes, rights and interests of the islanders." It also had to envisage the resurrection of the Executive and Legislative Councils of the previous island government, although on that point, the incorporation of a limited Argentine representation could be discussed. This was an essential requirement for British interests.

4. In any case, none of these alternatives could still receive serious consideration by the British Government, explained Pym, if

Argentina did not previously agree to comply with the requirements of Resolution 502. That is - if they did not evacuate their troops from the archipelago. Even the halting of the Task Force was irremediably subject to that precondition. Moreover, compliance with the Security Council request for withdrawal could not be delayed more than fifteen days because otherwise the main body of the British force would have already reached the zone of conflict and a confrontation would then be inevitable. Haig also received the news that day that the first British submarines had arrived in the vicinity of the islands and had received confirmation of the order to open fire on any Argentine ship which tried to violate the Exclusion Zone.

In a later meeting with Thatcher, Haig learnt from the Prime Minister herself that it was her decision not to go beyond the possibility of negotiations without a fixed term for completion and an interim administration linked to the prior withdrawal of Argentine troops. She further informed him that she would announce this decision to Parliament on Wednesday April 14th, only agreeing to maintain confidentiality on the actual terms of the negotiations. To sum up, she had said, there could be no more accommodation for the aggressors. Moreover, she advised the American Government, through Haig, that even a genuine peace-making effort had to have its limits.

There are signs, as demonstrated by newspaper leaks at the time, that Haig substantially altered the substance of his arguments on his second visit to London. In talking to Pym at the Foreign Office, as well as to both Pym and Margaret Thatcher at Number 10, he agreed to consider frankly the alternative in its various forms, of an open and early American support for the British cause. The British Foreign Secretary was later to declare himself confident, in a press conference which took place in the evening of that day that: "The United States will not remain neutral between a democracy and a dictatorship."

The Economist, which possesses excellent sources of information on the Conservative Government, stated in an editorial on that stage of the Haig mission:

"....for the United States, its interests in this dispute are more particular even than that. And just as we thought, it is now dawning on President Reagan that he cannot expect to be on both sides when the shooting starts. Nor will he be. By mid-week, the Argentines did not yet realise it, but it is now all but certain that if negotiations should fail and missiles start to fly, the United States will back Britain. Not with aircraft carriers, doubtless, but probably with economic sanctions equal to the telling, and admirable, ones invoked by Britain's partners in the European Community - and as time ticks by, perhaps with logistic support for the British fleet."[9]

And that is an exactly what happened some fifteen days later.
Moreover, the influential daily, *The Washington Post* included
an article in that day's edition signed by Carl Bernstein, one of the
journalists who exposed the Watergate scandal. In this, he reported a
leak from the Defense Department about the provision of American
intelligence information to Great Britain. He also identified Caspar
Weinberger as its principal promoter. Bernstein's report resulted in a
consultation by telephone between Costa Mendez and Haig, who denied
the report.

Haig and his advisers considered employing the same tactics as
he had in Argentina. These were to take what terms were offered and
return to Buenos Aires and so try to persuade the Junta simply to adjust
its requirements to what he had achieved. There was actually no need to
call Costa Mendez to sound him out, as the latter had anticipated this
approach.

It is not hard to imagine the difficulties the Argentine Foreign
Minister found in taking the initiative to make the call. There had been
at least two previous efforts. It took place about 10.30 pm, after a
meeting of the Military Committee, when Anaya introduced a new area
of disagreement. The negotiations that might follow an Argentine
withdrawal, explained Anaya, must not imply a repetion of the previous
seventeen years of frustration. The agreement, he demanded, had to
include a timetable for the transfer of sovereignty to Argentina; after all,
that was why the troops had been sent to the islands.

This new Argentine requirement was a great shock to Haig,
who considered it a "death blow" to his efforts. He did not hesitate in
telling Costa Mendez that a further journey by him to Buenos Aires
would be meaningless, given the new conditions. He suggested that
possibly his mediation should be concluded. After this bucket of cold
water, the Argentine Foreign Minister could only appeal for the peace
effort to continue - and this he did. "You must not abandon it," he insisted
to the Secretary of State. The latter's reply was non-committal. He made
no promise beyond saying he would put some thoughts in writing on this
difficult question and send them to Buenos Aires the next day.

The debate in the American team was heated. At that stage only
Enders and Walters were definitely for continuing the mediation.
Moreover, the issue of whether Costa Mendez was a reliable person with
whom to work was raised - a suspicion that would grow as the days
passed. The State Department officials concluded that the latest Argentine demand implied a substantial change in the terms the Foreign
Minister had agreed earlier. Haig adopted a compromise solution from

among those put forward by his aides: he would ask for a meeting with Margaret Thatcher the following morning, but would also travel to Washington. He could not continue under these circumstances if, after an overall analysis of the situation, Reagan did not renew his endorsement.

Another sixty minutes with Mrs Thatcher on the morning of Tuesday 13th produced meagre results. There was a lukewarm promise by the Prime Minister to consider any new ideas, it being clear that this would be only if the Secretary of State could think of them first.

The following two days were hard work for the mediator. Haig continued his contacts with the two parties while confronting domestic critics in the heart of the Republican Government. These were of two types: those who maintained that his effort had no future and that it only remained openly to support the British cause; and those who virtually accused him of not being a genuine mediator at all, but an agent of London. These last were very much in the minority.

After meeting the National Security Council, which was presided over by Clark and reported to President Reagan, it remained clear that there was still a consensus for continuing the search for a means to avoid a war. But on what basis? There were certainly not many new ways forward, so Haig drew up a five-point plan that implied a sort of separation of the differences. It was a formula to replace the attempt at bringing together the opposing parties which had been tried in vain up till then. Each of the parties would lose equally. The scheme very roughly was as follows:

1. Withdrawal of Argentine troops linked to a halt and subsequent pull-back of the British fleet by 1000 nautical miles over a period of fifteen days. Thus Great Britain obtained compliance with Resolution 502 and Argentina avoided the stigma of a unilateral withdrawal.

2. A tripartite interim administration, flying the flags of each one of its members: Argentina, Great Britain and the United States as mediator and guarantor. This form of government, which should include the island councils, would be in force until December 31st 1982, before which time a permanent solution would have to be found.

3. The removal of the Exclusion Zone - and the reciprocal sanctions - and the restoration of communications between the continent and the archipelago.

4. A system of direct negotiation between the parties to the conflict, assisted by the United States and according to the usual practice of the United Nations in such cases. The central issue to be the final status of the archipelago and its Dependencies.

5. Consultation through referendum with the islanders, to discover their wishes. The fixed period for a solution was unacceptable to London and likewise the referendum, as a significant element in the final outcome of the dispute, was equally unacceptable to Argentina. But at this stage one was "shuffling the cards and dealing again." It would be sufficient to obtain a rough agreement, with all objections ignored to begin with. And this, in fact, is how it proceeded. The consultations effected with London and later Buenos Aires made it necessary to amplify this basic scheme.

But this time Haig brought all the pressure at his command to bear on the Argentines. He began trying it with Costa Mendez. In both his telephone conversations and in the telex messages he sent, he invariably began with the greeting: "Dear Nicanor." In all of these, Haig brought in the possibility of a break-down, at the same time emphasizing the "many concessions" that in his opinion had been extracted from Prime Minister Thatcher.

Buenos Aires was ready to be receptive to the American arguments in spite of the positions taken up by the members of the Junta, in particular by Galtieri and Anaya. The possibility that the Americans might abandon the mediation did not bring joy to anyone within the power structure and least of all, the Foreign Minister, who had pinned his hopes in advance on Washington.

One incident among others illustrates the growing concern by the Military to achieve an agreement with American assistance. This was a concern which nevertheless was not to be found to the same degree among the members of the Junta. On April 14th, the Secretary of State believed he had reached a point where he could announce his return to Buenos Aires. On that day Vice-Admiral Lombardo moved to Puerto Belgrano from where, on the following day, the war fleet would set sail. The fleet had completed a period of re-provisioning and making ready, after the operation of April 2nd - this, according to a plan approved on April 12th.

On arriving, Lombardo informed the Commander of the Fleet, Rear-Admiral Gualter Allara, that he would make his official farewell to the company, but that, contrary to traditional practice, he was not thinking of doing it from the deck of the flag-ship - in this case the aircraft carrier *25 de Mayo*. "I am going to give my speech on board the corvette..... which is the only unit which suffered damage - and casualties," he told his subordinate.

Thus Lombardo said: "I came to the corvette, rather unusually, because you have had casualties and damage and I know you are shocked by your first experience of war. That is why I came to this ship, and I do so to show concern, because I believe that the most important function of an officer in charge of naval vessels is, more than the technical handling of equipment, to lead men."

"I want to say to you, therefore," added Lombardo, "that I hope, when you are at sea, that a settlement to this problem is reached, because that would be the only solution. Let no-one deceive himself: when we reach that agreement, it will mean giving something up. Because at this moment, in theory, we hold everything. We have sovereignty and government. But something will have to be given up to achieve a compromise."

In the astonished presence of some officers, among them Allara, Lombardo proceeded in - for these days - this unusually conciliatory vein:

"When we sign the agreement I know people will complain. They will say that we are over-generous, that we don't know how to keep what we have won. And the less a person knows, the more he will protest at these concessions. So you who have lost comrades recovering the islands are going to have to explain to such people why it was necessary to make these concessions."

Lombardo returned to his office at the base. Half an hour later Allara, who had remained talking with the members of the staff of the corvette, asked for a meeting. "Sir," he said to his superior, "I believe that some explanation is necessary. Did you say what you did to the fleet because you already know that an agreement has been signed and we don't know about it?"

The truth, however, was that the Chief of TOAS had been working from a private conviction which did not reflect any privileged information. "Look, Allara," he replied, "I have no news of any solution, but I think that the only sensible and reasonable thing is to come to an agreement. And we *are* going to reach that agreement - the more we delay the worse it will be."

That Wednesday there was another meeting of the Military Committee, in which drafts were approved for the new round of negotiations. The main conclusion for Buenos Aires was the need to offer Washington a show of Argentine goodwill. Thus it was decided to resort to another direct communication between the two presidents.

So that this concession might not appear a political retreat for Argentina, it was agreed that Galtieri should express a warning to Reagan and would put to him, in the usual elliptical formulas, the concern felt about American aid to Great Britain. He would also express displeasure at the declarations by some members of the American Government - such as the Defense Secretary, Weinberger - which were little less than openly favourable to London.

In the first case Galtieri would have to invoke the phantom of the Soviet Union - to which Reagan always showed himself to be sensitive - and in the second, to demand a re-affirmation of American neutrality. The American leader's emphasis in agreeing to provide this last assurance was noteworthy.

The dialogue began at 7 pm on April 15, scarcely three and a half hours before Haig's aircraft landed at Ezeiza. There was no reticence by Galtieri this time, as on the early morning of 2nd April; on the contrary, it was the Argentine's turn to be the one to ring the other's number. There was also no need for improvisation, as the contact had been agreed previously between the two foreign ministries, and the situation was similar to the first time.

In the course of the investigation, the authors obtained a copy of the recording of this conversation (in the Spanish version) which is reproduced below without modification:

"Good afternoon, Mr President. This is President Galtieri speaking. Let's see if you can hear me."[10]

"Mr President, I hear you very well; I am informed that you want to continue our conversations. I am very pleased to listen to you. I am at your service," replied Reagan.

"It really is a pleasure to talk to you again, Mr President, after the not very fruitful conversation we had on April 1st, during the night, when, practically speaking, from the Argentine Government's point of view, some very important matters had already been resolved and I could not meet your requirements. Let's see if you hear me. Over."

"I hear you well, Mr President."

"It is the desire, the deep desire, of the Argentine people and Government that there should not be a major deterioration in this situation. With the insistence of the United States on seeking a solution for both parties in accordance with UN Resolution 502; and taking into account existing antecedents to this problem - in bilateral form for 150 years, as well as the work done during the last seventeen years through the United Nations in respect of de-colonization.....let's see if you hear me, Mr President."

"Yes, I heard everything, Mr President. May I ask, Mr President, if you want me to make a reply at the moment or do you wish to add something more?" Reagan inquired.

"I prefer to add one more paragraph, Mr President: "There exists the best possible goodwill on the part of the Argentine Government, Mr President, but I would also wish you to realize that the advance of the British fleet and their measures towards the South Atlantic Ocean are not only making the situation in the South Atlantic between the two nations more and more dangerous - which of course concerns me greatly - but there is also the danger of involving other nations in this matter -

which should not involve the interests of anyone else. The relations established between our two governments, strengthened in recent times by the closeness of our two administrations....it is our firm desire to continue them in all aspects of international life, and I fear that if the English continue in their hostile intentions towards the South Atlantic, things could get out of hand and out of our control, becoming an extremely delicate matter for the whole world. I don't know if you understand me, Mr President?" Galtieri said, venturing a word of warning.

"Mr President, I heard you very well and therefore wanted to tell you that I personally remain committed to a peaceful solution to this dispute. This is of great importance because, as I have said in the past, it concerns the confrontation of two nations who are both our friends. Consequently we shall continue with our good offices towards both nations. Now, Secretary Haig is on his way and will be arriving in Buenos Aires in a few hours to continue our efforts. You know that Secretary Haig is my personal representative. In him I put my total faith and confidence in the matter. I must tell you, Mr President, that with all my heart I am committed to a peaceful solution to this quarrel. I agree that a war in this Hemisphere between two nations friendly to the United States is something unthinkable. It would be a tragedy, a disaster for the Western world. It would be a bitter legacy for future generations whether they be Argentine, British or American. The only party who would benefit in this type of conflict would be the Soviet Union and its slave allies; therefore I have hopes that we can arrive at a solution in the near future. Over."

"Thank you, Mr President. Tell him (in some places Galtieri seemed to address the interpreter) that I share his point of view. But while the hours pass and Great Britain's blockade of our coasts continues, and while the English fleet keeps advancing towards the South, any untoward event might occur. Some event not looked for by any other interested party in the world, which might be impossible to predict and which might aggravate the present situation. Besides, we must be very careful about this because evidently some people *are* trying to cause trouble. Newspaper articles in America and elsewhere in the world showed it yesterday: they are trying to cause rifts in the excellent relations established by our two governments and our two countries and our two administrations. I am afraid that as time passes they can start things which are difficult to control. Of course, I am grateful to the President for sending Mr Haig again to Buenos Aires. I shall of course make contact with him tomorrow and I shall speak to him at length about the problem that we have to deal with and which concerns us all. Over."

"Mr President, I naturally have hopes that we can reach an

agreement that may save the situation. I share your fears that some event may occur which will make controlling the situation difficult or from which it would be difficult to draw back. I also know that you and the British leaders want to arrive at a solution to the situation. They are people of the highest qualities of leadership. We can expect from them and we shall need both a flexible attitude and moderation in order that we may move towards a solution to this situation. But I want to make a firm stand on my belief and conviction that we need a peaceful working solution to this grave situation. A peaceful solution which takes account of the interests of the peoples involved and of the population of the islands, in a form acceptable to all parties. But as you have mentioned, in a few hours the Secretary of State will be in your country. I am certainly going to send the contents of this exchange to my own assistants and I again assure you, Mr President, that I consider the Secretary of State as my personal representative. This is an extremely difficult situation and I also realize that there is a propaganda effort to seek or perhaps provoke hostility between our two countries. We have done nothing, Mr President, at variance with the role we have assumed as neutral and objective intermediaries. Peace is our cause and our only objective, peace between two friendly nations, Argentina and Great Britain, and everything we do will relate to this objective. We must be careful to continue to be even-handed. There must be neutrality and friendship for both nations, because not to take this attitude would naturally prejudice our role as helper. Continuing with this non-partisan and objective stance clearly affects our capacity to help our friends in Argentina and Great Britain. Therefore I want you to know, Mr President, that we shall continue to play a neutral part in this matter, because if a conflict breaks out, it would naturally signify a very serious problem. Naturally, I have been the centre of criticism because our administration has maintained this even-handed line, but my intention is to continue with this neutrality while the negotiations proceed. Consequently I hope and pray to God that there be no conflict inadvertently caused by one party or another while we are dedicated to the solution of this situation. Over."

"I want to express my gratitude to you, Mr President, which is the main purpose of this call. I appreciate your kindness in continuing the dialogue we began on April 1st in this direct exchange between two presidents - maintaining the cordiality, friendship and understanding of both nations in order to seek solutions to the problems of the Western world and maintaining good relations. I only want to add that in 1776, the people of the United States, in the north of the Hemisphere, began the struggle against colonialism and achieved their independence. We here in the South, did the same though later than you. Only in the last century did we gain our partial independence and only on April 2nd, 1982 did we try to complete it - a little later than you in the United States. I want you to understand, Mr President, this sentiment of the Argentine people. Over."

"I understand your concern, Mr President, and I assure you that we shall continue in our role in order to reach a solution and also to maintain friendship between two nations of the Western world. Once again I want to thank you for your call and I await with enthusiasm and interest news from the Secretary of State after your negotiations tomorrow and this said I thank you and wish you good night."

"Good night, Mr President, until next time."

Naturally hopes grew inside the Military after that dialogue, even overcoming the recent shock felt by the Argentine strategists. On Wednesday, Prime Minister Thatcher had successfully mounted a new demonstration of determination, calling Parliament back from its recess in order to attend a new emergency session. She did it among rumours of the possibility that the House might pass a vote of no confidence, forcing her to resign.

Parliament, but especially the Conservative Members, seemed to have devided, as one London weekly put it, into a "war party" and a "peace party". Each of these being less in number than the undecided group in the middle[11].

The Prime Minister obtained majority support and the four principal parties - Conservative and Labour, Social Democrat and Liberal - accepted the proposal to recover the islands "by the diplomatic route, but with strong military support." The clearest support came from none other than the leader of the Labour Opposition, Michael Foot. The Argentine "analysts in uniform" consoled themselves simply by saying: perhaps it is better that way. It is always preferable to deal with someone who is in a politically strong position.

Haig arrived on Friday evening, and from Ezeiza airport at Buenos Aires appealed for: "a supreme effort in order to achieve a solution to this problem." He warned that this "would require a great flexibility on the part of both parties to the conflict, without either abandoning their principles but demonstrating the necessary flexibility." And the following morning he began discussions with Galtieri, who received him at the Casa Rosada.

The notes taken at that conversation - and to which the authors gained access during this investigation - allowed a reconstruction of some of its more important moments. After delivering a personal message from the President, drafted after his telephone conversation with Galtieri, the Secretary of State began to bring out his wares:

"We have prepared, Mr President," said Haig, "on the basis of a careful analysis of the positions of each of the parties and of the situation in London and Buenos Aires, a scheme containing seven principal points:

1. Withdrawal of Argentine troops and a halting of the British fleet.

2. The Argentine flag to remain on the islands, through a tripartite administration.

3. Considerable expansion of Argentina's role in the islands during the interim period.

4. Guarantee that negotiations for a long-term solution will be concluded before the end of the year.

5. I believe, Mr President, that we have the reluctant agreement of Mrs Thatcher to guide the process of negotiation according to the principles of de-colonization.

6. Normalization of communications between the continent and the islands.

7. Lifting of sanctions and a guarantee of American assistance during the whole procedure."

"In London," he continued, "I insisted that decisions should be taken by majority during the whole procedure, in order that the United States may be able to bring changes to the islands. Sincerely, I do not believe that either party can obtain all they desire, but we want to be sure of a successful solution," he concluded.

Galtieri showed interest, but emphasised that the Argentine Government had already made counter-offers and indicated that his Foreign Minister would be charged with negotiating the details. But he did not want to lose the opportunity of seeking clarification, as he had done with Reagan, though in a more direct form.

"There are things which certainly do not help," Galtieri began to complain. "My government received with displeasure the news of visa applications for Uruguay by all the officials of the American embassy here in Buenos Aires. We felt similarly about declarations by Secretary Weinberger of the support that the United States is prepared to lend Great Britain. I don't like it, Mr Haig, when American personnel ask for visas for Uruguay - personnel of the American embassy here. I don't know if this is a question of a summer holiday in Punta del Este (smiles).... but then there is the question of pressure from the United States. I don't understand it at all."

This was the consequence of the "Iran syndrome," but Haig prepared to ignore the problem, putting on a blank expression.

"You say they're American officials? That's terrible," feigned the Secretary of State.

"General, it was as if they had an instruction from Washington to prepare for the evacuation of the embassy." Galtieri guessed, correctly.

"But look, Mr President, remember what happened some time ago to the United States." (A presumed allusion to the case of the hostages in Iran.)

"I don't need to go back to the US to recognize that there are people of bad faith who are trying..." he said by way of a confused explanation, without finishing the sentence.

"No doubt, you identified it. We kept calm in a whole sector of government and we tried to keep the newspapers quiet too, as far as possible. We know that this is not the work of the American Government. But there are also the statements of the Secretary of Defense, Weinberger, which were not very encouraging," persisted Galtieri[12].

"Weinberger speaks without authority, Mr President. You know what President Reagan said," replied Haig. "We worked out what we were going to say very carefully and the British got very angry. I spoke with Mrs Thatcher by transatlantic telephone. There are people who don't understand that we have to maintain neutrality, balance. If a conflict comes, public opinion is going to push the United States towards Great Britain. This would be lamentable and we have to try to avoid it," warned the Secretary of State.

"We act from the best intentions in making every effort to seek a peaceful solution. But not for the reason you think. Not to do so would bring an explosion and separate America into two parts - above the Rio Grande and below it. Everyone is going to remember this, some more, some less. It will substantially worsen the world situation politically and strategically." Galtieri stated, in order to prove that he also could make veiled threats.

"We understand the problem," was the laconic reply of the Secretary of State.

"Look, General Haig, I am here all day. If anything comes up, while looking for a solution, Mr Secretary of State, don't hesitate to contact me. Although I hope that they do bring me solutions, not problems," the President hedged, resorting to humour.

"I want you to know, Mr President, that no-one in Washington, and particularly President Reagan, has the impression that people were intransigent here in Buenos Aires. On the contrary, there has been serious effort and good faith in trying to solve this problem," replied Haig, in the same conciliatory style.

The conversation turned to a possible solution and Haig told the President that in London there was no interest in any possible economic compensation - hitherto one of the major Argentine suggestions - or for that matter, future co-operation in the exploitation of the region's resources. Mrs Thatcher had been clear: one could not talk of money when principles were at stake.

At one moment in this conversation, Galtieri thought it opportune to return to the danger that an incident might be deliberately provoked inside the Exclusion Zone by a third country. Knowing the frame of mind of both conversants what other country could this be than the USSR?

Galtieri had already tried this with Reagan. In order to repeat it to Haig he took advantage of a naval report which said that the previous day an unidentified submarine had been detected in Falklands waters. The exchange went like this:

"The latest reply to American suggestions that we sent yesterday involves a mass of important things. Guarantees of rights and way of life; and guarantees of the personal financial interests of individuals wishing to remain on the islands, as well as for those wishing to leave. In the same way, we put forward matters concerning Britain's strategic interests as well as matters concerning the islands' population and economic interests. We've involved ourselves in a heap of things..." Galtieri confusedly summarized.

"I want to be sure, Mr President, that we all understand the British attitude. I know you are involved in other things, but I am now convinced that the attitude of Great Britain has nothing to do with economic interests. After years of occupation it is difficult for them to see only economic interests there," Haig said. He would have to confront that argument again on other occasions, notably when it came from Anaya, as we shall see later.

"Good!" Galtieri decided to change his tone. "What happened yesterday with my submarines?" he said, unexpectedly.

"I don't know," was Haig's startled reply.

It was on the same occasion that General Walters, who, as at previous times acted as translator, complied with what he understood to be the minimum rules of courtesy, and discreetly asked Galtieri's approval for the visit they were expecting to make to ex-President Arturo Frondizi, whom he met when accompanying Dwight Eisenhower on his official visit to Argentina during his period of office.

Galtieri did not of course make any objection. "It was a gesture I considered very elegant," recalled Walters afterwards. If the President had known the result of that courtesy visit by the American the following day to the head of the *Movimiento de Integracion y Desarrollo, (MID)*, he surely would have appeared less sympathetic. Walters and Frondizi spoke at length about the conflict and five days later the MID brought out the first document of an Argentine political party critical of the operation of April 2nd[13].

The brief meeting which took place that morning at the Casa Rosada was positively the last Haig had with the Argentines in which opinions were exchanged cordially and the atmosphere was quite agreeable. From then on, communication would become more complex with every hour; diplomatic warnings were transformed into virtual threats, the little mutual trust that remained evaporated, and both parties moved steadily along the road to breakdown. On only one further occasion did one glimpse something like agreement.

Having thus laid out the offer from the US Secretary of State, it is appropriate to include details of the Argentine position - a counter-proposal to the American's which was in his hands hours before his arrival in Buenos Aires. This is included as a record of the basic scheme approved by the Military Committee during their meeting of the night of Wednesday 14th. The authors had access to a copy of this document from which, inexplicably, point 8 had been omitted. With that proviso it is reproduced below. The text began:

"On the basis of Resolution 502 of the Security Council of the UN and the desire of the Argentine Republic (AR) and the United Kingdom (UK) to resolve the dispute that has emerged between them and renouncing the use of force, both governments agree:

1. An immediate cessation of hostilities.

2. As from..... hours of day..... the Argentine Republic and the United Kingdom will proceed to withdraw all naval units from the zone surrounding the Falkland Islands, South Georgia and the South Sandwich Islands (in the drafts of the agreement these names were translated into geographical coordinates). Within seven days from the date of the present agreement, the Argentine Republic will have withdrawn half its military forces from the islands to the continent and the UK will have withdrawn its naval units to a distance of not less than 3000 nautical miles from the islands.

Within 15 days from the date of the present agreement, the Argentine Republic and the UK will have withdrawn the whole of their units to their usual operational air bases.

3. The British Government will adopt measures necessary with respect to the Falkland Islands, South Georgia and the South Sandwich Islands to complete the decolonization of the same by 31st December 1982 in accordance with Resolutions 1514 (XV), 2065 (XX), 3160 (XXVIII) and 31/49, and others applicable to this case, of the General Assembly of the United Nations.

4. As from the date of this present accord, no military force will be introduced into the islands, nor the surrounding zone which will remain demilitarized until December 31st 1982.

5. The rights and guarantees that the inhabitants of the islands have enjoyed until now will be respected, especially those which concern freedom of religion, expression, education and movement; their property rights, sources of work, customs, life-style and traditional family, social and cultural ties with their country of origin."

6. The AR will be disposed to pay a just price for the properties of persons or companies not wishing to continue their activities in the Falkland Islands, South Georgia etc, thus giving compensation to those wishing to emigrate.

7. During the transition period that terminates on December 31st 1982, the administration of the islands will be as follows:

(a) The Governor will be appointed by the Argentine Government.

(b) The local administration, with the exception of the police force, will be retained. The Executive and Legislative Councils will also be retained, but will be broadened with the aim of including an equal number of members appointed by the Argentine Government. The said members will be selected preferably from the Argentine residents in the islands.

(c) The Governor will appoint the members of the police force who will include all the local members of the said force that were in service prior to April 2nd. The police will be under the authority of the Governor.

(d) Argentines from the continent and the inhabitants of the islands will enjoy equal rights and obligations.

(e) The Argentine flag will continue to fly over the islands.

9. Travel, transport, communications and all commerce between continental Argentina and the islands will be facilitated and promoted. As from the date of the present agreement all economic and financial measures related to the present dispute, including those relating to travel, transport, communications and transfer of funds between the two countries, will be annulled.

In the same way, the UK will ask third countries which have adopted similar measures to annul them also immediately.

10. A group composed of an equal number of representatives of Argentina, the United States and the UK will verify the carrying out of the terms of the present agreement.

11. The Government of the United States of America will guarantee the application of the present agreement."

Regarding point 8 (and in view of the order followed in the drafts of agreement that were drawn up on the basis of this scheme) it is worth mentioning that it was concerned with the establishment of a method of taking into consideration "the interests" of the islanders and the agreements that would have to be worked out to co-operate in the exploitation of natural resources.

The negotiations proceeded throughout the whole of that day in two sessions, being held up a few times in details that could seem to an unwary observer mere trivialities. On some matters, things seemed close, but practically each such position was achieved only when the discussion seemed on the point of collapse - and then not without Costa Mendez consulting Galtieri by telephone and Haig doing the same with Pym in London. Haig believed it appropriate on more than one occasion to warn that he was ready to call a halt to the whole procedure.

In the late afternoon, the Secretary of State made it clear that it would be necessary, if the negotiations were to continue at all, to have more flexibility from Argentina. This meant new consultations and at 7 pm Costa Mendez left the Palacio San Martin by a side entrance and made for the Casa Rosada, where he was awaited by Galtieri, Lami Dozo and Anaya.

The core of the question concerned a number of important matters on which London was continuing to make the following demands:

1. The "observers" that Argentina was proposing had to be truly only an interim tripartite authority. Argentine government could not be permitted to subsist there. Buenos Aires, in its turn, did not wish to have its role reduced in the interim period, if precise guarantees were not to be forthcoming of acquiring sovereignty after the interim.

2. The Island Councils, the traditional governing institutions, would have to be resurrected. Although London could accept the viability of an Argentine participation in them, it could not accept that this latter participation could be numerically similar to that of the *kelpers*. These institutions would be the voice of the local people in the first stage of the negotiations.

3. In these negotiations, it would have to be accepted that the "wishes and interests" of the islanders should be taken into account. (The first part of this formula was unacceptable to the Argentines, because it implied a renunciation of what had been achieved in the matter during the years of diplomatic battle in the UN.)

4. This last requirement had to be set out in the agreements reached, by means of the promise to carry out a sounding of the wishes of the islanders, according to the method duly determined by the interim authority.

The deliberations of the Military Committee that night of the 16th were tense as they tried to find formulas for rapprochement. Galtieri found himself in the crossfire again. The spreadshot coming from Anaya showed him to be opposed to any concession. He said that Haig was acting like an "advocate for the English" and that his threats were mere boasts that the American Government could not carry out. On the other side was the calculating pressure of Lami Dozo.

Moreover, the President then began to receive signals of unrest from his own backyard. The generals that he had sounded out, omitting anyone who might be a potential rival, were worried by the course of events and now did not hide it. Some of them were alarmed, not so much by the prospect of an armed confrontation as by the possibility of a total break with the United States. It was ironic that the same generals who had raved about the benefits of a "special relationship" with Washington, conceding even the possible costs of covert incursions into Central America, now threatened to become highly critical of such a relationship if ever cracks threatened to materialize within it.

From that meeting hardly any room for manoeuvre remained within which Haig's mediation could survive to another day. Argentina accepted the establishment of an interim government and the undertaking of further negotiations with American assistance. But it required that this be done within a framework that guaranteed the final acquisition of sovereignty and that Great Britain renounce the supremacy of the islanders' wishes. On these matters no compromise would be possible.

Costa Mendez went that same evening to the Sheraton Hotel where he apprised Haig of the changes in the position. The Secretary of State insisted that they were insufficient and advanced the need for him to be allowed to explain the situation at the centre of power, that is, to the Junta itself. He explained that he wanted to put to them the risks of failure in the talks.

And the Argentines acceded to his request. In the mid-morning, Galtieri, Anaya and Lami Dozo received Reagan's envoy at the Casa Rosada. It was this meeting, all witnesses agree, that was the true turning point and which sealed the fate of the drama, even though it continued for a few more days. If the mutual animosity had been latent up till then, cropping up only in some conversations, this time it was evident. American sources, moreover, agree in pointing out that the vicissitudes of that interview shattered any vestige of sympathy that they had been able to gain in the eyes of the rulers in Buenos Aires. For the Argentines in their turn, this would mark the beginning of the end of their "Western and Christian" fantasy, to characterize it with the same labels that they thought up themselves.

The discussion was tense, particularly during Anaya's contribution, and spare in its formulation by both parties. At one moment Haig complained of press leaks that stated that the Junta considered him to be pro-British. If he was expecting a diplomatic denial he was mistaken. Anaya set the tone of the conversation: "Those reports reflect a reality," he snapped.

The Secretary of State chose to return to arguing against the alternative of a war. He emphasized British military power and Thatcher's determination. Anaya again intervened with an exaggerated and unfortunate affirmation, as was to be seen afterwards:

"The Argentines are as determined as Mrs Thatcher. We have our courage and our blood to offer," the Admiral claimed. "I myself have a son among the troops and as a father I can assure you that it would be an honour to contribute his life confronting the colonial aggressor," he added, searching for a deliberately dramatic climax.

"I understand you, Admiral, but I also know that you can say that because you have never had the experience of seeing corpses coming back from the front in plastic bags." Haig replied.

Time would show the admiral the futility of appealing to grandiloquent rhetoric. A day after the surrender of Port Stanley, in General Walters' presence, he made an attempt by telephone to hasten the liberation of his son, an aviation lieutenant in the army, taken prisoner by the British.

Even in the requests which the protagonists made for conciliation it remained evident that that was almost impossible because there was no common language. Once more Anaya and Haig would be the ones to condemn this breach. In one moment of the conversation the Navy Commandant rose from his chair, while Haig was expounding to the members of the Junta some points of a memorandum assisted by Walters' translation.

Anaya approached Haig and interrupted him. Turning to Walters, he said:

"Explain to the Secretary of State that I understand the problem that confronts us perfectly well. The English are pressurising him because they want the Falklands oil. They must know that that cannot be an obstacle to peace. We are willing to find a formula in order that they can participate in this resource."

Haig's reply was not slow to come and was short: "I don't think the oil is important in present circumstances. The British, Admiral, are in this for the same as you. For the honour."

On seeing the way the exchange was going, Haig did not hesitate to employ all his ammunition. He did it with unusual awkwardness and thus the meeting came to a climax. If the situation was prolonged, the American stated, Argentina would have to confront the British military force. In this case Reagan's government would have no alternative but to support London, as the greater part of public opinion was loudly calling him to do. For Washington then, there would be no alternative but to follow the example given by the remaining members of NATO.

For Buenos Aires that would mean having to face a formidable adversary. To avoid such a battle, the American argued, NATO would have to do everything it could, even if it meant compromising the stability of the present Argentine regime. This was a threat, rather more than implied, and unacceptable for any government that maintained any self-esteem.

The meeting stalled an hour and a half after having started. The much-desired rapprochement was without doubt further away than before. Costa Mendez took advantage of the lunch which followed in his private residence in Coronel Diaz y Zenteno to try to unwind, but he did not have much success.

During that meeting, at which Miret, Moya and Iglesias were also present, the Secretary of State had not wanted to depart from his chosen line of argument. Thus, in the familiar atmosphere of the living room of his home, which featured an impressive library of predominantly English books, the Foreign Minister again heard from his foreign guest ominous forebodings about the future of the military administration.

The negotiations continued until the early hours without producing any substantial change of positions. No rest was possible and all the players in the drama tediously continued with their presentations into the Sunday. The only concession to that reality was when Haig played tennis at the residence of Ambassador Schlaudermann.

As a way of moving things along, the negotiators decided to give a separate push to those points on which differences had been reduced. For this reason Vice Admiral Leopoldo Suarez, Chief of the Joint Staff, was summoned to the discussions that Sunday, with the aim of agreeing the details of the military withdrawal.

Galtieri, for his part, showed how apprehension at the course of events had grown among the generals - by presiding over a meeting of senior officers. But in fact, the exceptional circumstances, more than the concerns of dissidents, prevented them from marshaling their criticisms. If, under normal conditions, the heirarchical organization of the Military obstructs internal control in the process of decision making, in a crisis it acquires overwhelming powers. In other systems of social organization, above all in the democracies, that control is assumed by the civil authority. But in the Argentina of 1982 that possibility was completely denied to its citizens.

Symbolic of the uncertainty in which the discussions took place were the contradictions which the Americans displayed each time they were asked about their plans. Haig on various occasions said that he had not decided what would be his next destination, nor when he would be leaving. On Sunday, the envoy's plane was prepared for departure, but afterwards some members of the team were seen changing dollars into Argentine currency in the *bureau de change* in the Sheraton, which seemed to argue against an imminent departure.

Discussions had not taken place in the Foreign Ministry at all that day, but took place instead at the Casa Rosada which was one more sign that the American had put on pressure at the centre of power, imposing on Costa Mendez ever more frequent consultations with Galtieri, and for Galtieri, himself, consultations with the Military Junta. Strictly speaking it is true to say that these conditions bore fruit on the Sunday night.

At 9.30 pm, Galtieri received the American envoy to talk to him for the last time. On that occasion a draft of a new Argentine proposal was delivered to Haig that in truth did contain some substantial concessions by comparison to the Junta's original position. The President-Commandant wanted to make it clear that in participating personally this text represented the bottom line as far as Argentine aspirations went. There could be no further retreat.

By this new document, Argentina accepted:

1. The Special Interim Authority in the terms London had originally demanded.

2. The restoration on the islands of an administration very similar to the original one, broadened to include Argentines, but with a reduced participation by these in respect to the original demand.

3. On mention of a "definitive solution" in the negotiations (according to Chapter XI of the UN Charter[14]), it is specified that this must take account of the *rights* of the inhabitants. To balance this concession, mention was also to be made of the commitment to respect the "principle of territorial integrity."

4. While still insisting on December 31st, 1982 as the final date for reaching an agreement, this draft did not contain a clause about any compulsory transfer of sovereignty.

This seemed a substantial advance. Galtieri proposed it to Haig, but the latter said he was not sure that the new Argentine approach would manage to satisfy London. The situation was still very dangerous.

The Argentine, who resented the threats, almost had an emotional outburst - "Look, Mr Haig You are like me, a general, and know what the first obligation of a general is when he is encircled: it is to break that circle. I ask you, please, not to fence me in, because I am likely to smash anything getting out of that circle". The word *anything* was of special significance; it could be nothing other than an allusion to the Soviet Union. It was an option Galtieri finished outlining hours beforehand to the army commanders: "The United States allied itself with the Soviet Union during the Second World War without selling her soul to the devil," he said to his generals.

Nevertheless, Galtieri was mistaken: what he ended up presenting to the American was not an unalterable position. That same night the Junta, in a meeting which lasted until the early hours, introduced a new and fundamental change on whose behalf, Anaya brought all his influence. After an agitated debate, the proposal was made to include a final clause:

"As from December 31st 1982, and until such time as the agreement on the final status comes into force, the leadership of the government and administration will be exercised by an official appointed by the Argentine Government."

This news was like a bucket of cold water not only on the spirits of the mediator, who was notified the following morning, but on more than one of the Argentine negotiators too. On learning of it, the reaction of one of them served to give a permanent nickname to the proposal: "But what are they after now with this mad clause?" he asked an official at the Palacio San Martin, in the presence of another colleague.

News of the "mad clause" was not the only disturbing thing that Costa Mendez conveyed to Haig on the morning of Monday 19th. The progress of the British Task Force, the bulk of which had reached Ascension Island, obliged Argentina to ask for a consultative meeting of the IATRA to be called.

The American replied, saying that things were going back to "square nought" and announced his immediate return to Washington. From that moment public opinion began to show signs of the march of events: during the morning and part of the afternoon, the turbines of the Secretary of State's aircraft were alternately started and stopped, several times.

Haig demanded one last effort of Costa Mendez with the Military Junta in order that at least the coercive condition might be eliminated. The Foreign Minister, although he could not declare it explicitly to his colleague, agreed that coercion was inappropriate. But he could only agree, without much hope, to make an attempt.

A little after 5 pm the Secretary of State read, in an admonitory tone, a brief statement that reflected the drama of the moment. "I am more convinced than ever," his conclusion said, "that war in the South Atlantic would be the greatest of tragedies and that in fact time is running out."

The cold and drizzle was a depressing influence on Buenos Aires at that moment and contributed to the dismal scene. Costa Mendez took his colleague by the arm and whilst they both slowly and deliberately covered the tarmac to the aircraft steps, he gave him the latest news. Haig's face became tenser still.

There would be no revision of the final clause of the proposal, he told him. Moreover, in the next few hours, Buenos Aires would ask for a meeting of American Foreign Ministers within the framework of the Rio Pact. Haig briefly tried a new argument against this last option: "Don't do it," he asked Costa Mendez. He claimed to know that "something is going to happen in Central America." There were, according to the Secretary of State, signs of an imminent armed action by Nicaragua against Honduras. If the two problems exploded in the OAS at the same time, it would be equivalent to a catastrophe.

In fact the American was mistaken in at least two of his assessments that afternoon: there was no Nicaraguan aggression and the time had already run out - at least the time for his attempts at negotiating. The "greatest of tragedies" was already at hand.

NOTES

1. *The Crisis of the South Atlantic: Antecedents, Consequences, Documentation*. Thomas Enders, Joint Secretary of State for Inter-American Affairs, Sub-Committee of Inter-American Affairs in the House of Representatives of the United States, Washington, DC. August 5th, 1982. p 6.

2. According to a source consulted by the authors in the United States, the possibility of the gendarmerie replacing troops of the armed forces in the archipelago was a point of dispute. The Americans considered the gendarmerie as "paramilitary forces" and consequently

with "excessive combat capability." This characteristic was contrary to the original withdrawal proposals.

3. The Haig mission constituted the only part of the multiple negotiations which were held in order to avoid the war - which finally did take place - in which London was disposed to a solution including South Georgia and the South Sandwich Islands. The British themselves had facilitated this part of the Argentine demands by having changed those two archipelagoes into dependencies of the Falklands for administrative reasons. Once the Secretary of State's effort failed, the British Government revised this original concept and in both the initiative by Belauade Terry and that of the Secretary-General of the UN, Perez de Cuellar, refused to consider any Argentine claims for sovereignty over South Georgia and the South Sandwich Islands, further increasing the distance between the positions of the parties. See Enders op.cit.

4. Chapter XII of the Charter of the United Nations deals with an "International Trusteeship System," and its Article 75 "establishes under its authority an international regimen of trustee administration for the administration and overseeing of territories which can be placed under the said regimen in virtue of special subsequent agreements. The said territories will be named "trust territories". The following article states that among the objectives of this regimen is that of "promoting the political, economic and educational advancement of the inhabitants of the trust territories, and their progressive development towards self-government or independence as may be appropriate to the particular circumstances of each territory and its peoples and the freely expressed wishes of the people concerned, and as may be provided by the terms of each trusteeship agreement."

5. In the middle forties, when Juan Domingo Peron was preparing for his accession to power and the social revolution was being carried out in Argentina, the then American ambassador in Buenos Aires, Spruille Braden, embarked on a political and personal crusade against the young colonel. Without the least embarrassment, and violating virtually every one of the forms and standards of practical diplomacy, he joined the established political parties in opposing the new phenomenon. On moving to Washington to occupy himself in Inter-American affairs at the State Department, he had the rather unfortunate idea of giving publicity to a certain dossier shortly before the elections which gave Peron the Presidency. The dossier was intended to prove the fascist ideology of the Argentine military leader and his connections with the defeated Nazism of Germany. The followers of Peron transformed this accusation into a weapon of publicity, manufacturing the slogan "Braden or Peron." According to the opinion of several historians, this American action was one of the determining factors in the

electoral triumph which Peron achieved that year (1946).

Since then there were many Argentine military rulers who, openly or secretly, often cherished the fantasy of repeating this phenomenon each time they confronted one of the frequent crises between Argentina and the United States. The last of these was the first President of the *Process of National Reorganization*, Jorge Rafael Videla. In 1977, while Argentina was continually being hounded as a result of the covert repression, he speculated in public with the new choice: "Carter or Videla."

6. *The Battle for the Falklands* Max Hastings and Simon Jenkins, Michael Joseph, London 1983, p 110.

7. Rear Admiral Moya went into retirement at the end of 1982 as a consequence of a public argument in which he virtually stated those who criticized the political and military conduct of the war with Great Britain were traitors. At the end of his military career he was in agreement with the argument used by Galtieri, whom he advised throughout. The argument was set out in his last speech on June 15th. Moya agreed with the view of the conflict that Galtieri always maintained.

8. *How the British Think*, survey by Market and Opinion Research International (MORI) published by *The Economist*, April 17th 1982, p 23.

9. "The Principle." *The Economist*, op.cit. p 15.

10. This conversation took place by telephone with the "scrambler," which jumbles words into unintelligible sounds and then reassembles them at the other end of the line for security purposes. In this way each one of the conversants must wait patiently until the other has finished before speaking himself. This is the reason for using the radio term "over" at the end of each contribution.

11. "Jaw-jaw continues as war-war approaches." *The Economist*, April 24th 1982, p 24.

12. The opinions of Weinberger, who, moreover, made his own effort with Haig in the Reagan administration, would be one of the much disputed points concerning those days. Even after the ending of the Haig mission, the Secretary of Defense took the lead in another episode which contributed to a further worsening in the relationship between the two countries at that delicate moment.

On May 5th a news release carrying the letterhead of the Assistant Secretary of State for Public Affairs in the Defense Department - entitled: *Comments by Secretary of State, Caspar Weinberger, on the support for Great Britain* and numbered 217-282 attributed to him, among others, the following assessments:

"The time has now arrived when Washington cannot now look

upon the present conflict between Argentina and Great Britain like a 19th Century comedy. The United States has found itself in an unenviable position, but is not incapable of resolving this complicated situation. We are confronting the problem of complying with our obligations as allies to Great Britain as much as to those we have towards Argentina within the framework of the OAS. From the beginning of the shuttle diplomacy of Secretary of State Haig, I took the position that that mission could not contribute to maintaining our policy by means of a diplomatic settlement of the conflict. According to my opinion, the conflict between Argentina and Great Britain could have a negative impact on the role of the US as leading country in NATO and we are very conscious of that. From that point of view I defended the giving of all our military assistance and all our support to our British ally."

That text also alluded to the "stubborn and selfish attitude of Argentina," and to the necessity of "preserving the unity of NATO" and even made references that could be interpreted as an American incursion into Great Britain's internal affairs. According to a copy of the *Foreign Affairs Note*, one of the State Department publications dated Washington, April 1983, the news release was the product of "a manoeuvre of Soviet falsification and disinformation." This was a conclusion extracted from presumed incorrect idiomatic expressions and from the argument that the serial number of the document corresponded to information concerning contracts awarded by the Defense Communications Agency. The Americans maintain that the assumed comments by Weinberger were not intended for publication - copies would not have been circulated to members of the diplomatic corps - but included in cables that embassies sent to their foreign ministries. The curious thing is that the content of the news release was not too different from the real thinking of Weinberger on the problem.

13. The declaration of the MID fell like a bucket of cold water on the military authorities because it posed disquieting questions. "It is false," it said in one of its paragraphs, "that when there is an international conflict one has to be quiet about the anomalies in government that have put that action in motion, and even stirred up the trouble.... our initial misgivings have grown with the events that followed the early enthusiasm. There are questions which only by being posed can shed light on the political decision taken to put the operation into effect and to conduct the diplomatic negotiations. If the Government does not put them to itself, it is necessary to do it now, in order that we may find a better way forward.

Did they evaluate the relationship of international forces, not only military but also political and diplomatic? Did they evaluate the economic and social consequences of the conflict, not only the cost of the operation, but also in regard to reprisals and similar measures of other countries? Was the debilitating effect on the country of the economic crisis in which we found ourselves considered? Did they reflect on the risks of breaking the coherence of the strategic position of the country within the Western camp and the tactics regarding the conflict? Did one take into account that there are Argentines who think that territorial sovereignty has the counter-weight of a growing loss of our economic and political sovereignty in virtue of the programme that has been applied since 1976? [When the Military took over from Isabel Peron.]

14. Chapter XI of the UN Charter consists of the "Declaration concerning non-autonomous territories" and is composed of two articles:

Article 73 refers to the obligation of those countries which are signatories to the Charter who "assume responsibilities for the administration of territories whose peoples have not yet attained a full measure of self-government," to recognize "the principle that the interests of the inhabitants of these territories are paramount," assuring their "well-being.....the due respect for the culture of the peoples concerned, their political, economic, social and educational advancement; the development of "self-government, to take due account of the political aspirations of the peoples;" the promotion of "international peace and security;" the promotion of "constructive measures of development," and the transmission to the Secretary-General of the UN of "statistical and other information of a technical nature relating to economic, social and educational conditions in the territories."

Article 74 establishes that "the members of the UN also agree that their policy in respect of the territories to which this Chapter applies, no less than in respect of their metropolitan areas, must be based on the general principle of good neighbourliness, due account being taken of the interests and well-being of the rest of the world, in social, economic and commercial matters."

Chapter 9

THE END OF THE FANTASY

It is not an exaggeration to say that the overall result of Alexander Haig's second journey to Buenos Aires was to produce "several crises inside a crisis," - as one American source close to the Secretary of State's mission recalled. And the description applies to what happened in Buenos Aires, London and Washington too. In order to understand later developments it is necessary to examine these events.

For the Argentine Military Government, the possibility that the United States would place a protective umbrella over their action in the Falklands was fading. This had been fervently desired by Costa Mendez in particular and was now disappearing over the horizon like the immature fantasy it had been. This process was directly proportional in form and speed to the rate at which the British fleet was closing in upon the Falklands from Ascension Island.

To say that there were men in the hierarchy who were confused by the course of events was an understatement. The same military officers and civilian officials who scarcely ten days before had rejected any anxiety by the reporters over the approach of the British, were perplexed. Theirs had been the off-hand: "No reason for alarm! The fleet is moving at diplomatic speed; in fact it's not thinking of reaching here." These same officers shunned any contact now.

Almost all the signs foretold new problems and of major gravity too. The Junta needed only a few hours after Haig's departure to grasp that the mediation was collapsing. That same Monday 19th, Haig, on board his aircraft on his return home, wrote to his Argentine colleague:

"Dear Nicanor:
1. I have the first British reaction to the paper drafted in Buenos Aires. It is a disappointment. London, of course, concedes that it is worth

185

careful study, but it finds the basis for a mutual withdrawal very inequitable.

2. The question of sovereignty is stated too explicitly, and it finds that the wishes of the islanders have not been taken into account sufficiently.

3. London will issue a press release, placing emphasis on the failure to consider the wishes of the islanders as paramount, but it has not closed the door.

4. Tomorrow I shall be in a better position to advise you, but I would urge you to pass on this first reaction to your colleagues in the Government.

5. It is clear to me that a substantial mutual adjustment of position will have to be made if war is to be avoided. When I have seen the British proposal in detail I shall get into contact again concerning future steps.

Warm regards. Al Haig. April 19, 1982[1]."

Nevertheless, there is evidence that one of the members of the Junta conceived the idea, though in no very clear way, of introducing a new "substantial adjustment." But any notion of Lami Dozo's in this direction was to be shattered against the intransigence of Anaya and his deep resentment with his formerly much admired colleagues from the north who had launched Galtieri in the first place. Evidence in the newspapers at the time indicates that the air force chief actually expressed the anxieties of his senior officers when they began to detect that a clash with Washington, at least a political one, was coming very close.

This argument was nourished more by the fondness the Argentine Military used to feel for everything American - though the same feeling had rarely been reciprocated - than by any urgency to avoid war. This, however, was now beginning to assume concrete form in Buenos Aires. Moreover, Anaya had already passed the point of no return. Accordingly, he discovered a new argument: "Haig is playing for time so that the English can get their fleet in position. One must not," he argued, "let oneself get trapped by this delaying tactic. On the contrary, one has to reach out immediately for any resort that is open."

And that resort was Latin America. It was that same part of the American Hemisphere that the *Process of National Reorganisation* had watched over and tried to manipulate sometimes with systematic contempt, when not grossly interfering in the internal affairs of its constituent countries. Thus the basic principle of solidarity was ignored, whether for excessive ambition, as with Bolivia,[2] or on behalf of the interests of third parties, as in the case of Central America.

It was within this framework that the Foreign Minister chose to try to gain time for the American peace effort. He maintained to his chiefs that it should still be possible to find some opening; there was nothing to be got from an early breakdown. The final decision was, as often happens in these cases, a compromise. The clumsy attitude of the Reagan administration was not imitated, but new diplomatic pressure points were opened up. Until this moment, these had been kept in reserve in the secret hope that they would never have to be used. This was so, not only in the case of Latin American relations, but also those within the Movement of the Non-Aligned Countries.

For his part, Haig returned to Washington to confront his own domestic front - which was thoroughly disturbed. On landing at Andrews Air Force Base, he had completed 32,965 miles in twelve days - a new record for shuttle diplomacy. But unlike Kissinger, he could not show results. The bulk of conservatives, as well as the majority of liberals, expressed open criticism of the Secretary of State. Worse still, because of his admitted failure in the South Atlantic question, they began likewise to judge the whole of his performance in government.

During his absence, newspapers and magazines had pictured Haig trying to restrain the infuriated British lion, while protecting with his body a swarthy military officer with a heavy moustache, adorned with innumerable decorations and an enormous sword. This last figure was the stereotype of the banana republic dictator which Galtieri and his colleagues evoked in American public opinion. Indeed, an opinion poll conducted at the end of April would produce a crushing result: 60 per cent of Americans consulted declared themselves in favour of Great Britain and scarcely 19 per cent expressed some sympathy for Argentina[3]. Even the influential *New York Times* in one of its editorials advised in a tone half-mocking and half-paternal: "Al Haig, stay home."

Everything then pointed to the likelihood that the Republican Government would not be able to delay a decision to support London much longer, if it did not want to pay a political price for its ambiguity on the question. In a short essay, an American investigator described the circumstances that brought his compatriots, whether conservative or liberal, to demand Washington's support for the British. He concluded that everyone in his own way opposed Haig's conduct to some degree: "One heard conservatives expressing consternation that the Secretary of State had abruptly changed sides instead of quietly returning from the fruitless negotiations. This would have permitted the Reagan administration to announce its decision at a later date. Many liberals felt that

187

given that support for Britain was inevitable from the beginning, Haig was mistaken to offer his good offices at all. As a result of this, the wish of the United States to postpone support for Great Britain simply encouraged the hard-liners in Argentina to hold to their position, so delaying any agreement."[4] Moreover, the Secretary of State discovered that this wealth of criticism finished the working relationship he had with some of his colleagues. He learned that the American ambassador to the UN, Jeane Kirkpatrick, was rapidly becoming a sort of political arch-enemy. She had taken the liberty of activating parallel channels of communication, another way of betting on the failure of the mediation.

Kirkpatrick, kept deliberately on the side-lines during the mediation by Haig himself, chose to work out an alternative approach with her British colleague, Anthony Parsons, her Argentine colleague, Eduardo Roca, and the Secretary-General of the UN, Javier Perez de Cuellar. In this she took advantage of her influential personal situation. Besides enjoying the confidence and ear of Reagan - which has already been mentioned - Kirkpatrick was not simply an ambassador. Her responsibilities included a seat in Reagan's cabinet, which in some ways put her on the same level as the Secretary of State. As if this were not enough, something had also materialised which would later become a solid political alliance of this influential official with the President's National Security Adviser, William Clark.

With this initiative coming from the White House, Perez de Cuellar appointed one of his assistants, the Pakistani, Rafee Ahmed, to set up and put to work a team intended to compile the relevant documentation and study the development of the conflict. This was in mid-April and was done with a view to a possible intervention by the Secretary-General.

The concern of the Secretary-General of the UN was reiterated in an informal note of April 17 1982, which was delivered to the delegations of both countries in the conflict, but produced no immediate reaction. In this, Perez de Cuellar indicated his conviction that "the timely application of Resolution 502 will bring a rapid reduction in the tensions in the area [of the South Atlantic]."

The Peruvian diplomat put on record that nothing should interfere with the American Secretary of State's mission, but also that, "at the same time, it is incumbent upon the Secretary-General to concern himself directly with the development of the situation that provoked the action that the Security Council has taken. This is in accordance with his responsibilities for the maintenance of peace and international security."

In the same note he suggested that "it would be possible to employ an appropriate UN presence for any of the following purposes, or for a continuation of the same:

"Observe, verify and certify the withdrawal, as may be agreed, of armed forces from the area.

"Observe, verify and certify the withdrawal, complete or partial, as may be agreed, of civilian and administrative personnel.

"Observe, verify and certify the continued observance in a specific period of the above mentioned arrangements.

"Observe, verify and certify the application of the administrative arrangements which may be agreed upon.

"Provide the cover of the United Nations for these administrative arrangements.

"Provide a temporary UN administration."

The informal note also speculated on some details of the probable participation of the UN, although recognising that this would be conditioned by the "nature of the accord achieved by the two parties." He added that: "When the mandate of the said UN presence has been determined, the establishment of the said presence could follow, *mutatis mutandis*, the usual guide-lines of the Security Council, including the responsibility of the Secretary-General for assuring the integrity, impartiality and efficiency of a participation of this type by the UN."

This participation of the international organization had been part of the baggage that the American mediator carried in his role as travelling peace salesman to London and Buenos Aires. But in the Secretary of State's scheme of things, the assistance of the UN would only be sought when the agreement had effectively been achieved, and not before. Haig was decided that no one should divest him, even partially, of the credit that would attend his triumph.

As if this were not enough, the contacts that he maintained with his British counterpart left little room for optimism. Pym struggled in Thatcher's Cabinet to make the case for the continuation of the American intervention only to earn the disgust of some of his colleagues, the anger of the military High Command and the suspicion of the Prime Minister. More mistrust still was provoked in the mind of Margaret Thatcher by the equivocal behaviour of the Foreign Secretary: in the intimacy of Cabinet debates Pym expressed dove-like arguments, while before the press or Parliament he did not hesitate to appear as a hawk. Thatcher believed she could see in these tactics traces of an attempt to replace her as head of the Government.

The members of the so-called War Cabinet saw in the efforts to prolong Washington's intervention, the veiled intention of blocking the operation to recover South Georgia - a decision that had already been adopted - for which purpose some units of the Task Force had been ordered to separate and head for that objective. The general climate in Great Britain was, moreover, distinctly bellicose. The London newspapers spelt out war in every headline, for example, *The Express*, which demanded: "No To Surrender," or the *Daily Star*, which proclaimed: "Let's End the War of Politics."

Nor could the Opposition divorce itself from this trend. The Labour Leader, Michael Foot, momentarily appeared to abandon his advocacy of the diplomatic path - his demands for more activity in the UN and more time for negotiations. He joined the band-wagon for whom the conflict already appeared inevitable. He even agreed to discipline three of his fellow-Parliamentarians, Tam Dalyell, John Tilley and Andrew Faulds: implacable critics of Margaret Thatcher. All of them were relieved of their duties as spokesmen of the Labour Shadow Cabinet in the fields of Science, Home Affairs and the Arts.[5] It was clear that there was no room for dissidents.

Still less was there any acceptance in London for a public defence of American disengagement which was being viewed with frank suspicion. Together with a war fever with which some of the papers chose to fill their pages, the British press began to make swipes at Haig. The newspapers gave so much emphasis to these two stories that 10 Downing Street at one point discreetly asked the editors to "take into account the risks that the British fleet is running.[6]"

There was little Pym could achieve in such fierce rapids - a grudging agreement allowed him to go to Washington to submit the differences between the parties to a new process of rapprochement as a final attempt at a solution. However, at least one newspaper, the *Daily Telegraph*, did find it reasonable that the Foreign Secretary should travel there - "rather than expect Mr Haig to add another leg to his already marathon journey across the time zones.[7]"

According to those who know him, Haig is a man who does not easily tolerate contradiction, still less when this occurs in public. For that reason, and because he had invested too much of his own political capital in the mission for it to end in a notorious failure, he persisted with his objective. On Wednesday 21st he sent a new message to Costa Mendez reassuring him about the continuation of his mission.

After the now routine, but to Argentine eyes absurdly intimate, greeting: "Dear Nicanor," Haig said:

"As you know, Pym will come here [to Washington] on Thursday and Friday to hold discussions on the document worked out in Buenos Aires which, contrary to newspaper reports from London, has not been rejected."

"Pym will send us his amendments in advance," he added.

"I have urged him to reduce these to an absolute minimum, in view of what we have all been through," he revealed to Costa Mendez.

He also included a plea for trust in him from Buenos Aires: "I now believe myself to be completely aware of the Argentine anxieties and I shall be able to respect these entirely in our discussions. Some modification to the document from Buenos Aires is inevitable," he reiterated in continuation of his advice, but he was still of the belief that it was the right framework in which to continue searching for a solution.

The Argentines supposed that given the picture, IATRA would put pressure on the British, through the United States. This was the veiled threat that Galtieri had hinted at to Haig of "dividing the continent, above and below the Rio Grande." In this calculation, as in many others at the time, they mistakenly encouraged undue expectations. If Latin American solidarity were to function effectively it would be because history and common interests imposed their own dynamic and because the military power had been conscious of it.

Paradoxically, some lessons were learnt in the wake of the experience. One such emerged from the fact that the Junta had had to ask for the support of the Sandinista Government of Nicaragua at that stage of diplomacy, against whom only months before, it had been willing to invoke the provisions of the same treaty concerning "Hemispheric security," in order to please the Americans. Perhaps, when that last case had arisen, the IATRA might have functioned efficiently, because it concerned an instrument conceived to protect the interests of the ideological model Washington proposes. But the case of the Falklands, far from the intentions of those who originated the treaty, was a case of anti-colonial struggle, a characteristic destined to enter into collision with the essence of the treaty itself.

The characteristics of IATRA are nothing if not the classic product of an international re-structuring during the post-war period and it is hence bound to reflect the new antagonisms and hegemonies that manifested themselves. Since its inception during a conference of Foreign Ministers of the Americas held in Rio de Janeiro in 1947, it has become one of the most useful instruments of United States foreign policy. The USA positively conferred on it the unacknowledged title of *anti-Soviet pact*. Its support of the Americans during the missile crisis of 1962 and, two years later, its promotion of sanctions against the Cuban socialist regime are eloquent proofs of such.

The security zone defined in Article 4 of IATRA explicitly includes the archipelagoes of the Falklands, South Georgia and the South Sandwich Islands. At the time, their inclusion constituted a diplomatic triumph for the Argentine delegation at the Rio Conference. This delegation was headed by the Peronist Foreign Minister, Luis Atilio

Bramuglia.

The essence of the Rio Pact is contained in its third Article, which states:

"The High Contracting Parties agree that an armed attack by any State against a State Party shall be considered an attack against all the State Parties and consequently, each of them undertakes to assist in meeting any such attack in the exercise of the inherent right of individual or collective self-defence recognized by Article 51 of the Charter of the UN.[8]"

This solidarity is made subject to a decision of the Organ of Consultation (Article 3, Clause 2) - that is, the Committee of Foreign Ministers of the signatory American countries[9], although a certain margin of flexibility is reserved in order that State Parties may adopt individual measures of co-operation at the request of the State or States attacked.

The Organ of Consultation, the IATRA text states, must meet "without delay" (Article 3, Clause 4) if summoned by the Permanent Council of the OAS, in all cases of aggression against a State Party, "until the Security Council of the UN has taken the measures necessary to maintain international peace and security." (Article 3, Clause 6).

The collective measures which may be taken must be supported by "the vote of two thirds of the Signatory States which have ratified the treaty (Article 17), which establishes a minimum of fourteen votes out of a total of a possible twenty-one, and can comprise one or more of the following possibilities:

"The recall of chiefs of missions; breaking of diplomatic relations; breaking of Consular relations; partial or complete interruption of economic relations or rail, sea, air, postal, telegraphic, telephonic, radio-telephonic or radio-telegraphic, or other means of communication; and use of armed force." (Article 8).

The IATRA defines aggression as "the use of armed force by a State against the sovereignty, territorial integrity or political independence of another State, or in any other manner inconsistent with the Charter of the UN, the Charter of the OAS or this Treaty." (Article 9, Clause 1).

On making a request to the Permanent Council, the Argentine representative, Raul Quijano invoked Articles 6 and 13 and mentioned "the imminence of an armed attack announced by Great Britain[10]." He was, however, careful to clarify the fact that "this must not be interpreted as being against the continuation of negotiations or as a sign that the efforts of Secretary of State Haig have failed. Argentina values these efforts." On Tuesday April 20th, eighteen of the signatory countries voted in favour of calling a consultative meeting of the IATRA whilst three countries - the United States, Colombia and Trinidad and Tobago, abstained.

The modifications by Pym to the "document worked out in Buenos Aires," the summary of the consultative committee of the IATRA and, especially, information on the military front narrowed Quijano's room for manoeuvre with every second that passed. In fact, a part of the Task Force was at that moment closing on South Georgia. And a day before receiving his British colleague, on Wednesday 21st, he conceived a new move: to meet the parties on the neutral territory of the American capital to have a face to face encounter.

Pym would be two days in Washington and Costa Mendez had to travel to be present at the IATRA meeting. In spite of having no explicit acceptance by Pym for arranging a meeting of this nature, he sounded out the Argentines by diplomatic channels, although not personally. The Secretary of State thought that this direct contact would be the most suitable setting possible to present his last proposal, hereafter given the generic designation: *Haig II*.

The idea caught the imagination of the professional Argentine negotiators, including Costa Mendez. In Washington, it was cautiously promoted by the Argentine Embassy - the channel used for the initiative - and by the Argentine mission to the OAS.[11] The benefits from the point of view of the State Department were well-known: if at the week-end, or even before, the beginnings of an agreement began to appear, one could hold off any military action. In that case, the meeting of the IATRA, due to begin on the Monday, would be unnecessary and its deliberations mere formalities.

But the foolhardy effort lasted only a few hours - that is until it succumbed to the two military perspectives: one in Buenos Aires, and the other, the uncompromising logic of the Prime Minister in London.

Costa Mendez put it to the Junta for consideration. But for the Commandants - and there is no suggestion of disagreement between them on this matter - the possibility of a personal dialogue with the "enemy" was equivalent, at this stage, to demonstrating weakness.

On the other hand, there are signs that Francis Pym was initially in favour of the idea, but when he presented it to the Cabinet, hours before leaving to meet Haig, it provoked an angry reaction from the Prime Minister, Margaret Thatcher. One did not "talk to the aggressor" was the forceful reply of the British Premier.

Another phase of the peace effort was thus aborted. Haig wrote to Costa Mendez on Friday 23rd, the same day on which he met Pym and one day before he travelled to Washington. He spoke of anticipating the difficulties that still had to be overcome, but also of putting on record the need to maintain a new personal contact.

That same day in New York the Argentine representative at the UN, Eduardo Roca, obtained a declaration from the Bureau of Co-ordination of the Movement of Non-Aligned Countries. In this, its members expressed solidarity for the "just claim of the Argentine Republic" over the Falkland Islands and an appeal to the parties to: "avoid any use of force or threat of the use of force that can put the peace and security of the region in danger."

It was the first favourable outcome that Argentina had achieved in this forum since the crisis started. It was also the first sign of international re-adjustment that Argentina began to effect, before thinking its policies out in the light of events.

Already by then the Argentine diplomatic representations in Washington and in New York were showing - according to a description by one of its members - "the peculiar individuality of the different efforts that each were making." Whilst Ambassadors Takacs and Quijano were taking care to keep the American channel "open and in good condition," Roca and his people were talking daily to their colleagues in the Non-Aligned group and the representatives of the Soviet Union.

In time, the Argentines at the UN mission began to allude in teasing fashion to their companions in the American capital, mainly Takacs and Quijano, as "the Washington widows," for the dialectical efforts that they were making in trying to mitigate the effect on the Reagan administration of the "swing to the left" in Buenos Aires diplomacy.

On Saturday 24th, with the British fifty-four nautical miles from South Georgia, the Foreign Minister set off, accompanied by a team formed by Ambassadors Figueroa, Erhardt del Campo y Listre, and the "mini-senate" composed of Miret, Iglesias and Moya.

Some days before the Foreign Minister's departure, the Junta had despatched to Washington a sort of unofficial advance party. It was formed of various political leaders that agreed to plead the Argentine cause to the Government, institutions and American VIPs, in an effort to demonstrate that this cause was not the exclusive property of the *de facto* Government. Another had gone to Europe, where for example the men of the *Democracia Cristiana* employed their best arguments in trying to convince their sceptical Italian co-religionists.

In the United States, the *Justicialistas*, Antonio Cafiero and Ricardo Guardo, the *Radical*, Fernando de la Rua and the *Centrista*, Francisco Manrique tried it. The impresario Amalia Fortabat and her friend, Colonel Luis Premoli, an ex-government official under General

Juan Carlos Ongania in the sixties, also went on their own accord, but without being able to speak with any authority.

To say that the fruits of all this effort were less than meagre would not be an exaggeration. The Argentine diplomats discovered that in general, the politicians lacked any significant contacts of their own. Their feeling of helplessness made it necessary for the majority of the interviews to be arranged through the Argentine embassy. Even in the few reliable cases where this was not so, the American reception of the Argentine political argument oscillated between coldness and frank hostility.

Or, as happened to Manrique, everything ended in as much disarray as the main negotiations. This ex-marine and ex-Minister of Social Welfare had a card up his sleeve and at the opportune moment, he played it. Using Quijano's secretary, and dropping some names which were "linked with English Masonic lodges," he obtained an interview with John Ure, Pym's Chief of Staff. John Ure formed the team which accompanied the Foreign Secretary on his journey to Washington.

The meeting was fixed for 6 pm on Friday 23rd, and Manrique asked the ambassador to the OAS for the assistance of an official to act as interpreter. Quijano was less than convinced of the usefulness of the contact, but could not refuse the request. He allocated an embassy Secretary for the task.

The meeting took place in a private home in Connecticut Avenue, in the district where live many members of the diplomatic corps accredited to the US Government. The reception which Ure lavished upon the Argentines was formally impeccable, but icy. This did not dent Manrique's spirits, and he began to unload his arguments onto the Englishman.

The *Federalista* leader spoke of the "sad paradox" represented by the "present confrontation between two countries who have traditionally had such good relations."

I am sorry," he added, in very personal fashion, "as I have been in Great Britain and I have a British daughter-in-law. And besides, we are both Western and Christian countries," he pursued.

At this stage of the argument Ure, who had listened in silence, thought it necessary to intervene:

"Personally I am in agreement with what you say and that is why my government is ready to consider any reasonable solution. Have you any proposal?" he inquired in an effort to reach the nub of the question.

"Firstly I want you to know that we politicians are separate from the Military Government in Argentina. I personally have been the spokesman for our adherence to this national cause with President

Galtieri," the Argentine explained, with undisguisable fatuity. "But I made it clear," he added, "that this support is conditional on what is the first priority - not to put at risk the Western and Christian identity of the Argentines. Our way of life, the values that we share with the West."

Ure looked deliberately at his watch, while Manrique finished his statement. He pointedly commented that in a few minutes he had a meeting with the Foreign Secretary, and then asked:

"I should like to know, Sir, in what way you think you can collaborate in the solution of the problem."

"I have channels that could be used in case the present negotiations fail..." the Argentine vaguely suggested.

"Which - the Junta, the President?" insisted Ure, determined not to give a respite.

"Channels at all the levels you mention. But I would also like to convey to you the fact that President Galtieri is a very determined man," said the Argentine, varying the line of his argument.

"I do not doubt it. But Mrs Thatcher is noted for her determination too. In particular, the only solution possible that I can see is compliance by your country with Resolution 502. Otherwise our Task Force will enforce a solution," was the British diplomat's cutting reply. He rose from the chair. "You will have to excuse me," he apologised, "but I have a meeting with my Minister."

The Englishman ended the interview in an almost brusque fashion and accompanied his visitor to the door. As he went through the door, Manrique left him a card. Ure accepted it, thanking him, but also let slip: "As you will understand, it is not very probable that we shall call each other."

On his return to the mission building, Manrique made an optimistic report to Quijano anyway. When the politician left, the ambassador closed his office door and, turning to a subordinate who had been present at the encounter, asked:

"Tell me; it was a cock-up wasn't it?"

Whilst this was happening in the American capital, the Argentine political parties themselves were beginning to become deeply anxious about the certain clash that events were pointing to.

Upon the alarm being sounded by the *Desarrollistas*, the *Radicales* joined in, but they used a confidential channel. According to testimonies obtained during the investigation, the President of the National Committee of the UCR, Carlos Contin, got into contact with the Assistant Secretary of the Interior, Colonel Menendez - at that time the link between the Government and the political leadership.

Contin was extremely worried because he considered it irrational to arrive at a warlike confrontation - an argument with which the military official was not in agreement. But Contin went on and suggested to Menendez that he might explain to his superiors that the *UCR* were ready to adopt a posture favouring Argentine concessions thus promoting the negotiating option over the route to war.

As happened in those days, the suggestion fell on deaf ears. There is evidence, however, that a move similar to that proposed by the Radicals actually took place with Brigadier Lami Dozo. Once again, official silence was the answer to the politicians' unease.

In the early hours of April 25th, British artillery opened fire on Grytviken, substantially altering the situation, or at all events acting as a catalyst. The old submarine *Santa Fe*, anchored in the harbour, was severely damaged. Lt. Commander Alfredo Astiz, chief of the Argentine troops, who after this attack would obtain an unenviable notoriety, had ordered a withdrawal to Port Leith to "continue combat" according to Communiques 27 to 32 inclusive issued by the Junta.

As on so many occasions at the time, the truth was not even touched on by the rhetoric of official communiques.

Communique No 31 stated that the naval officer had decided to "burn his boats" and destroy his radio equipment, so isolating himself voluntarily from headquarters, before taking up resistance. In fact, less than two hours after the British attack began, Astiz ordered the white flag to be raised next to the National Ensign and proceeded to surrender the place, almost without firing a shot.

Was this a personal decision by Astiz to avoid combat? There are signs which point to a different conclusion. Once the attack had been made, military spokesmen made considerable efforts to convince reporters that "it was not a surprise to the Junta." What is certain is that President Galtieri himself, three days earlier during his visit to the islands, told the military governor of the Falklands and his officers that an armed confrontation would be inevitable before the then failing negotiations could be revitalized.

None of the sources consulted could, or would, confirm the possibility that one or all of the members of the Junta believed that the British would be satisfied with recovering South Georgia, thus salving their wounded pride. But neither did they completely reject the idea. After having saved face, London might be better disposed towards a negotiated solution, although this might be proposed in radically different terms, since the British would then have a foot-hold in the region.

Had this been the case, the sacrifice of Astiz and his "lizards" in action would have been useless. ["*Lizards*" *(Lagartos)*: the nickname of the men of the Argentine detachment in South Georgia derived from their earlier participation in the clandestine repression.] Still, if this speculation went on within the Military, it was kept dark. On the very day when a bearded and obedient Astiz put a flourish to his signature on the document of surrender at Grytviken, far away in Washington one of Costa Mendez's team was speaking to one of the present authors about the Commander of the Lizards. "The English are not going to cart *him* off. That boy is very tricky and he isn't going to give in like that," he claimed.

The darkest of premonitions that Foreign Minister Costa Mendez brought with him from Buenos Aires were confirmed as soon as he landed at John F Kennedy airport at New York, at mid-morning on Sunday April 25th. Ambassador Roca entered the first class cabin of the Aerolineas Argentinas Jumbo Jet. He showed signs of agitation and without preliminaries gave him the news: the British had allowed war to break out. The ambassador's anxiety was justified: it would have been disastrous if his friend and chief had been allowed to confront the cameras and microphones without knowing the dramatic news himself. For some reason, that Costa Mendez himself later judged to be "without importance," no-one in Buenos Aires had thought of using the aircraft radio to send news of the hostilities to him.

The plans that Costa Mendez and his advisers had meticulously worked on during the flight were half-forgotten in this new anxiety. The Foreign Minister, without yet knowing the effect that the battle had produced on the domestic military front, outlined a compromise formula for discussion in his statement. He condemned the attack, "carried out when the negotiations were still in progress," and declared dialogue with the British at an end, though carefully making clear that "the same [dialogue] with the United States remains open."

Having scarcely arrived in Washington, Costa Mendez spoke to Galtieri on the phone and learnt how far his plans had been altered by the British attack on the submarine *Sante Fe*. The President ordered him to cancel the meeting arranged for that Sunday with Haig at the State Department. Animosity towards Washington reached its peak in those hours.

Galtieri, on instructing his Minister for Foreign Affairs, bore very much in mind an argument used by Anaya in the Military Junta. He had said that Haig's warnings about what would happen if a solution was not found - which up till then had been acted upon with amazing correctness - confirmed suspicions that the Secretary of State had behaved not as an impartial mediator, but actually as a representative of the British.

A few hours later, Haig heard of this comment from Anaya, which made him explode with rage. "How can he dare think I'm not a free agent?" the American said indignantly. He even considered not attending the meeting of the OAS, and this was signalled to various Latin American missions. His absence might have given a bad impression, as various of the Foreign Ministers who had gathered in Washington for the session of IATRA[12] made known to him. It would have meant the *coup de grace* for his efforts at mediation. In spite of all the agonising, Haig was not yet disposed to confess failure.

The Argentine-American connection hung literally by a thread during those hours. Nor was there agreement upon the need to preserve it in either of the two governments. This fact was clearly visible in the Argentine delegation. Whilst Takacs, for example, was resorting to any means within reach to resurrect the Costa Mendez-Haig dialogue, Rear-Admiral Moya, Anaya's faithful disciple throughout the conflict, reported that in Buenos Aires the flames of intransigence were burning brightly. On the morning of Monday 26th when the Argentines received confirmation that Haig would attend the inaugural session of IATRA, one of the diplomats tried a joke:

"Perhaps Canoro might not greet him when he passes him [i.e. Haig] in the corridor," he speculated.

Moya, who was present at that meeting in the embassy, replied in a sombre tone as if his questioner might have been speaking seriously:

"If the Foreign Minister greets him, perhaps he won't be Foreign Minister for much longer."

Costa Mendez arrived at the enormous OAS building weighed down by circumstances. In the space of a few hours the war had obliged him to revise the line he was thinking of taking before the assembly. With sights always set on the Haig mission, his diplomatic corps had prepared a strategy for IATRA which deliberately avoided stretching Latin American solidarity too far. The resolution that the signatory countries adopted would have to serve to bring pressure on the mediator, but without going so far as to get in the way of his efforts.

Moreover, that solidarity had very precise limits, as Costa Mendez discovered in earlier consultations with the different capitals. The least qualified support for the Argentine cause came from countries whose governments possessed a militant foreign policy, such as Panama and the Sandinista regime in Nicaragua, or who were involved in similar disputes to the one which brought Argentina to arms - such as Venezuela or Guatemala[13].

But the rest of Latin America remained cautious. Brazil being the clearest example of this attitude, or, as happened with the Colombian

Government of Julio Cesar Turbay Ayala, succumbed to pressure from Washington. The Chilean regime, with the unsettled Beagle Channel dispute in mind, gloried in a spoiling attitude towards any defence of Argentina, except when it came to the rhetoric of the delegates.

Such limitations did not discomfort Costa Mendez initially. After all, the draft resolution that he had brought from Buenos Aires - planned so as to win the two thirds vote required by IATRA for its approval - only contained a handful of points, none of which would commit pact members to active support. There were three imperatives:

1. Explicit recognition of Argentine sovereignty over the Falkland Islands [the OAS had not yet delivered this].
2. Condemnation of the British attitude, and
3. A plea for the solution to the dispute to be arrived at by way of negotiation.

The Argentines only wished to obviate, if possible, any reference to Resolution 502, but they were also disposed to accept reference to Haig's mission in terms of high praise. Everything Argentina was fighting for would be covered by the appropriate Article 6 of the Rio Treaty concerning the preservation of peace in the Hemisphere.

The truth is that there were few antecedents upon which to base the proposal. The OAS had never made a pronouncement on Argentine sovereignty over the Falklands. There only existed a resolution to that effect by the Inter-American Judicial Committee - an advisory body[14].

But the British military action had substantially altered the expectations the military commanders had of the Foreign Minister. With their characteristic ignorance of international realities they now suggested to him that the requirements be increased.

Fate ordained that fresh spring morning in Washington that Moya's indirect warning to Costa Mendez should prove useless. He arrived at the OAS and went to greet Secretary-General Alejandro Orfila in his office, next to the Hall of the Americas, where the first plenary session was being held. On leaving he passed Haig, who was entering the place at that very moment.

With his characteristic lack of inhibition, the Secretary of State stopped the Argentine and extended his hand. At the same time, without formalities, he told him that it was urgent for them to meet as soon as possible. Time was almost running out but still there was a possibility of one new proposal. Costa Mendez replied in vague terms, speaking of the need to consult his government, and finally managed to extricate himself from this embarrassing offer - to which he had no real reply.

In the hall and corridors a swarm of delegates, reporters and onlookers exchanged greetings and comments. There were also Manrique, la Fortabat and Premoli, all of whom wore the grey badge that identified them as delegates. If this distinguishing mark had reflected realities, and not been merely a courtesy from the Argentine mission and the OAS towards their visitors, one might have expected the Argentine cause to have been irredeemably lost on that occasion. Two anecdotes, among many reported that day by the journalists, serve to satisfy this assertion.

Manrique offered various "master classes" on the virtues of Argentine submarines - "I know what I'm talking about, they are my boys," he affirmed, recalling his days as a naval instructor. The Latin American reporters were sceptical, in view of what had happened to the submarine *Santa Fe* in Grytviken. He only broke off his delivery when he suddenly spotted Haig. Without being intimidated by the smoothly operating protective screen surrounding the Secretary of State, Manrique walked up to Haig and offered his hand, which the latter accepted as a reflex action. At the same time, the Argentine's specially-contracted photographer snapped the occasion. Hours later, without even a blush, Manrique repeatedly referred to "my interview with the Secretary of State," when speaking to various reporters.

The behaviour of the impresario Fortabat and of Colonel Premoli was not markedly different from that of Manrique, the *Centrista* politician. They both poured out trivialities to the press tape recorders from an early hour. Finally, when there were only a few minutes left before the start of proceedings, Fortabat insisted to her companion: "We must make more statements, Luis," as if the mere accumulation of them could favour the situation.

They soon got their chance. A Colombian reporter approached the couple who had not yet taken their seats in the hall, and interviewed them: what would happen, he wanted to know, if Argentina did not obtain the necessary seventeen votes for the resolution?

"It is to help to make sure that doesn't happen that we have come here," replied the impresario confidently. Already the first debate - in which Costa Mendez was the first speaker - sharply transformed the prevailing climate. The Argentine produced an authentic anti-colonialist outburst: "It is enough to run through a little history of this century and the last one," he reminded the audience, "to show the similarity of this British aggression to other invasions and to the two blockades suffered by the young Argentine Republic. And too, the bombardment of Venezuela, the Suez aggression, the oppression of half the African continent as well as a great part of Asia - to prove what Great Britain is and how it behaves."

It was Argentina that was going back to its historic roots, he said, ironically for a self-confessed admirer of the old British lion. "We have not transgressed against order and international law," the Foreign Minister denied. "We have acted against a peculiar type of order of things, an order intended to preserve an oligarchic view of the international system; the *status quo* of the international system."

Haig listened in silence, looking fixedly at the Argentine's face. He witnessed the ovation with which his Latin American colleagues received him, headed by the Nicaraguan, Father Miguel d'Escoto, who did not hesitate to stand up to applaud. He also endured a long, substantial and hostile speech from the Venezuelan Zambrano Velazco. Then came his turn[15].

The American tried a new balancing act, adopting a line of argument that suggested neutrality as far as possible. His speech did not contain a single mention of the Falklands or *Malvinas*. The only solid argument was that of the need to comply with Resolution 502. But his speech was ineffective and his contribution received no applause at all.

"In a world where they don't stint on applause, almost deliver it as a courtesy, Haig's piece was a fiasco," said one experienced operator in the assembly.

While these three speeches were taking place, the American ambassador to the OAS, William Middendorf, was sent to explain again to his colleague, Quijano, the urgency of a meeting between their respective chiefs. About 4 pm, and after offering excuses to the Panamanian, Javier Illueca, who was preparing to make his speech, Costa Mendez went to Orfila's office, from where he contacted Galtieri. Ambassador Schlaudermann had applied his personal pressure in Buenos Aires in such a way that after a brief exchange, the Argentine Foreign Minister received the authorization to speak to his American counterpart.

The meeting, which took place in the office of the Secretary General of the OAS, was brief, but dramatic. Haig said a British military action on East Falkland was imminent. He also announced that he had a new proposal to put to the Argentine Government. He even indicated his willingness to return personally to Buenos Aires, if it should be necessary to discuss it with the members of the Junta. If London were to see him making the journey, he suggested, perhaps it might be possible to halt the escalation towards war.

Costa Mendez knew that he had no grounds for proposing a new visit by Haig to the Junta. Both men agreed that the text of the proposal would be simultaneously delivered to the Argentines in Washington, through ambassador Takacs, and in Buenos Aires, through Schlaudermann. In fact, Costa Mendez made only one promise: the reply would be sent "as early as possible."

A few hours later the Argentine negotiators were acquainted with the so-called *Haig II* text:

1. The establishment of the tripartite Special Interim Authority on which the government of the islands would henceforth depend in order to be able to adopt "decisions, laws and regulations."

2. The "local traditional administration" would be re-established, but would incorporate in the Executive and Legislative Councils two representatives appointed by the Argentine Government and at least one more in each body to represent Argentine inhabitants resident on the islands.

3. The flags of the three members of the Interim Authority would be flown, which implied that Argentina would not lower hers.

4. On December 31st 1982, the "provisional period" would be concluded, during which negotiations would have to be completed in order to transfer "the islands to the list of Non Self-Governing Territories under Chapter XI of the UN Charter and on mutually agreed conditions for their final status, including due consideration for the rights of the inhabitants and the principle of territorial integrity..."

5. The Authority had to present "proposals and specific recommendations," after previous consultation with the Council, to the two governments in order to establish :

(a) "The manner in which the desires and interests of the inhabitants of the islands will be taken into account, on the basis of a survey of opinion of inhabitants, carried out in respect of the questions which are the object of the negotiations in a form to be determined by the Authority."

(b) The questions relating to the exploitation of the resources and the future role of the Falkland Islands Company and

(c) The questions relating to the possible indemnifications to the inhabitants.

6. In relation to the mechanisms to guarantee attention to the "desires and interests" of the inhabitants, the proposal established that these would not affect the respective positions of the governments concerning the "force of law" which will be granted to such opinion in the achievement of a final solution.

7. If it should not be possible to reach a final solution before the end of the period fixed, an extension of six months would automatically be established.

It was extremely difficult to reconstruct the train of events following the simultaneous delivery of the proposal which was carried out on the morning of the 28th in Buenos Aires and Washington. These were cities in which both power and the Argentine negotiators were divided. This was still more true if one takes into account that Costa Mendez and his collaborators had to attend to two fronts almost simultaneously: activity within the framework of IATRA as well as the analysis of *Haig II*.

To complicate matters still further, the warning the Secretary of State gave to Costa Mendez on the imminence of a massive British attack began to be confirmed in both Argentina and Great Britain. This obliged the Foreign Minister to denounce the threat and demand that deliberations in the plenary session on Tuesday morning be speeded up. Earlier he had a meeting with the then Argentine delegate to the Inter-American Defence Council.

The fact is that *Haig II* contained substantial changes to the initial ideas put forward by the mediator on his two journeys to the capitals involved in the crisis. They represented an undoubted improvement for Argentine interests. Today in retrospect, they might still be judged insufficient, but they cannot be ignored.

In the different branches of the Military Government various approaches were becoming clearly defined with the course of events. Ambassador Quijano, for example, recalled having hurriedly produced a document of ten pages at the Foreign Minister's request. This contained a decidedly favourable opinion on the contents of *Haig II*, though it did suggest some minor points for negotiation.

Quijano did not keep a copy of the document - most of the papers that the experts worked on in those days were classified as strictly secret - but he indicated several of the points within it:

(a) The interim form of administration emerging from the proposal indicated that the colonial British government would not be restored.

(b) It accepted that negotiations had to be carried out according to the principles of decolonialisation of the UN.

(c) Mention of the wishes of the islanders, a word which caused much irritation to the Argentines, appeared to be balanced by the explicit reference to the "principle of territorial integrity."

But above all, Quijano, stated that:

(d) an explicit promise was obtained of a United States guarantee not only for the negotiation process but also for the interests of the parties concerned.

On Tuesday, Margaret Thatcher insisted on defending her tough line before Parliament and public opinion. But the pressure of arms London exercised on the Military Junta, far from producing the desired effect, was provoking a dramatically opposite reaction. This tough line stemmed from Margaret Thatcher's announced policy of "seeking a solution by diplomatic channels, but with a strong military back-up."

Such was the climate prevailing in Great Britain, that the Labour Opposition attempted a timid break from the consensus of support that the parties gave the Prime Minister. Michael Foot on five occasions demanded the sending of Francis Pym to New York. This was in order to ask for the mediation of the Secretary-General, before any new bellicose escalation could be launched.

From the area of military operations, Admiral John Woodward stoked up the fire by stating: "We are in the preliminary stages of a great engagement which in my opinion must be a triumph."

On examining the balance sheet of the conflict, many of the American authorities whom the authors consulted criticized this British approach with the same vehemence that they applied to the initial Argentine decision to invade the archipelago.

The military trio who accompanied Costa Mendez knew little of the proposal and once the respective consultations with their superiors in Buenos Aires were completed, Iglesias, Miret and Moya all began to point out to reporters that *Haig II* contained clauses unacceptable to Argentina[16].

Costa Mendez was left with hardly any room for manoeuvre to try to save the situation. From the consultations he had with President Galtieri, and through his small "military senate," it clearly emerged that Buenos Aires would not even produce a counter-offer to place before the impatient Haig.

And in the early hours of the 28th, the Organ of Consultation gave the *coup de grace* to the precarious situation - without their members realising it - in approving by seventeen votes and four abstentions (Colombia, Trinidad-Tobago, Chile and the United States), the terms of the resolution so arduously negotiated[17]. throughout the whole of the previous day in the working parties.

The Latin American Foreign Ministers left it on record that "they had to take into account the Argentine Republic's rights of sovereignty over the Falklands, as expressed in important resolutions emanating from different international forums, among them the Inter-American Juridical Committee as expressed on 16 January 1976..." In these documents, on the other hand, it may be seen that they refer to: "Resolution 502 (1982) of the Security Council of the United Nations, which must be complied with in all its aspects."

In the seven points of the resolution it proposed:

1. To urge the Government of the United Kingdom and Northern Ireland to cease immediately the hostilities they are carrying out in the security region defined by Article 4 of the IATRA, and further to abstain from any act that might affect Inter-American peace and security.

2. To urge the Government of the Argentine Republic also to abstain from carrying out any action which may aggravate the situation.

3. To press the said governments to establish immediately a truce that permits a resumption of the normal development of negotiations leading to a peaceful solution of the conflict, taking into account the rights of sovereignty of the Argentine Republic over the Falklands, as well as the interests of its population.

4. To take note of the information received concerning the important efforts by the US Secretary of State and to express its good wishes that they will contribute effectively to a peaceful solution of the conflict.

5. To deplore the adoption by members of the European Economic Community and other states, of coercive measures of an economic and political character which harm the Argentine people, and to exhort them to remove the said measures, pointing out that they constitute a grave precedent and are not protected by Resolution 502 (1982) of the UN Security Council, and are incompatible with the Charters of the UN and the OAS and with GATT.

6. To charge the President of the Twentieth Consultative Meeting with presenting formally and immediately to the President of the Security Council of the UN this resolution in order to make it known to members of the Council[18].

7. To keep open the Twentieth Consultative Meeting, with the special object of keeping watch over faithful compliance with this Resolution, and of taking such additional measures that are thought necessary to re-establish and preserve peace and to resolve the conflict that has arisen by peaceful means.

The results obtained within the framework of IATRA were without doubt important, but they did not even remotely constitute the "miracle" that the Argentine Government had hoped to bring about in world opinion. The recovery of a Latin American identity suddenly burst upon the consciousness of a vast part of Argentine society which had previously preferred to conceal it with disdain, when not actually denying it.

In fact, Latin American solidarity had grown in spite of that attitude and above all in spite of the last six years of military government. This government had adopted as one of the basic assumptions for its conduct of international affairs the acceptance of Spanish-American Balkanization and even its active promotion. There was, however, a belief among Argentina's neighbours that this historical trend could be reversed. As the then Foreign Minister of Panama expressed in one of his contributions to the conference: "Latin America turns its eyes towards Argentina in the belief that Argentina will also look towards Latin America."

For the Military in Buenos Aires, the OAS vote was a necessary political tonic that stopped the encouragement of non-cooperation. For the Americans, it was a warning about "the course of political disaster that events were following," according to one diplomatic source.

The principal American newspapers demanded a decision from Reagan to put an end to the efforts by the Secretary of State but in fact, they were demanding that the US should align itself with Great Britain. Congress, after listening to Francis Pym on April 23rd[19], threatened to intervene directly in the question. This was through a scheme presented by the Democratic Senator for New York, Patrick Moynihan, demanding the imposition of a commercial embargo on Argentina. Even the section of the Republican administration which argued in favour of Washington protecting its Latin American front called a retreat.

The drums of war beat out still more loudly that Wednesday, when Costa Mendez crossed the large hall of the State Department, accompanied by his Chief of Staff, to meet Haig for the last time during the war. A little before, Margaret Thatcher had announced in London the strengthening of the Exclusion Zone - 200 miles around the islands - making it absolute by adding an air blockade to the naval blockade already in force.

Costa Mendez had not too many arguments at his disposal; scarcely enough to moderate the effect of the negative signs coming from Buenos Aires and from his own team and, with luck, to agree some way of concealing the inevitable forthcoming rejection. Once more it was a question of gaining time.

But Haig was not in a mood to offer it. The meeting lasted an hour and a half and concluded not only with the application of the "American option," but also with the collapse of the friendship that had been developing between the two men. The dialogue, if one can call it that, was extremely tense, involving prolonged silences from which neither knew how to escape.

Haig refused to accept that Argentina was not disposed to give its approval to his proposals and reproached Costa Mendez for the way in which, in his judgement, the Junta had condemned his mission to failure. The temperature rose to the point where the host turned to threaten:

"It will not be Great Britain alone," he warned. "The United States will support her, and together with NATO we will bring pressure to bear so that inevitably the Argentine Military Government is going to fall. Be sure of that."

Costa Mendez's reply did not leave room for hope and marked the collapse of the talks.

"That threat, Sir, is unworthy of a Secretary of State."

The Argentine diplomats were careful to spell out the tenor as well as the outcome of that last contact. The least camouflaged account available to Argentine reporters came from Figueroa's room in Embassy Row: "It was a clash of two very strong personalities," suggested the Chief of Staff at the Palacio San Martin - in the manner of a figure of speech.

It had been an untiring attempt, but insufficient. One floor below in the same building, a version was awaiting the special envoys which had more points of contact with reality. This time it was offered by Brigadier Miret. This time, the air force officer disclosed not only the facts, but also the disquiet at the course of events that was already bothering him, and which had begun to distance him from his two colleagues: Moya and Iglesias.

Miret used the presence of the reporters to reflect aloud. He certainly did not question the decision to reject *Haig II*, but he did not conceal the future lack of direction that it would produce among those who had accepted it.

During the conversation, Miret, the Military Government's Secretary for Planning, took out a copy of a working document describing the vicissitudes of the conflict on the battle front and some "conclusions"[20]. Among the latter, it suggested that "Britain planned to recover the islands, whatever the cost - with US support. The British fleet could not return defeated after such an effort as this would produce serious problems for the British Government and the US Government too." These would seem like platitudes to an observer, but up till then, no official had dared to say them out loud.

He also stated that: "While British power increases, the capacity for an Argentine response diminishes."

When the originator of this document was asked: "What can Argentina do?" He replied that there were three possibilities:

1. "To withdraw from the islands by agreement and to continue the struggle, at least diplomatically. For that to be a solution, the question of sovereignty could not be raised at the negotiating table because it would lead to the failure of the negotiations.

2. "To continue the struggle, which would mean the destruction

of all the forces stationed on the island and also of the Argentine combat air force. To continue along this path would be to extend the war by no more than forty-five days.

3. "To make an alliance with a more powerful country. The implications of such an alliance are beyond the scope of this analysis, but a rough approximation of what could happen would be as follows:

(a) The Falklands would become a second Vietnam.

(b) The implications of an Argentine agreement with other countries would raise a very serious problem for the US.

(c) The South American and British positions would run the serious risk of provoking a world war."

The same day, Costa Mendez made a statement to the BBC in which he said: "I believe that the Falklands can result in a Vietnam for Great Britain. The place is located 10,000 miles from London and is very difficult for the British to defend."

Costa Mendez proved that the die was cast but, trying to maintain some consistency with what he had himself said to the US mediator, he wanted to preserve some room for manoeuvre. He drafted him a reply in careful terms in which he stated that he had carried out an in-depth examination of the document, *[Haig II]*, "comparing it with our previous proposals and with the points of view that we have put forward in our various meetings. From that analysis," he added, "significant differences have emerged, some of which raise difficulties that it is essential to overcome."

"As my government has already shown, Mr Secretary, the objective that Argentina set is the recognition of its sovereignty over the Falkland Islands. That central element of our discussions is the ultimate justification for the actions undertaken by my country, and as I have already had occasion to express to you many times, it constitutes for us an unrenounceable aim," he added.

Costa Mendez' text also questioned the following: **a.** the "imprecision" of the American proposal concerning the recognition of Argentina's claims to sovereignty; **b.** the absence of "mechanisms" that would grant Buenos Aires "greater facilities for the administration of the islands" during the provisional period; **c.** the provisions for incorporating Argentine representatives in the Executive and Legislative Councils and **d.** the implicit establishment of a referendum to sound out the wishes of the islanders, which he judged "in open contradiction" to the contents of Resolution 2065 of the UN General Assembly.

The penultimate paragraph contained a reference to the Argentine readiness to continue negotiating, but in no part of the note was there included anything amounting to a counter-proposal. And this was what condemned to failure Costa Mendez's last attempt to keep the American alternative open. The Argentine military power had nothing to offer but a "no."

With this text under his arm a distressed Takacs entered the office of the Assistant Secretary of State for Inter-American Affairs, Thomas Enders, at about midday. The latter recalled that Takacs was visibly troubled by the task that overwhelmed him at that moment and also by the reaction of Haig and his deputies on learning of the contents of the reply. "It was like a bucket of cold water over us all," he said to the authors when they interviewed him.

The Argentines left Washington for New York, that Thursday morning, amid gloomy omens. The signs were everywhere. In London, *The Daily Telegraph* stated in a long article[21], that: "After a slow start, America is backing Britain as never before since the Second World War," and warned that "should President Reagan's latest diplomatic efforts,launched yesterday, fail to avert war, powerful voices in Congress and within his own Administration will urge all-out support for Britain..." Quoting an influential columnist of the *New York Times*, James Reston, the British journal indicated that: "Washington will have to tell the [Argentine] generals that Mr Haig has done the best he can to avoid the clash, and that if they reject US mediation and defy the UN resolution, then the US will oppose them, declare economic sanctions and give the British Navy all the aid at its disposal."

The American Senate - whose Foreign Affairs Committee had listened to a report from Haig behind closed doors - met that morning and quickly approved by the overwhelming margin of seventy-nine votes to one, a resolution calling for Argentina to withdraw her troops from the islands. The only negative vote was that of the extreme right-winger Jesse Helms. Such was the value of Argentine shares in the political market of the West.

In the UN, the Argentine Foreign Minister found a propitious atmosphere for summoning the Security Council. Nevertheless, he did nothing personally to encourage it. His instructions were that Argentina should forbear from making such a request, since whichever party to the conflict did so would be admitting that its position was compromised. Besides, the obstacles would be enormous, as London did not want the Council to meet. Margaret Thatcher had already declared that her country would not accept a new resolution from the Council - compliance ought first to be obtained with 502, she warned - and that her delegation would veto any attempt to demand a cease-fire that was not linked to an immediate withdrawal of Argentine troops from the islands.

While Costa Mendez conferred with his colleagues from Nicaragua, Panama and elsewhere, Ambassador Kirkpatrick from the

American delegation to the UN, tried a political move of her own on the confused chess-board. That morning she had participated in a special session of the UN Security Council in which it was decided to end Haig's mission and apply sanctions upon Argentina.

Without consulting the Secretary of State - which did not imply that she had not spoken to the White House - she conveyed the news to the Secretary-General of the UN, encouraging him to act. Haig learnt of this later and his reaction was to increase his old aversion for the ambassador.

Perez de Cuellar, for his part, lost no time, and a few hours afterwards received the Argentine Minister. He made an offer to him of his own good offices in the dispute though the offer was only verbal at this stage. Costa Mendez did not then compromise himself, but was careful to leave the option open.

At the same time, Ambassador Takacs was leaving the office of his legation in Washington to make the journey to the State Department once more, where he received official notification of the American decision. Enders informed him that the announcement would be made public at 10 am the following morning.

However much this may have been foreseen by the Argentines, its effect on the delegates' spirits was obvious. A group of reporters returning from a dinner in a restaurant in the picturesque New York district of Little Italy met a taciturn Miret at the door of the UN Plaza, where they were all staying. He was nervous and pulling hard on his cigarette.

The Brigadier did not return their greetings. He limited himself to saying loudly that: "The Americans are opening up," as if he was continuing a conversation and not starting it. The reporters were unsure at first whether to carry on listening to the anguished officer's reflections or to run to the nearest telephone to hold up the front pages of their respective newspapers. They finally opted for the second alternative, knowing that in spite of the hour it was not only the day that was ending at that moment. Another stage in the drama was ending too.

NOTES

1. The version given is a translation from the original English, in which the *tuteo* or *voceo* (the familiar forms of address) do not exist. Nevertheless, the degree of familiarity employed by the Secretary of State in his writing - note the forms of address in these messages - suggest the use of that form in Spanish as an equivalent.

2. A diplomatic source revealed that on his journey of December 1981, when Walters visited Buenos Aires, he expressed to Galtieri and the other members of the Military Government, the concern of the USA at the Argentine assistance to the *de facto* regime in Bolivia.

This was one of the principal causes of disquiet in Washington, because the authorities in La Paz, including the dictator, Garcia Meza, were linked with the multi-million dollar drugs traffic. The USA was the most important market for these drugs. Some days afterwards the Army Commander-in-Chief boasted to some of his generals that he had told the itinerant ambassador: "In Bolivia, I decide who and when to put in power and when to remove him."

3. Opinion poll by Lou Harris, April 29, 1982.

4. *US reaction to the Malvinas War: An Informal Assessment.* Mark Falcoff - American Enterprise Institute for Public Policy Research - Washington 1982.

5. *The Battle for the Falklands* Max Hastings and Simon Jenkins. Michael Joseph, London, 1983, p 136. For a detailed discussion of the episode, see also *One Man's Falklands* by Tam Dalyell. Cecil Woolf, London, p 87 et seq. London, 1982.

6. Ibid (4) p135.

7. "Pym's Brief" *Daily Telegraph* April 21, 1982, London.

8. Inter-American Treaty of Reciprocal Assistance. Signed at the Inter-American Conference for the Maintenance of Continental Peace and Security, Rio de Janeiro, August 15 - Sept 2, 1947. The IATRA suffered some modifications in 1975 during another meeting of Foreign Ministers held in San Jose, Costa Rica after a long process of opposition on the part of the Latin American countries to its character of "holy alliance" with the US.

9. The contracting parties of IATRA are: Argentina, Bolivia, Brazil, Colombia, Costa Rica, Chile, Ecuador, El Salvador, United States, Guatemala, Haiti, Honduras, Mexico, Nicaragua, Panama, Para-

guay, Peru, Dominican Republic, Trinidad-Tobago, Venezuela and Uruguay.

They are all members of the OAS, but the following have not joined IATRA: Antigua and Barbuda, Barbados, Grenada, Jamaica, Bahamas, Santa Lucia and Surinam. Consequently they do not have a vote in either the meetings of the Permanent Council of the OAS on questions relating to IATRA, or in the sessions of that pact. In those cases the delegates of these countries attend as observers.

10. Article 5 of IATRA states: "If the inviolability or the integrity of the territory or the sovereignty or political independence of any State Party should be affected by an act of aggression as determined in accordance with Article 9 of this Treaty that does not fall within the scope of Article 3 or by a conflict or serious event that might endanger the peace of America, the Organ of Consultation shall meet immediately to agree on the measures that must be taken to assist the affected State Party and the measures and steps that should be taken for the common defence and for the maintenance of peace and security in the Hemisphere."

Article 13 reads: "The consultations will be initiated at the request of the Permanent Council of the OAS or of any of the Signatory States that have ratified the Treaty".

11. Cardoso, Oscar Raul: "Pym y Costa Mendez" *Clarin*, April 22, 1982, p 8.

12. In the interview in which Foreign Minister Jose Alberto Zambrano Velazco greeted him after arriving in Washington from Caracas, Haig suggested the possibility that his commitments might prevent his attendance at the deliberations of the Organ of Consultation. The Venezuelan did not ignore the matter and rapped out in a heart-felt manner: "If you don't go you will be doing Hemispheric unity a bad turn."

13. Venezuela has long maintained a dispute with Guyana over the sovereignty of the region of the Esequibo, whilst Guatemala for its part does not accept the "independence" granted by Great Britain to Belize.

14. The resolution of the Inter-American Juridical Committee was arrived at on 16 January 1976 at a meeting held in Rio de Janeiro, when Argentina denounced the Shackleton mission that Great Britain had sent to the Falklands. In its first clause, the declaration of this Committee states: "That the Argentine Republic has an unquestionable right of sovereignty over the Falklands, and therefore the fundamental question to be resolved is the procedure to be followed for the re-integration of its territory."

15. Observers of the OAS agree in describing the speech of the

Venezuelan as "one of the most important pieces of oratory" that had been produced in the history of the organization. Zambrano Velazco did not limit himself to analysing the present situation and attempted severe criticism of the international juridical system. See record of the First General Session (OAS Series F/II Document 20/82 - April 26 1982).

16. On the basis of these unofficial comments *Clarin* newspaper headlined the edition of 28 April: "La Junta Rechazo la Propuesta de Ronald Reagan" (The Junta rejected Ronald Reagan's proposal) which complicated the manoeuvre Costa Mendez was employing in order to avoid an *impasse* in the negotiations. In Washington the Foreign Minister appealed to the press, using any argument he could lay his hands on to change the "rejection" into "partial objections".

17. Resolution: "Grave Situation arisen in the South Atlantic." Document 28/82 Revision 1, 28 April 1982. See also "Consultative Meeting of Foreign Ministers" OAS/Series F II.20, 27 April 1982. The motion for the original resolution was presented by the delegations of Peru and Brazil, with the co-sponsorship of Costa Rica and Honduras.

18. The British Government responded to this declaration by the Inter-American system through a note presented on April 29, 1982 to the Security Council of the United Nations, with the signature of its permanent representative, Anthony Parsons. In its reply, London rejected recognition of Argentine sovereignty over the islands and the accusations regarding the economic sanctions applied to Buenos Aires. But an intelligent welcome was given to the part in the declaration which refers to Resolution 502 of the Security Council and "the interests" of the islanders.

19. The Argentine embassy sounded out its contacts in Congress in order for Costa Mendez to be able to make representation at the Senate Foreign Relations Committee in the same way as his British colleague had done. But the consultations disclosed the existence of such a hostile atmosphere that the Argentine dropped the idea. See *"Un Paso Difficil"* (A difficult step) *Clarin* April 24, 1982, p10.

20. The copy, three pages long, that Miret exhibited did not have identification marks showing its origin and its pagination showed that one or more leaves had been removed. But it was clearly a "working paper." Its title was: *The Strategic Situation of Argentina and England in the Falklands Conflict.*

21. "Sail on, Oh Union firm and great." *Daily Telegraph*, April 29, 1982, London.

Chapter 10

"SINK THE BELGRANO!"

Almost without noticing it towards the end of April, Argentina was drifting into armed conflict with Great Britain. There were sufficient data at that stage of events to infer that the Task Force had not arrived in these distant regions merely to intimidate. A naval contingent of impressive size and capability had crossed the South Atlantic and perhaps the last hope of avoiding a clash was buried when the Royal Navy left Ascension Island. From that moment, events seemed to devour the calendar and on April 25th Argentines learnt that on a grey and rainy Sunday, firing had broken out on South Georgia. While official reports maintained the fantasy of a non-existent resistance, the Junta seemed oblivious to everything: the dispute in the Falklands had reached a point of no return.

In reality, the inactivity of the Argentine Military did have some explanation. The armed forces were operating at a level greatly subordinated to the Intelligence Services. Thus the High Command's first confirmation of the presence of the British fleet in the South Atlantic was obtained by a Boeing 707 under the command of Vice-Commodore Fontaine. It detected the ships at the latitude of Cape Frio in Brazil, but on being intercepted by a Sea Harrier, which took off from one of the aircraft carriers, the Boeing had to retire.

Neither was Argentina able to count on satellite information from the Soviet Union - at least there was never any sign of it. Great Britain, on the other hand, had developed its own information system, invaluably enriched by the open assistance of the United States.

Four days after the attack on South Georgia an incident occurred in Argentina which demonstrated the inadequacy of the conditions under which Argentina was operating. It showed how the Junta was still not persuaded that it was inexorably forcing the country towards an unequal war. On the morning of April 29th, the Chief of TOAS, Vice-Admiral Lombardo, decided to travel from Comodoro

Rivadavia to Buenos Aires, to submit a report to the three commandants. On board his aircraft, and while he was revising some notes, he received an urgent radio message which informed him that a Neptune reconnaissance aircraft had spotted three enormous boats heading for the South American mainland. Lombardo reacted with a certain incredulity. He knew that these planes, many years in service, did not produce reliable information - any sudden climatic change affected the radar equipment - and some of the pilots, transferred by the impresario Amalia Fortabat, lacked expertise in this type of work.

The Chief of TOAS, by that time approaching Buenos Aires, ordered a renewed inspection, which produced results identical to the first time. Now there could be no doubt: three British ships (there had been no authorization for Argentine ships to cross that zone) were trying to shell the mainland. This was a fear which gained ground in those days particularly in the most southerly towns and which was strongly sustained by the Commander of Air Defence, Brigadier Augusto Hughes. As soon as he landed, Lombardo set off for the Libertad building to inform Anaya of what had happened and to ask for authorization to organize a counter-attack.

Although it may seem incredible, the commandants had not worked out, even then, a policy on when to open fire. That is to say, the military chiefs on the mainland and in the islands did not know for certain when they could attack the enemy. And now it was almost war. Anaya gave Lombardo the O.K. for an advance upon the supposed British ships and obtained the consent of Lami Dozo, who ordered his aircraft to be made ready for a massive attack.

Galtieri's authorisation remained to be obtained, however. The President, upon being requested over the telephone by Anaya, appeared reluctant and expressed the view that "it is better to see what happens." Like a man obsessed, the naval chief warned him: "Look, Lami Dozo also agrees; so it's two to one," [Decisions within the Junta had to be majority ones]. It was already almost mid-day when Galtieri asked Lombardo to come and visit him at Government House. The Commander of TOAS, a determined man, waited a long time in the ante-room, and when he entered the Presidential office, he found a sleepy Galtieri in shorts. He was untidy and unkempt.

"General; we can't wait any longer. The ships are going to attack the mainland. We must order a counter-attack," urged Lombardo.

"You think so?" the President managed to reply. "Afterwards we can lay the blame on the aggressors. But I don't know..." he stammered.

It was while they were deliberating that Lombardo was to answer a telephone call from Comodoro Rivadavia: it had all been a false alarm, he was told. The boats were in fact three fishing vessels of Argentine registration which had had to make for that port for technical reasons. Such authoritarian bungles were a distinctive feature of the Military Junta.

Much has been said, especially in the foreign press about the supposed firmness of Galtieri and Anaya in decision making, and of the corresponding weakness shown by Lami Dozo. The facts show the opposite to be true. Overwhelmed, perhaps, by responsibilities which appeared too much for them, Galtieri frequently sank into deep depressions, while Lami Dozo rapidly alternated between attitudes of toughness and flexibility. The most stubbornly well-balanced seemed to be Anaya, who nevertheless also fell into indiscretions.

The fact is that the 30th April was a milestone on the long road to the Falklands conflict. On that day, the US shelved its neutralist posture and laid charges at the door of Argentina. Alexander Haig announced, for example, economic and military sanctions on the nation. These last were a mere extension of those in force since 1978 due to the Humphrey-Kennedy amendment. They signalled an alert for the "probable large-scale military actions" in the Falkland Islands. President Reagan went further when, from the White House, he told reporters that he considered Argentina to be the true aggressor.

There was then no room for doubt. At 4.40 am on May 1st, Vulcans, and then Sea Harriers, began their attacks on Port Stanley. This marked the start of hostilities that would only cease on June 14th when General Menendez surrendered the capital of the archipelago. That day also marked the beginning of a new diplomatic effort - after the successive failures of Haig and the inefficacy of the United Nations. As never before during the conflict, this effort had intimate links with what was happening on the battle front.

Costa Mendez was returning from New York and during the stop in Rio de Janeiro, he was informed of the British attack on the islands. The Foreign Minister was deeply affected. But in fact, he still believed that the US decision to abandon efforts to find a negotiated solution to the South Atlantic crisis would open more diplomatic doors than it closed. He speculated on the possibility of a meeting of the Security Council. At the same time, this same Costa Mendez carried hidden in his briefcase an indirect proposal from the UN Secretary General, Javier Perez de Cuellar. This was for a possible mediation between the countries in conflict.

Public opinion had switched attention from the diplomatic front to events in the war. These were presented by the Government with a marked triumphalist flavour. The Joint Staff, incidentally, made a "calm evaluation," in those first hours - so the communique said - of the events in the war and dared to indicate "serious errors of a professional order," in the British forces. Accordingly, it announced the first day of battle to be an "Argentine triumph."

It was therefore not strange that a simplistic feeling of success infected broad fringes of society. A Gallup Poll proved revealing: according to a sample taken in all districts of the Federal capital, 90% of those consulted described themselves in favour of the war, with only 8% against. This in spite of the fact that in the capital, the war figured only as some very distant story. Furthermore, some 82% discounted any possibility of negotiation with Great Britain while only 15% took the opposite view.

In any case, it was the US that had been most interested in pumping oxygen into the negotiations, because in the last resort it did not want to have to choose between Argentina and Great Britain - as in fact, it finally did have to do. Even after taking up the British side, the Reagan administration encouraged the Peruvian Government of the architect, Fernando Belaunde Terry to become a voluntary mediator. The Peruvian President had made a very solid relationship with the US, especially in financial matters.

However, not everyone shared the idea that Reagan's hand could be seen behind the Peruvian offer. It was Ambassador Jeane Kirkpatrick herself who confirmed that impression to the authors. "It was a new undercover Haig mission," she managed to admit.

At 10 pm on May 1st Costa Mendez received a call from Javier Arias Stella, his Peruvian opposite number. With generous diplomatic tact, Stella used their close personal relationship to learn what the Argentine attitude would be to any eventual offer of help. At the time, the Argentine Military were bragging about what in their judgment had been a day of victory on the battle front. The Foreign Minister had to press hard, therefore, for Galtieri to accept a dialogue with Belaunde Terry at all. The Argentine President was seeking to avoid this, on the grounds of having "too much work." The President of Peru's mission, however, had its origins at some earlier time. A representative of the *petite bourgeoisie*, Belaunde was always an enthusiast for the problematic concept of *Latin America* and a protagonist - more theoretical than active - for regional unity.

For that reason it is not surprising that the man from *Accion Popular* who re-established constitutional life in his country should so emphatically take up the work of mediation, thus going far beyond the nod he had received from the US. A few days after the passing of Resolution 502 by the Security Council, Belaunde had demanded that Argentina and Great Britain should cease hostilities. It seemed at the time a formality because at that stage the Royal Navy was far from the

Falklands and the possibility of a war seemed out of the question, at least to many Argentines. Belaunde nevertheless gave his explanation: "That exhortation was necessary, so that when they were face to face, they wouldn't shoot it out[1]."

Very early on May 1st the President of Peru contacted Haig, who immediately raised the possibility of establishing a new bridge between Argentina and Great Britain through Lima. Haig knew of the friendship between Peru and Argentina - perhaps one of the few things the Secretary of State knew about Latin American history - and suggested to Belaunde that he might get in touch with Galtieri. "To propose what?" was the architect's reply, knowing as he did the reasons for the failure of the Haig mission. Nevertheless, both did begin work, using as a basis the various ideas that had not been accepted by the Argentine Government during the extended April negotiations. With a certain finesse, however, Belaunde made suggestions for improvements that might make the proposal more palatable to the Military Junta.

On more than one occasion he warned Haig to relax the rigidity of principle he was displaying, because Argentina had converted the Falklands into a fortress and it was essential to avoid a massacre. Haig was forthright in his reply: "Mr President," he warned, "I am a soldier. The British will win. they have sent five ships and if one is sunk, they will send three to replace it. If an aircraft is shot down, they will send four."

And he concluded: "The British have very sophisticated armaments that the defenders of the islands, valiant though their resistance may be, will not be able to counter[2]."

Finally Galtieri accepted the call from Belaunde - whom he repeatedly called "Doctor" - a term of address selected from his limited military vocabulary. This was in spite of the faces pulled by the Foreign Minister in efforts to make him understand that Belaunde was an *architect*. This was only a minor error but, at the same time, it was symptomatic of that tendency towards over-simplification beloved by the Military. It was as if, for the Military, society could be divided into two: doctors and officers.

Belaunde thought he could see in Galtieri a man who was likely to accept help. This impression was in direct contrast to the Argentine's off-hand attitude in dealing with the Peruvian President. The idea of mediation was accepted by Galtieri, who in any case preferred the details of any proposed solution to be sorted out with Costa Mendez. In fact, Belaunde had secretly sketched out such details with Haig.

The President of Peru set out a seven point Peace Plan that the Foreign Ministry received through a confidential telex from the ambassador in Lima, Luis Pedro Sanchez Moreno. The plan proposed the following:

> **1.** Immediate cessation of hostilities.
>
> **2.** Immediate and mutual withdrawal of forces.
>
> **3.** The presence of representatives other than from the two parties in conflict for the temporary government of the islands.
>
> **4.** The two governments to recognize the existence of differing positions on the status of the islands.
>
> **5.** The two governments to recognize that the points of view and interests of the local inhabitants have to be taken into account in the final solution of the problem.
>
> **6.** The group of nations which would immediately intervene in the negotiations to implement this accord to be composed of Brazil, the Federal Republic of Germany, and the USA.
>
> **7.** Before April 30th 1983, a final agreement to be reached under the aegis of the group of countries mentioned above.

Costa Mendez read the little document carefully and was very enthusiastic, even though he was convinced that he would still have to make a great effort for the proposal to be acceptable on the military front. The mediating effort seemed to have come to life again in the space of a few hours, but the negotiations began to run into trouble with the fifth paragraph of the plan and the chances of success began to be a race against the clock.

Haig had sent the proposal to the British Foreign Secretary, Francis Pym, who immediately made his objections known: the British Government would not accept the phrase: "points of view and interests." At first sight, this objection from London seemed to be no more than a mere linguistic caprice. But it was not so in reality. The objection pointed up the very basis of the Falklands conflict which both nations had not managed to resolve after decades of futile negotiations.

Not by chance, Argentina also made a stand on this same point in the Peace Plan. It first questioned "points of view," and asked for it to be replaced by "aspirations." Then, in the face of British intransigence, it chose to stick to Belaunde's initial formula. What was in contention behind the subtleties of language was possible recognition of Argentine sovereignty in the archipelago.

It is known that during the last years of the negotiation there had been little advance towards agreement between Argentina and Great Britain. Despite UN Resolution 2065 which was passed by virtue of the efforts of Doctor Miguel Angel Zavala Ortiz, one of the most significant dates occurred during a meeting in Rome in 1977. On that occasion, the British authorities admitted for the first time in a hundred and fifty years that the problem of sovereignty "is a subject" for the consideration of the parties - as the official record of those days reads.

What seemed in principle a step forward turned out to be a delaying tactic by the British, since in later meetings, Her Majesty's delegates - often deliberately reduced in strength to deprive them of authority - began to cling to the principle of self-determination for the islanders. This was insisted upon as a condition *sine qua non* for the determination of the dispute.

This battle over a word while the crude realities of war were looming was not, apparently, an idle one. The British covered themselves with the argument for respecting: "the wishes of the *kelpers*," because in sophisticated diplomatic language that could imply the recognition of self-determination by the UN. Great Britain endorsed that idea with the UN Resolution of November 1976. This accepted the principle of self-determination for Belize, whose formal independence was finalized in September 1981.

Nevertheless, precedents for the Falklands case, hardly existed. The two cases constituted perhaps the last vestiges of colonialism on the American continent and had in common the fact that Great Britain exercised the power of dominion over each territory. But the similarities did not extend beyond these facts.

In Belize there was a native population as well as its original Spanish-speaking inhabitants which dated back to the end of the 17th century. Although they had links with Spanish sovereignty, they also identified themselves with the British settlements which themselves lacked any clearly defined relationship to their own mother country. Spain's gradual abandonment of empire, however, gradually led to the acceptance of this British presence and, as a consequence, to the consolidation of the administrative structure of a new British dominion.

With the Falklands, nothing similar had occurred. In 1833 a British occupation force had taken power in the archipelago, ignoring Spanish titles and possession and established an enclave with citizens brought from Great Britain.

Argentina for that reason never recognized the principle of self-determination, arguing that such a claim could not be exercised over an alien territory. Argentina also relies on some valid antecedents arising in the United Nations: Resolution 1514 of December 14, 1960, which urged that body "to put an end to colonialism in all its parts and in all its forms," and stated that in non-autonomous territories, "immediate measures must be taken without conditions or reservations, to transfer all powers to the peoples of those territories, in conformity with their will and desires freely expressed."

This instrument, although it observed the necessity of de-colonization, became in time an obstacle for Argentine diplomatic efforts by its heavy emphasis on the principle of self-determination.

When a special committee was constituted for the de-colonization process - called the Committee of 24 because of the number of countries comprising it - Argentina put the case for the Falklands before it, and afterwards put it before the UN General Assembly. This was done with a view to an eventual referendum to legalize the *de facto* situation through a literal application of Resolution 1514.

It thus managed to get Resolution 2065 passed which declared that the General Assembly, "taking note of the existence of a dispute between the governments of Argentina and the United Kingdom over the sovereignty of the said islands, invites these governments to pursue without delay the negotiations recommended by the Special Committee." In the text of the resolution, it especially recognizes that the Falklands is an example of colonialism which must be ended.

In 1973, the UN passed Resolution 3160, which expressed "grave concern" at the time that had passed without progress in the negotiations over the Falklands. On November 15, 1976 a new resolution was approved by a large majority: 94 to 1 with 32 abstentions. It required the concept of "territorial integrity" in the case of the Falklands to be respected. In fact, that implied down-grading the principle of self-determination and a tacit recognition of the necessity to restore Argentine sovereignty over the archipelago. At the present time, with the war concluded, Great Britain has confirmed its absolute dominion over the islands, but has left a flank open on the diplomatic side, in accepting the principle that negotiations may be renewed at some time in the future.

Triumph in war obliged the British to change the islanders' status into that of British citizens - something long desired by the kelpers themselves - and this move towards integration only weakened Britain's best argument in the international forum: that of self-determination. It seems obvious that a difference between Argentina and Great Britain cannot now be subordinated to the will of a single group of those British citizens. That would be equivalent to conferring on them the unacceptable status of being both parties to the dispute and judges in it[3].

That morning of May 2nd, the telephone calls from President Belaunde Terry to the Argentine Government became almost obsessive. He had already talked to Galtieri in the morning and at midday he continued without let up. With evident urgency - the Argentines did not quite understand why - the Peruvian asked for a reply to his Peace Plan. But the bureaucracy of the Argentine military power - a characteristic of the *Proceso* which appeared on the scene in 1976 - hindered any speedy results. Galtieri remained in a somewhat uncomfortable position *vis-a-vis* Belaunde - losing himself in digressions without managing to give a reply. Whilst he tried to summon the Military Junta he delegated responsibility for negotiations to Costa Mendez.

Between 12 noon and 2 pm, Belaunde spoke on three occasions with the Foreign Minister. Argentina continued to defend its argument for not including the word "desires" in the draft accord. It also objected to the presence of the United States as one of the members of the group of countries listed. Great Britain, for its part, had asked for the exclusion of Peru in the same way, suspecting a certain partiality towards Argentine interests.

Belaunde had by then a telephone at each ear. On one side he listened to the suggestions of Haig, who had an open line to London through Foreign Secretary Pym, who was visiting him in his office in Washington. On the other, he was listening impatiently for the O.K. from Buenos Aires. Costa Mendez was rather seduced by the Peruvian President's proposal and even risked saying during one of the conversations that they were on the threshold of an agreement: "I cannot tell you yes or no, Mr Architect," commented Costa Mendez, knowing that in the end everything would be subordinated to the opinion of the Military. And he added: "If we exclude one or two little things I believe it's going to work."

"Let me take the document to the Junta, who are meeting this evening - and don't worry," he almost begged.

In one of these dialogues, Costa Mendez stretched the concessions to the limit. The final part of it - recorded at both ends of the line, as were all conversations at this level during the conflict - developed in the following manner:

"The US ambassador has called me and asks me two small things. First, that we use the Spanish version, because the English version was prepared here and everything is not as careful as it should be," explained Belaunde Terry.

"Very good, that's no problem," replied Costa Mendez.

"He also asked me for point five of the Spanish version - where it says "points of view and interests of the islanders" - to be changed to: "desires and interests of the islanders," said the Peruvian leader, once again raising the most critical question of all.

"That is impossible for us," cut in the Argentine Foreign Minister, and argued: "for us the word *desires* is unacceptable. This has already been discussed on various occasions in the UN. It was always thrown out there by an overwhelming majority, and the word *interests* substituted as representing everything that we should have to take into account."

"The English version says *the views and interests*. Perhaps we

223

could accept the formula *"the views concerning the interests."* Thus it would become: *"the two governments acknowledge taking into account the views concerning the interests,"* suggested Belaunde in an effort to overcome the stumbling block.

"It could be acceptable," admitted the Argentine, in an effort at conciliation. And in reality it was, as supposedly in part at least, it retraced the steps of Argentine demands at the UN.

"Good; I'm noting that, Doctor," said the President of Peru.

Belaunde was not happy with this promise and spoke once more with Galtieri who at this stage was finding it difficult to contain his irritation.

"Yes; of course, what you said to Costa Mendez is O.K. But don't try to make me give you a reply because I can't. Look, I also have my Senate and must consult it," commented the President, trying not to let his forced amiability crack. Galtieri was referring, of course, to the Junta. Belaunde would say afterwards that he understood the situation: "A Senate with stripes is a very serious matter," he explained[4]. Perhaps his ability to pick the right phrase was born of his own experiences. It escaped nobody's notice that in Peru as well as in Argentina, the armed forces adopted no very respectful attitude to political authority.

At 4.30 pm Belaunde again spoke to Costa Mendez, who did not really have much new to offer, beyond his efforts to encourage the Peruvian President on the feasibility of finding a solution. The Foreign Minister did once confess his regret for perhaps paying insufficient attention to his conversations with Belaunde that 2nd May.

Running through his notes, Costa Mendez recalled later that during that particularly tragic day for Argentines, Belaunde was "excessively anxious" and that in one part of the talks he had warned "Look; I've been told that something can happen..."

That surely now explains - and with a vengeance - the Peruvian President's haste while he was trying to extract a reply for his Peace Plan. This was never understood by the Argentine authorities. It is also useful to remember that Belaunde had Haig permanently on another line, and the US Secretary of State was ensconced in his office with the British Foreign Secretary, Francis Pym. In London, meanwhile, Margaret Thatcher's War Cabinet was deliberating.

No-one can doubt, in the light of the foregoing, that Belaunde sensed the anxiety that Haig conveyed to him over the telephone, and that Haig, in his turn, noticed Pym's restlessness, being in communication with Chequers, where the fate of the cruiser in the South Atlantic would be decided.

Paul Foot, a journalist on the staff of the *Daily Mail*, was of the opinion that the cruiser, *Belgrano*, was sunk in order to put obstacles in the way of positive progress in Peru's mediation attempt. He maintained that Pym and Haig were "heatedly" discussing points for nine hours in the search for a possible solution and that in the interim, the Argentine ship was torpedoed. Pym, on the other hand, though he admitted that Haig had told him about the possible basis for a solution the Peruvians and Americans were working on, never seemed to have real confidence in the effort.

"There were only promising guidelines for other negotiations," affirmed Margaret Thatcher's Foreign Secretary, and he added that Haig had also recognized that for this plan to be brought forward, it would require more time than was available.

Pym also said that the proposal from Peru did not differ much from schemes that Argentina had already rejected, revealing, in his view, the lack of consistency that the negotiations showed[5]. The British viewpoint had little in common with the expectations that Belaunde's mediation awakened in Argentina and Peru. Perhaps that clash of attitudes serves to explain how at that stage the determination of the British Conservative Government to negotiate seemed to be lacking.

If not, how can one understand the pursuit of the cruiser, *Belgrano*, by the nuclear submarine, *Conqueror*, for more than 30 hours? Why carry out the attack when Argentina, at least, believed itself to be near a solution? Why do it outside the announced Exclusion Zone?

The question marks lead almost inevitably to a strengthening of the hypothesis that Great Britain, having settled the matter of South Georgia, and having sent its fleet to the South Atlantic, never seriously believed in the possibility of concluding the dispute by recourse to diplomatic channels.

The built-in replies to all these questions are locked up in official British documents - where they will remain many years, safe from curious eyes - and in the consciences of those taking part. But there are some signs which afford an explanation if put together correctly:

1. In the first place, the crisis of the South Atlantic granted the British Admiralty an invaluable opportunity to defend its surface fleet against Government cuts. It was planned to be replaced by Trident nuclear submarines. Margaret Thatcher and her Defence Minister, John Nott, were determined on transforming the Royal Navy into a mere appendage to the NATO forces, with hardly any capacity to operate outside that framework. The arguments of the naval commanders, advocating the retention of surface units, had invariably foundered against the firm convictions of the Conservative Government.

2. Moreover, the *Iron Lady* had done honour to the toughness which had earned her the nickname, dispatching the Task Force scarcely hours after the Argentine landing. She demanded, and then obtained, the consensus of the population. She knew that she could not make it turn round half-way without a clear victory, as from the very beginning she made her confrontation with Argentina into an over-riding matter of domestic politics. As Winston Churchill had confronted Nazi Germany, she was now going to do likewise with the Argentine "fascists." She would not repeat Suez in the decade of the 80's.

After the war, Costa Mendez outlined another theory: he supposed that the decision to torpedo the Belgrano was adopted in order to exercise pressure on the Junta and oblige it to accept Belaunde's proposal with expedition.

But the Argentine Military had advanced too far into the conflict, in deeds as well as words, to retreat abruptly at the first important set-back. It was therefore unthinkable that the sinking of the Belgrano would work to reduce tension. Quite the opposite: there would be, as finally did occur, an exacerbation in the war fever.

Another testimony, that of Geoffrey Underwood, author of *Our Falklands War*, confirmed the belief that the attack was carried out premeditatedly, at the exact moment necessary to sink any possibility of a diplomatic rapprochement. In support of this, the Labour MP, Tam Dalyell, made the following statement in Parliament: "I understand from two members of the crew I am not prepared to name that [....] HMS Conqueror detected the General Belgrano and her escorts at least twenty-four hours before 14.57 hours South Atlantic time, 8 pm London time on May 2nd [the first official sighting]."

He also quoted from the official report: "Concerned that *HMS Conqueror* might lose the *General Belgrano*.....the Task Force Commander sought and obtained a change in the rules of engagement to allow an attack outside the 200 mile Exclusion Zone"[6]

In the sessions of the House of Commons of 4th and 5th May 1982, the Defence Minister, John Nott, had stated that the Belgrano was detected at 8 pm London time on the 2nd (3 pm Argentine time). A similar piece of information is evidenced in the report produced by the Commander-in-Chief of the Fleet, Sir John Fieldhouse, at the conclusion of the conflict. The BBC, in its *Newsnight* TV programme, also made an investigation into the sinking of the Belgrano and in it it stated that on May 2nd, in Pym's presence, the American Secretary of State contacted Margaret Thatcher by telephone to tell her that the Peruvian plan was on the point of being accepted by Buenos Aires.

The coincidences are apparently sufficiently convincing, at least in quantity, as to suggest that the attack on the *Belgrano* was intended not only to gain military advantage but also to reduce the scope for a negotiated solution. Nevertheless, Belaunde Terry believed in a negotiated solution until the last moment. For this reason, at 8 pm, Lima time - 6 pm, Buenos Aires time - he summoned a press conference in his office to announce an Argentine-British accord.

In Buenos Aires at that hour, there was scarcely a hint of the sinking of the cruiser, and great was the surprise in the newspaper offices when the Associated Press Agency announced that as reported from Lima, the bilateral document would be signed "in a few hours." In New York, on the other hand, the possibility of an accord did not seem to be taken into account at all. Almost at the same time as the attack on the *Belgrano*, and whilst the peace effort of the Peruvian President was proceeding, the Secretary General of the UN, Perez de Cuellar, summoned the representatives of Argentina and Great Britain: Eduardo Roca and Anthony Parsons.

He proposed his own good offices as mediator to seek a way out of the conflict, and great was Costa Mendez' surprise when he learned of this offer. No-one could understand how two peace efforts could be superimposed - coincidentally, both brought into being by Peruvians. For, although Belaunde's proposal certainly seemed destined to failure, no-one, at least at that time, was yet persuaded of the fact.

The investigations carried out by the present authors serve to throw light on this question of the two peace moves that continues to be a great unknown for the principal Argentine participants in the conflict.

The explanation has to be sought in the internal politics of the US and in the power struggles in the White House, especially between Alexander Haig and Jeane Kirkpatrick. The ambassador to the UN and adviser to President Reagan had been deliberately left on one side by Haig during the peace mission. "During that time," she confessed, "I spoke with neither Argentines nor British." It happens that the dual role played by Kirkpatrick never pleased Haig: on one hand she reported to the Secretary of State on events in the UN, but on the other she had direct and confidential access to Reagan as a member of his Cabinet. Moreover, Kirkpatrick had a different view to Haig's on the dispute. The ambassador encouraged a neutral stance for the US and not a "pro-British one like that of Haig" - this according to a description given by sources close to the ambassador.

As far as Kirkpatrick was concerned, Haig did not understand - neither then nor now - the Latin American point of view, although she granted him a measure of determination in seeking an agreement. Contrary to the opinion of many, Kirkpatrick also maintained that Thomas Enders only knew the region superficially, and that in fact only Vernon Walters - who, in her judgment, had only a marginal role to play - was familiar with the subject.

227

Perhaps one may suppose, with a certain amount of reason, that Kirkpatrick's opinions are coloured by a marked partiality, bearing in mind the rancour she showed towards Haig. But there is one fact which speaks for itself and lends authority to the ambassador's views: of all American officials, she is certainly one of the most knowledgeable about the ethos of Latin America[7]. On the other hand, one can well disagree with her opinion on the role of Walters. What for many seemed marginal was not really so - above all this became clear after the checks carried out by the authors mentioned in chapter one. What is certain is that it was Kirkpatrick herself who encouraged Perez de Cuellar's intervention, as she guessed that Belaunde Terry's mission was running into the ground. Kirkpatrick had put her plan to Reagan, though she recognizes that although it had the support of the White House, this was: "not exactly that of the President."

Nevertheless, according to investigation, there was a consensus in the White House in favour of the move by Perez de Cuellar. This situation infuriated Haig, and he had it out with Kirkpatrick openly and finally. In regard to the go-ahead hinted at by the ambassador, other sources consulted pointed towards William P. Clark, the previous though still influential, National Security Adviser to President Reagan.

The impression that the agreement promoted by Belaunde was evaporating grew in Buenos Aires as well, in spite of the premature announcement made by the Peruvian President. There was an enormous gap between that expression of optimism and the depression to be seen among the Argentine diplomatic officials. At 7 pm, Costa Mendez entered the *Libertador* building, headquarters of the Army. Slowly, Lami Dozo and Galtieri himself appeared. The Foreign Minister was continuing work on the Peruvian document, but nothing could be resolved because without warning, and contrary to his habit, Admiral Anaya was not on time that day.

He arrived 45 minutes after the time arranged. He entered looking pale, with a solemn face. Costa Mendez had hardly begun to mention Belaunde's proposal when the Admiral stopped him abruptly: "The navy is withdrawing from the negotiations. They have sunk the Belgrano." He carried in his right hand a telex of only two lines.

There was only a faint light colouring the sky over the South Atlantic when a Douglas A4Q of the Argentine Navy took off from the aircraft carrier, *25 de Mayo*, located in the region of the Gulf of San Jorge. It was May 1st, and some hours beforehand war had broken out between Argentina and Great Britain. The navy's sea fleet was stationed in defensive positions which would remain almost unchanged throughout the conflict, and was alerted by the message that had been received from the mainland. At 1 am on that day, Vice-Admiral Lombardo, Chief of TOAS, had advised: "Do not take up positions outside the protection zone."

The behaviour of the fleet generated much discussion after the conflict. The majority of opinion - except that of the public who were not acquainted with the facts - was biased by vested interests. Nobody can be unaware that the air force took a firm stand on more than one occasion over the passivity of the navy during the war, just as the latter service took on the job of de-mythicising the exploits of the airmen. For example, naval sources said that the attack on the *Hermes* by a small Pucara, supposedly piloted by Lt. Daniel Jukic never took place, because the pilot had died the previous day in the British bombardment of Darwin.

Meanwhile the army blamed both these forces for its own failure to defend Port Stanley. From the authors' investigations it emerges that at no time was there any political conditioning of Admiral Anaya, who acted with greater independence than his peers in taking decisions during the conflict.

The naval commanders explained that the conduct of the navy, after the landing on the Falklands on April 2nd, could not be anything but desultory. Lombardo himself had indicated as much to the Military Committee in the meeting of April 6th, when he rejected the use of the fleet as an effective way of impeding the approach of the British to the islands. In that encounter, the chief of TOAS had set out the difficulties that the defence of the archipelago presented. The British submarines, in his opinion, prevented any movement of ships. The air force and naval air arm were going to be able to operate (with difficulty) from the mainland. This was because their range permitted the establishment of a brief air superiority over the Falklands. Besides, the air strip at Port Stanley could not accommodate combat aircraft except for the Pucaras, which were really designed for fighting against guerillas and not for battle on this scale.

Thus the Royal Navy could position itself, as it did during the war, at the limits of the range of its aircraft and in that way neutralize the most rewarding method that Argentina had of prosecuting the armed conflict. Nor was it possible to propose air combat to the armed forces. For that it would have been necessary to possess permanent patrol aircraft with the ability to enter into action immediately. That was really impossible: the aircraft carrier - vital in such cases - could not penetrate the Exclusion Zone in the face of a threat from nuclear submarines. Six of these were patrolling the Zone, among them *Conqueror*, *Spartan* and

Splendid. and any aircraft that set off from the mainland would take approximately two hours to arrive at the Falklands. In that period the adaptable Sea Harrier could well overfly and bombard the Falklands with complete ease.

There was only one hypothesis, among the thousand that the Military shuffled through in those days, that favoured Argentina's plans: if the British tried a landing, their fleet would be split up inevitably and have to remain at fixed points for several hours. Consequently the Argentine fleet was divided, from April 29, into three task groups: *GT1* stationed near Cape Tres Puntas, made up of *Hercules, Santisima Trinidad,* the aircraft carrier, *25 de Mayo,* and two destroyers; *GT2* stationed to the north of the Gulf of San Jorge, comprising *Drummond* and the corvettes, *Granville* and *Guerrico,* and *GT3,* near the island of Los Estados, with the cruiser, *General Belgrano,* and the destroyers, *Piedrabuena* and *Bouchard.*

The naval chiefs imagined that the fleet would only engage in small combat operations, because it was not equal to taking on the bulk of the enemy force. Moreover, they maintained, with doubtful reasoning, that the dispute with Chile over the Beagle Channel could not be ignored, and they did not exclude the possibility of an audacious move by Pinochet's Government.

That is the reason why *GT3* was stationed so far south, they say. It was led by the cruiser, *Belgrano* - an old ship that had been re-equipped with six-inch guns for naval and land bombardment, five inch guns for naval and anti-aircraft work, 40 mm machine guns and batteries of Sea Cat missiles of short range (approximately 4000 metres). In reality a supposed intervention by Chile, taking advantage of Argentina's involvement in the war with Great Britain, was also in the minds of military and diplomatic personnel. But, to tell the truth, there is no evidence that the Pinochet regime had thought of anything on these lines.

The only concrete report on this was made by the British journalist, Robert Fox of the BBC, author of *Eye Witness Falklands,* who states the the British knew the position of the *General Belgrano* thanks to a message that the Commander of the Chilean Navy at Punta Arenas sent to the British military attache in Santiago. The message, according to Fox, said, "A1 information. One heavy unit, two light units in the sea. 13.00 - 14.00 Zulu. Latitude 54 degrees south and longitude 65 degrees 40 minutes. Direction evasive - 335 degrees."

Perhaps the only fact which lends credit to Robert Fox's information concerns the position of the cruiser, *Belgrano,* which is very similar to that which appears in official secret reports (55 degrees 18 minutes latitude and 61 degrees 07 minutes longitude). Anyhow, the only active involvement of Chile during the Argentine-British conflict seems to have been limited to a psychological campaign. It was very frequent for the radios of Argentine ships to suffer interference by Chilean radio enthusiasts who extolled British power and resorted to phrases which did not exactly look forward to a happy future such as: "They are going to make shit out of you."

One doubt did hang in the air however, and it concerned the appearance of the Sea King helicopter in Punta Arenas, rapidly hidden from view by the gendarmes when the first reporters arrived on the spot. The Argentine Navy maintains that this helicopter could not have come from the British fleet, situated as it was to the north of the Falklands, because it lacked the range to fly such long distances. One is inclined to think, on the other hand, that some British ship, perhaps winked at by the Chileans, was sailing in the Pacific and used such helicopters to carry out espionage tasks. Finally, it must not be forgotten, Argentine air operations of heavy transport were executed invariably from the mainland.

Nevertheless, one version has it that the appearance of the Sea King on trans-Andean soil was in reality the advance party of a hazardous mission by eight members of the Special Air Service (SAS) into Argentine territory. The purpose of such a mission would be to obtain information about planned air manoeuvres[8]. The Douglas A4Q aircraft that slipped away in the dawn reported, after careful reconnaissance, that the British fleet seemed disposed to try to make a landing in the Falklands.

By this time, Port Stanley had been withstanding a naval and air bombardment for some hours. Lombardo received the message from the Douglas in Comodoro Rivadavia and immediately began to contact the Governor of the islands, General Menendez. He made a report which impressed Lombardo: he put forward the proposition that the British were planning to disembark at the very gates of the capital of the archipelago. In reality the chief of TOAS was very sceptical regarding any such premature and open attempt by the Royal Marines.

He was seriously persuaded of the might and professionalism of the British and in this sense he differed from some of the Military, among them General Ramon Camps, who breezily declared that the British fleet "was pure scrap metal." He had always supposed, in his forward planning, that the British would not attempt an early landing, still less in the capital of the islands, where the power of the Argentine armed forces was concentrated.

Before ordering the fleet to advance, he preferred to make sure and once again spoke to Menendez, who replied undauntedly: "We are ready for the defence."

Faced with the evidence - the fleet was divided and was

attempting a landing - Lombardo sent a telex at 3.55 pm to the Commander of the Fleet, Rear Admiral Gualter Allara, aboard the aircraft carrier, *25 de Mayo*: "Enemy at anchor. You have liberty of action," he transmitted. From that moment the three task groups of the Argentine fleet began to advance towards the north of East Falkland, where the supposed British operation was taking shape.

The reports that were arriving at Comodoro Rivadavia from the islands were frankly optimistic and announced the shooting down of British aeroplanes and helicopters and a landing attempt beaten off with grave enemy losses. Lombardo demanded details - the remains of a crashed aircraft, its registration number, the name of a captured soldier -but such replies were "delayed." At one time, he thought, but could not believe, that everything was just the result of imagination and inexperience. And so it proved to be.

About midnight, the chief of TOAS thought it imprudent to pursue the advance of the fleet, to whom he had suggested hours earlier the possibility of a massive attack. The military chiefs on the islands still failed to send any news so that the original threat of a landing seemed finally to have disappeared. This was so because for several hours the British had ceased their harassment of the Falklands - which was, in fact, only to be renewed two days later.

Lombardo himself, days afterwards, made a lengthy evaluation of the episode in a document submitted to the Military Committee on May 15. It followed a personal statement which the military triumvirate did not take into account - and which in one part reports:

"The first important British action of May 1st seemed to be an invasion attempt that was successfully repulsed by our forces. Serious enemy casualties were estimated due to aerial attack. The theatre commander's present appreciation is, however, that this was not an invasion attempt, but a dummy run mounted by the enemy force to test our capacity and training.

"This appreciation is based on the following:

"The enemy has demonstrated in all previous and subsequent actions that it acts with the utmost prudence, with large numbers of men of a good professional level. If it had really intended an invasion, none of those conditions would have been met. In spite of searches and dredging, no remains or signs of landings, boats, helicopters, live or dead personnel, nor any other evidence of the reported landing have appeared.

"To summarise, this supposed rebuffed invasion and the supposed important losses inflicted on the enemy merely reaffirmed our own optimism. The mass media stirred up the fervour of the public, who saw an easy Argentine victory and great fighting strength in our forces.

"The enemy, however, merely withdrew their forces, continued receiving their reinforcements and carried out other measures, probably studying and refining plans of action.

"It is logical that this force which had set sail with such speed needed a period for evaluation and analysis in the area of operations. This would be so as to organize the forces that were going to take part and also to receive political directives for action."

The three groups of the Sea Fleet were near the Exclusion Zone by midnight - it took a day to cover the 250 miles to East Falkland - when Lombardo alerted Allara: "There have been no aerial attacks over the Falklands since 1900 hours. I don't know the position of the aircraft carrier. The enemy is not at anchor and so constitutes a serious threat for the fleet."

The ships, advancing at full speed, were closing the distance. Allara then began to analyze the risks involved in a possible attack on the enemy.

The C-in-C of the Fleet calculated that even at the risk of finding a greater opposing force than expected, an operation was viable if the aircraft could take off from the carrier with a full load: six bombs each and tanks marked "full" on the instrument panel. For the planes to be able to take off in these conditions it was essential, in his judgment, to have a tail-wind of at least 25 knots. At that time the wind intensity was scarcely greater than 5 knots. Allara reported his conclusions to TOAS and about 1 am on May 2nd, he proceeded to order the withdrawal of the fleet.

From that moment, the fleet virtually retired from the conflict. There would later be one unsuccessful operation with submarines and various other discarded proposals, among them that of launching the fleet *en masse* as well as a quantity of merchant ships, on the Royal Navy Task Force.

The return to the security zone was slow and serene. Nobody believed an enemy attack possible, much less one outside the Exclusion Zone. Nevertheless, Lombardo, the chief of TOAS prepared to protect his ships to the maximum and after mid-day he notified GT3: "Bring Luis to Miguel."

In this coded message, Lombardo had ordered the *Belgrano* and the destroyers to withdraw to positions of less depth in the rear - not more than 120 metres, in fact - to avoid nuclear submarines that cannot manoeuvre easily in these conditions. The *Belgrano* - survivor of the Japanese attack on Pearl Harbour on December 7, 1941; participant in the Battle of Leyte which ended in the latitudes of Japan; and which suffered only two fatal casualties in all its history - moved forward at low speed, and 10 kilometers behind followed the *Piedrabuena* and the

Bouchard. The light was fading and the sea was draped in heavy mist.

The destroyers had shut off radio communication and were trying to maintain maximum distance from the cruiser. There was an explanation for this. The *Piedrabuena* and the *Bouchard* - the best anti-submarine ships in the fleet - needed almost sepulchral silence to secure maximum range for their hydrophones so as to detect any British submarines.

The *Belgrano* had been the only member of all the fleet that a year earlier had completed on time, and without problems, a crossing from Puerto Belgrano Naval Base south of Buenos Aires to Rio de Janeiro. In spite of this, the *Belgrano* was just the opposite of silent. Its boilers and its old motors were much more like a noisy hell.

There was both calm and tension among the Argentine crews. Nothing had happened up till that moment, but every war generates a sensation of anguish difficult to overcome, even in hours of greatest serenity. Of the 1701 crew members, a third were resting and the remainder on routine work or making preparation for combat.

A little after 4 pm, the *Bouchard* thought it detected a torpedo attack. Its hull vibrated and only minutes later TOAS was receiving its first message: "Torpedo attack. I am beginning withdrawal."

The truth was otherwise. A minute after 4 pm the British submarine *Conqueror* discharged three torpedoes at the cruiser *Belgrano*. Two hit the target and the explosion raised the warship to an angle of 45 degrees. This is because the torpedoes do not embed themselves in the target but explode underneath it. The third one missed. The commander of the ship, Hector Elias Bonzo, reported the moment of the attack:

"The first impact holed four decks upwards as far as the main deck. Thus all decks were affected vertically. That was a tragedy, because one deck can be kept watertight from another by closing doors and partitions, but not when the decks are holed. The ship was sailing at that moment in a choppy sea. I left my cabin to go to the bridge and then I felt a vibration in the ship and a sensation like climbing a mountain of sand. A low sound, then a thud, and suddenly silence came. The ship stopped. Simultaneously all the lights went out and an acrid smell began to fill the whole ship. The second explosion occurred a little distance from where I was: that torpedo produced a total drop at the bows of 15 to 20 metres.

"At seven or eight minutes after the impact, the boat was listing between 13 and 15 degrees. As the torpedo had attacked the port side, the list was towards port. At the same time, the hole was bigger in the stern, which was also sinking. There was no chance of getting the water out. The bilge pumps had been affected. There was no power.

"The emergency generators had been put out of action by an explosion in the instrument panel of the electricity distribution system. There were people who wanted to get the generators working, but the machines had become dislodged from their bases[9]."

Conqueror had approached to within half a mile of the cruiser. It fired three Mk8 torpedoes, two of which hit the target, and then left at speed to avoid a response from the *Piedrabuena* and *Bouchard*[10].

The two Argentine vessels, according to testimonies from both countries - which agree - fired depth charges, but only as a reflex action. In reality they were not aware of the presence of the nuclear submarine until the shock waves from the attack on the *Belgrano* reached them.

Argentine experts also maintain nowadays that it is very difficult to explain this episode. Captain Bonzo, in agreement with the the Fleet Commander, Rear Admiral Allara, believed that the torpedoes fired by the submarine were not of conventional type, and argues: "The ship possesses protective armour plating to avoid penetration by a projectile. On the sides it has armour three metres wide and fifteen centimetres thick, suitable for withstanding torpedoes of the period when the ship was built in 1939." He adds: "In my judgment, *Conqueror* did not use Mk8's. They were Tiger Fish. It is the only explanation for such a rapid sinking. If one of those torpedoes had hit a World War II ship, I don't believe it would have taken more than fifteen minutes to sink it."[11]

At 4.35 pm the *Bouchard* notified TOAS that the cruiser was adrift. "Assessment difficult. No explosions or smoke observed. I do not know if it was torpedoed. I request support for verifying the situation."

At 6.36 pm the *Bouchard* insisted that communications were cut and signalled that after a withdrawal to 20 miles, it was picking up contact again with the area from a distance of 14 miles.

This behaviour by the escort ships - that they left the area after the attack - generated heated discussion not only among the public but also among naval chiefs in Argentina and Great Britain. Admiral Woodward, Chief of the Task Force, said on one occasion that the strategy of the *Piedrabuena* and *Bouchard* hindered the rescue of a greater number of the ship-wrecked seamen.

Nevertheless, there is one anecdote - to which Argentine naval chiefs instantly turn - that explains in some way the conduct of these escort ships. It occurred during the First World War, in which the first submarine action of any magnitude in contemporary history took place. Three American cruisers were sailing through the English Channel in those days and were detected by a German submarine. The first torpedoes hit one of the ships, which began to sink. The other two gathered to rescue the victims and were successfully torpedoed and sunk, leaving more than two thousand shipwrecked in the water.

Since then, sailors agree, the professionals know that when a ship is sunk, the escorts must withdraw and drop depth charges to cover their flight. These explosives have a dissuasive effect more than anything: it is unlikely in such cases that they can expect to strike the enemy. What is certain is that when the *Piedrabuena* and *Bouchard* returned to the scene of the attack there remained only some turbulent water and life-rafts scattered in the sea as testimony to the tragedy. The old cruiser *Belgrano* had been devoured. In hardly an hour its enormous hull foundered and with it the last possibility of agreement between Argentina and Great Britain. Belaunde Terry's proposal had also been wrecked.

A profound depression was perceptible in the ruling circles of the Argentine Government. The meeting of the Military Committee had been abruptly halted and military intransigence - explicable on an emotional level and resulting from the attack on the *Belgrano* - caused the Foreign Minister to file away Belaunde's proposal. But this was not without previously warning the three commandants: "Let's keep this document. It's very important; let's not forget it."

Neither Galtieri, Anaya nor Lami Dozo paid much attention to the Foreign Minister's appeal, for without exception they had been too deeply shaken. Perhaps a thirst for vengeance unknown until then had been awakened.

Now, around midnight, Galtieri was still in his office at the Casa Rosada, a characteristic of his brief administration. The President, his detractors allege, was very disorderly and erratic in work, which obliged him to make greater efforts still. If it was normal to see lights burning at late hours in the windows giving onto the Plaza Colon, it was even more so at this time when the country was sinking into its first war of the century.

Once more, as during the whole of May 2nd, President Belaunde Terry's voice appeared at the other end of the Presidential telephone line. It was, in fact, half past midnight of day 3, when Galtieri again spoke to his Peruvian colleague. The dialogue marked the break in the mediating effort, though at the same time it made way for a new appeal for negotiations that would later be unsuccessfully attempted.

The authors had access to the text of the dialogue between the presidents. It is worth reproducing, because it throws light on details which assist in an understanding of the attitudes by the parties involved at this stage of the conflict: Argentina, Great Britain, the United States, and Peru.

"Good evening, Mr President. I very much want to talk to you and am rather concerned," said Belaunde, starting up the conversation.

"I am more concerned than you," replied Galtieri energetically, "because you know perfectly well, following what I told you yesterday afternoon, that here in Buenos Aires at 7 pm - 5 pm in Lima - the Military Junta had a meeting at which we were going to discuss the proposal your Government was going to put to the Argentine Government after contacting Washington concerning peace in the South Atlantic. In fact, the seven points you listed were closely analyzed within the available time and we had agreed to continue examining them further, given that the subject involves peace and Argentine sovereignty in the Falklands and South Georgia. But all this, Mr President, has been totally transformed by the British attitude in torpedoing the cruiser *Belgrano* of the Argentine Navy. As far as we are concerned this happened outside the United Kingdom's own 200 mile limit, which moreover, we do not accept. Clearly this situation not only does not help matters but in the face of such military pressure, the Argentine Government is not disposed to accept any negotiations concerning peace in the South Atlantic under such conditions."

"We prefer to die on our feet than live on our knees," he insisted, resorting to a phrase once used by the Spanish Communist Deputy, Dolores Ibarruri, known as *La Pasionaria* during the civil war in her country. "I don't know if you heard me?" asked the Argentine President after his monologue.

"I understand you perfectly, Mr President; I was informed of this matter in the evening and naturally I understand that that creates an extremely grave situation," said Belaunde, with an air of resignation.

"Consequently, Mr President," Galtieri resumed, "In the morning, I would like to send to you the Secretary-General of the Presidency, my personal delegate, Mr Iglesias, if you consider it appropriate. He will explain to you and to the commanders of the armed forces, the Argentine position as fully as possible - something we have fruitlessly tried to agree with Washington since the first days of April. He will also explain all the ins and outs of the documents that have been studied, so that we can reach a complete understanding of the situation we have arrived at."

"I understand you very well," said Belaunde. "I appreciate that there was a tacit understanding that whilst there was some possibility of negotiations, those English gentlemen would abstain from an aggressive act, is that right? That is elementary, and that much has been put to Secretary of State Haig, hasn't it? I was very encouraged that in the morning, no hostile act had occurred. As far as I am concerned, it was a disagreeable surprise and I was extremely angry at this attack taking place.

"I am grateful to you Mr President, for this undertaking on your part, and I have no doubt that as Latin Americans, all of us South of the Rio Grande, all who have Spanish blood in our veins must feel as you feel: indignation at these events." replied Galtieri, appealing to the new regional sentiment that was beginning to imbue military spirits in those days.

"Now, Mr President; how many victims are there expected to be in the *Belgrano*?" asked Belaunde anxiously.

"Look," said Galtieri, to get out of trouble, "I have no precise information. I know it has been torpedoed; it is not sunk; (in fact it was sunk at 5.01 pm the previous day) I believe that it is drifting; other boats are going to its help; this is the latest news I have at the moment. The *Belgrano* has been out of communication because of the damage suffered; so I can't be more precise, Mr President[12].

"Well, be assured of my complete support in this affair which I consider is a tragedy for all Latin America and I do understand that our fervent efforts to find a quick way out of the problem will necessarily have to go into cold storage for a while," indicated the President of Peru.

"If you wish," insisted Galtieri, taking up the idea that had not yet had a reply, "considering the respect for your Government and the Peruvian people due from the Argentine Government and people, first thing in the morning I will send you the Secretary-General of the Presidency in order to place himself at your disposal and at that of the Council of the Senior Commanders or who you believe..."

"With great pleasure, Mr President, with great pleasure. Clearly in a moment of such emergency I would not want, unless absolutely necessary, to deprive you of a close assistant. But any emissary of yours will always be well received at any time and in any circumstances," accepted Belaunde, in order to be accommodating.

"Mr President, for me that is no trouble. Anyway, we shall be in touch tomorrow morning," Galtieri emphasised in an attempt to end the conversation.

"We shall be in touch. I am going to call Secretary Haig. I am bringing this forward because he called me in a very distraught mood in the evening and told me something about the loss of a ship. I naturally expressed my amazement to him. And I told him that I was expecting your call and that as soon as I had received it I would let him have your reply, which I naturally understand has to be one that the circumstances demand. We are going to suspend things for the present, but I don't despair of being able to do something more to achieve peace. Look, if this peace had been achieved, as I was hoping, at 10 o'clock this morning, the loss of the *Belgrano* would not have happened. So I know the importance that hours and minutes have in these things," said Belaunde, in an oblique reproach for the unending proceedings on the part of the Argentine Military which had followed his peace proposals.

And he added: "Actually, last night we thought that we were hitting the nail on the head, didn't we? But as you know it's a matter of extreme urgency to try anything that may bring a cease fire, isn't it? Because there are so many lives at stake. We even announced a little prematurely that it might be possible to reach an accord and some rather eager reporters put out the news that this had already taken place. This was rectified, of course. But with what has happened now I understand that your worries are of a different kind. Nevertheless, while you face up to your delicate responsibilities we here, less overburdened, are going to continue working and are going to see what can be done. Count on my support for any step you may be able to take, perhaps by other methods or under different conditions, in order to shorten any period of danger or alarm there may be."

"I thank you and I repeat my gratitude, Mr Architect. I repeat this because I know your enormous predisposition - personal as well as that of the Peruvian Government, but..." said the Argentine President without finishing his sentence because Belaunde immediately took up the thread of the conversation again.

"I am now studying the way to communicate with the US President, to put to him some thoughts on the necessity of a change in the mistaken policy that he is pursuing," said Belaunde.

"Look; I thank you because I believe that an expression of views in that direction by the Peruvian Government is very important and more so if made public. But it is regrettable, really regrettable, and it's going to take several decades of American history to repair this situation brought on by the US Government. This is because it is incomprehensible that given its capacity and its power it cannot make its influence felt in such a delicate situation within the American continent," declared Galtieri, irritated by United States "treachery."

"Look, I have noticed in the course of the day - and this may interest you - I have noticed a change in General Haig's attitude. He was actually almost euphoric in searching for terms that might be acceptable to the parties and he seemed to me disposed to bring pressure on Great Britain," Belaunde estimated, with a touch of ingenuity. "But evidently," he continued, "this news and various other reports that there was a bombardment of the Falklands or an attempted landing has changed the situation." Then he changed his attitude to one of frustration and so he now presents Mr Pym as a man who has no interest in peace but simply in obtaining greater facilities for continuing the war. "And evidently," he insisted, "Mrs Thatcher is very stubborn in this affair, so that we shall all see what door opens to us. But I repeated to the American ambassador who has just brought me a letter from Reagan, that the darkest hour is the one just before dawn. And I say this to you in all sincerity, to help get you through these difficult times."

"Thank you for your sentiments, Mr President. The Argentine people thank you," said Galtieri, "because this is not a problem of any particular president of the moment who happens to be occupying the Presidency of the Argentine nation. This is the historic calling of the nation and is shared by all sectors of political life; whether of the Government or of its opponents, and by all sections of industry and commerce of the Argentine Nation - at every level. Therefore, really, when you tell me that General Haig feels frustrated, I feel alarmed. I feel alarmed because he must know me very well and has all the necessary powers to enable him to control and guide the behaviour of the Government of Great Britain by political, economic and military means. Consequently I don't understand, I don't begin to understand and the Argentine nation and population does not begin to understand the attitude of the United States," added the Argentine President with transparent impotence."

"Well," Belaunde tried calmingly, "I am now going to call Haig. To tell them that, though you are all well disposed to study the points in my proposal, you feel obliged to put them aside in view of the events which occurred this afternoon. That is the essence of what I can tell him, isn't it?"

"That's it. Beyond that the seven points could be in some respects reconsidered and modified, Mr Architect. But I again repeat: though we are reconsidering some aspects of the seven points, the news of the cruiser *Belgrano* now sets all study and reasoning aside in the face of this action, which, beyond the merely military aspect, is psychologically and politically so far-reaching for the public of the Argentine nation."

After the inevitable salutations, Galtieri and Belaunde concluded their conversation and the Argentine President immediately contacted General Iglesias and Rear Admiral Moya in order to entrust them with the mission to Peru.

Very early that May 3rd, Foreign Minister Costa Mendez received a call from the Peruvian Minister Javier Arias Stella, who told him that the British ambassador in Lima - no-one knew for certain whether it was with honesty or black humour - had delivered to him a note in which London stated that: "The door is not completely closed within the framework of what has been put forward."

Costa Mendez was surprised by the revelation - it was not 12 hours since the British had sunk the *Belgrano* - and communicated in passing the indignation of the Military at what was seen as a clear US satellite role in the episode of the attack on the Argentine cruiser.

What is certain is that the Argentine military commanders explored the possibility that day of an aerial attack that might inflict damage on the enemy and at the same time put life into a flagging Government and a public opinion to which the idea of a prolonged war was already beginning to have little appeal. The 4th was truly an important day for the conflict. About mid-day and while British Sea Harrier aircraft were attacking Darwin and the Royal Navy was concentrating its attention at that point too, a squadron formed of three supersonic Mirage fighter-bombers and a Super Etendard launched an attack on two ships situated 40 miles east of East Falkland.

The Super Etendard - the novelty of world-renown that was to mark this violent clash between Argentina and Great Britain - fired an Exocet missile while protected by the Mirage jets. The missile travelled 35 kilometers until it struck the *Sheffield*, one of the most modern ships in the British fleet, with 268 crew and a sophisticated armament.

Not a few personalities closely involved in the conflict with Great Britain have expressed to the authors after the war was over, the view that that Argentine success in battle was perhaps the final blow to achieving any negotiated solution.

The spirit of the Argentine Military was re-invigorated and it was not accidental that Galtieri's envoys to Lima exhibited a triumphalist attitude which was hardly justified by an objective analysis of what might actually be achieved.

President Belaunde Terry explained carefully that except for Brigadier Garcia, Moya and Iglesias stuck firmly to an optimistic line, rejecting any possibility of agreement. "The Falklands are a bastion," they were given to repeating before the incredulous gaze of the Peruvian Head of State.

"I told them," said the Peruvian President, "that you *know* when you are really winning. You might be celebrating victory but perhaps inside 24 hours things could be different. Of course, after that the Argentine optimism began to fade away, but even when the British had landed in the Falklands we were still negotiating a settlement. I had hopes of being able to get - rather symbolically - a hundred British soldiers and a hundred Argentine soldiers onto a Hercules aircraft that would take them to Punta Arenas - we could count on Chile's authorization."[13]

Belaunde, in a simplistic way, interpreted the sinking of the *Sheffield* as a sort of "equalizer" in the clash of forces. He therefore contacted Haig again and suggested an initial proposal that amounted to a cessation of hostilities and envisaged that the future administration of the archipelago could remain in the hands of the United Nations.

"But the Buenos Aires Government finally resolved to put everything to do with the problem to the UN, which took the negotiations out of our hands," explained Belaunde[14].

Already at that stage, the Argentine Government had placed the fate of the negotiations in the hands of the Secretary-General of the UN, Javier Perez de Cuellar. It did not believe in Belaunde, nor in the many offers to mediate - among them that of King Juan Carlos of Spain himself - and seemed to have directed its fortunes towards the battlefront.

In spite of this, the Peruvian leader persisted in his attempt, accompanied this time by Venezuela and Colombia, without fortune providing him with any better results than those already obtained. On May 20, Belaunde Terry approached Argentina with a document named "New Peace Formula for the South Atlantic," in which he tried to rescue the achievements of the Secretary-General of the UN in bringing the positions of the parties somewhat closer. That same day, the latter had publicly ended his efforts at mediation in a letter to the President of the Security Council, Ling Qing.

This last proposal, known in diplomatic jargon as *Belaunde IV*, consisted in the following:

1. Each one of the parties in dispute would unilaterally subscribe to the last proposal presented by Perez de Cuellar. 2. The Secretary-General of the UN would proceed to carry out the clauses in which there was agreement (withdrawal of troops, interim administration for the islands, etc). 3. The Secretary-General and the member countries of the "Contact Group" would take charge of organizing and presiding over the negotiating meetings.

The epicentre of the whole affair had been moved to the battle front where a well-aimed blow - the sinking of the *Sheffield* - warmed the spirits of the troops, and the fantasy of a victory returned to seduce many military chiefs.

NOTES

1. Felix Luna: "Habla el Presidente del Peru." in the journal *Todo es Historia*, number 191, p.33.

2. Ibid. p. 30.

3. Rodolfo Terragno. *Clarin*, May 24, 1983.

4. Ibid. 1 p. 30.

5. *Clarin*, May 22, 1983.

6. Official Report 29th November, 1982 Vol 33 c104. Quoted in Hansard 12 May, 1983.

7. Jeane Kirkpatrick wrote her doctoral thesis on Peronism, later published as a book under the title "Leadership and Vanguard in Mass Society." She is, moreover, the author of many essays on Latin America.

8. *Daily Express*, March 14, 1983.

9. Ana Baron and Mario Markic: Report on Captain Hector Bonzo in journal *Gente y la Actualidad* pp. 34-35. April 21, 1983.

10. Ana Baron *Gente y la Actualidad*, p.79, April 14th 1983.

11. Ibid. 9.

12. The authors received from an absolutely reliable source a copy of the textual recording of the conversation between Galtieri and Belaunde Terry which is reproduced in the present volume. Nevertheless they afterwards had access to the version of this same dialogue which the ex-members of the Military Junta delivered to the "Rattenbach Commission." From this last version, Galtieri's statement that the cruiser *Belgrano* was "adrift" had been deleted.

13. Ibid.1.

14. Ibid.1.

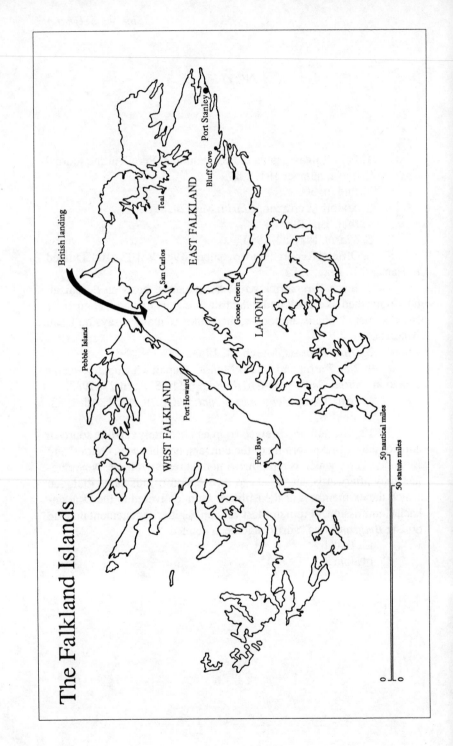

The Falkland Islands

British landing

Pebble Island

WEST FALKLAND

Port Howard

Fox Bay

San Carlos

Teal

EAST FALKLAND

Bluff Cove

Port Stanley

Goose Green

LAFONIA

50 nautical miles

50 statute miles

Chapter 11

THE WRECK OF DIPLOMACY

On the morning of 30th April, Alexander Haig confronted the television cameras provided with a text of less than four pages in length. The Secretary of State's stern expression did not completely disguise the displeasure that it was causing him to make announcements which, in effect, implied an admission of his own failure.

By way of introduction he warned in a firm tone that the crisis was about to "enter a new and dangerous phase during which it is probable that military action on a large scale will take place." In connection with this, he recalled the "extraordinary effort" made by the United States in searching for a negotiated solution to the conflict - this in an attempt to preserve "human lives and the international order."

He stayed true to the ideological stance of his own country when alluding to the recent decision of the community of this Hemisphere under the Rio Pact. "We have also," he said, "made this effort because the crisis prompted demonstrations of Hemispheric solidarity, vital at a moment when the Communist adversaries are looking for positions of influence on the American continent and when simmering territorial disputes throughout a great part of the Hemisphere demand unity and firm defence of principles."

He recalled his last proposal which he stated "represented our best appreciation of what one could reasonably hope that both parties would accept and was based on complete equity; on our principles and concern for the rule of law."

Then came the first blow: "We had reasons to believe," Haig maintained, "that the United Kingdom would consider an agreement along the lines of our proposal, but Argentina informed us yesterday that she could not accept it. The position of Argentina continues to be that she must receive present assurances of her eventual sovereignty, or else an extension of the *de facto* role concerning the government of the islands."

The paragraph contained a piece of information which helped

damage the Argentine position in world public opinion, but it could not be avoided. When Haig presented his proposal to Argentina he could not at the time be certain that it would be accepted by the British *in toto*. Strictly speaking, London had initially indicated that on a first examination, it would appear to be necessary to have "certain modifications" in order to make it feasible in general terms[1].

The reply from Buenos Aires had been different: it had considered the proposal "unacceptable" for which reason it was even simpler to place on Argentina the entire responsibility for the failure, while simultaneously one could praise the willingness of the British to co-operate. It was another price that the Argentines had to pay in full.

And penalties followed the reproaches. Haig announced: "... the President has ordered:

1. The suspension of all military exports to Argentina,
2. The retention of the certification of Argentine eligibility for military sales[2].
3. The suspension of new credits and guarantees from the Export-Import Bank and
4. The suspension of credits from the Commodity Credit Corporation."

The list was completed with another blow of more immediate effect: "The President has also determined that the United States will respond positively to requests for material support from the British forces."

In spite of the rhetoric with which the Argentine Military Government explained this away, it was impossible to disguise the profound impact the American decision had on the spirits of senior officials. The reality is that although the generals, admirals and brigadiers that conceived and carried out the *Process of National Reorganization* from 1976 onwards were accustomed to having its ideology rejected - the Carter Administration and Western Europe in general had harassed them politically - this new announcement brought an emptiness similar to absolute solitude.

This was in part what the Secretary of State had intended. He wanted to create conditions in which a new presentation of *Haig II* had a chance of success. Counting on the effect of this blow he renewed his political gamble, though this time only briefly. As he clearly could not do it in the same direct fashion as previously, he now resorted to a Latin American channel.

The choice fell upon the Peruvian leader Belaunde Terry, the details of whose intervention are related in the chapter, *Sink the*

Belgrano! Nevertheless, there are some details which can usefully be described so as to help in understanding later events.

There are signs that in order to achieve his purpose, Haig had various consultations which included the Colombian Government and the Secretary-General of the OAS, Alejandro Orfila. In the first case there was no hope of any results. After the virtual condemnation of Argentina by representatives of President Turbay Ayala during the IATRA deliberations, it was most improbable that Buenos Aires would accede to any suggestion that stemmed from Bogota.

Orfila's position was extremely delicate - besides being head of the inter-American forum he was a member of the Argentine Foreign Service with the rank of ambassador. On the other hand, Secretary-General Orfila was to be heard muttering discontent at the time over the decision of the Military Government to keep him out of the affair completely or at most to consult him only occasionally. The truth is that this international official, a man with excellent links with the establishment, supposed that he would be called to take a more significant part in the crisis than the one which actually fell to him.

But at least three key factors combined to prevent Haig reaching success on this occasion:

1. The American stand scored a direct hit on the sensibilities of the Junta, but had not necessarily made its members inclined to come to an agreement.

2. Haig no longer had a free hand as he had had at the beginning of his endeavours. Other powerful, or at least well-known influences, were taking advantage of the weakness of his position in order to impose their own efforts in the search for peace. They were mindful of the political fortune which might accrue to whoever achieved that peace.

3. Another factor to emerge during those fateful days is the consolidation of Margaret Thatcher's inflexibility. "Our boys" - as she used to refer to the British troops in the Task Force - were already able to launch a massive offensive against Argentine positions. Her ministers as much as her War Cabinet had almost completely ceased to perturb with arguments in favour of negotiations. In this they were doubtless influenced by the bellicose climate encouraged in the press. The explicit support of the United States strengthened the feeling of British omnipotence. Pym himself even announced his return to Washington, with the fundamental aim of agreeing the details of the promised American assistance. The tragedies of the *General Belgrano* and *HMS Sheffield* scarcely damped this euphoria.

Before returning to Buenos Aires, the Argentine delegation,

headed by Costa Mendez, worked together in New York drawing up a document in reply to Reagan. It was read a day later in Buenos Aires by the Minister of the Interior, Alfredo Saint Jean.

Apart from the Foreign Minister, who chose to maintain his presence of mind, the rest of the members of his team could not help displaying the consternation overwhelming them. Miret confusedly alluded to "the strange ideas that Schlaudermann seemed to have put into Galtieri's head."

This unflattering reference - whose real meaning was never clarified - originated in a report telephoned by Lami Dozo, in which he referred to the visit the US ambassador made to the Casa Rosada. This was to deliver formal confirmation of the abandonment of the US efforts at conciliation.

Schlaudermann confirmed for the present authors during their research that on that occasion - the last on which he spoke to Galtieri - he was accompanied by his military attache who was in uniform to underline the nature of his presence. Nevertheless, Schlaudermann did not want to enter into details on the conversation that he had.

The session in New York - on the night of April 28th - during which the contents of the Argentine reply were debated, produced the beginning of what would become an interminable clash of opinion between Miret and Moya. The differences deepened while the conflict proceeded and while the chance of a peaceful solution became more and more of a pipe dream. The airman - in line with his friend and superior - inclined towards concessions, while the sailor, no less loyal to *his* chief, made a defence out of his very intransigence.

The exchange of opinion between these two men - while the civilian diplomats cautiously abstained and Iglesias sank into a state of dismay - degenerated more than once into outright argument. Miret would later confess when the aftermath began that: "Moya seemed very much like a nightmare to me."

One of those sessions must have influenced the mind of Moya on the evening of the 30th - hours before travelling to Buenos Aires - and caused him to cross the border into comedy, earning him a nickname which stuck. The naval officer left the ambassador's office, in which he had just finished holding a meeting and made for the large hall of the mission building - at that time brimming with Argentine and foreign reporters with their cameras, microphones and recorders.

At first, no-one noticed the small figure of the sailor in civilian dress and carrying a briefcase. After all, his face was familiar only to Argentines and the latter had already heard enough of his rhetoric to want to avoid it. Anyhow, the large groups of people seemed to confuse Moya who - addressing no-one in particular - said hoarsely and in a loud voice

"I have to go to the hotel immediately."

The phrase attracted the attention of the reporters, who began to follow his movements while he, rather disorientated, looked for the way out.

From the hall of the embassy there is access to various offices, to an inner passage and to an outer one which leads to the lifts. The double doors that open onto the latter are notably larger than the others, and one of them has a built-in closed-circuit television camera. The receptionist controls entry in this way. In accordance with the New York City regulations, they display an enormous plastic notice with the red inscription *EXIT*.

Moya looked around several times and hesitated. Finally he went straight towards the inner passage and stopped in front of a pair of sliding doors. Was he looking for an overcoat in this, the only cupboard of the room?

No, he opened them, and with determination tried to enter the confined space. There were no laughs - the spectators were as confused by his efforts as he was himself. But Moya was conscious of the scrutiny to which he was silently submitting himself and this disturbed him even more. He turned rapidly and moved off, this time ending up in the office of a female administrative assistant. He backed off wearing an expression which was a silent plea for help. In order to end the farce, the receptionist overcame her diffidence and approached Moya. With a maternal gesture she guided him to the way out. It was at that moment that his compatriots of the press baptized him "Admiral Exit."

Haig pursued his "Peruvian channel," but while doing this, other wheels began turning. On May 1st Kirkpatrick began whispering exclusive information in the ear of Perez de Cuellar. This happened on a couple of occasions: the first was to advise him of Belaunde Terry's intervention and the second to alert him to the latest failure by the Secretary of State.

Both pieces of information excited him equally. Some testimonies suggest that an old antipathy exists between these two prominent Peruvians and on this occasion that sentiment became transformed into a silent rivalry. If Perez de Cuellar intervened while the President was trying to achieve success, Belaunde Terry, for his part, appeared on the scene with a new idea each time the UN Secretary-General failed.

Besides events on the official level and these formal contacts, others of a different nature were taking place. The open collision with the US generated disquiet in the Argentine business sector. A part of this sector had solid economic ties with controlling interests in the north and the inevitable network of contacts included some of the more conspicuous figures. Others like Ambassador Takacs, at this point reduced to silent criticism of the actions of the Junta, took advantage of this opportunity to exert his influence with many American friends. These were either on the fringes of power or actually part of it.

The clearest example of the first type was the lawyer, Wenceslas Bunge, a Harvard graduate who enjoyed the confidence of Lami Dozo and was a personal friend of Kirkpatrick and Enders, among others. Takacs in his turn communicated on different occasions with Clark, Reagan's National Security Adviser and with various Congressmen, among others, Paul Laxalt.

Furthermore, Bunge and Takacs were personal friends. Many of the moves they made were through the American, William D. Rogers, ex-Assistant Secretary for Inter-American Affairs, and one of the few men of influence in US circles of power who pleaded the case for Argentina. In the second half of April, Rogers published an article on the editorial page of the *Washington Post* entitled *Sovereignty is not the Question*, which was considered a modest success by Buenos Aires, and in which he maintained that Great Britain could not question, or even try to question, the Argentine title to sovereignty over the Falklands.

Rogers, who remains in the circle of close associates of his ex-chief, Henry Kissinger, travelled to Brazil in the latter days of the conflict and at that time a meeting was attempted between the American and Lami Dozo, possibly in Puerto Iguazu, but it did not succeed.

The action of this informal lobby generated other, more concrete outcomes, which are detailed later in this account, but all were equally unfruitful.

On May 2nd, it was open war and the sinking of the cruiser, *Belgrano*, produced the final justification that Perez de Cuellar needed. Together with his advisers, he prepared an *aide memoire* destined to provide the basis for his future offer of *good offices*. The opportunity to formalize his offer came that same day when Francis Pym agreed to make a stop-over in New York on his return to London from the American capital. As had been arranged, the Foreign Secretary and Perez de Cuellar were dining that day at the residence of Ambassador Parsons.

Mindful of the formalities, the Secretary-General held a previous meeting at his home - located in the exclusive Sutton Place Avenue in Manhattan - with the Argentine representative, Eduardo Roca, who came accompanied by the First Secretary, Nestor Martinez. On that occasion, both diplomats took up the challenge with an undertaking to obtain a response from Buenos Aires as quickly as possible.

Perez de Cuellar gave the interview after adequate press notification and consequently reporters mounted vigil in front of the doors of his house. When Roca was about to leave - courteously accompanied by the Peruvian - he noticed that his second-in-command was carrying in his hand the envelope containing the *aide memoire*. Knowing the ability of reporters to identify details, he told him: "Keep that in your pocket, Martinez. The reporters saw us go in with our hands empty and now, if they see us with that they will be sure to begin to ask questions."

The text was simple and followed the general lines of his previous "informal note" of April 17, which was delivered two days later to the respective ambassadors. As to the suggested points of agreement - as could not have been otherwise - they had much in common with what Haig had been trying to do..... "The Secretary General," said the *aide memoire*, "wishes to suggest that the two governments should simultaneously adopt the measures enunciated below, which are conceived as provisional measures, and which will not prejudice the rights, demands or positions of the parties:

"It is proposed that from H-hour it is specified that:

1. The Government of Argentina commences the withdrawal of its troops from the Falkland Islands and the Government of the United Kingdom, the redeployment of its naval forces and commences their withdrawal from the Falkland Islands zone; both Governments to complete their withdrawals by an agreed date.

2. The two Governments to commence negotiations for the purpose of achieving a diplomatic solution to their differences within an agreed period.

3. The two Governments to revoke their respective announcements of blockades and exclusion zones and put an end to all acts of hostility.

4. The two Governments to put an end to all economic sanctions.

5. Transition arrangements to come into force for supervising compliance with the measures indicated, and to attend to administrative needs."

Perez de Cuellar also stated in his presentation that: "The practical arrangements relating to any UN role can be put into effect rapidly, with the consent of the parties concerned and the prior decision of the Security Council.

In his conversation with Pym, the Secretary-General discussed at length the advisability of summoning the Security Council in order that it might formalize the Peruvian's initiative with an appropriate mandate.

Perez de Cuellar thought that this would be the best move,

conscious as he was of the political risks that were run by acting without the support of the executive organ of the UN. This was particularly significant in his own case, since his election to the post was the consequence of a political compromise between opposing groups and did not represent a consensus.

Nevertheless, Pym produced forceful counter-arguments. He reasoned that London would accept a new unofficial peace effort, but not a new Security Council pronouncement: London's policy was to abide strictly by the terms of Resolution 502. Besides, there was always the possibility that if the Council discussed the granting of the mandate, there might be an attempt to promote a cease-fire, in which case Britain's unchanging stance would necessarily condemn the whole exercise to failure.

It was therefore advisable to manoeuvre in order to postpone any formal meeting of the Security Council. Without knowing it, the Irish representative, Noel Dorr, a diplomat with an undisguised inclination towards the theatrical, was on the point of provoking the collapse of this scheme. This was to happen that same evening, by virtue of an accelerated move by Dorr and his colleagues to cause the summoning of the Council. This set in train a series of informal scenes behind closed doors in which Parsons made it clear that his country would not suspend military operations[3].

The reaction to these events on the part of some European allies - who began to suggest conditions for their support - gave new weight to Pym's arguments on the necessity of adopting measures that would not put the "international consensus" in danger. The Foreign Office chief could then also hint in public at the Government's acceptance of a UN trustee status - a proposal suggested from time to time by the Opposition through Denis Healey[4].

The consultations did not last too long in either of the capitals and Roca was able to deliver a reply on the 5th, whilst Parsons made his own the following day.

That Wednesday was a very special day for the Argentine. He not only sent a vital message to the Secretary-General - the acceptance of his good offices - but obtained a new favourable pronouncement from the Bureau of Co-ordination of the Movement of Non-Aligned Countries. This was after addressing a message to its members that would cause a transitory furore in Argentina and make a considerable impact on the mind of the diplomat himself.

The text ratified the pronouncement of April 26 and confirmed "the support manifested in the communique for Argentine sovereignty over the Falkland Islands, reaffirming the findings of all the meetings at summit and at ministerial level of the Movement, since the Declaration of the Conference of Ministers of Foreign Relations held in Lima (Peru) in August 1975."[5]

Driven by its own urgent needs, the military regime was discovering and employing third world and revolutionary rhetoric that only a short while earlier had grated on military ears. Roca made it reach new heights on the morning of May 5th:

"The blind obstinacy of the British Government in desperately seeking a military triumph on which to base its prestige in the midst of its decadence," he said in one part of his speech, "has cost a new batch of young men's lives [.....] but there is another fact which by its singular importance, by its gravity and perfidy, is worth exposing separately from the preceding chronological scheme. I refer, Mr President, to the attitude of the Government of the United States of America, which won for the United Kingdom the necessary time for the punitive fleet to arrive at its destination and which, once this objective was achieved, turned its face on its own promises of impartiality, lied about our proposal, deceived its own public opinion and now gives economic and military assistance to the colonial aggressor.

"It is not only this spurious political alliance," he continued, "which merits our rejection, but also the fact that it betrays our own legitimate and bold attempt at solving a very old problem. As my Foreign Minister would say, the Argentine people will neither understand nor forget that in one of the most critical hours of its history, in contrast to the solidarity in all corners of the continent, the United States preferred to take the side of a power alien to the Hemisphere, co-operating with its aggressive designs."

A few hours after this outburst, Roca received two Argentine reporters in the meeting hall of the mission. One of them, being acquainted with the diplomat's political and ideological background said to him in jocular tone: "Congratulations, Ambassador. I have just spoken to Buenos Aires and they tell me that your speech is on the front pages of the evening newspapers. It seems to me that you have outdone Father Miguel D'Escoto," (the Nicaraguan Foreign Minister).

Visibly surprised, Roca sank into his chair, looked at his questioners and instinctively covered his face in his hands before replying with candour:

"They are going to throw me out of all the clubs!"

Just then one of his assistants advised the ambassador that the Foreign Minister was calling him by *carola* telephone. Without disguising his nervousness, Roca went into his office next to the hall without closing the separating door. The visitors listened to him voicing the doubts that had grown in him in the last few minutes.

"I am worried, Canoro. Some friends tell me here that that speech caused a commotion. I don't want to increase our problems," he explained to Costa Mendez.

After the conversation he returned to where the reporters awaited him and - visibly relieved - Roca confessed:

"Costa Mendez told me literally - if I were in your place, Eduardo, I wouldn't worry - and I'm not going to."

During this dialogue with his chief, Roca was also notified that the Deputy Foreign Minister, Enrique Ros, had been nominated to take charge of the negotiations. At the Palacio San Martin, Ros was the expert on the Falklands *par excellence*. From that moment Roca was, in practice, to become subordinate to Ros. Britain on the other hand would be represented by Parsons.

Strictly speaking it was Roca himself who asked for Ros's presence, acting on the advice of his own aides. In the course of our investigation, and with the benefit of hindsight, the ex-Argentine ambassador to the UN found reasons to regret his request: "I asked for advice on the matter and the officials of the mission reacted as they always do in such circumstances. They are reluctant to tackle delicate questions without having some superior involved at the same time. Perhaps it may not have been the best thing to do," he admitted. In view of what happened one has to agree that this reflection contains a grain of truth.

Ros arrived on Friday May 7th, encased in his habitual circumspection and numerous private prejudices. The result of his February round of negotiations and the communique of March 1st worked a deep transformation in his mind. According to one of his colleagues in the Foreign Service, these had led him nowhere. This man, whose diplomatic career had been obsessed with the danger of making a slip or some indiscretion, now decided that there would be no more "cordial climates," no more excessive shows of flexibility to the adversary.

Thus in his first informal conversation with reporters, whom he could never meet without leaving the impression of a sense of vertigo, he firmly contradicted a comment made by one of them.

The journalist had referred to the need to "seek peace":

"I have come to seek peace, but it only interests me if it is a peace with dignity," Ros had replied.

This "dignity" became an unstated assumption in the conversation. In bringing it to the surface, Ros began indirectly to emphasize the limitations that had been imposed on him in Buenos Aires as much as those other constraints which marked his sense of political survival.

The possessor of excellent colloquial English, he replied on one occasion: "No more Mr Nice Guy!" when opening up to a colleague who had pleaded in favour of moderation.

A day after Ros's arrival in New York, Margaret Thatcher took a fundamental decision. At Chequers she approved the proposal of her War Cabinet that the infantry forces necessary for the landing, then still stationed on Ascension Island, should join the fleet in the South Atlantic[6]. London linked this new escalation to the acceptance of the "good offices" of Perez de Cuellar.

It was one more expression of Margaret Thatcher's dual policy - diplomacy with military support. It was a move that reflected caution. If American acquiescence was desirable in carrying out the final assault, one had to give Washington enough evidence of a willingness to negotiate. As one of the Prime Minister's entourage admitted:

"We must not and we shall not repeat the terrible mistake of Sir Anthony Eden in Suez in 1956, when he brought Britain to war without the support of the United States [.....] one cannot operate militarily in the southern Hemisphere without the consent, explicit or implicit, of the United States."[7]

The British Government had also taken into account, when deciding upon a reply to the UN Secretary-General's offer, how latest events in the theatre of battle had affected public opinion. On the same day that it was discussed sending the Marines to make a landing in the Falklands, the *Sunday Times* in one of its editorials urged Margaret Thatcher to recognize that: "... the task of recapturing the islands is too difficult and presumably too costly in human life."[8]

Caution was not the exclusive prerogative of London. On Sunday May 9th, on an Argentine television channel, where a team from the American CBS network had hired a studio, the Argentine Foreign Minister confronted a group of American reporters in the programme: *Face the Nation*. That day he introduced an appreciable shift in the position of the Military Government which nevertheless passed almost unnoticed by the Argentine media. During the questioning, Costa Mendez stated that Argentine sovereignty over the archipelago had to be the "objective" of negotiations necessary if a cessation of hostilities was to be agreed and not, as previously, "a prior condition."

This re-definition marked a substantial shift in the position that Argentina had held at the time of the Haig mission. Throughout, it had insisted on concrete guarantees of sovereignty or at least a formula which would permit the retaining of effective control over the islands during any interim period.

Perez de Cuellar used as a basis for his efforts, the small shifts in the instructions which Parsons and Ros received from their respective governments concerning their dialogue through the UN Secretary-General. In the case of Parsons, it was the British Government's readiness to explore the area of "trustee status" over the islands under the aegis of the United Nations. This indirectly implied an abandonment of their previous requirement to consider as "paramount" the wishes of the islanders. Now no demand was being made to sound out the kelpers' opinion. As for Ros, he no longer insisted on prior assurances that Argentine sovereignty would be recognized.

On Monday 10th, an important thing occurred of which public opinion was almost unaware. That day, the roving ambassador, Vernon Walters arrived on board a half-empty Pan-American flight - in the unobtrusive manner that marked his style of operation. In a few hours he had spoken with President Galtieri and the other two commandants, with various members of the military hierarchy, and with men of the public and business sector. Nevertheless, he refrained from meeting Costa Mendez, whom Washington had begun to regard with resentment and mistrust.

Even when the press revealed the presence of the envoy a few days later, the State Department never admitted it officially. In the interview granted to the authors in Washington, Walters confirmed that he had made the journey but described it simply as: "An effort to avoid the complete collapse of bilateral relations." Although he did not wish to identify them to his questioners on that occasion, he assured them that he found "many understanding people of goodwill." The authors' investigation nevertheless revealed some evidence that goes to explain the reasons for sending Walters and also identifies some of the results of his contacts.

The course of events was beginning to concern Washington, especially the repercussions in Latin America of the US decision to support Great Britain. With this concern, internal feuding returned - it was not exactly muted. Jeane Kirkpatrick reacted angrily, according to some reporters at the time, after listening to a report by Haig during a Cabinet meeting: "The foreign policy of the United States," she had said, "is designed for British dressed in American clothes."

No information links the two following events, but what is certain is that scarcely twenty-four hours after Walters made his fleeting tour through the inner circles of Argentine power, Ros notified Perez de Cuellar of his government's consent to a formula "under which the results of diplomatic negotiation would not be prejudged from its beginning."[9] That same day, the Argentine envoy would rather cryptically describe to a reporter the stage that negotiations had reached as: one in which the parties were running "a calculated risk." The Argentine presentation was formally a reply to new pressure from the Secretary-

General. Perez de Cuellar had put to the Argentines the formula mentioned above and had demanded that it be accepted quickly.

A few hours after returning to Washington, the American specialist in "discrete missions" completed the job started in the Argentine capital with one of his rare public statements: "The conflict between Argentina and Great Britain over the Falklands," he said, " is a silly war... the *machismo* of women is even more sensitive than that of men."[10]

In those days, critical references to Argentina were not a novelty in the United States. On the other hand, those whose main target was the British Prime Minister certainly were, especially if coming from a man of such a position in the Government. On that same occasion, Walters took it upon himself to remind his audience that: "Argentina has the most pro-Western government that we have seen for a long time."

These tactics would nevertheless have insufficient results. Discussions continued without pause - the UN Secretary-General held two or more meetings daily with each of the parties - and the tense climate began to erode the nerves of the protagonists as much as their basic differences. The procedure chosen by the Peruvian - perhaps the only one possible under the circumstances - was in itself exhausting. There were no tripartite meetings, no direct confrontations of the arguments of the two parties. The mediator received the ideas and comments and before passing them on, analysed them occasionally introducing some variations.

More than one of the testimonies gathered by the authors, provide confirmation that Perez de Cuellar began to feel irritated by the obsession with which Ros lingered over details, often at the price of postponing the settlement of key points in the negotiations. The Secretary-General thus developed a growing dissatisfaction with the Argentine negotiator. In the extremity of his frustration, this caused him to say in desperation while in conversation with some of his assistants that the Deputy Foreign Minister "was the least suitable man that Argentina could have chosen for the mission."

Roca, at this time Ros's principal assistant, did not dissent much from the opinion that Perez de Cuellar formed of the Argentine principal negotiator. But he recalled that on many occasions, the latter's concern for questions - apparently only of form - originated from instructions he received from the Palacio San Martin. It was these which showed an "exasperating tendency to underline details." What is certain is that these efforts lasted a further couple of days, without succeeding in overcoming some basic difficulties:

1. The insistence of Great Britain that the final solution should

be consistent with Article 73 of the UN Charter, whose provisions among other things speak of "developing self-government," and "duly taking into account the political aspirations of the inhabitants," of non-autonomous countries - a definition which included the Falklands. London maintained that its colonial administration of the archipelago had helped the population to develop and consolidate its "own democratic institutions" in accordance with the mandate of the Charter. It maintained that these would have to be consulted before settling the final status of the territory.

2. Buenos Aires could not accept this possibility. For the Junta this was merely another way of demanding the right of self-determination for the islanders. Its stand was to demand an interim authority of the United Nations, assisted by the British, Argentines and islanders from both countries of origin, with the proviso that the opinion of the latter should not in any way affect the final solution.

3. The refusal of London to include in the agreement the islands of South Georgia and South Sandwich, also claimed by Argentina. Without intending it, London had encouraged this claim by Buenos Aires by considering both archipelagoes, for the purposes of administration, as "Falkland Island Dependencies." During Haig's mission, as previously explained, Great Britain accepted formulas which included these territories, but later modified this position, claiming that South Georgia and the South Sandwich Islands were "entirely different cases," and that "the British title to these islands" had an "entirely different" character to that of the Falklands.

The negotiations entered an agonizing stage. Perez de Cuellar felt the need to show some results, given that his position was particularly delicate, not having an express mandate for what he was doing. He met the members of the Security Council in a secret session and confessed to them: "The time for peace is running out."

Nevertheless, on Thursday 13th, Parsons and his colleague accredited to the White House, Sir Nicholas Henderson, were summoned urgently to London. What was the reason for this call? Certain events had renewed domestic and international pressure on Margaret Thatcher and she had accepted Pym's suggestion, and that of other members of the team, to make a "last effort" before finally unleashing the military potential that the UK Government had built up in the vicinity of the islands.

Among those reasons, it is necessary to emphasise the following: the frightening prospect of the "final battle" - with a correspondingly large number of casualties - which strengthened the element of good sense within the public opinion of both countries; the decision of

Ireland and Italy not to renew their economic sanctions against Argentina; but more fundamentally, the latest insistence of Washington upon a major diplomatic effort from London.

The reality is that alarm at the deterioration the US position was suffering in the Hemisphere - continually voiced by Kirkpatrick and Clark - convinced Reagan of the need to share out political pressure more evenly between the two capitals. The prospect of an emotional reaction in an "Argentina with leaders humiliated by British military power," as Kirkpatrick put it, was a nightmare for the group of Presidential aides who were afraid that the results of the South Atlantic war would influence the Central American crisis.

Haig firmly opposed this approach and all the subsequent efforts that were made. "Having failed in his own effort, he doesn't want anyone else to be successful where he was not," said an American diplomatic source to the present authors. In that respect, his arguments were ignored. Nor did it help his position that some of his subordinates, such as Enders and Walters, shared Kirkpatrick's apprehensions.

At the end of a week which Parsons spent in London and Chequers deep in deliberations with Margaret Thatcher and with members of both the Cabinet and the War Cabinet, a document emerged which represented the last chance to avoid, by diplomatic means, the tragedy which finally did occur. This was a proposal for an agreement presented by Great Britain to Perez de Cuellar on May 17th.

This new proposal would have an extremely brief life, scarcely two days, but it would be rich in revealing episodes.

There is evidence that even before the formal delivery of the text to the UN mediator, the British Government revealed its contents to the Americans and they, appealing more to unofficial channels than official ones, tried to achieve its acceptance by Argentina.

The proposal prepared by the British Conservative Government had the following distinguishing features:

1. The accord would be in agreement with the terms of Article 73 of the UN Charter.

2. Its provisions would not affect the respective positions of the parties in dispute, nor the final solution.

3. It would provide, in detail, conditions for carrying out the demilitarization of the zone, a procedure for which compliance would be verified by the UN.

4. Both nations would undertake jointly to sponsor a resolution of the Security Council in order that the latter should take note of the accord and grant the necessary mandate to Perez de Cuellar to assist the parties in the final negotiation.

5. The Secretary-General would designate, with the consent of the parties, an official who would take charge of the interim administration.

6. This delegate would have to ensure "the uninterrupted administration of the government of the islands," consulting with the "representative institutions" of the islanders, to each of which councils an Argentine representative would be added. The "traditional laws and practices" in force in the islands would be the basis for actions by the administrator.

7. The parties would start negotiations under the auspices of the Secretary General, so as to arrive at a final solution, with the undertaking to conclude them by December 31st 1982.

8. If, however, this should not prove possible, the provisional accord would remain fully in force until that solution was found.

While London's pronouncement was nervously awaited in New York and Buenos Aires, other actors entered the scene. One of them was the lawyer, Bunge, who at that time found himself in Washington, on one of his frequent business trips.

In the early morning of May 17, Bunge received a call at his hotel from his old friend Ambassador Kirkpatrick, who without hiding the urgency asked him to come to her residence in Washington that evening. She also revealed to him that having read the new British offer, she believed this time everything would turn out well. Time had virtually run out and there was not a minute to lose.

Bunge waited patiently for the ambassador, who arrived at nightfall; she had been talking with Reagan and Clark about the crucial negotiations. The Argentine for his part had taken soundings among his friends in his own government, among them Lami Dozo.

It was Bunge who commented to Kirkpatrick that Argentina would respond quickly, perhaps that very night. "It is essential that they are not pressurized," she cried, and added: "I believe peace is at hand if this opportunity is handled well."

What the diplomat was indirectly signalling was the necessity for Argentina not to reply with a categorical rejection, in that way precipitating the outcome she believed to be facing that country.

Applying another turn of the screw, Kirkpatrick asked her companion to get in touch with Roca in New York, so that they might meet that same evening to discuss the possibility of an accord over the papers.

Then began a race against the clock. Bunge was taken to the Washington National Airport in Ambassador Takacs' car, from whose telephone he had tried unsuccessfully to contact the Argentine mission to the UN and advise Roca about the meeting.

Finally, while Kirkpatrick was boarding the aircraft which would take her to New York, Bunge managed to make contact from the public kiosk at the airport. He only managed to tell Roca "I am coming with Jeane. Wait for me at the Harvard Club to dine with us."

Gasping for breath from the effort, the lawyer did not miss the plane. He sat beside the ambassador during the flight and discussed what he would try to do.

Calling him by his familiar name, Kirkpatrick said: "Wences, I think, that the British proposal was made to be accepted. It's written all over it. We must force that acceptance. Although it doesn't include South Georgia and the Sandwich Islands, it is done in an acceptable fashion." She paused and continued, saying: "Our task is to make it digestible."

They arrived in New York at 9 pm. Roca, distressed, had preferred to wait for them at La Guardia airport. After a brief greeting, Kirkpatrick changed the place for their meeting: it would be in her apartment at the Waldorf Towers, half an hour later.

Bunge, who stayed alone with Roca, summarized the conversation with the American. At 6 pm that day, the ambassador had received the proposal from the hands of the Secretary-General with the warning that London was expecting a reply in the exceptionally short period of forty-eight hours. He agreed to take part in the meeting, but said "I can't go alone. I must tell you that Ros has to be there because he is virtually the Argentine Government negotiator for discussions with Perez de Cuellar.

Finally, at the agreed time, Roca, Ros and Bunge met their hostess, accompanied by Jorge Sorzano, one of her closest assistants, at the Waldorf Towers. Bunge thought it necessary to explain his presence at the negotiating table, indicating that his aim had been to encourage the meeting. After finishing his introduction he tried to rise, but Ros and Kirkpatrick asked him to stay with them.

After the formalities, they got to work on the text of the British proposal, the method was chosen by the Argentine Deputy Foreign Minister. His objections accumulated during the conversations.

Kirkpatrick tried a change of tack and began to write some modifications on the British proposal to make it more digestible for Ros. For his part, Ros, who was acting without instructions from the Foreign Minister - something which terrified him - did not want to move a millimetre from the official Argentine position. The dialogue became arid and tedious, and fatigue sank into the participants' bones.

The American began to feel a growing irritation with Ros and his punctilious manner of examining the clauses of the accord. From this, it seemed, only disagreement could emerge. True to her temperament, Kirkpatrick did not worry about hiding her feelings.

But she was not defeated. Taking the text of the proposal she suggested to Ros: "Let's introduce the necessary corrections here and you'll see that this proposal can be accepted by Argentina." In the last Article she sought to reduce the requirement for the restoration of the system of government and of the laws in force in the islands before April 2nd.

This effort also proved useless, and at three o'clock in the morning, everyone agreed to end the fruitless session. Bunge, exhausted, returned to his hotel, but before being able to get any sleep he received another call from Kirkpatrick.

She confessed to her friend that she couldn't get to sleep, that her thoughts kept returning again and again to the various alternatives of that long day and asked him to return to her apartment to continue the analysis. Bunge agreed, and morning having already arrived, this new effort produced a brief memorandum in which the concessions which in the opinion of both had been extracted from Great Britain were identified and assimilated. Their eight points indicated:

1. The United Kingdom Government had agreed not to reintroduce the British administration to the islands.

2. It had agreed to a short interim period with a specific final date for the negotiations.

3. It had accepted an interim administration for the islands.

4. It had abandoned the demand for Argentine recognition of British sovereignty over the islands.

5. It had agreed to the simultaneous withdrawal of forces in place of demanding a prior Argentine withdrawal.

6. It agreed that the Legislative and Executive Councils would each have two representatives from the 30 Argentine residents and six representatives from the 1800 British residents.

7. It had acceded to the verification of the withdrawal of forces by the United Nations in place of the United Kingdom.

8. It had agreed to the presence of an Argentine observer.

With this brief text, Kirkpatrick took up new consultations with Perez de Cuellar and with Parsons. From the first, she was greeted by a sombre picture of the course of events, while the British representative returned her memo with a handwritten note of no less ominous content:

"These concessions go much further than many might have hoped," Parsons pointed out, and added: "They will be considered a complete surrender by many members of the House of Commons."

In reality time ran out when on Wednesday 19th, Ros delivered to Perez de Cuellar an Argentine counter-offer, which the latter quickly sent to London's negotiator.

Its most salient points were:

1. South Georgia and the South Sandwich Islands to be included in the agreement.

2. The interim administration to remain in the exclusive charge of the United Nations, assisted by "observers" of the parties and others chosen among the islanders.

3. In spite of the above, it was accepted that the administrator had to carry out his task on the basis of legislation in force at April 1st 1982.

4. It was demanded that the UN Resolutions 1514 (XV), 2065 (XX) and other references to the question in the General Assembly should form the framework for the final negotiations, for which purpose New York City was to be the established venue.

5. It was demanded that the interim period should be until December 31 1982, but explicitly accepted a single option of an extension up to June 30 1983.

6. In the event of this later date being reached without a solution having been arrived at, the proceedings would be turned over to the General Assembly, which would then resolve the question.

Perez de Cuellar immediately grasped that this marked the inevitable end of the process, so that, taking advantage of the time needed for London to send its formal reply, he kept up his contacts with both Galtieri and Margaret Thatcher to whom he made the same request: more concessions. It was late for everything and on finishing the last of his discussions on the night of the 20th, he took the inevitable decision: he called for a meeting of the Security Council to inform it of the failure of the attempt at mediation.

That same day, Kirkpatrick called Bunge for another urgent meeting, this time to tell him: "This is total war, Wences. The only thing is for Argentina immediately to announce that it accepts the proposal. It is the only hope and we must find the way to make it happen."

Bunge knew that this would be far beyond his personal influence and he explained as much. The American did not accept this and exhorted him to assume the responsibility of informing public opinion in his country: "Go public, Wences! Go public!" she told him. "This is being managed by people who are not seriously looking for an agreement, and the Argentines have the right to know it," she reasoned.

Bunge, conscious of the risks, did not follow the advice of his friend. But nevertheless, after leaving his office, he stopped at the first public telephone he found - on the corner of First Avenue - and made a call to Lami Dozo.

From that unusual place, in full public view, he tried to convey to the Air Force Commandant the same urgency that he had detected in Kirkpatrick's words: "Arturo," he said in familiar fashion to the member of the Junta, "believe me if I tell you that Jeane was categorical. It is acceptance or out-and-out war!"

From a distance, Lami Dozo seemed unable to understand or share the distress that had overcome his friend. He spoke of the impossibility of acceptance if at the very least, London did not agree to withdraw the reference to Article 73. Nevertheless, on Bunge's insistence he promised to put forward the idea to the Junta: "Calm yourself, Wences. I'll talk to the President and Anaya straight away and call you immediately at your hotel."

In his room at the Harvard Club, Bunge received several calls from Kirkpatrick, who spoke in ever more pressing tones. He also made other calls to Buenos Aires, until he learnt from Lami Dozo's lips that nothing had changed. Neither Galtieri nor Anaya showed any disposition to revise the Argentine position. For his part, Costa Mendez insisted that accepting the principle of accordance with Article 73 was equivalent to returning the islands to the British.

About 10 pm he spoke for the last time to the American ambassador to tell her the unfavourable news. She was crushing: "There's nothing you can do, then. Your compatriots have changed a diplomatic victory into a military defeat." Possessing excellent military intelligence, she revealed to the Argentine: "London has already given the order for the final attack."

A few hours later, British troops landed and consolidated a beachhead at San Carlos, confirming Kirkpatrick's mournful prophesy.

After Perez de Cuellar's confession to the Security Council - "My efforts now do not serve the objective of peace," he said - the assembly immersed itself in the search for a ceasefire that might stop the slaughter on the battle front and perhaps bring a pause for reflection.

From the first sessions it emerged quite sharply that Great Britain was firmly decided on blocking any such move with its power of veto. The conflicting parties spoke clearly of the speedy progress made by the landing force and Margaret Thatcher clearly did not want anyone to deprive her of the victory that "my boys" were winning with their lives.

None of the public appeals changed the situation one iota - among them the Irishman Dorr's dramatic intervention: "Someone must say it's enough!" The frequent exercise of each speaker's right of reply resulted in debates in which Parsons and the Foreign Minister of Panama, Illueca, bordered on insult.

Four delegations presented plans for a resolution of the conflict. Two of them - sponsored by Panama and Brazil - required a cessation of hostilities; the others - prepared by the Irish and Japanese missions - avoided that requirement and limited themselves to granting Perez de Cuellar a mandate to undertake a new peace attempt.

Buenos Aires meanwhile fell back on putting pressure on Washington. A new request for a meeting of IATRA was made and sent to Takacs and to the State Department with a note which hinted at the withdrawal of delegates from the *Junta Interamericana de Defensa* (Inter-American Defense Council) - and the breaking of bilateral relations. Further still, it was rumoured that Costa Mendez would head the Argentine delegation to the meeting of the Bureau of Co-ordination of the Movement of Non-Aligned Countries, which was expected on May 31st in Havana.

Kirkpatrick - reluctant to give up the undertaking - continued her efforts and again consulted Bunge in Buenos Aires on the text of her speech to the Security Council on Saturday 22nd. The drafts came and went via telex - from the mission building on First Avenue in New York to the 18th floor of a building in the calle San Martin, where Bunge had his office.

"The United States," said Kirkpatrick at the end of her so carefully prepared speech, "is disposed to support every initiative that can help Argentina and Britain to achieve an honourable peace."

Though her message did not have any decisive effect, at least it confirmed her in the eyes of the Argentine Military as the only valid person with whom to speak. Thus Lami Dozo commissioned Miret, who was once more accompanying Costa Mendez, to maintain permanent contact with the American diplomat.

The Secretary of Planning was the only one of the Argentine negotiators for whom Kirkpatrick retained respect. "He seemed the least influenced by triumphalist rhetoric. And this was the most noticeable characteristic of the other Argentines - .'. spite of all the evidence," she recalled during the investigation.

But not even with Lami Dozo was dialogue simple. On one occasion the ambassador, Jose Sorzano, felt exasperated by his chief's failure to convince Miret that an Argentine defeat was little less than imminent. Worn down by the stubbornness of the officer - who only referred everything back to Buenos Aires - the Cuban-born diplomat appealed to his maternal Spanish in search of a suitably robust phrase. "The English are going to kick the shit out of them," was the one he found.(*"Los ingleses los van a cagar a patadas!"*)

On the night of Wednesday 26th, a little after approving Resolution 505, Miret convinced Costa Mendez to come to one of his meetings with Kirkpatrick. Resolution 505 was a compromise text derived from the Irish plan which allowed seven more days for Perez de Cuellar to make a further peace effort[11].

This attempt at a rapport ended in another fiasco. First there was the argument over the Argentine decision - already adopted, but not yet announced in public - to send the Foreign Minister to Havana:

"Are you going to Cuba after having fought Leftist subversion for five years?" argued the indignant Kirkpatrick.

"Yes. Perhaps then, you weren't fighting German Nazism when you allied yourselves with the Soviet Union?" retorted Miret[12]. But when the dialogue seemed to be turning more conciliatory in tone - Kirkpatrick spoke of: ".....the friends, like Clark, those whom Argentina could continue counting on in Washington....." - one of her assistants interrupted her to inform her that the Secretary of State was on the line.

Kirkpatrick excused herself and went into another room for one of her more violent exchanges of opinion - one of the many that she had those days with Haig. He had learnt of the meeting with Costa Mendez and began to reproach her for the initiative, accusing her of acting behind his back. The discussion was prolonged and at the end of half an hour, the Foreign Minister rose and left with Miret without taking his leave of his hostess. "I can't wait any longer. If the ambassador wishes to speak to me, she knows where to find me," he snapped curtly to one of Kirkpatrick's assistants.

The renewed deliberations of IATRA in the early hours of Saturday 29th, produced a new resolution of political value to Argentina, but it was light on content. Its principal points were a condemnation of the "unjustified and disproportionate" British attack, and the request to its member states to "lend the Argentine Republic the support that each judges appropriate." In the event, this was not much more than verbal support.

That same day, Costa Mendez returned from Washington in the special plane of Aerolineas Argentinas that the Government had chartered for the occasion, believing for many reasons that Argentina should be represented at the Havana meeting by a delegation of top-level people. But he also harboured reasonable doubts about how this would be viewed on the military front. This was no time to cause division in the forces when they were involved in an armed struggle against Great Britain.

The authors' research showed that there was evident military dissatisfaction regarding the move in Cuba, but also that the dramatic circumstances through which the country was living inhibited any general expression of opposition. After the war, however, it was common to hear condemnation of the cordial dealings between Costa Mendez and Fidel Castro, as also of the later journey of President Bignone to India and his meeting with Yasser Arafat, though the Military felt obliged to swallow it.

In spite of everything, the Foreign Minister asserted that the decision to go to Havana was unanimously accepted by the Junta, and that it in no way constituted a "traumatic decision."

Anyway, the reality for the armed forces was that during the whole *Process of National Reorganization*, they had disowned the Third World, some of whose countries were considered "real enemies of the Fatherland," for having supposedly fostered subversive activities in Argentina.

Costa Mendez arrived at Ezeiza airport at about 10.30 pm on Saturday 29th, and his greatest wish at the time was to shut himself away in his comfortable apartment in Palermo Chico. Nevertheless, he was met with a surprise: a limousine of the Presidency of the Nation awaited him. Galtieri wanted to see him immediately.

The Foreign Minister, in the company of his military "mini-senate" set off for Galtieri's residence in Campo de Mayo - the army's most powerful support garrison, on the outskirts of Buenos Aires.

The President idly awaited him in his easy chair in the living room of his house, slowly smoking his low-tar cigarettes. When the Foreign Minister walked through the door, he got up and gave him an effusive embrace.

Costa Mendez enlarged on all the moves made in the United States. Galtieri seemed enthusiastic with the results, which in reality did not alter Argentina's uncomfortable international situation.

With evident excitement, the President interrupted the Foreign Minister. After getting on his feet he exclaimed:

"Good... now you are going to Havana." He paused for a moment and added:

"With my friend, Fidel Castro, we shall bring Thatcher to her knees."

Miret, recovering from his initial stupefaction, observed:

"General, I don't think I have anything to do with the delegation that is going to Cuba. Besides, I must talk the matter over with my commandant."

Galtieri did not place great importance on this statement. He preferred to rely on the mute assent of Iglesias and Moya. Nevertheless, for Miret, his words had a special significance. Well-informed about the workings of the Military, he imagined that sooner or later his career could be cut short by that journey to the Caribbean island.

The meeting over, Costa Mendez was able to get some rest, but Miret, almost overwhelmed by events, set off by car for the private residence of Lami Dozo. It was past 1 am and the commandant was surprised at his unexpected visitor.

Miret briefly related what had happened in Washington and New York, and immediately advised his chief of his wish not to be sent to Havana. In fact, however, he had been more shaken by the impression the President had given him minutes earlier.

"Look Arturo - Galtieri's state of mind surprised me. Think it over, but I think we are in the hands of an Ayatollah. But an Ayatollah without religion..." he confided to Lami Dozo.

In fact, Brigadier Miret was only a peripheral member of the delegation, whose sole military representative was General Iglesias - another of the men trusted by the President.

On Wednesday June 2nd in the afternoon, the Argentine mission touched Cuban soil and thus began one of the most audacious diplomatic gambles of the military *Process*. It was not so much the manner in which it was planned - the realities forced a move of this kind - but the absolute nature of the reversal, in such a short time, of a foreign policy which had been solely dedicated to "Western and Christian" principles.

It was this perhaps, together with the stand taken by the United States, which produced most upset in the inner circle of the armed forces. But in their different ways, one as much as the other had to be accepted by the Argentine Military.

Havana was in the grip of a cyclone at that time and the visitors scarcely had time to reach their hotel, change clothes and set off for the Palace of the Revolution. At the Palace, a reception was being held for delegations taking part in the meeting of the Non-Aligned Countries.

Costa Mendez received preferential treatment from the moment of his arrival. In an office on the upper floor of the very building where the gathering was being held he had his first private interview with Fidel Castro.

The Cuban leader gave an analysis of the special circumstances in Latin America which greatly impressed his guests. General Iglesias frequently glanced at Costa Mendez showing his surprise - he would never accept that there was also a modicum of admiration - but the Foreign Minister avoided any sign that might be perceived by Castro as one of weakness or lack of expertise on the subject.

At one time, Castro rose to his feet. On a large map he located the Falkland Islands and began to question Iglesias about the military precautions adopted in order to resist the final attack of a Western power.

It seems the explanations of the Argentine general did not

measure up to the Cuban leader's view of the situation. His predictions of what would occur in actual battle was found to be close to events, according to the recollection of those present at the meeting.

Iglesias stuck to the defence arguments - which were simply to fortify the area adjacent to Port Stanley. At one point, the Foreign Minister intervened so as to make it clear: "We have not come to ask for military aid."

Castro replied without losing his composure but also without hiding a certain relief: "I am glad that you're not asking this of me. Because it would be neither appropriate for me nor yourselves."

He immediately asked for how long the Argentine Military were thinking of prolonging the armed confrontation with Great Britain. Costa Mendez deferred to Iglesias - as he did each time a military matter arose while he was abroad - but his explanation again seemed to leave Castro dissatisfied.

The Cuban leader then stressed that the Falklands cause fitted into his understanding of a war of national liberation, and made a fiery tribute to Argentine conduct prior to the conflict.

But he at once made clear:

"You must understand that no war of national liberation is lost, so long as one is really ready to fight it."

In this last warning, Castro let his doubts show concerning the extent of the Argentine Military's strength of will in embarking upon the adventure: "Whoever wins the battle for those mountains will have won the match," Castro pronounced, pointing to them on the map.

Iglesias' reply was evasive. In the first place he felt constrained by the forceful military presentation that Castro was giving; in the second place he really did not know what the military preparations were for the defences of the Falklands capital.

Turning to Costa Mendez, Castro asked him what kind of general Menendez was. The Foreign Minister was surprised by the question, but guessed its meaning. Avoiding a definite description he said that Menendez was "dark and small," trying to get off the hook with a physical description of the Military Governor.

Castro stopped him dead and went straight to the point: "What I am asking you is - is Menendez a general who fights or one of those who surrenders."

Costa Mendez preferred not to reply, choosing instead to let the conversation drift to another subject - after an embarrassing silence.

The delegates of the Non-Aligned Countries were conversing animatedly in a large room, when the sound of a door opening alerted them.

Costa Mendez appeared first and then, a few steps behind, Fidel

Castro. the Foreign Minister began to descend the staircase and the Cuban leader, in a rather unusual gesture, came up to him and accompanied him as far as the exit, taking him by the arm.

On arriving at the way out, a fine and persistent drizzle could be felt which caused Castro to remark: "Rain and snow are needed to beat the British in the Falklands. Don't you think so, General?" he enquired of Iglesias.

The latter's reply was an imperceptible grimace, and when Costa Mendez prepared to climb into his car, Castro made another gesture that inspired a thousand comments. He took a step forward, opened the door for him and took his leave of him with an effusive embrace.

On the following day, the Argentine Foreign Minister spoke to the Bureau of the Non-Aligned Countries and denounced what he called a tripartite alliance consisting of Great Britain, the United States and South Africa, whose object, he claimed, was to install an American base in the Falklands!

That statement, perhaps less spectacular in tone than the pronouncements in the OAS and UN, nevertheless served to assuage the doubts of the African countries, and this had immediate repercussions in the Security Council, as it enabled nine votes for the cease-fire resolution to be obtained, obliging Great Britain to exercise its veto.

Nevertheless, while this was happening, the Argentine delegates tried to bring in a preliminary motion for a resolution that would severely condemn Great Britain and the United States. This, however, was resisted by the Caribbean anglophone countries, headed by Jamaica.

That same day, Costa Mendez and Castro had a further meeting in a corridor of the Palace of Conventions which only served to nourish the expectations of reporters, who surrounded the two men in a matter of seconds.

On their return to Argentina, the delegation made a stop in Caracas, and there Costa Mendez took the opportunity to make clear that: "We shall not have a socialist Fatherland." He also described the position of Argentina as intermediate between the Third World and the First World neither of which accepts us, nor has ever accepted us."

The Foreign Minister believed that it was necessary to make these points clear, which in reality were intended for the Military. At that stage, no-one could be in any doubt about the real significance of the mission to Cuba, nor of the very warm but sceptical support offered by Fidel Castro.

In New York, Perez de Cuellar's second peace effort reached impasse - more quickly this time than the previous occasion - and, faithful to the terms of his mandate, the Secretary-General threw the ball back to the Security Council on June 1st. Thus, once more, he left its members to tackle the challenge of changing the disastrous course events were taking.

A day before, Reagan had travelled to Versailles to be present at the annual summit of the developed countries: a forum made up of Italy, France, West Germany, Japan and Canada, as well as the United States and Great Britain. There, Reagan tried in vain to convince Margaret Thatcher that the humiliation of the Argentine Military would, in the long run, do no good to the "Western cause."

On Wednesday 2nd, Miret, Moya and Mallea Gil (Iglesias' replacement - he was accompanying Costa Mendez in Cuba) returned to the UN offices. Their instructions were to renew threats of a break with Washington - which up till then had not materialized.

As well as this, the Foreign Minister arrived to announce officially - a day before the adoption of Resolution 505 - the withdrawal of its delegate to the Inter-American Defence Council. But this decision was later changed in Buenos Aires and the Foreign Minister then had to try numerous ploys to cover the confusion.

At that stage, the differences at the heart of the Military were more than noteworthy. Miret used various methods to get round the "vigilance" of Moya and Mallea Gil when establishing his contacts. Mallea Gil for his part preserved a certain independence from the group. Moya limited himself merely to *not* losing contact with his team companions; after all, unlike them, he had no-one to question him.

In the course of the Thursday session, later suspended to permit some delegations to prepare a motion for the cessation of hostilities, Miret approached an Argentine reporter and in a low voice said to him: "Do me a favour. In a minute or two come to the Argentine delegation and invite me to lunch in front of the others. I'll explain later."

Without understanding the reason for this unusual request, the journalist did what was asked. That same night the air force officer returned the favour: "I had a meeting with Kissinger," he confided, "and I wanted to go alone." Whilst he related the details of this encounter to the reporter, Mallea Gil knocked at the door of the room Miret occupied at the UN Plaza Hotel. Making a grimace, Miret indicated the bathroom, demanding silence. "Give us a few minutes to use the lift and then leave yourself," he instructed the reporter in a low voice.

The consultations on Friday 4th produced an innocuous text - an amendment of a scheme originally sponsored by Panama - in which a cessation of hostilities was demanded, but made conditional upon a renewed intervention by Perez de Cuellar.

The text obtained the nine votes necessary (Spain, Panama, China, USSR, Poland, Ireland, Japan, Uganda and Zaire); four abstentions: (France, Jordan, Guyana and Togo) but was condemned by the vetoes of Great Britain and the US.

In justifying her own action, Kirkpatrick surprisingly announced in a tone of mixed anger and frustration that: "My assistants inform me that according to the provisional rules of the Council, it is impossible to change a vote after it has been given. Nevertheless I have received instructions from my Government to put it on record that if it had been possible to make that change the vote would have been altered from a veto to an abstention."

What had happened? Research permitted the following reconstruction of the various details of the events. Kirkpatrick tried all day long to obtain a change of her instructions. A veto would be uselessly irritating to the Argentines, she argued, and would be unnecessary because Great Britain would employ hers with the same effect of cutting short the peace effort. Moreover, she constantly sounded other delegations out and in successive cables transmitted the decisions of Japan and Ireland to abstain.

This attempt - not easy if one takes into account that Reagan and Haig were in Paris and the latter was not disposed to give the least respite to his political rival - was pursued even after the Council was in session. A permanently open telephone line carried the news of the debate to the Paris hotel room where Haig was staying.

Kirkpatrick, for her part, kept in permanent contact with Walter Stoessel - who was replacing Haig at the State Department - and with Thomas Enders. These in their turn did the same with the Secretary of State.

Five minutes before the vote, Stoessel told Kirkpatrick:

"Look, Jeane. It is perfectly clear that up to this moment there is no change of instructions, so you will have to vote against the motion."

That seemed to have been the end of the matter. But she had hardly raised her hand to indicate her country's veto when one of her assistants conveyed to her the news: Haig (in France) had ordered the vote to be changed. Kirkpatrick replied that that was technically impossible, but the Secretary of State insisted that at least she had to put on record the US wish to change its vote.

At first she thought of not complying with this last order. But, believing it to be a sign of a manoeuvre by her enemy, she changed her mind. "The Argentines had threatened to break off relations; if I had not reported the change they could have done it and Haig would have had an excellent opportunity to blame me and perhaps to press the President to remove me from the post." She reluctantly informed the Council concerning this new order.

Far from these speculations, the Soviet ambassador, Oleg

Troianovsky, left the Council Chamber and approached the astonished Argentine journalists.

"What was that?" he asked them, somewhat amused.

"I don't know; perhaps it was for show," replied one of them.

"I think it was for show," the diplomat observed categorically[13].

Whatever it had been, it annihilated the last breath of peace.

NOTES

1. During this time, a British weekly correctly commented of *Haig II*: "Mrs Thatcher finds much in the [American] plan that is unsatisfactory; it will almost be easier for her if Buenos Aires rejects it." Article: "Time runs out." *The Economist* May 1st, 1982.

2. The sales of American arms to Argentina were, strictly speaking, prohibited from 1978 under the rules of the "Humphrey-Kennedy Amendment" to the Act of Foreign Assistance. This was a sanction against the violation of human rights by the Argentine military regime. The new restriction merely confirmed the pre-existing one.

3. Anthony Parsons: *The Falkland crisis in the United Nations. 31 March - 14 June 1982*. International Affairs - Chatham House p 173 London, February 1983.

4. Max Hastings and Simon Jenkins, *The Battle for the Falklands*, p 168, Michael Joseph, London, 1983.

5. The Movement of Non-Aligned Countries, of which Argentina is a full member since 1974, pronounced in favour of Argentine sovereignty over the Falklands in its documents of Lima (Conference of Foreign Ministers, August 25-30, 1975); Colombo (Vth Conference of Chiefs of State or Government, August 16-19, 1976); New Delhi (Ministerial meeting of the Bureau of Co-ordination, April 7-11, 1977); Havana (Ministerial meeting of the Bureau of Co-ordination, May 5-20, 1978); Belgrade (Conference of Ministers of Foreign Affairs, July 15-30, 1978); Colombo (Ministerial meeting of the Bureau of Coordination June 4-9. 1979), and more recently in Havana (Ministerial Meeting of the Bureau of Coordination, May 31 - June 5, 1982) and in New Delhi (VIIth Heads of State or Government, March 1983). See *Two Decades of Non-Alignment* (Documents of the gatherings of the Non-Aligned Countries 1961-82), a publication from the Ministry of Foreign Affairs of the Government of India, New Delhi, 1983.

6. Ibid (4), p 169.

7. "Two Hollow Victories at Sea" *Time*, Vol 119, No 20, p 13.

New York, May 17. 1982.

8. "More War or More Jaw" *The Sunday Times*, May 9, 1982.

9. Ibid (3) p 173.

10. "Critico Vernon Walters a los dos paises," *Clarin* p 10, May 11 1982.

11. "Reaffirming its resolution 502 (1982) of April 3, 1982.

"Observing with the deepest concern that the situation in the region of the Falklands Islands has gravely deteriorated;

"Having listened to the declaration made by the Secretary-General to the Security Council in its 2.360 session, held on May 21 1982, as well as the declarations formulated in the course of the debate by the representatives of Argentina and the United Kingdom of Great Britain and Northern Ireland;

"Concerned to achieve as a matter of the greatest urgency, a cessation of hostilities and the termination of the present conflict between the armed forces of Argentina and the United Kingdom of Great Britain and Northern Ireland:

1. Expresses its recognition to the Secretary General for his efforts that he has already made to achieve an agreement between the parties, to achieve compliance with Resolution 502 (1982) of the Security Council and in this way re-establish peace in the region;

2. Asks the Secretary-General on the basis of the present resolution, to undertake a renewed mission of good offices, bearing in mind Resolution 502 (1982) of the Security Council and the approach outlined in the declaration that he formulated on 21st May 1982;

3. Exhorts the parties in conflict to co-operate fully with the Secretary-General in his mission with the aim to put an end to the present hostilities in the Falkland Islands and in their vicinity;

4. Asks the Secretary General to take up immediate contact with the parties with the aim of negotiating mutually acceptable conditions for a cease-fire, including, on being necessary, the adoption of measures for sending observers of the United Nations in order to watch over the compliance with the conditions of the cease fire;

5. Asks the Secretary-General to present a provisional report as soon as possible and in any case not more than seven days after the approval of the present resolution."

12. Cardoso, Oscar Raul "Contactos Reservados" *Clarin* p 12, May 27 1982.

13. Cardoso, Oscar Raul "Una Puesta en Escena" *Clarin* p 4, June 5 1982.

Chapter 12

ANOTHER ALCAZAR OF TOLEDO?

That 10th April, Menendez prepared to receive the first official visit to the Falklands. The Argentine Governor had been there for almost a week, and his activities had been reduced to purely administrative affairs which in every way caused him more than a headache. For example, the change to driving on the right in the streets of Port Stanley provoked a wave of protest from the kelpers, to the point that the bishop of the islands had to intervene. "Do you know what it means to a person aged 50, who has been driving on the left for 30 years to change his habits at a stroke?" the prelate argued. But his plea was met with only the inflexibility of the Argentine Military.

Menendez had spent his time organizing the one thousand soldiers scattered over the archipelago and occupying himself in governing in the manner advised by Galtieri at the beginning of March. He had to think of schools, the development of a system of justice, the gradual introduction of the Argentine peso to replace the Falklands pound, and also to be on the watch for acts of sabotage that rebel locals were likely to commit against the new inhabitants of the islands. Some, for example, threw the keys of tractors and jeeps into the sea.

Nor was the Governor able to think of the possibility of war with Great Britain. The news that did reach him, above all through the few reporters who still had authorization to visit the islands, was frankly far from reassuring. The Royal Navy had set sail and the precautions taken by the Argentines in the Falklands did not remotely meet the requirements for an eventual armed clash with one of the Western Powers.

His surprise was therefore great when on the morning of the 10th, he met the Chief of Theatre of Operations in the South Atlantic (TOAS), Rear-Admiral Lombardo, who was the bearer of instructions prepared on the mainland.

Menendez had worked with Lombardo, Garcia, Plessl and Suarez del Cerro on the drawing up of documents that set out the steps to be followed upon the recovery of the Falklands. In these, a special point was made of the diplomatic action to be deployed in the face of the inevitable and violent reaction by Great Britain in the international forums and - but only as a remote possibility - the study of any eventual military riposte from Margaret Thatcher's Government.

Suddenly, the priorities had changed for the Argentine Military and during that day, Menendez learnt - not without a certain shiver - that those original documents had been superseded. The war was not now being looked upon as a mere possibility, and Admiral Lombardo suggested to the Governor the need to reinforce key points in the Falklands.

"Well, so what are we going to do now?" asked Menendez.

"You have complete freedom of action. Look: I brought directives, but from the mainland I can't do much. I am Theatre Commander. My concern is with the fleet, with the air force..." replied Lombardo.

"I understand, but alone we can't do anything here without support. What can *you* do?" he said, almost pleading.

"Look General, you are going to have to resist as best you can. Support from land is complicated. Understand that we have to face nuclear submarines." explained the Chief of TOAS.

"Well, but you *are* going to do something?" insisted Menendez.

"Yes, of course... If the British attempt a landing just wait a few days, then the fleet can try an attack." said Lombardo, reassuringly.

The Chief of TOAS made a rapid evaluation of the manpower stationed on the Falklands and arrived at the conclusion that some reinforcements were essential.

"What do you feel about another brigade, General?" asked Lombardo.

"Well, it would be wonderful, but one has to know for what purpose. We lack mobility....." Menendez pointed out, very little attracted by the new proposal.

"With a force like that the British are going to have to think again. They are already preparing ships to come here....." pronounced Lombardo, putting an end to the conversation.

On the following day, an unexpected Hercules transport descended to the still intact landing strip at Port Stanley airport. Suddenly the plane began to empty, and from its interior emerged hundreds of soldiers. Menendez was urgently summoned because no-one knew what to do with this, the 3rd Infantry Regiment.

"What are you doing here, Lt. Colonel?" asked a perplexed Menendez.

"Er....look, General; we've been sent here," said the officer.

276

"Who sent you? Is anyone else coming?" inquired the Governor.

"I think the whole brigade is coming." persisted Lt. Colonel Comini.

That afternoon, Menendez and Brig. General Americo Daher - deputy to Menendez as Commander of Land Forces in the islands - were conversing in the Governor's residence when the telephone began to ring insistently. The military chiefs were studying plans spread out on a large glossy wooden table and no-one paid attention to the intermittent sound. Colonel Machinandiarena went to pick up the receiver. Moments later Menendez took the phone and heard: "This is General Jofre, Sir."

"Hallo Tiny! How are you?" asked Menendez, who was an old acquaintance of his.

"What is this *how are you?*" asked Brig. General Oscar Jofre in an unfriendly voice.

"Yes, er ... how are you ... where are you speaking from?" the Governor just managed to say, hesitatingly.

"I am speaking to you from here, at the airport where I have just arrived and there is no-one to meet me." said Jofre.

"Shit! I'll send you an estate car," exclaimed Menendez.

Jofre did not look very pleased. He arrived at the Governor's residence, and Menendez excused himself with "Forgive me, but I didn't know about your arrival." Then without losing any time, they began to plan the distribution of the new men and to solve the logistic problems that the unexpected reinforcement posed.

The Governor had first to get round the problem of seniority. Jofre was a more senior general than Daher and the latter was unavoidably displaced in the new set-up. When the news filtered out of the arrival of Jofre and his troops, the officers of the brigade commanded by "Turk" Daher began quietly to show their disapproval at what they considered the unjustified displacement of their chief.

Daher himself put it in those terms to Menendez asking for his authorization to make a formal complaint, which would involve returning to the mainland to put his case to Major General Garcia. The Governor tried to dissuade him and, as a last resort offered him the post of Chief of Staff. It was not sufficient; in any case, that designation implied being moved from second to third in the chain of command. Moreover, and in spite of differences in seniority, the three - Menendez, Jofre and Daher - were brigadier generals who normally have colonels as their chiefs of staff.

Menendez understood the difficult situation in which Daher had been placed - he realised he would have reacted in the same way - besides he did not want to take over a problem for which he had no responsibility whatever. He authorized Daher to go to Comodoro Rivadavia, where he met Garcia. The situation was not improved for the displaced general, but at least he obtained a few considerate words from Garcia. He accepted that there was a problem. But Daher, since it was scarcely a matter of necessity, insisted that in some way it had to be interpreted as a judgment on his professional capacity. No, Garcia replied in a solemn tone. Accordingly, Daher had to return to Port Stanley to carry out his duties and ignore this small inconvenience. After all, Garcia said, it was a minor matter compared with the importance of the mission which the country had entrusted to him.

And so it was. Daher returned to assume his new post of Chief of Staff for all the army units stationed on the islands, but not before letting it be known among the officer corps how Garcia had showered him with praise. The journey to the mainland did not restore Daher to the status that his functions had had before Jofre's arrival, but at least it permitted him to save face before his subordinates. The Daher episode provoked long discussions as to who should be on the right of whom in the march-pasts and other official ceremonies. Successive members of the Junta had instituted these from March 1976 onwards and they were held on innumerable occasions throughout their rule.

What is certain is that Menendez immediately began to receive artillery groups, anti-aircraft defence units, and a number of regiments which rapidly raised the total of soldiers stationed on the islands to 10,000. The first half of April had already gone and war was beginning to appear more likely than the possibility of a negotiated solution.

On the 19th, Admiral Anaya presented himself on the Falklands. With his habitual frugality, the navy chief said very little and also refused an invitation to see more of the islands.

The commanders were rather surprised and a sense of anguish came over them when they asked Anaya about the results of the diplomatic efforts. "They continue talking," was all he would say to a group of officers who wanted to know with certainty if they still had to prepare themselves for a combat of blood and fire.

General Jofre carefully detailed the various precautionary measures adopted. Apart from the large body of men garrisoning the islands, he pointed out the barbed wire entanglements, the mining of fields and beaches and the installation of anti-aircraft defences in the neighbourhood of the capital.

For the first time Anaya abandoned his aloofness and commented with unusual enthusiasm: "This is going to be like the Alcazar of Toledo"[1]. Jofre did not want to be less enthusiastic and with exaggerated optimism he added: "The Alcazar of Toledo will be nothing to this... Admiral," for which he received the reward of a rare smile from

Anaya.

On April 22nd, Galtieri arrived on a visit to the Falklands - Lami Dozo had preceded him two days earlier - and sparing no efforts he asked the Governor for a rapid tour of the archipelago. Menendez as an obedient subordinate complied and scarcely forty minutes after having arrived at Port Stanley, the President was already installed in the helicopter that would take him to the most remote points on the islands.

The first part of the flight lasted almost fifty minutes - as far as Fox Bay, passing over the central mountain range towards the heights of Darwin and then to Falkland Sound. Galtieri at one moment seemed impatient and in a grumbling tone exclaimed: "This helicopter is rubbish. How slow!"

Menendez explained to him that the Falklands were 250 km from East to West, and approximately 110 from North to South with an area of 11,600 sq. kms. "More than half Tucuman," he ventured, referring to a province of Argentina that he got to know like the back of his hand during the repression of the guerillas.

He also warned that during the fifty minutes of the flight, the helicopter could have been shot down up to seventeen times by a British Sea Harrier. Galtieri's eyes seemed to grow larger, and in a tone of mixed surprise and fright, he exclaimed: "Of course.....How big the islands are!"

"Do you think the British will come to Port Stanley?" he asked almost immediately, without a pause.

"Look, General, the objective of the British campaign must be Port Stanley. But they can disembark in any distant part of the islands. There are many suitable places and we cannot defend them all," replied Menendez.

General Jofre, who was travelling at Galtieri's side, insisted on pointing out the difficulties of the terrain - the undergrowth, the broken coastline, the boggy stretches - and remarked on the problems of mobility that the Argentine troops would have. Menendez, accompanied by General Senorans, also described these features to the point of tedium, but Galtieri for some reason was more concerned about the heights of a particular northern peninsula which still remained unprotected.

Thus when the Puma was ready to descend to the airport, he asked that the journey be extended to go to that area. After flying over it for fifteen minutes, Galtieri ordered: "A brigade should be stationed here to prevent any landing." Menendez listened without replying, because this bright idea of the President did not seem to make any sense. The coastline he pointed out would present serious difficulties for any supposed British landing and would only be accessible by air.

279

On the way back to Port Stanley Galtieri ordered a meeting of the military commanders assigned to organizing the defence.

In a small room previously used by the Royal Marines, everyone gathered: Galtieri, with the members of his General Staff - Menendez, Jofre, Daher and Brigadier Castellanos as well as colonels, naval captains, commodores and even some of lesser rank.

It was difficult even to breathe, but that did not matter to Galtieri. Amid the acclaim, he began to describe the situation with a self-sufficiency which attracted the attention of many.

"Well, gentlemen; everything that is happening was foreseen." (At that moment, Menendez was tempted to intervene because he remembered Galtieri's first instructions in March: full of simplicity and optimism, but he contained himself: "Be quiet, Benjamin, it's better if you keep quiet!" he convinced himself).

"The discussions with Mr Haig have not produced results," he added, "so that the British Government's commitment is becoming greater all the time. Inevitably there is going to be an armed collision. After that, I believe we shall enter into a new stage of negotiations. We will have to wait for that collision and allow time and space for the continued search for a diplomatic solution."

After this, Galtieri and Menendez stayed behind, away from the others for a time, and made plans for the defence. The Governor explained that it would be difficult to increase the radius of the defensive perimeter round Port Stanley because of lack of transport. The President insisted on the advisability of sending more regiments - as if an accumulation of men could guarantee a more efficient defence - and it also seemed useful to him to "put some soldiers" on West Falkland, on the other side of Falkland Sound.

In reality, this idea had been initiated by Lami Dozo, supported by Anaya during a meeting of the Junta.

Menendez made a new plan for the deployment of troops on the islands and presented it to General Garcia, who promptly rejected it.

"Forgive me, General, but the only thing which seems to interests you is the defence of Port Stanley," Garcia criticized.

"Well....that was the original idea," replied the Governor timidly.

"I agree, but we have to change tack. That's war. West Falkland is not well protected. We shall have to send more men," ordered Garcia.

Suddenly General Jofre, who was also there, interceded: "General, it would be good if you could send us helicopters. If not, the transport of soldiers will be impossible."

Menendez took up the thread again: "Look, General; what worries me is that if the British do what Admiral Lombardo and I believe

- if they come from the north of East Falkland and attack the capital - the forces on the other side of the Sound will be isolated and will be useless. On the other hand, it would be right to reinforce Darwin, which is connected to Port Stanley."

Garcia lost patience and ended the dialogue in cutting fashion: "Well, look; it's Galtieri's decision. Don't discuss it any more. The question is closed."

Galtieri returned from his inspection of the Falklands brimming with enthusiasm. In fact, he had gone with a pre-conception because only hours before the President went there, Anaya himself had spoken to him of the marvels of the fortifications at Port Stanley.

"I found the defensive position very strong," explained Anaya, "because when you talk of a landing operation, the ratio of forces has to be between five and eight times to have any chance of success. If we put more than five thousand soldiers in Port Stanley, the British will have to have a landing force of at least twenty-five thousand men. That's not possible."

In reality Anaya was clinging to a fragile argument often wielded by Argentine naval officers during the first stages of the war. The authors were present on various occasions at meetings held by the Joint Chiefs of Staff in those days. In these, Rear Admiral Salvio Menendez was given to revealing his thoughts on the development of events.

In fact, one of his favourite ideas was that of persuading the reporters of the non-feasibility of a British landing in the Falklands. To that would be added constant references to the rigours of the South Atlantic climate (Salvio Menendez used to refer to help by "Admiral Winter"). In his opinion, support for the Royal Marines would be difficult - forgetting that they were NATO professionals who were used to training in the Arctic at temperatures below minus sixty degrees Celsius. Moreover, the prolonged stay on board ships to which Argentine resistance would compel them would not exhaust them psychologically, as he claimed. Rear Admiral Menendez was forgetting that the NATO fleet stays at sea for periods of up to six months continuously.

In the Falklands, Governor Menendez continued receiving reinforcements in Port Stanley, but the requirements for logistic support - helicopters, land vehicles etc. did not appear, and - to tell the truth - this situation was not to alter much until the surrender.

General Menendez insisted many times after the war was over that the British acted just as he had foreseen: that is to say, they disembarked at some point of their own choice on East Falkland and began their advance towards the capital.

Nevertheless, Galtieri claims that Menendez always supposed

that the attack would come from the sea - and that only at the last moment did he warn that the offensive was being made by land[2].

The man who was Governor of the Falklands denies this interpretation. Moreover, he states that he had a perfect knowledge of the archipelago and knew of all the ungarrisoned places where enemy forces could penetrate.

"I expressly indicated these to the three commandants when they visited the islands," remarks Menendez.

Nevertheless, Galtieri states that during his brief stay on the Falklands he had the sensation that the then Governor was not in touch with what was happening and that he was not moving in the field of operations with sufficient security[3].

Except for a single contact with General Garcia, which took place on April 24th, the Governor of the Falklands had no further personal meetings with the top military authorities until the end of the struggle. Henceforth, communication would be by telex or telephone.

In the early hours of May 1st, British shells burst on the islands. Following that, euphoria broke out among the troops stationed there when an anti-aircraft battery, after several failed attempts, brought down a Sea Harrier on the Falklands mud.

The Royal Navy also began operations which then suddenly stopped, in what the great majority of the Argentine Military interpreted as a successful repulse of the British offensive.

Nevertheless, that morning of the 1st May an event occurred which was worth taking into account but which was wrongly evaluated by the High Command. Menendez was inspecting the defensive positions in the capital, when he was approached on the sea front at Port Stanley by a radio operator who had been listening in at the communications centre.

"General, Admiral Woodward offers surrender!" reported the official, almost breathless.

The Governor smiled complacently, but before replying he asked:

"Are you sure?"

"Yes, General," replied the operator.

In this next part of the incident, versions of events differ. Reports published at the time by all the media, followed the line laid down by a dispatch from the official news agency TELAM, and indicated that Menendez made a scathing reply to the British Admiral:

"We won't surrender, because we are winning. Bring the little Prince (that is, Prince Andrew, who was aboard the carrier, *Invincible*) and come and look for us."

Menendez, on the other hand, attributes that response to the radio operator himself, whom he says, he reproached for his behaviour, ("But clarifications are pointless now," he explained). The request for surrender was repeated after midday and again ignored. The British action at the time was the subject for examination that day by the Chief of TOAS, Rear Admiral Lombardo, who stated that enemy forces were testing Argentine resistance and had, above all, an intimidatory aim. [See: Chapter 10, *Sink the Belgrano!*]

After May 2nd when the Belgrano was sunk, actions in the field diminished, but the sophisticated British technology began to wear down the will of the Argentine soldiers.

For example, during the night of the 4th, radar at Port Stanley detected an impressive landing of British forces. What followed was a "red alert" broadcast all over the islands and almost 10,000 men did not get a wink of sleep. The air force was not in a position to carry out night operations and so at that moment there could only have been a land response to the invading troops.

More than six hours went by and the radar continued to indicate the landing with such perfection in terms of distances and movements that it began to look suspicious to some officers. After a few days it was discovered that it had only been a mock landing by the British, using decoys and computers which interfered with the radar signal that the Argentine detection equipment was tuned to - similar in fact to the video games in evidence all over the world.

British guns continued their harassment of Darwin and Port Stanley, and the impression began to grow that the day of the final battle was coming dangerously close.

Menendez pressed his colleagues on the mainland about the lack of naval support and the intermittent participation of the air force. Thus on May 12th he called Comodoro Rivadavia and demanded of Lombardo that fast patrol boats be sent which, in the view of Admiral Otero in Port Stanley, could be useful in preventing the prolonged harassment of the island capital by the British fleet.

The navy had only two such craft equipped with torpedoes and rapid-fire cannon but declined to send them because of "technical difficulties" - among them the lack of suitable fuel in the Falklands for their provisioning.

Menendez then asked for two Hoffman cannons, of 9 tonnes, each of which were then transported in a Hercules C-130 aircraft.

The Governor by that time was hoping for new directives, but in fact the only thing he received was a negative reply to his suggestion for altering the operational plans of the air force: "The policy of only making attacks on very profitable targets will be maintained," said the order from the military triumvirate.

The inflexibility of this strategy exasperated the Governor to such an extent that on the 14th he prepared a memorandum to the Junta - which never received a reply - demanding that he take part in the making of such decisions and called for clarification of the meaning of "profitable targets."

On the 15th, the British carried out on Pebble Island one of their most successful commando raids, destroying a fleet of Pucara ground attack aircraft and blowing up a munitions dump of vital importance to the Argentine forces.

This impelled Menendez on the 16th to prepare a long document in which he set out all the logistic difficulties. The 3rd Brigade, for example, had arrived on the islands with only light clothing and equipment. There was lack of military intelligence and a shortage of fuel which made the operation of radar impossible and restricted the use of helicopters. There was too the worsening of climatic conditions as well as the lack of food reserves and a perceptible lowering of the fighting spirit of the troops. Menendez also urged a re-instatement of the air bridge between the archipelago and the mainland, which had been disrupted for the previous fifteen days.

This document coincided with another from Lombardo, sent to the Junta, in which there was a description of the conflict so far, and a less than optimistic assessment of the outlook.

The Junta's reply to Menendez was not long in coming and ordered the formation in Comodoro Rivadavia of a Centre of Joint Operations (CEOPECON), under the charge of General Garcia. This implied the *de facto* disappearance of TOAS, and with it the eclipse of Vice-Admiral Lombardo, whose severe but realistic evaluation of events much displeased Galtieri, Anaya and Lami Dozo.

The President also promised Menendez that fishing boats would be sent with essential supplies - at that stage the Argentine soldiers used to hunt sheep, whose meat was valuable in providing indispensable calories to combat the cold - and he also made one thing clear: "Look, General," the President said, "from now on, deal with Garcia."

The Argentine Military were occupied upon such matters when from London came the announcement on the 19th of "an early British landing," to which few paid attention. Some officers insisted that it was only part of a campaign of psychological warfare.

Anyhow, on the islands themselves, some precautions were taken and some 70 soldiers who were dug in at Darwin were transported by helicopter to the neighbourhood of San Carlos.

The movement was fortunate because it was just this contingent under the command of Lieutenant Esteban which detected signs of a landing on the beaches of San Carlos. A radio message alerted General.

Menendez at 8.30 am on the 21st and the Junta was warned of the imminent final battle for the Falklands.

The governor of the islands, without even considering the extent of the British advance, ordered a reconnaissance flight by Naval Lieutenant Owen Critta. This advance was to be systematically denied on mainland Argentina through the reports made available to the public by the Joint Staff. Critta went in search of the four ships which, according to Esteban's information, had approached the shore at San Carlos, but on making the turn to take in the mouth of the bay, he met the main contingent of the Royal Navy. No less than twelve ships had taken up strategic positions and some of them were occupied in systematically shelling the Argentine positions at Darwin - which were not exactly well fortified.

Critta was surprised at the scale of the enemy force. There was no time for any doubts: making the sign of the Cross, he made a level flight and directed his Aeromacchi towards the fleet so managing to leave a British frigate seriously damaged. Common sense did not suggest a repeat performance, as only a miracle - perhaps his invocation to God - had permitted him to escape safe and sound the first time.

When he returned to Port Stanley, he could hardly find the words to describe what he had seen. He insisted on getting his machine ready to take off again, but the Aeromacchi did not want to move. Anything more was impossible from the islands themselves, because air power at that stage had been visibly decimated. Meanwhile, the enemy fleet continued to manoeuvre with relative ease and the calm in San Carlos was only broken around mid-day, when planes of the air force began to operate from the mainland.

Menendez was completely astonished and went running to his office at the residence, where he asked for a telephone line to Galtieri.

"They've landed - are there many of them?" were the President's first words.

"Don't worry, General. It was within our expectations. They have landed in an undefended place. And, well..... we are doing what we can," replied the Governor.

Galtieri did not seem to be in good spirits that day and some of his close associates confided that the news of the landing had made him sink into one of his periodic depressions.

The man most worried seemed to be General Garcia, who called the Governor of the archipelago insistently from his brand-new post in Comodoro Rivadavia. Actually it was never possible to know with certainty whether he acted on his own initiative or was egged on by the members of the Junta.

"And now what are we going to do?" was one of the first

questions that Garcia put to Menendez.

"Well, I have already explained that we can't do much more. We have studied the possibility of sending a contingent of the 12th regiment to the hilly area, and have also moved heavy mortars to increase fire power. Later we are going to try some limited action. We have a plan to climb the hills but there is a risk that the British with their helicopters would trap us there in a sort of sandwich. We also have some soldiers scattered on Pebble Island, where there was a British commando attack, and we have sacrificed two helicopters rescuing them. Perez Cometo's Puma was able to fly at night to bring the men in," the Governor said, making a great effort, and trying to seek some understanding from his silent questioner.

By the afternoon it was already established that the beach-head secured by the British was really important and that San Carlos sheltered more than two thousand soldiers and a vast quantity of sophisticated war materiel. With these facts in mind, Menendez imagined that the British would not delay much in beginning to move against Port Stanley and that Darwin certainly had to be the first objective.

That area was the key to wearing down the British in their effort to reach Port Stanley, but really it was far from being much of a serious threat to them. The Governor urgently called for a task force to be sent by air and to be stationed in the neighbourhood of Darwin.

The air force considered that operation to be of high risk and offered to send a contingent to Port Stanley from whence the soldiers could be ferried by helicopter to Darwin. The military commanders on the islands would not accept the proposal, because at the speed of operation of the air bridge between the islands and mainland they would need to deploy the whole of the men available for the defence of the capital, considering that the Royal Marines would already have overrun the positions in Darwin.

The situation remained unchanged, that is to say without solution, until the early hours of the 26th. It was drizzling and very cold in Port Stanley, when in the middle of the night a soldier arrived at the Governor's residence, where Menendez was sleeping.

The knocks at the old wooden door roused the military chief.

"General, there's an urgent call for you at the communications centre," the soldier informed him.

"Where from?" he asked, surprised, whilst noting that his watch said only four o'clock.

"From Comodoro Rivadavia, General," replied the messenger.

Menendez quickly put on his overcoat, boarded a jeep and set off for the communications room. Something serious must have taken place, he speculated during the journey, because otherwise they would not still be awake at this hour in the morning. He fondly imagined that it might be a diplomatic accord - though how this could have arisen, he did not know - or perhaps there might be some crisis at the heart of the armed forces.

But it was neither of these things. At the other end of the line was General Garcia who without much courtesy gave Menendez the order: "A counter-attack on San Carlos must be commenced." The Governor thought he was not hearing properly and that his sleepy state was affecting his senses: "A counter-attack on San Carlos, you said?" he asked, almost reflectively.

Garcia explained that a surprise attack, well executed, could have great internal and international impact - he even said it would help Perez de Cuellar's diplomatic effort - and that a success in the field of battle would help strengthen public opinion, that was beginning to doubt the seriousness with which the Military had entered the war.

"Look, Menendez," he said, "take men from Port Stanley, and use the troops who are on the other island as well - and also those at Darwin - and send them against the British."

"But .....why this sudden decision now?" was all the Governor managed to stammer.

"Well," Garcia insisted,"I already explained to you that there are political reasons. Moreover, we must keep up the good name of the army. The navy has already contributed its share of blood and people keep commenting on what the air force pilots are doing. So we have to do something. You understand?"

Menendez couldn't sleep another wink and decided to share this misfortune with a group of close aides. Between *mate* and *mate*, he passed on the bad news and pressed them to prepare a list of the minimum requirements for mounting a counter-offensive.

At night, Menendez spoke to Garcia and advised him of the contents of the plan they would be sending him the following morning. In it, everything from soldiers' back packs to a solid air and naval support would be needed in order for him to go in search of the enemy forces. He also pointed out that the operation could not be mounted quickly. This was because the distance between Port Stanley and San Carlos was more than 90 km and eight to ten days would be necessary to cover it, when you took into account the difficulties of the terrain.

The Governor had still been left with egg on his face, however, for during the conversation, Garcia pointed out the inefficacy of his strategy for the defence of Port Stanley. While his aides were thinking up a counter-attack, Menendez decided to send a one-page refutation of Garcia's assessment to his superiors, the initial objectives of which plan had been overtaken by events.

The Governor explained that his idea was not simply to deter the British from making a landing at the approaches to the capital, and, in passing, he formulated a series of questions concerning the order for the counter-offensive on the beach-head.

Menendez emphasised that among other things the destination of the Royal Marines aboard the *Queen Elizabeth II* was still unknown, and that in those circumstances, to launch oneself on San Carlos, leaving the defence of the capital to no more than two units, would be an imprudence difficult to accept. He insisted on the continuing lack of air and naval cover for the islands. He concluded with two forcefully expressed points which were very badly received by the mainland commanders, and only served to sharpen the confrontation between the political and strategic conduct of the war.

Menendez was completely convinced that a counter-attack on San Carlos could not be mounted - unless measures were to be taken that could reverse the course of events - and he demanded that any action in the field should be the subject of prior consultation with the commandant of the islands.

The final paragraph revealed the depth of the crisis: "In the event that my opinions are not considered reasonable, I request an opportunity to discuss the operational problems and others of a personal nature."

The Governor had another meeting with his aides, to whom he announced that in his opinion the scheme proposed by the mainland was complete madness.

"I have despatched the plan and the list of requirements needed to carry it out. But with it I sent a personal message giving my point of view. In it I say they either approve it or I am ready to present my request to be relieved."

His aides did not take this very seriously, which produced the following warning from Menendez: "Perhaps tomorrow you will have a new commander," he said.

That plan, like so many others, came to nothing and a few days afterward, on May 30th, Darwin surrendered to the British, in spite of Argentine efforts to reinforce their positions. The fall of this strongpoint was a hard blow for the Argentine troops to take, who with reason saw that the enemy was advancing towards the capital - and how he was getting round obstacles with greater ease than foreseen.

From that moment on, the military commanders spent their time thinking about the final defence of Port Stanley and its nearby heights. At the same time, attempts by commando patrols were made to infiltrate British positions, but this type of action had logistic difficulties - such as lack of fuel which restricted the movement of helicopters. In fact, that was not the only problem suffered by the Argentine soldiers. At that stage the shortage of supplies was severe, not only among the Military, but also among the civilian population.

Because of the war, Great Britain had decided to suspend the supply ship chartered by the Falkland Islands Company. It had been coming from London but was detained in Brazil on April 16th. The kelpers had been putting up with the shortages, but now, in the first days of June, the situation was coming to a head. There was a lack of flour, sugar, powdered milk and meat, so that the arrival of the hospital ship, *Almirante Irizar*, was like a balm in the straightened conditions in the archipelago.

The Military gave priority to the provisioning of the civil population. In this way, some battalions posted far from Port Stanley did not receive essential food supplies until the battle was almost over.

The British advance was pressed relentlessly and Menendez suggested to Garcia the possibility of mounting an operation on San Carlos from the mainland. The idea was to attack the rearguard of the British forces, already in possession of Darwin.

The Governor knew that there was little time to execute this action and so he pestered Garcia for replies, but typically these were of the type: "The plan is very interesting. We are studying it."

Menendez considered each day that passed to be a gift to the British, and told Garcia that it would be advisable if General Daher, Chief of Staff on the islands, went to Comodoro Rivadavia to give a full account of the plan and to re-state the objectives in the defence of Port Stanley.

Galtieri was also attracted to the idea of the meeting and therefore Daher attempted to travel almost right away, but weather conditions had put the island airport out of action. Nevertheless, the urgency remained and at 8 pm the Chief of Staff in the Falklands risked taking off from Port Stanley in an aircraft which flew him to Tierra del Fuego. From there he changed planes and continued to Comodoro Rivadavia, where at 9 pm he met all the military chiefs.

The President, meanwhile, was returning from an inspection of the 2nd Army Corps HQ in Rosario when it occurred to him that it might be useful to have a meeting with Daher. He summoned him for the following day. Also present were Colonels Cerro and Caceres as well as other army officers.

This meeting stirred up a fierce argument among Argentines after the war was over. Galtieri said on one occasion that he asked Daher if there were any problems on the islands which were being overlooked and which were standing in the way of offering the maximum resistance to the British attack. The latter replied that: "The only things needed are ten thousand pairs of bootees and long underpants as a change of clothes."[3]

The authors managed to reconstruct this meeting which in terms of content and development really does seem to have exceeded the partial assessment made of it by the ex-President. Daher certainly did demand a re-supply of clothing, but he also presented a three-part plan of operation that Galtieri never took into account. Perhaps he had good reason, because the plan probably seemed beyond all possibility during this armed struggle.

Before Daher delivered the document, Galtieri made a statement and gave the army officers the benefit of his advice:

"There has to be a dynamic defence. Move from here to there. Don't keep fixed positions, don't stay tied to the ground, advance on San Carlos. Understand me, General?"

Daher tried to explain all the logistical problems that there were on the islands - scarcity of fuel, hardly two trouble-free jeeps working - but Galtieri took no notice, until finally he exclaimed: "For God's sake, Daher! With a little will and imagination you can do anything."

Galtieri looked for support from some officers sitting embarrassed at the meeting and asked one of them: "Look, you, the infantry colonel, can we work like this or not?"

The officer hesitated a moment and scarcely managed to say: "Look, Sir, the conditions do not seem..."

Galtieri seemed to feel this reply not sufficiently encouraging and cut him dead. "Well, what about you, Colonel? You, in the cavalry. Explain to us."

"Sir," he tried to say, "I consider it right to make a precise preliminary assessment of the actual situation on the battle front."

This officer could not continue either because Galtieri realized straight away that he was not finding the required echo. Then, sticking to his over-simplified version of reality, he finished off his instructions with: "Well then, carry on as you are. Anyway, with the drubbing we gave them the other day in Bluff Cove they are not going to be able to do anything until the 20th at least."[4]

Faced with such a perspective, Daher chose to abandon the document he was putting forward. His proposals would have been:

1. Attack the frigates in the San Carlos Strait with submarines supported by two corvettes and two fast patrol boats (*La Intrepida* and *La Indomita*), which would reduce the British pressure on the advance positions because of the attack on their rear.

(As verified by the authors, this particular item was specifically prepared by Admiral Otero, the chief of the naval component in the General Staff, Falklands. Otero it was who when Daher raised the query: "Is this feasible?" replied:

"If it was not I would not have put it forward, Admiral.")

2. Launching of a parachute task force 30 km south of Darwin and Goose Green. Here the danger to the air force of this manoeuvre was also pointed out. They would have needed at least 40 transport aircraft in the movement of men. At the same time, an attempt would have been necessary to infiltrate commandos into San Carlos to distract the enemy's attention.

This operation with parachutists foresaw casualties of 30 per cent and a similar loss of equipment because, although the men would have had to land in a relatively flat area, it would have had to be at night, committing many transport planes. There is evidence that General Julio Fernando Torres, the then head of the 4th Brigade of Air-Transported Infantry - troops specialised in this type of action - would have objected energetically to this plan. The above schemes 1 and 2 foresaw the landing of tactical divers to sabotage logistic supply dumps.

3. Requesting military assistance from countries in the region. This would involve other nations in the conflict and would achieve a demonstration of Latin American solidarity. It could modify the image of "Argentina against the world," that characterised this conflict.

This point illustrates the lack of information on the islands. The military leadership was convinced that having applied to IATRA, the signatory countries would be obliged to lend concrete military support. Thus, it was believed, this request from Daher would mean that Brazil had to contribute its deep sea fleet; Cuba its air force; Peru its submarines...

At this stage the military commanders on the mainland seemed resigned to the course of events and incapable of providing new responses in the armed struggle. Menendez persisted in making new requests for logistic reinforcement, but in the face of the exasperating silence from the commanders, he asked for another communication with Galtieri.

"Did you speak with Daher, Sir," asked the Governor.

"Yes, yes; I have already spoken to him. He put his points of view to me. We are making plans for the measures to be adopted." said Galtieri.

"Well, General; you will have an idea of the effort needed to be made..." commented Menendez.

"Yes; don't worry. We are going to do everything possible," promised the President.

On the 10th, Galtieri and Menendez again conversed.

"How are things going, General?" asked the President, as if he was somehow outside the war.

"The air force has had some good successes. It carried out a bombardment. Also two planes with support material were able to reach the islands. It is very little, Sir," observed the Governor.

"Well, but you know we are doing everything possible..." confessed Galtieri.

"I do not deny it, Sir, but neither is it sufficient," replied Menendez, slightly raising his tone of voice.

"Well, but that's what we can do," said Galtieri, becoming irritated.

"Very well, General. If that is all you can do..." Menendez said pointedly, with resignation.

Until the 13th, all contact with the mainland was, for practical purposes, cut off. The Military - the whole country, in fact - were occupied attending to His Holiness, Pope John Paul II, whose presence in Argentina moved and motivated a people who now felt anguished by war.

Meanwhile, British troops broke through the Argentine defences around Port Stanley, which were positioned on the mounts Two Sisters, Challenger and Kent.

During the day in question, Menendez again asked for a word with Galtieri.

"General; the first massive attack on our defences has been made," said Menendez.

"Well, don't slacken off. Tell me, Menendez: where is the front line?" asked the President, becoming interested.[5]

"That is not very clear, General. They have come close to the capital, but I think there is still fighting further over in the hills," explained Menendez.

"Good, but watch out for them coming from the south," warned Galtieri.

"Yes, we have already received that information. We have reinforced the positions. We are sending a company of the 3rd Regiment there, another of the 7th Regiment; we have made up the strength of the 4th Regiment and we are provisioning some other groups," Menendez stated.

"You have to put in all you've got," Galtieri ordered.

"Look, General," said Menendez in an exhausted voice, "I want to clear up two points. In the first place, we have achieved a solid position in the Mount William area with the 5th Battalion of Marine Infantry, (BIM) and reinforced Regiment 7. We have taken precautions and are going to hold on. But I also want to assure you that judging by the activity that the British have displayed during the day, this very night they will launch the final attack and consequently between today and tomorrow the fate of Port Stanley will be in the balance. If we lose those two heights now there will be nothing more we can do.

"Very well.... Put everything you have around the capital. We shall make the stand there," concluded Galtieri with hopes of epic proportions.

Menendez tried to think up fortifications which were already futile by any reckoning. He hardly even insisted on maximum protection for the airport, even though its loss could mean the beginning of the end. The island capital was a picturesque but in fact precarious little town with small wooden houses reminiscent of London suburbs. It was crammed with Argentine soldiers unsuccessfully trying to find somewhere to stay.

The Governor was certain that the inevitable finale was approaching and the shortage of water at nightfall made the situation still more dramatic for both kelpers and Argentine troops.

After midnight, the collapse of defences was obvious, but a counter-attack by 6th Company in the hills, ordered by Major Ianella, momentarily halted the British advance and encouraged Menendez in the hope of being able to hold out a few more hours.

"Hold out for what?" the Governor used to ask himself at every moment. In reality that option lacked any purpose, because no-one by then cherished any hope of a negotiated settlement.

When the southern sky was brightening slightly, a persistent light snow began to fall on Port Stanley. This feeble light was swallowed by thick black storm clouds, however, and sudden darkness became perhaps an omen of the final defeat. The Chief of the 5th BIM, Captain Robacio, had already notified General Jofre that the British were "in sight." His men had not been able to defend Mounts William and Tumbledown and the counter-attack of Regiment 6 had been blocked by enemy forces.

At 8.30 am on that 14th day of June, the greater part of the men retreated before the British fire in such numbers that Regiment 3 under Colonel Comini, could not bring off an attempted rearguard action because of the people converging on the town.

The radars were also detecting the threatening approach of Royal Navy frigates and the men had fallen back almost as far as the Falklands Hospital, situated in the heart of Port Stanley.

At 9.30 am, Menendez got into contact with General Garcia in Comodoro Rivadavia from his centre of communications.

"Look, General, we are still fighting, but it doesn't amount to

293

much. I think we have no choice and it is urgent that we take measures to get out of all this," explained the Governor in distress.

"I understand you, I understand you," Garcia repeated, to cover up any lack of reply. "I am going to speak to Galtieri. But these things take time."

"I only ask you to get a move on, because there is nothing to wait for...." begged Menendez.

With this dialogue scarcely ended, he set off towards his residence and on the way saw the procession of his soldiers broken by adversity. Men were wandering along with their guns drooping, looking lost, as if awaiting - perhaps even wishing for - an outcome of any sort.

Menendez arrived at his residence when the shelling from the British ships was becoming unendurable. The idea of talking to Galtieri immediately was momentarily frustrated because a direct hit had left Port Stanley without electricity. He then went to an old shed where the auxiliary communications equipment had been very well protected.

"General, we have reached the limit of our capabilities. The British are surrounding the town and our heavy artillery has been put out of action. Our soldiers moreover, can't go on any more; they are worn out..." Menendez reported.

"The British are also worn out, Menendez. You have to put up with it, you have to impel the troops to go on. You don't pull them out of trouble to retreat, you pull them out of trouble to go forward. You should counter-attack with spirit!" ordered Galtieri.

"I don't believe you understand, General. I told you that we were going to hold on, and we have done so all night. But we can't do any more." replied the Governor.

"Regroup the troops and go forward. You have to fight, Menendez," insisted the President, without much foundation.

"General, Admiral Otero has just told me that 5th BIM has arrived here with scarcely one commando and only one section. Artillery Group 4 has disappeared. We have lost all the positions in the hills..." Menendez vainly tried to persuade his chief.

"The only thing I can say to you is to fight..." said Galtieri obstinately.

"General, I would seriously recommend that you look at the possibility of accepting Resolution 502," demanded Menendez[6].

"No, please; that is impossible." replied Galtieri.

"Well, I don't know of anything more that can be done..." confessed Menendez, in the hope of some offer of salvation.

"After all, you are the Governor of the islands and know what your responsibilities are," snapped the President.

"I know them perfectly. There is no need to remind me. I have been exercising them now for two and a half months and I am going to exercise them once more," Menendez answered with pronounced irritation, and in a threatening tone.

The abrupt end to the conversation coincided with the entry into the shed of a naval officer: Captain Melbourne Hussey: "General, I have received a communication from the British which offers surrender."

The Governor felt a sudden relief, because until that moment he had not the least idea of how he could put and end to the conflict. Without losing time he sent a telex to General Garcia to whom he reported the news and informed him of the conversation he had had with Galtieri.

The Chief of CEOPECON seemed enthusiastic at the idea of accepting Resolution 502. "Lamentably Galtieri does not agree," he warned Menendez - and he promised to persist in order to bring home the realities of the battle before the President.

"The British have just offered me a dialogue," the Governor reported to him.

"Good; accept it," authorized Garcia.

Shortly afterwards, in his office, Menendez received a message from Galtieri which ratified Garcia's authorization for contact with the British, but warned him that he must not accept any condition that might signify a "political compromise" for the country, and "much less Resolution 502."

Menendez, accompanied by Captain Hussey and Commodore Bloomer Reeve then met a British officer, Lt. Colonel Rose, with his interpreter, Captain Roderick Bell in the offices of the Town Hall. Meanwhile Galtieri, desperate, contacted his Foreign Minister from Government House. He wanted to know what a possible surrender would mean. Perhaps the capitulation of all Argentina?

Under these circumstances Costa Mendez tried to calm him. One had to keep a cool head not to sink further into the bog. For the rest, he added, he could stop worrying: the surrender in the Falklands did not mean that the Union Jack would also fly in the Plaza de Mayo.

The Foreign Minister, alerted about this turn of events by military and media sources, asked his legal department for a memorandum explaining the scope and implications of a petition for a cease-fire. Ambassador Candioti set out in a brief summary the position that in accordance with international law surrender in the islands did not apply beyond that geographical area.

The British officer quickly proposed the surrender, and Menendez frowned because he did not imagine finding himself faced with such a crucial decision so quickly. By way of a small courtesy or else as a simple reflection of the truth, the representative of the Royal Navy praised "the bravery and courage" with which the Argentine troops had fought, and specially emphasized the conduct of the marines[7].

For more than three hours Menendez and the British officer discussed the terms of the capitulation which Argentina believed would have to be in accordance with the Geneva Convention. Menendez successfully proposed that Argentine officers might resume command of their troops and in passing suggested that they could also keep possession of their arms. The British officer accepted, but indicated that the arms were going to have to be given up before leaving the islands, because during the conquest of April 2nd the Royal Marines had been obliged to leave all theirs behind.

In short, the essential points agreed in the surrender were the following:

1. Units would keep their flags.
2. Officers would keep their arms while they were on the islands.
3. The administration and government of the Argentine troops would be exercised by their own commanders.
4. Mixed work groups would be formed to resolve and coordinate problems of personnel and logistics.
5. The return of Argentine personnel to the mainland could be carried out in ships of Argentine registration.
6. Argentine troops would have to be grouped in the region of the airport, but would leave Port Stanley only on the following day.

They also agreed upon the formation of special groups for organizing the soldiers - there were more than fourteen thousand in a town built for nine hundred residents - for burials and the clearance of the minefields laid during April.

The hour fixed for the signing of the surrender document was 7 pm and in the interim, Menendez began to receive a flow of messages from the mainland. In the first of them he was advised "not to sign any paper," and in a later one from Galtieri he was ordered not to arrange a capitulation, but an "agreement between parties." A true "gentleman's pact" the President even suggested.

Menendez thought for a moment that Galtieri was keeping his sense of humour in spite of everything and after bathing and shaving - a gesture of tidiness not approved of by many Argentines - he went to his meeting with Maj. General Jeremy Moore, chief of the British land forces.

The officers were alone, without the presence of reporters at the request of the Argentines, since the memory of the photograph of

Lieutenant Commander Astiz signing the capitulation in South Georgia was still fresh. It had appeared in newspapers all round the world. They exchanged pleasantries and when Menendez took the document in his hands he found to his surprise that it spoke of an "unconditional surrender."

He immediately reacted: "This is not what was agreed."

"Well, it's already written." answered Moore.

"The agreement was a surrender with conditions. I am not signing it like this. We shall continue fighting; I don't know how, but we shall continue..." said Menendez.

"This is the solution." Moore intervened.

Menendez then made his bequest "unconditional" and inserted another idiomatic expression of his own that did not seem inappropriate. He put away his ball-point pen, shook Moore's hand and left the place.

The dream of re-conquest had ended on its 74th day.

NOTES

1. The battle of the "Alcazar of Toledo" was one of the most important in the Spanish Civil War and its story one of heroism *par excellence*. During July 1936, in a castle which was an old residence of Carlos V, some of Franco's troops had fortified themselves under the command of Colonel Moscardo, and were besieged by Republican militias. More than the siege itself, the evocation of the "Alcazar" refers to the dialogue that took place on the 23rd of that month between Moscardo and the militia chief who had taken prisoner the nationalist officer's son. The Republican demanded by telephone the surrender of the fortress in the peremptory period of ten minutes, threatening to shoot the young Luis Moscardo. As a reply the Colonel instructed his son to prepare to die and to his enemy he said: "You can save yourself the time you have given me, as the Alcazar will never surrender."

2. Report of an interview by the journalist Juan Bautista Jofre with General Galtieri, published by *Clarin* newspaper, op.cit.

3. Ibid. (2).

4. On June 8, 1982 Argentine forces repulsed an attempted British landing at Fitzroy and Bluff Cove. In the action that developed, the troop transport, *Sir Galahad*, was sunk and her sister ship, *Sir*

Tristram, and the frigate, *Plymouth*, were seriously damaged. The scene was filmed by the British from the ships - some of which were included in special programmes on the conflict on the BBC and ITN. They showed that the Argentines faced up to the counter-attack with few resources, but in spite of this, they were successful.

5. In military language the "front line" defines the area in which the two adversaries are involved in frontal combat.

6. Menendez's proposal was, although he did not know it, too late, and was meant to propose compliance with the UN Security Council mandate, approved on April 3, 1982. This provided for the withdrawal of Argentine troops from the archipelago. Nevertheless at this stage, with its Task Force in operation, Great Britain did not want anything less than a military victory.

7. *The Falklands Campaign - the Lessons*. A document presented to Parliament by the Secretary of State for Defence, London, December 1982. In paragraph 127, it states: "The second phase took place on the night of 13-14th June. In the north, in another superbly executed night attack, 2 Para captured Wireless Ridge. Further south the Scots Guards had a hard fight to capture Tumbledown Mountain from a regular Argentine Marine battalion whose heavily defended machine gun emplacements put up fierce resistance for a number of hours. (H.M. Government White Paper, CMD 8758, 14 Dec 82.)

Chapter 13

THE COLLAPSE

The news of the surrender of Port Stanley came like a bombshell for Galtieri. Stunned by the news he could not grasp the scale of what had happened. Months later he would express his disgust because he never imagined resistance would be so brief[1]. Muttering hoarsely he issued harsh judgments on the Military in the islands, but he could not grasp the heart of the matter: Menendez' decision would also end his government.

He thought that he would be affected by the hard blow, but he also thought of a formula straight away which he believed would allow him to turn the situation to his advantage. Before everything else he had to regain the lost initiative. The most suitable way seemed to be to lay blame on the generals in the Falklands for the hasty capitulation. Perhaps he would also charge the navy with their presumed desertion of the battle for control of the sea.

His narrow political vision caused him to confuse the popular, honest support for the action in the Falklands with a supposed support for his own conduct. On the basis of this error he put in action a plan prepared with Admiral Moya under pressure. At that stage, Moya had become his principal political and spiritual adviser. His influence on Galtieri - mentioned on two previous occasions in the present account - rose steadily during the war and became much more marked in the final days of the battle, when the President sank into periods of prolonged depression. It was the Military Attache to the Presidency who took on the task of raising his spirits, accompanying him in his solitude and presenting ministers and officials to him in his office with the object of giving encouragement.

The plan consisted in calling on the political parties - in essence the largest (*Peronist* and *Radical*) - to organize a great ceremony in the Plaza de Mayo. There the intention to continue the armed struggle could be ratified. Meanwhile, Galtieri would try to keep the Army High Command occupied on the work of evaluation of the events.

That same afternoon he began his task: he met with the major generals and explained to them the reasons for the fall of Port Stanley.

The testimonies collected by the authors concerning that conclave are in agreement on one point: Galtieri spoke in an almost triumphant tone and claimed that it was only a matter of one lost battle. If Port Stanley was a Cancha Rayada, a Maipu would come next, he had argued at the time[2]. In essence, Argentine troops had been defeated by Great Britain and the US, two powers of the first rank.

Those present at the meeting remained silent throughout. The atmosphere was tense, but no-one took it into his head to make reproaches, nor to challenge the forceful speech of the army chief.

Galtieri, using what he thought was a clever ruse, entrusted the generals with the work of making an assessment of three alternative courses of action:

1. Continue the war.

2. Continue the war and negotiate at the same time.

3. Negotiate with the British, with or without the intervention of the United States.

This was a simple intellectual exercise, an entertainment that the Commandant set his senior officers. But at that time reality meant more than any imaginary project, because the loss of the islands was already irreversible.

Long afterwards, in a conversation with one of his closest collaborators, the Commandant confided: "In moments of crisis you mustn't let the generals think. Give them work so that they are occupied."

It was natural that Galtieri should be mistrustful. He was not sure of the response he would get from his subordinates. He therefore preferred to make a personal check of the state of mind of the brigadier generals - the rank immediately below that of major-general - where he supposed he would find a better response for his plans.

Within this complicated context, there were also several intelligence reports concerning a mysterious journey by Vernon Walters to Argentina, five days before the capitulation of the archipelago. There are contradictory versions of the objectives of Reagan's "phantom ambassador," but all agree that the American representative was actually in Buenos Aires.

In conversation with the authors, Walters, said he "did not recall" that journey to Buenos Aires. Ambassador Harry Schlaudermann, for his part, denied having any knowledge of the episode either. But no-one emphatically denied that the visitor did appear surreptitiously. Galtieri declared that he was unaware that Walters had passed through Buenos Aires at the time[3]. But qualified official sources stated that the Navy Chief, Admiral Anaya alerted him to the conversations Walters was having with serving military officers.

One of the leading members of the government of the day confided to the authors that Anaya on one occasion criticized Galtieri for this. "If my officers spoke with Walters as yours do, I would already have reprimanded them in double quick time," said the Navy Chief in his characteristic style - so far removed from diplomacy.

Anaya's refutation nevertheless contradicted a telephone conversation he had with General Walters the day after the fall of the Falklands capital. In the research for this book the authors confirmed in Washington that contact had occurred between Anaya and Walters, and that this was linked with the situation of the Argentine prisoners on the islands - among whom was the son of the Navy Commandant himself. Anaya requested a "special effort" by the White House official with the British, so as to secure the speedy release of the young officer. The admiral making this call to Washington was the same man who had speculated with Haig about the pride he would feel if his son had had to offer his life in battle. [See Chapter 9]

One of those special relationships which curiously unite all military men enabled Galtieri, for example, to maintain correspondence with the ex-Deputy Director of the CIA - as would become evident in Washington. These "special relationships" are those which endure - and they do so in spite of criticism, for example - such as Walters made of Galtieri. In his interview with the authors, which took place in the State Department, the itinerant ambassador pointed, on two separate occasions, to the same display cabinets: the first to show a silver gaucho knife, cleverly worked, that had been presented to him by Viola and the other to show a set of *boleadoras* - also with decoration worked in silver - that Galtieri had given him as a mark of recognition. On the same occasion, Walters revealed another item with almost ironic pride: a small ash-tray with the legend: "The Falklands are and will always be Argentine" was adorning a coffee-table.

"He was clever to deceive us," said Walters of the ex-President of Argentina, referring to the war which he himself had contributed to causing[4]. Testimonies indicate that Walters had sounded out the Argentine Military over the solidity of the alliance that sustained Galtieri[5].

The Americans possessed first-hand military information: they knew that the defences of Port Stanley were being weakened by the British shelling from land-based and naval artillery, as well as by virtue of the air supremacy that they had established over the archipelago.

They encouraged a last, almost desperate intervention by Javier Perez de Cuellar, to stop the final battle, for which a massacre was forecast. That effort by the UN Secretary-General once more demonstrated a constantly-repeated feature which was true throughout the whole negotiation: Perez de Cuellar invariably entered the dialogue hours before some large-scale British military action.

On Saturday June 5th, the then Argentine Charge d'Affaires at the UN, Arnoldo Listre, was exhausted. He had refused an invitation to dine with some friends and was preparing to go to bed early in the apartment near to the UN Building that Roca had made over to him on Third Avenue and 48th Street, when he received a telephone call. It was Alvaro de Soto, right-hand man of Perez de Cuellar, who wanted to talk to him urgently.

Listre agreed to a meeting at the office of the Argentine mission and went there in the certainty that he would have something to transmit to Buenos Aires. In fact de Soto delivered a letter to him from Perez de Cuellar addressed to Galtieri with a last proposal, which consisted in a pull-back of the troops on the battlefield.

The letter upset the Military Junta, which was preparing to receive John Paul II, who would arrive on Saturday 12th in Argentina. "They are conditions for surrender," argued Anaya at the meeting of the Junta and added: "Ambassador Listre should not have accepted this letter. He should have rejected it immediately." Costa Mendez, who was present at the time, defended the diplomat and explained didactically to the Navy Chief that Listre had simply been a channel for a letter from the UN Secretary-General to the President of Argentina.

The proposal was rejected. But no-one grasped the message that was underlying the communication from Perez de Cuellar: if he was sending it, it ought to be supposed that something grave was about to occur in Port Stanley. This would be nothing less than the final battle.

But what did this proposal, which meant an admission of defeat by the Argentine Government, consist in? The answer was to be found from various sources. The fact that the UN Secretary-General had exact military information was underscored by a paragraph in the proposal:

"The armed conflict in the region of the Falkland Islands is threatening to enter a new and extremely dangerous phase, that will probably result in a great loss of life for both parties - that would gravely compromise for the foreseeable future any prospect of settling the underlying controversy. The tension and conflict would continue, in contradiction to the interests of the parties involved."

On the basis of this perspective, the Secretary-General went on to make a "direct call... [in the hope]... that it may still be possible to find a way of putting an end to the fighting and initiate negotiations with a view to resolving this crisis."

He continued, saying that: "At this late stage, it is doubtful whether additional exchanges with the parties would be productive. Therefore I wish to suggest to you the following plan, which should be considered as a whole:

1. A truce to come into force from 1100 hours, New York time, on Monday June 7, 1982.

2. On Wednesday June 9, the two military commanders in the islands will meet in the presence of a representative of the Secretary-General with the aim of agreeing arrangements for a cease-fire, which has to be in force at 1100 hours New York time, on Friday 11th June.

3. Simultaneous with the cease-fire the withdrawal of Argentine troops from the islands will commence, which must be completed within a period of 15 days. Argentina to inform the Secretary-General on the programme for withdrawal.

4. Within this period, the United Kingdom is to inform the Secretary-General about the reduction of forces in the region of the Falkland Islands. In the light of those plans, the Secretary-General will initiate consultations on the possibility of establishing security arrangements under the auspices of the UN."

He then indicated that direct Argentine-British negotiations must be entered into with a maximum period of up to December 31 1982, but they could be extended by agreement of both parties.

This plan, in order to be effective, would require both governments to reply giving their acceptance "without reservations..[by]...20.00 hours, New York time, on Sunday, June 6, 1982."

As already mentioned, the Argentine reply was in the negative. It was made on the day specified, though one hour overdue[6].

From the strictly political and diplomatic point of view, an expert in this type of negotiation would immediately predict that after the time limit specified by Perez de Cuellar an abyss would open up. But on the other hand, the Argentine military leadership refused to believe that the defences of Port Stanley could be rapidly breached.

It is important to emphasize another point: when John Paul II arrived in Argentina a high official of the United Nations also came, an emissary of the Secretary-General who had arranged an audience with the Holy Father. It was Alvaro de Soto.

In a small gap in his crowded programme, the Pope granted de Soto a few minutes. The interview took place in the office of the Papal Nuncio and there was no information, official or unofficial, given out concerning this meeting. Furthermore, it was only during the research for this book that the authors learned of the visit of this high UN official at all.

"What was his objective?" The most plausible hypothesis suggests an attempt to persuade the Pope to intercede with the Argentinians to gain their acceptance of Perez de Cuellar's plan. Ecclesiastical sources consulted said they were unaware of any such construction.

In the search for information, the authors found opinion unanimous among the military and political hierarchy concerning the Holy Father's mission. This opinion considered it a pastoral visit: alerting the Argentines to the fearful nature of war.

Some have maintained that the Pope came to Buenos Aires to prepare Argentine spirits to accept defeat, a defeat which was to be precipitated scarcely two days after the departure of John Paul II.

On the other hand, it is incontrovertible that the announcement of the Pope's visit to Great Britain gravely disturbed the Argentine Government. There were fruitless attempts by the official machinery of "psychological warfare" to get the media to criticise the Holy See for the London visit. None of the media in private hands agreed to this request. They recognised it as an unofficial suggestion, as such moves usually are.

It was Cardinals Juan Carlos Aramburu and Raul Primatesta who informed the Pope at the Vatican of the negative impact on Argentine public opinion caused by his visit to the United Kingdom. And so he decided on his marathon trip to Buenos Aires. The Pope had to arrive there before the final push by the British infantry.

On that occasion, a group of civilians tried to find a political way out of the morass in which the Government had got itself stuck. The concern began with Alfredo Critto, a sociologist of Catholic background who had an interview with Lucio Garcia del Solar - ex-President Arturo Illia's one-time ambassador to the United Nations, and a man belonging to the political and diplomatic elite of Argentina. Critto showed him from the results of a survey, that eighty per cent of the people consulted would agree to a withdrawal of Argentine troops from the Falklands - in spite of the triumphalist climate ruling in the country - in order to avoid what was being presented as the "final battle."

The "Critto Plan," prepared with the arrival of the Pope in mind, consisted of a public call to Galtieri for the withdrawal of troops, explaining to the country the impossibility of continuing the fighting with an enemy superior in preparedness and military technology.

Critto had even prepared a draft of the speech, pointing out the positive aspects: one had struggled for a just cause, for an ideal (sovereignty); one had made sacrifices; but to continue fighting a powerful adversary, assisted by the United States, would be absolutely useless. What one had achieved was very great and one had to preserve it for the negotiating table.

The key point consisted in taking advantage of John Paul II's presence to order the withdrawal of the troops, whilst the Pope provided a setting of Christian peace and understanding to the decision to bring the soldiers to the mainland and put an end to the war. Garcia del Solar openly supported this plan.

Possessed of good connections, a friend of Costa Mendez and of political leaders at the highest level, he put himself to work in order to open a channel for Critto into the power structure. The latter, for his part, began to sound out the politicians, with the argument that if the Junta accepted the initiative it would be a good move for the parties to receive it with enthusiasm also.

Garcia Solar met Raul Alfonsin. The latter listened to him attentively and said that the initiative was "most important," that one had to support it passionately. And when the ex-ambassador explained to him that a call of that type would touch the hearts of the people, Alfonsin's eyes filled with tears.

"Excuse me, Lucio, but this moves me. You don't know how much..." the *Radical* leader said.

The consultations went on deep inside the *Radical* party, where the certainty of an imminent defeat had begun to grow like an olive-oil stain. Encouraged by these results, Critto and Garcia del Solar met with Costa Mendez, who received them in his office at the Foreign Ministry, ordering his private secretary not to let anyone else disturb them.

The Foreign Minister gave great importance to the proposal and immediately called on Ambassador Ros, who had just returned from the United States, to join in the conversation. They both agreed that the plan should be taken to Galtieri without delay.

In a conversation with the authors afterwards, Garcia del Solar revealed that Costa Mendez' attitude to the proposal had surprised him. On being asked about this, the ex-Foreign Minister said: "I know enough to realise when to take something seriously and when not to." The Minister put the papers in a briefcase and took them to the Casa Rosada.

One day later, Garcia del Solar called Costa Mendez by telephone to discover the fate of his proposal. The minister disclosed to him that the idea "had not been badly received," and that on the contrary, Galtieri had shown a certain receptivity.

Critto, for his part, did not remain quiet. He presented his plan to a senior retired air force officer - Brigadier Osvaldo Cacciatore, ex-mayor of the city of Buenos Aires, who had agreed with the rationale behind the scheme - in order that it might be shown to Lami Dozo. According to the testimonies collected, the Air Force Chief also showed enthusiasm.

"I believe that I obtained a better reception from Lami Dozo than from Galtieri," Critto confessed to Garcia del Solar at the time.

Twenty-four hours later, everything collapsed. Costa Mendez was charged with notifying them that the "scheme has bounced." The opposition to the scheme came from Anaya once more, though one doubts whether Galtieri was much disposed to carry it out.

The truth was that the naval chief was really excited about the great blow delivered by the Argentine air force at Bluff Cove on the British transport ships, *Sir Galahad* and *Sir Tristram*, with severe casualties among the troops of the Task Force.

It was while he was discussing the Critto-Garcia del Solar plan, which might have been encouraged by the Church hierarchy, that Anaya reminded Costa Mendez that: "Argentina is winning and you want to negotiate...?" Galtieri also had an inflated view of the disaster at Bluff Cove. He thought that the British plans would be delayed considerably thereby and that the battle for Port Stanley would be postponed. There are serious indications that the Argentine High Command thought that the British would not be in a condition to return to the attack on the defences of Port Stanley until June 20.

If the "Critto Plan" did not work it must have been because the Argentine Government had already taken a decision that no retreat was possible. The spectre of a noisy collapse of the Galtieri administration was naturally the most serious threat that the regime's strategists considered, should they think at that time of withdrawing the troops from the Falklands.

But this provides further evidence of what in various ways presented a grave picture of the course of the war. The greatest mistake was to believe that sudden successful attacks, with their enormous effect on public morale, meant that the war was being won. In reality, at that stage it was clear that, save a miracle, defeat would come sooner or later.

Nevertheless, it is incorrect to think that there were no attempts at other negotiations. The possibility was even considered at that stage of the war of a face to face meeting between Margaret Thatcher and Galtieri. Although this may appear an outrageous proposal, it is true that serious thought went into it and concrete soundings were made to realize this "summit."

There was also the Mexican President, Jose Lopez Portillo, who offered himself as a "bridge" between London and Buenos Aires, in order to try for a rapprochement.

Argentine-Mexican relations had deteriorated considerably because of Argentine equivocation in granting safe conduct to Juan Manuel Abal Medina, ex-Secretary-General of the Peronist Movement.

The Military accused Medina of being one of the principal ideologues of the Leftist guerillas - these having been virtually exterminated in the "dirty war." Abal Medina took sanctuary in the Mexican legation on March 24 1976, the day the constitutional government of Peron's widow Isabel was overthrown. By the time the struggle for the Falklands broke out, Medina had broken the record for a fugitive in a foreign embassy - even beating the one established in Lima by the legendary Victor Haya de la Torre.

Mexico was one of the countries which strongly criticized the Military and welcomed thousands of refugees into their territory who had fled from the repression in Argentina. That fact aggravated the tension between Buenos Aires and Mexico City. One episode which was never cleared up concerned the presumed presence of an Argentine commando, denounced by one of the members of his group, who deserted on arriving on Mexican territory[4]. This was kept quiet by Lopez Portillo's Government, but there was always the possibility of that country's Foreign Ministry making it public.

On the other hand the influence of Mexico in the Latin American community is great. In order to achieve their outright support for the Argentine position over the Falklands, Costa Mendez tried to modify the Military's intransigence over the safe passage for Abal Medina. At the same time, in telephone conversations with Lopez Portillo, outlines of the scheme to try for a meeting of Galtieri with Margaret Thatcher were being drawn up.

The place suggested for this was the beach at Cancun, an exclusive Mexican tourist centre lying on the Pacific coast.

Abal Medina was freed in a lightning operation[7] that went unnoticed by almost the whole Argentine press, but no-one today can give any reliable explanation for the failure of the Lopez Portillo manoeuvre.

Galtieri himself[8], in the interview previously mentioned, admitted that such a meeting was under consideration, indicating that the countries where it could have been held were Mexico and Switzerland.

One can very reasonably infer that one of two things may have occurred: 1. that Margaret Thatcher flatly rejected the Mexican proposal - which is entirely plausible, and in addition, 2. Lopez Portillo, on finding it to be useless, may have discontinued with his attempt.

It should also be noted that these moves were not endorsed by all the members of the Junta. They were simply exploratory efforts by certain members of the Government, later nullified by intransigence of one or more of the three commandants.

All these earlier events passed through the exhausted mind of

Galtieri. When he arose on June 15 he prepared himself to pursue the only chance he had left - he had to shake up the military command structure; divide the country into "loyalists" and "traitors," and hint at a popular political uprising. It was already too late.

That morning the Plaza de Mayo was slowly filling with people. Those who gathered there had read the front pages of the morning newspapers which headlined the "catastrophe" - that four generals and 11,000 men were in British hands; that the Argentine flag had been taken down after the capitulation of Menendez - and that everything was finished.

The cries from the crowds were: "Cowards! We want guns! No surrender!" No answer came from the stone balconies of the Casa Rosada. Violence was in the air.

Alarmed by the situation, the mayor of Buenos Aires, Guillermo del Cioppo, spoke to Colonel Menendez by telephone, warning him of what would occur if the police were to unleash repressive forces. The assessment of the Assistant Secretary of the Interior was similar and he spoke to the chief of the Federal Police to express the same concern to him. It was already too late: the tear-gas and truncheons were being distributed freely, then and there before Government House.

Soon State-controlled radio and TV began to broadcast a notice of a meeting at the same place, to hear an address by the President.

Galtieri was, for practical purposes, overwhelmed by events. Admiral Moya, and to a lesser degree, General Iglesias, gave him moral support and encouraged him to carry on.

The air force and the navy, each acting independently, faced the call squarely and openly rejected it. The Government was already sliding towards collapse.

Foreign Minister, Costa Mendez, thought it appropriate for the Cabinet to resign as a whole: some heads would have to be sacrificed in order to achieve a minimum reduction of political tension. He met the Minister of the Interior, who expressed agreement. Nevertheless, when the moment of truth arrived, this same General Saint Jean did not resign but sheltered instead under the questionable argument that he was an officer on active service and had to take orders from his superior.

Costa Mendez and Sergio Martini, Minister of Public Works, offered verbal resignations to Galtieri, who refused to accept them. Nevertheless, the Foreign Minister pressed the matter before the full Cabinet, appealing for a collective resignation. Martini and Roberto Alemann, the Minister for the Economy, supported him. The rest of the ministerial team remained silent - a similar silence to that maintained by certain people when the fate of President Viola was debated. On both occasions there were ministers who passed the time examining the ceiling.

At that stage, a silent struggle was developing between on the one hand the small group who supported Galtieri, and on the other, the Interior Minister and his Assistant Secretary, Menendez, who struggled to prevent the President speaking. The confusion grew hour by hour: Galtieri, under pressure, tried to avoid the mass meeting in the Plaza de Mayo. It was his only concession. He would speak to the country using the text that Moya and Iglesias had prepared for him.

Against all hopes people were making for the Plaza de Mayo. The pain and frustration that they vented that day on their compatriots who had loyally taken part in the national effort in the Falklands were enormous. They were marching once more so that someone might explain to them this massive disappointment which was so completely disorientating. No-one came out on the balcony of the Casa Rosada, however. There was one isolated police incident which caused a disturbance to break out. The consequent repression was, once again, hard and cruel.

When tear gas was still floating over the centre of Buenos Aires, Galtieri appeared on television to give his version of the capitulation. Still President of the Nation, Galtieri roared: "There will be no place for speculation, nor for deception. Idleness will be a crime. Taking advantage of the situation will be seen as an affront to the blood of those who fought, and defeatism will be treason."

His message was clear: no-one should doubt what had been done by the High Command of the Military during the war. That would be treason.

On concluding his harangue, Galtieri went to the eighth floor of the offices of the Army Commander-in-Chief. The top brass of his arm of the services awaited him in an angry mood. Present were: Jose Vaquero, Chief of the General Staff; Cristino Nicolaides, Chief of 1st Corps (its 10th brigade had fought in the Falklands); Juan Carlos Trimaro, Chief of 2nd Corps; Eugenio Guanabens Perello, Chief of the 3rd; Llamil Reston, of the 4th; Osvaldo Garcia of the 5th; Horacio Varela Ortiz, Chief of *Fabricaciones Militares*; Luis Martella, Chief of the Federal Police; Edgardo Calvi, Commander of the Military Institutes; and Saint Jean.

The meeting was stormy. The commanders rose up roundly against Galtieri. The first to lead the assault on the tottering Commandant was General Calvi, who complained resentfully about not having been consulted on the landing in the islands, nor when negotiations were still open, and above all during the Haig Missions.

Galtieri's counter-attack was predictable: there were no consultations with the commanders of any of the three forces because it was an operation whose success depended on secrecy.

Calvi refuted these arguments, maintaining that a war could not reasonably be decided upon in secret by the three Commandants alone. Galtieri returned to the attack, claiming that during the conflict, Calvi had preferred to keep his mouth shut during meetings of generals that were held then.

To the support of the Chief of Military Institutes, came Generals Reston and Varela Ortiz in mutual agreement. The first was a defender to the death of the United States who procured the retirement of General Ricardo Flouret after the war when the latter had dared to question him in a comradely meeting on the subject. For Reston, the world since Potsdam and Yalta had been divided into the hegemonies of the super-powers and whoever dared to argue against that premise would be certain to suffer for it. That, in Reston's opinion is what had happened to Argentina.

Galtieri became furious at this attack from Reston, Varela Ortiz and Calvi. He maintained that the war had been lost essentially because of "Washington's treachery," and recalled the "services" lent by the Argentine army to American strategy in Central America.

Reston appealed to his hobby horse once more: "Yalta exists, General," and added: "we can't confront the greatest power in the Western world."

Galtieri wanted to halt this discussion without further ado. "Well, gentlemen, I am the Commandant. He who is not in agreement knows what he has to do." The meaning was clear: Calvi, Reston and Varela Ortiz had to ask for retirement from the army.

Calvi, beside himself, asked for it immediately. Reston and Varela Ortiz rapidly followed him.

The climate was getting more tense all the time. Galtieri decided to end the meeting and descended to the third floor, to the office of the Commandant. His second-in-command, General Vaquero, stayed some time with the generals, trying to cool them down. When he considered that the situation was under control, he went to see Galtieri. His object was to calm him as well, to return things to a rational level.

He was received immediately by a Galtieri, who was still furious. Thumping his desk, he revealed his plan: "I am going to reorganize the Command completely. I shall retire Calvi, Reston and Varela Ortiz and any that go along with them." While Vaquero was delicately trying to calm Galtieri's hot temper, the Commandant's aide informed him that the three generals who had confronted him in the meeting wanted to speak to him.

Vaquero left the office and went to join a meeting with the officers of the General Staff, who were also deliberating. Galtieri, for his part, received the rebels.

Afterwards he related what happened during those conversations. "I received them in order of seniority. The first was Reston. He came in, saying: "Are you going to offer me a whisky? In the conversation he told me, just like the others did later, that the argument was the result of nerves, and that one should not give it great importance. I replied that it was possible, that we were all tired out by the effort we had made. I agreed with the three that we should forget the matter of retirement. Nevertheless, I asked myself: "How will they behave tomorrow when they again appear with all the other generals?"

But the siege of the Commandant-President would not allow him any rest that night of June 15th. The last of them had barely left when the steely voice of Vaquero came over on Galtieri's intercom: he was with the officers of the General Staff and they wanted to discuss the situation with him.

Perhaps at that moment he realised that his chance had arrived. If he managed to convince them, he would have a good military base for bringing about a restructuring of the High Command. He considered, with a certain logic, that the members of the General Staff, who in some manner or other had taken part in the war, would not differ greatly from this approach.

It was to be another disappointment. When he entered the meeting, he met Generals Wehner, Deputy Chief of General Staff; Podesta, Chief of Personnel; Sotera, Chief of Intelligence; Meli, Chief of Operations; Esposito, Chief of Logistics and Philips, Chief of Mobilization. They had worked out a common position. It was strongly critical of the whole conduct of the army during the war.

They accused Galtieri of not having consulted them on the decision to land in the Falklands; of not having negotiated seriously enough when the United States was intervening - here they included harsh criticism of the behaviour of Foreign Minister Costa Mendez - and of having established links with countries which had aided the guerillas in Argentina, such as Libya and Cuba. They castigated him for the decision to summon the people to the Plaza de Mayo and for having included in his speech a description of those who disagreed with his conduct of affairs as "traitors to the Fatherland."

There was direct pressure on him to secure an accommodation at all costs with the United States.

Galtieri related what happened in this manner: "The meeting began at 1 am and ended at 3.30 am. After a short time a series of questions were put regarding the support that we were receiving from countries or leaders who, directly or indirectly, had aided subversion: Cuba and Libya, for example."[9].

The Commandant persisted in his argument: the United States, he said, had openly collaborated with the British during the war. How could the generals of an army which had been defeated now demand an accord with the principal ally of the country which had been victorious?" The most critical moment was a verbal confrontation between Galtieri and Esposito, who had had an excellent personal relationship, so much so that afterwards the Commandant would remark that one of the things which hurt him most was the attitude that this officer assumed.

"Look, Esposito. You are making judgments which to me are worthy of a 2nd Lieutenant," said Galtieri.

"Remember that you are talking to a General of the Nation," replied Esposito.

On perceiving the turn of events, Galtieri decided to cut his losses and proposed to the brigadier-generals: "To continue in command I need the express support of the army. In my judgment, important measures have to be taken and that requires the consensus of the major-generals." The message was transparent: if the lower echelons put up with him, he would sack the High Command. Those present would become the new management of the army.

Whilst Galtieri was sleeping at the Casa Rosada, political leaders and some retired Military continued deliberating. It was obvious that he was mortally wounded; one had to think how to replace him.

An important role among the retired generals was played by ex-President Viola, who saw before him the chance to take revenge on Galtieri. In reality, since before the fall of Port Stanley he had been working on a plan which assumed that the Government would collapse as a result of the Falklands conflict.

There were civilian and military plans. the civilian one had several people involved. It was Raul Alfonsin, of the *Radicales*, who was to give the first impetus to the plan: the Government would have to be taken over by a political leader who had general acceptance - he proposed ex-President Arturo Illia, in a transitional Government of National Unity. This would carry out the necessary tasks for democratization. A comparison might be made with the case of Greece at the time of the collapse of the Colonels' Regime.

Illia would be the "Karamanlis" of Argentina, to replace - as in Greece - the Military Junta[10].

Alfonsin's fundamental assumption was that the Falklands adventure would end badly. In the event, strong political action would be necessary to achieve a democratic way out of the morass into which the Military had landed them.

But at the same time, as has already been said, Galtieri would hang on to his dreams of becoming a popular leader to the last.

A discussion took place between Colonel Menendez and Ricardo Yofre during the mediation of the conflict. Ricardo Yofre displayed great activity among the political leaders of the time and the discussion is illustrative.

Strong words were exchanged, resulting from the intransigence of the Military when confronting the politicians' point of view over the progress of the war. It developed in the following terms:

"This is going to be a disaster," said Yofre.

"I don't agree, Doctor," the Colonel replied.

"You continue to question Alfonsin, Leon and Saadi. May I remind you that they will still be around, and perhaps one day one may be President, when you have been sent into retirement," Yofre foretold.

"The problem is of a difference in approach, Doctor," the Colonel suggested.

"Look, Menendez. You are going to be judged like Ionnides, Papadopoulos and the others were judged in Greece. Just as in Greece, the firing squad will be replaced by life imprisonment. They are going to bring disaster upon us - but unlike Greece, we here have no Karamanlis to take over government after the disaster," insisted this one-time official of Videla's government.

"Don't believe I haven't thought of what happened in Greece," replied the Assistant Secretary of the Interior, crushingly.

"I believe that you have launched yourself into all this for two reasons: 1. You needed political leeway, and 2. to have succeeded would have projected Galtieri as a national leader," continued Yofre.

"You have a point there," conceded the Colonel.

But now the situation for Galtieri was very serious. Taken to task by his commanders, prevented from achieving an illusory contact with the people in the Plaza de Mayo - who would undoubtedly have reacted badly if he had dared to appear on the balcony - he continued playing the cards he did hold. But his chances of remaining in the Casa Rosada were minimal.

On the morning of June 16th, Minister Saint Jean received the political leaders. But the most important parties - the *Peronistas* and the *Radicales* - as well as their fellow members in the *Multipartidaria* (*Democristianos Desarollistas* and *Intransigentes*) did not keep the appointment. And it would be essential for these parties to be present for Galtieri's chances to have any hope at all.

Saint Jean got out of the jam as best he could. He promised those who came to the Ministry of the Interior that the meeting could be postponed until the following day: he had obtained the promise of Deolindo Bittel, Chief of *Justicialismo* and of Carlos Contin of the *Union Civica Radical*, that they would appear without fail. Arturo

Frondizi, of the *Movimiento de Integracion y Desarrollo*, had also given his word.

A lot of pressure was consequently brought to bear upon these leaders not to go to the meeting at the Casa Rosada. Various retired military officers converged on the *Radicales*. At a meeting held at the residence of the ex-deputy, Ricardo Natale, there were present: Contin, Facundo Suarez and Horacio Hueyo. There were also Generals Reynaldo Bignone, Domingo Bussi and Adam Alonso - all retired by Galtieri. They urged the politicians not to go to the discussions with the Government[11].

They put forward the view that a "strong government, with a reliable person at the head and with all the ministers military men," was necessary.

They did not manage to change Contin's decision. Nevertheless, Rogelio Frigerio, the influential leader of *Desarrollismo*, persuaded Frondizi to change his mind: the *MID* would not go to the Casa Rosada.

A similar effort by Antonio Cafiero, of the *Peronismo*, achieved Bittel's defection and Antonio Troccoli of the *Radicalismo* influenced Contin to step back from his initial intention to talk to the Government.

In Troccoli's study in the vicinity of the Palacio de Tribunales, the representatives of the five groupings of the *Multipartidaria* gathered: they decided not to attend on the 17th, giving Galtieri's Government another push towards the abyss.

But the President still wanted to do battle. He ordered General Vaquero to ask the major-generals and brigadier-generals for their opinion on whether he could count on the support of the army. So out of touch with reality was Galtieri that he gave them seven days to answer, when in fact he was only to remain in power a few hours more.

Now in the early hours of Thursday 17th, Galtieri asked Vaquero to represent him at a meeting of the Junta, so overcoming the brief reluctance of this Chief of the General Staff. The President left for Campo de Mayo, his usual residence, but beforehand he whispered in General Iglesias' ear: "All this smells bad."

Vaquero decided to put an end to the comedy. On his own responsibility he suspended the meeting of the Junta, and going against Galtieri's orders, he summoned the major-generals and discussed with them a way out of the crisis.

Except for Osvaldo Garcia and Eugenio Guanabens Perello, who were in the interior of the country, everyone attended. Everyone there agreed - with the exception of Saint Jean, who stood up for his commandant - on the necessity of removing Galtieri and taking away his right to name his successor in the army.

After obtaining the support of the two absent generals by telephone, Vaquero went to Campo de Mayo to notify Galtieri that he was President no longer, and likewise that he was no longer Commander-in-Chief of the army.

Galtieri was sleeping and, still in a dreamy state, he received Vaquero seated on his bed. The latter informed him of what had happened. Still Galtieri resisted. In an emotional outburst he asked Vaquero to summon the generals to discuss the situation.

"It is too late now; there's no sense to it, Leopoldo," argued Vaquero in a paternal fashion. Admitting defeat, Galtieri began to sink into a deep depression. He managed, however, to obtain a formal concession: he could personally deliver the Army Command and the Presidency to his interim replacement, General St Jean.

He had no choice, nor the will to fight. He explained it graphically: "In the face of these events, [that is, his overthrow] I had two alternatives. One, to accept the request for my resignation and go - as I did. The other, to bring about the removal of the Army High Command by calling on some brigadier-generals who supported me, with their men and their fire-power. I did not do this because I was afraid of causing such a convulsion."[12]

The rise and fall had been completed. The man who once declared that he did not want to mix with politics, and who had come to consider himself as "the spoilt child of the Americans," that had listened for a moment to the music of the people in the Plaza de Mayo and who had so deceived himself, was now alone - with his own conscience.

Even his greatest military friends who had promised him everything had abandoned him. Anaya, the intransigent naval chief, against whose myopia so many hopeful chances for negotiation were smashed, also went into retirement.

Lami Dozo, who stammered his disagreement on some decisive questions during the conflict and who could never impose his view, fell once again into error; he gambled that the bravery and example of his aircrews during the conflict would serve as a launching-pad for his own political take-off.

In the end, the three military chiefs of the war were tamely devoured by history.

NOTES

1. Interview with Galtieri, *Clarin* April 2 1983.
2. Allusion to battles during the liberation of Argentina and Chile from Spain. In Cancha Rayada, troops of San Martin were defeated. In Maipu they later obtained a resounding triumph. That argument was much used by the Military in their justification for the defeat suffered in the Falklands. Various works published by retired chiefs used this stereotyped example.
3. Ibid. 1.
4. Morales Sola, Joaquin. *"La Caida de Galtieri. El comienzo de un largo calvario."* in *Clarin*, June 17 1983.
5. Other details of the relationship which Vernon Walters maintained with Argentine military officers can be found in *"Falklands, Whose Crisis?"* Latin American Bureau Special Brief, p 81, London, 1982.
6. *Clarin* was the only Argentine newspaper which discovered this last proposal of Perez de Cuellar, publishing the confirmation in the edition of June 8 1982. p 3.
7. Ibid. (1)
8. Ibid. (1)
9. Ibid (1)
10. The comparison with the Greek situation, in the fall of the Colonel's Regime, was assiduously cited in political circles during that period. Raymond Aron, the prestigious French political commentator, also referred to the historical analogy between the Argentine situation and the one Athens passed through in 1974: "The Argentine military will begin to search for their Constantino Karamanlis." Karamanlis was a conservative Prime Minister who had been displaced by the King in 1964. To shore up their political fragility, the Greek Colonels invaded Cyprus, leading to a confrontation with Turkey in a war. The United States withdrew their support from the Athens administration. It was the beginning of the end. The Colonels called Karamanlis by telephone, who was exiled in Paris, to ask him to take charge of the Government. See also Cardoso, Oscar Raul: *"El Caso Karamanlis; Las analogias de la historia."* In *Clarin* p 7 June 22. 1982.
11. Ex-President Viola maintained intense activity to bring his

influence to bear to cause the replacement of Galtieri. He had his candidates: General Horacio Tomas Liendo, General Reynaldo Bignone, General Jose Rogelio Villareal, General Antonio Bussi and General Oscar Bartolome Gallino.

12. Ibid. (1).

INDEX

318

323